The "I Love Lucy" Book

In Memory of Lucille Ball Arnaz,

August 6, 1911–April 26, 1989

THE "I Love Lucy" BOOK

Bart Andrews

DOUBLEDAY

NEW YORK LONDON TORONTO SYDNEY AUCKLAND

PUBLISHED BY DOUBLEDAY
a division of Bantam Doubleday Dell Publishing Group, Inc.
666 Fifth Avenue, New York, New York 10103

DOUBLEDAY and the portrayal of an anchor with a dolphin
are trademarks of Doubleday, a division of Bantam Doubleday Dell
Publishing Group, Inc.

Title and Log Page created by Julie Linden
Designed by Judith Neuman

Library of Congress Cataloging in Publication Data
Andrews, Bart.
The "I love Lucy" book.
 ISBN 0-385-19033-6
 Rev. ed. of: Lucy & Ricky & Fred & Ethel. 1st ed. c1976.
 Includes index.
 1. I love Lucy (Television program) I. Andrews, Bart.
Lucy & Ricky & Fred & Ethel. II. Title.
PN1992.77.I253A45 1985   791.45'72   84-6033

 9 11 13 14 12 10 8

BG

This Book Is Dedicated To

Vivian Vance

July 26, 1912–August 17, 1979

Foreword by Jess Oppenheimer

It's hard to realize that it's been almost thirty years since Madelyn Pugh, Bob Carroll, and I wrote "I Love Lucy." The two Bobs, Schiller and Weiskopf, joined us for the fifth year. Most things that a person has done thirty years before are relegated to memory, and maybe a yellowed clipping in an old file, but "I Love Lucy" is as alive and kicking as can be, seen in hundreds of television markets every day, and several times a day in some places.

The most-often-asked question, at least to me, about "I Love Lucy" is "What was the secret? What made it so different from all the other sitcoms of the time that caused its unheard-of longevity?" My answer: Luck. Pure, unadulterated luck.

I'd better qualify that somewhat. The first and most important piece of luck was building the show around Lucille Ball. More about that later. You will find, if you examine any runaway hit, that everything, almost miraculously, breaks just right for it. Somehow, a particular group of special talents just happens to be available and in the right spot at precisely the right time in history. It is the perfect moment for that particular project. There are hundreds of talented people working in the entertainment field, and some of them will perfectly complement certain others and make a wonderful writing or acting team *if* they happen to meet and get together. Most don't. But in the lucky, star-struck few, the supernovas of the entertainment business, everybody is just perfect for everyone else. In the case of "I Love Lucy," the kind of writing that came easiest and most natural to us was exactly what the performers understood best, appreciated, and played most skillfully and happily. Also, we had the luxury of having tuned our relationship for three years on radio, with "My Favorite Husband."

Vivian and Bill fell right out of the blue into our laps. They were the perfect people for those parts in that property. A few weeks into the series, we had a script idea which depended on Viv and Bill being able to sing and dance a little. With great trepidation, we approached them. With our luck, we shouldn't have worried. To our complete delight they revealed that they had both been stars in the musical theater. That news opened up a lot of story ideas, I can tell you. All of our casting and hiring of technical people fell into place the same way. Desi turned out to be a charming foil.

We had planned to shoot a "Lucy" every other week. Instead, because the sponsor wanted us to shoot in New York and we wanted to stay put in L.A., negotiations resulted in its being done once a week, and on film. On film guaranteed quality shows to be rerun. Had we been on kinescope, like "Your Show of Shows," there would have been no second use of the shows. Another bit of "I Love Lucy" luck.

And the timing. Television was in its infancy, and anything would make an impact. But our time slot, can you believe it, was immediately following Arthur Godfrey, the number one show in the country. Nobody had to search around to find us. Arthur Godfrey asked his audience to stay tuned, and we popped right on to most of the sets in the country, and into first place within twelve weeks. Talk about luck.

Even though the entire world loved "I Love Lucy," everyone on "I Love Lucy" didn't love everyone else on "I Love Lucy." Luckily—there's that word again—all the interpersonal problems didn't show through the performances. Lucy and Desi were having a whole set of domestic problems, which ended in their divorce; Vivian couldn't stomach Bill, mainly because she failed to understand how anyone could believe she was married to "that old man"; Bill reacted in typical fashion, referring to her figure as "a sack of doorknobs"; and Desi and I had a running series of spats, mostly ticked off when I picked up the trade papers and found he had taken credit for something I had done. But, luckily (again), it could not be seen on the screen, and there was no blowup which destroyed the team.

To get back to the first element of luck—Lucy herself. Take all the elements of the show. Take the writers, take the other actors, take the cameraman, take the producer, the director, the editors. Take everybody. Take them and roll them up together and flush them down the toilet. There was nothing without Lucille Ball. Hers was an unbelievable talent. She was everywoman; her little expressions and inflections stimulated the shock of recognition in the audience. Their hysterical reaction was their way of saying, "We know, Lucy. We know. We've been there." Lucy had a universal quality with which everyone could identify. She could play a common street tough as honestly as she could a pillar of high society. It was very difficult, after watching her turn a routine transitory scene into a comedy gem, to keep from thinking what a great writer you were.

Thirty years later, we are still running in luck. "I Love Lucy" has not lost its popularity, and for several reasons. When a child controls the set and chooses "I Love Lucy," the adult who is forced to watch can enjoy it too. It is clean. We operated under a different set of rules concerning subject matter for television comedy in those days. A mother who lets her child watch "I Love Lucy" knows that her darling is not going to come back with questions about such current sitcom themes as adultery, homosexuality, bigotry, sexual permissiveness, and other amusing little traits; questions with which the parent may not be prepared to deal. With "I Love Lucy," she is home free!

In short, or maybe in long, the ones who really loved Lucy the best, and still do, were those who worked the show. We knew the kind of luck we had to have her as our star. We knew that "I Love Anyone-else-but-Lucy" would have been a dog.

Preface

At a posh dinner party in New York's elegant Gramercy Park district in mid-1951, the prominent public relations representative for a giant tobacco company was overheard to say, "We've just bought a little thing being made out on the Coast . . . a situation comedy with Lucille Ball and her husband—whatsizname. I don't know if it will amount to anything."

That "little thing" turned out to be the most popular, most watched, most talked about television program of the 1950s: "I Love Lucy." And "whatsizname"—Desi Arnaz, of course—soon became TV's most successful entrepreneur of mirth, the brains behind not only Miss Ball's million-dollar laugh machine, but also forty or fifty other prime-time series like "Our Miss Brooks," "The Untouchables," "December Bride," etc., etc., etc.—enough film to stretch all the way from Hollywood to Nigeria, where, incidentally, "I Love Lucy" is still running.

The Desilu empire, dissolved officially in 1967 when it was sold to the Gulf & Western conglomerate, blossomed from a tiny, inauspicious stripling of a situation comedy that, just prior to its debut on October 15, 1951, *TV Guide* modestly described as a show "revolving around problems arising in a household where the wife is stage-struck and the orchestra leader husband thinks she should stay home." Hardly something to rush right out and buy a new twelve-inch Motorola for.

But in a short six months, or twenty-six episodes later, "I Love Lucy" became the first television program to be seen in 10 million homes. In fact, the April 7, 1952, broadcast ("The Marriage License") was viewed in 10,600,000 households, according to the American Research Bureau (ARB), one of the five rating services operating in the early 1950s. That figure might not seem overwhelming by today's mass media standards, but remember that at the start of 1952 there were only 15 million TV sets in operation in the United States.

In New York, "Lucy" was the number one show after only four months, ranking well ahead of Arthur Godfrey, "Your Show of Shows," Milton Berle, and "Fireside Theatre."

Writing about the Lucille Ball–Desi Arnaz show in the New York *Times,* the dean of TV critics, Jack Gould, observed: "The series has engendered as much public interest as anything since the days when the world stood still every evening to hear 'Amos 'n' Andy' on the radio."

For, indeed, if the world stood still for "Amos 'n' Andy," America came to a grinding halt every Monday night when "I Love Lucy" came on the air.

The "Lucy" mania was so widespread that telephone companies actually reported a "substantial reduction" in calls during that half-hour period. Families without TV sets crowded into neighbors' living rooms to watch their favorite redhead. If the set happened to be a taxi ride away, fans in New York might have been out of luck: Cabbies disappeared into bars to catch a glimpse of Lucy and Ricky and Fred and Ethel uncoiling their latest plot, and didn't turn on their ignitions again until 9:30 P.M.

The mammoth Marshall Field department store in Chicago switched its evening shopping hours from Mondays to Thursdays when it became financially clear that the biggest clearance sale in the store's history was no match for "Lucy." So that customers and employees could watch the show, the management put up a sign in the window on State Street declaring: "We love Lucy, too, so we're closing on Monday nights."

Likewise, doctors and dentists in many cities changed their Monday-evening visiting hours to prevent cancellation of appointments by "Lucy" fans.

PTA leaders in Lynn, Massachusetts, picketed their local CBS affiliate, demanding that "I Love Lucy" be broadcast at an earlier hour so school-children could get to bed at a reasonable hour.

Members of a Lions Club in Santa Barbara, California, chipped in and bought a TV set, then installed it in their meeting room, declaring a half-hour recess so everybody could watch "Lucy."

Such mass devotion did not go unrewarded. The series won more than two hundred awards, including five Emmys (it was nominated twenty-three times) and the coveted George Foster Peabody Award for "recognition of distinguished achievement in television."

Once, when presidential candidate Adlai Stevenson cut in on "I Love Lucy" for a five-minute campaign pitch in the fall of 1952, his office was flooded with hate mail. One lady, obviously a Republican, wrote: "I love Lucy. I like Ike. Drop dead." Stevenson chose not to preempt "Lucy" when he ran again in 1956.

On February 10, 1966, the United States Senate was conducting hearings on the Vietnam conflict during which former Ambassador George Kennan was being interrogated by Senator J. William Fulbright. Feeling a moral compunction, Fred W. Friendly, president of CBS News, wanted to preempt a morning rerun of "I Love Lucy" in order to air the hearings live, as ABC and NBC were doing. His immediate superior, John A. Schneider, would not permit it.

"Not running 'Lucy,' " Friendly bitterly recalls, "would have meant a loss of about five thousand dollars." Five days later, Friendly resigned.

Interestingly, "Lucy" did enjoy a better rating than the Senate hearings televised by the competition. But perhaps that is not so surprising. Thirteen years earlier, more people watched "I Love Lucy" on the occasion of Little

Ricky's birth than the 1953 inauguration of the thirty-fourth President of the United States, Dwight D. Eisenhower, or the coronation of Queen Elizabeth five months later.

Hedda Hopper, who was in the capital the night Ricky, Jr., was born (January 19, 1953), said, "I remember that the inauguration party that Colonel Robert R. McCormick, publisher of the Chicago *Tribune,* gave came to a temporary halt while everybody had to watch 'I Love Lucy' in silence. Bertie was wild about the show and wanted to see the birth."

As you can see, "Lucy" fans are, from all available indications, a diverse and hearty lot. When WNEW-TV, New York City's Channel 5, decided to cancel the twice-daily telecasts of the vintage series in September 1975, a picket line formed in front of the station's East Sixty-seventh Street studio. Mail poured in, ordering Lucy's immediate reinstatement.

One letter, handwritten in pencil by a young fan from New Jersey and addressed to the "Program Manger [sic]," said, "Dear Sir: I am eight and a half years old. I am writing to find out why you took off my favorite TV show. . . . It was a very bad idea to take off Lucy. She has the best show. Even my mother watches the show. So you better put it back on because evryone [sic] loves Lucy."

TV writer Harold Mehling once speculated: "At last report there was no one left in the United States who has not seen at least one of Lucy's escapades, and arrangements may shortly be made to exhibit them to the newborn as soon as they can see."

These so-called escapades (193 of them), if screened in succession without interruption, would consume four days, seven hours, and forty-five minutes. They are also available dubbed in Japanese, Portuguese, Italian, French, and Spanish (*"Yo Quiero a Lucy"*) from Viacom (formerly CBS Films, Inc.), which promotes the reruns to TV stations by claiming: "Today more than ever, Lucy's madcap antics with Desi Arnaz, Vivian Vance, and William Frawley are praised as priceless performances with timeless appeal. Show a new generation of viewers the queen of comedy in her finest half hours. They'll repay you with an audience worth a king's ransom."

The "I Love Lucy" phenomenon—there's no better word for it—grows in magnitude every year. The intensity of fans' loyalty to the show borders on the bizarre. In a Manhattan art gallery, an oil painting titled "Teensy and Weensy Go Off into the Sunset" (referring to characters in the 1955 episode "Tennessee Bound") was being exhibited. Also in the Big Apple, at a club for aspiring comics, a young comedian was doing his stand-up act and getting no laughs. Suddenly he chanted, "Ethel to Tillie . . . Ethel to Tillie" (referring to the episode "The Séance"), and brought down the house. A Brandeis University student phoned CBS in New York for assistance in the preparation of her Master's thesis; the subject—you guessed it—"I Love Lucy." Lucille Ball herself has inspired the formation in 1977 of a fan club, We Love Lucy, that boasts nearly one thousand members worldwide and meets occasionally in Los Angeles for marathon screenings and meetings (Box 480216, Los Angeles, California 90048).

On her seventy-second birthday on August 6, 1983, Los Angeles TV station KTTV honored the comedienne by airing a thirteen-hour "I Love Lucy" marathon that began at nine o'clock on that Saturday morning and ran, uninterrupted, until 10 P.M. Twenty-six classic "Lucy" episodes— everything from "The Freezer" to "Lucy Does a TV Commercial" to "Lucy's Italian Movie"—were aired. The marathon pulled Channel 11 to the number one position in the ratings for the entire day, and, in fact, won every half-hour in the 1:30 to 7 P.M. time period. Featured throughout the tribute were on-camera birthday messages from such stars as Gale Gordon, Johnny Carson, Bob Hope, Jack Lemmon, and the cast of "Three's Company." The special, which was done with the cooperation of Lucy's husband, Gary Morton, was the brainchild of a young man of Cuban descent who works at the station. Alex Escarano arrived in the United States from Cuba in 1967 at age nine. The first thing he saw on TV was a "Lucy" rerun and the series instantly became a daily habit. Alex credits the show with helping him master the English language as quickly as he did.

Three thousand miles away and eight months later, Lucy was honored again—this time at the prestigious Museum of Broadcasting in New York where the nine-year-old, privately funded repository of vintage radio and TV programs staged an exhibition titled "Lucille Ball: First Lady of Comedy." Consisting of eighty hours of programming (including four hours of Ball's "My Favorite Husband" radio sitcom and her and Desi's first joint TV appearance on "The Ed Wynn Show") and three Lucy-hosted seminars, the tribute garnered incredible worldwide press coverage. Lucille Ball aficio-nados started queuing up to buy tickets at three o'clock in the morning after it was announced she would make a trio of appearances to kick off the five-month-long exhibition. Ron Simon, thirty, curator of the Museum's TV collection, said, "Space was limited to only six hundred and fifty people. We received phone calls from thousands of fans, each with a story more bizarre than the next: 'I lost my ticket,' 'I'm an old friend of Lucy's and she'll expect me there,' 'I'm an actor and attending a seminar is important to my career.' Fans tried any ploy to crash one of the events!" Scenes from "L.A. at Last" (William Holden), "Job Switching" (candy factory), "Harpo Marx," and "Lucy's Italian Movie" (wine vat) were screened, prompting Miss Ball to remark, teary-eyed, "God, I had fun on that show."

In California, where personalized auto license plates are all the rage, such six- and seven-digit messages as LUCY FAN, BABALU, DESILU, LCY BALL, and I LV LCY are in evidence on the streets and freeways of Southern California, bringing many a smile to the lips of amused motorists.

In and around Los Angeles, new businesses have cropped up with such derivative names as I Love Sushi, a Japanese restaurant in Malibu; I Love

Ricky, a chic shop specializing in fashion styling; and my favorite, a health food restaurant on trendy Melrose Avenue in Hollywood—I Love Juicy.

Recently, Lucy-mania has taken the form of merchandise reminiscent of the mid-fifties when such items as Little Ricky dolls, "I Love Lucy" aprons, and Lucy and Ricky matching pajamas were hot sellers. While the older items fetch a pretty penny at swap meets and garage sales, the newer items such as records ("Disco Lucy," "Hey, Ricky," and Desi Arnaz's album "Musical Moments from 'I Love Lucy' "); postcards depicting classic "Lucy" scenes; T-shirts with everything from the famous heart logo to such sayings as "Forget Lucy, I love Ethel"; videotapes of Philip Morris commercials featuring Lucy and Desi; and a commemorative "I Love Lucy" plate (signed by Miss Ball and numbered) are being sold at an amazing rate.

What made "I Love Lucy" one of TV's four all-time hits, according to media specialists and television historians (the others are Milton Berle, "The Beverly Hillbillies," and "All in the Family")?

TV writer Jack Sher and his wife, Madeline, put it this way: "The captivating thing about Lucy and Ricky is the fact that they hold a mirror up to every married couple in America. Not a regular mirror that reflects the truth, nor a magic mirror that portrays fantasy. But a Coney Island kind of mirror that distorts, exaggerates, and makes vastly amusing every little incident, foible, and idiosyncrasy of married life."

Jess Oppenheimer, one of the show's three creators, harbors the same opinion: "The funniest single line ever uttered on 'I Love Lucy' came when Lucy summed up in epigram what happens to a lot of marriages: 'Since we said, "I do," there are so many things we don't.' "

In Jess's learned opinion, the line was not particularly funny in itself, but it gave viewers a sudden, deep insight into themselves—a shock relieved by means of laughter. An interesting sidelight is that this line was contained in the premiere episode of the series, "The Girls Want to Go to a Nightclub."

After so many years, "Lucy" still lives in the hearts of millions because it was—no, is—funny. It's as simple as that. After the first season of "I Love Lucy," the astute Jack Gould of the New York *Times* analyzed: "The distinction lies in its skillful presentation of the basic element of familiarity. If there is one universal theme that knows no age limitations and is recognizable to young and old, it is the institution of marriage—and more particularly the day-to-day trials of husband and wife. It is this single story line above all others with which the audience can most readily identify itself.

" 'I Love Lucy' has no monopoly on the humor inherent in marriage," Gould continued in his New York-based column. "The idea is as old as the theatre itself. But it is the extraordinary discipline and intuitive understanding of farce that gives 'Lucy' its engaging lilt and lift.

"Every installment begins with a plausible and logical premise. Casually the groundwork is laid for the essential motivation: Lucy *vs.* Ricky. Only after a firm foundation of credibility has been established is the element of absurdity introduced. It is in the smooth transition from sense to nonsense that 'I Love Lucy' imparts both a warmth and a reality to the slapstick romp which comes as the climax.''

Put more simply again, "Lucy" was marriage projected to larger-than-life size, but never distorted so that it lost its hold on the viewer. Through the art of cleverly devised exaggeration, Lucy and Ricky put marriage into sharp focus.

As Desi Arnaz says, " 'I Love Lucy' wasn't slick or cerebral—it never insulted anybody. It had one mission: to make people laugh honestly.''

Acknowledgments

On October 15, 1976—the twenty-fifth anniversary of the premiere of "I Love Lucy"—E. P. Dutton & Company published my labor of love, *Lucy & Ricky & Fred & Ethel: The Story of "I Love Lucy."* My editor, Bill Whitehead, who deservingly is now editor-in-chief of that house, couldn't quite fathom how widespread the audience for that book would be. I kept insisting, "There are a lot of people out there watching those reruns!" The book did, indeed, find a large and loyal following, far beyond what we all imagined.

Since publication eight years ago, more material has been gathered in interviews and via additional research. And in response to the countless letters I have received from devoted "Lucy" fans since then, I decided to rewrite the book, making it as thorough and comprehensive a study of "I Love Lucy" as I could possibly do. The result is *The "I Love Lucy" Book.*

It, obviously, could not have happened without the extraordinary influence of Lucille Ball, Desi Arnaz, Vivian Vance, and William Frawley. Equally significant have been the incredible contributions made to the TV sitcom form by Jess Oppenheimer, Madelyn Pugh Martin Davis, and Bob Carroll, Jr.—the three creators of "I Love Lucy"—who were clearly the unsung heroes in this holocaust of hilarity. To them all, I owe my greatest, most heartfelt debt of gratitude.

I must thank the entire staff of Viacom for its cooperation and assistance, above and beyond the call of duty, particularly the late Todd Gaulocher, who was so instrumental in helping me put together the original book in 1976. I know I join many others who miss Todd; he left us much too early.

Thanks also to all those persons who granted interviews in connection with the research for this volume, especially Marc Daniels, Bill Asher, Eliot Daniel, Jerry Hausner, Ross Elliott, Maurice Marsac, Bob Carroll, Jr., Madelyn Davis, Jess Oppenheimer, Bob Schiller, Bob Weiskopf, Jay Sandrich, Elois Jenssen, Al Simon, Herb Browar, Jerry Miggins, Doris Singleton, and Ralph Levy, to name just a few; nods to Mary McCartney, William V. Dunn, Don DeMesquita, Stuart Shokus, Larry Ashmead, William R. Behanna, and Brad Dunning for their assorted favors and kindnesses; a special vote of appreciation to William Ballin of American Export Lines for helping me track down Allison S. Graham, the company's former publicity director; to Maurine Christopher, the talented radio/TV editor of *Advertising Age;* and to the staffs of the Margaret Herrick Library at the Academy of Motion Picture Arts and Sciences and *TV Guide*/Hollywood.

To the scores of "I Love Lucy" aficionados who have written to me expressing their mutual affection for the redhead, thank you. Several who have suggested ways of revising the original text deserve special mention: Bruce Adams, Judine Benche, Jim Bergmann, Jeffrey W. Bowan, Bill Budris, Rick Carl, Dennis Composto, Jim Hall, Vicki Lee Hampton, Peggy Henry, Charles W. Knoll, George Light, Eddie Lucas, Robert R. McJilton, Jr., Kathy Rakel-Ferguson, Sean Rockburn, Tom Rygh, Ken Schoenwetter, Patty Schutte, Gregg Alan Simon, Judy and Jerry Smay, Keith A. Thomas, Mark Towner, Frederick M. Tucker, Neil Wilburn, Jenni Wilkins, and Angel Zadarnowski.

Finally, I wish to express my deepest appreciation to a few very special people: the Doubleday contingent—Laura Van Wormer, the editor who wanted the book and hung in there waiting for it; Paul Bresnick, the editor who inherited it when Laura decided to join the ranks of us freelancers; and the person who held it all together from beginning to end, Nell Hanson; my agent and partner Sherry Robb, whose belief in me literally keeps me going; Marco DeLeon, whose devotion and loyalty mean more to me than he'll ever know; and Thomas J. Watson, my friend and compatriot in all things "Lucy," who did a yeoman's job helping me with the research for this new edition.

To everyone—again—thank you.

                                                             Bart Andrews

Los Angeles, California
June 1, 1984

Contents

The "I Love Lucy" Book

1 On the Road

Lucille Ball and Desi Arnaz had been married nearly a decade in 1950 when CBS informed their agent, Donald W. Sharpe: "We want to transfer Lucy's radio show, 'My Favorite Husband,' to television. Jell-O will continue its sponsorship but only if Lucy and Richard Denning continue as the leads."

Disenchanted with her fifteen-year-old film career, Lucy had escaped to radio in July 1948 to headline a comedy series based on Isabel Scott Rorick's novel *Mr. and Mrs. Cugat,* in which Ball played the role of Liz to Dick Denning's George, her fictional banker husband. The situation comedy was well into its second season when the network tendered the TV offer, realizing that the new *visual* medium was about to blossom in a big way (from 1949 to 1950, the number of TV sets in existence quadrupled from 1 million to 4 million).

"I had never given television any thought until CBS came to me with the offer," recalls Lucille Ball. "I had already done Ed Wynn's show—it was the first time I ever did anything on TV. So frightening, but so wonderful. I'd never been in such a hurried, chaotic setting with these monstrous television cameras all over the stage and not enough rehearsal. But it was great fun."

Despite the enjoyment Lucy experienced from Wynn's *live* TV show—the first to be produced by CBS on the West Coast—and a few subsequent video appearances, she was not thrilled with the idea of turning "My Favorite Husband" into a television show, at least not with Richard Denning. Her initial reluctance did not bother the CBS brass, who recognized the obvious possibilities of turning the successful radio show into an even more successful television program. Confident Lucy would ultimately change her mind, they commissioned the "My Favorite Husband" writers to write an "audition" script to star Lucille Ball and Richard Denning that, to this day, remains unproduced in a desk drawer in Madelyn Pugh Davis and Bob Carroll, Jr.'s office.

Lucy had nothing against Denning, whom she liked very much and with whom she worked very well, but she wanted her real-life husband Desi to play her "favorite husband" in the projected video version. "Richard Denning was playing a typical Midwestern American," Lucy continues. "So far as radio was concerned, the show firmly established my type of man—whatever *that* is!—as a nice gent from Minneapolis, certainly not—great heavens—Desi Arnaz from Cuba!"

William S. Paley, who ran CBS from its corporate headquarters at 485 Madison Avenue in New York, tried his best to change Lucy's mind about Desi: "He's a bandleader, Lucy. He can't act. What'll we do with him?"

"Bill, I'm sorry," Lucy told her broadcasting boss, explaining that Desi spent most of his time traveling around the country on one-nighters with his orchestra and that she wanted more than anything a stable married life and a child. The then thirty-eight-year-old Mrs. Arnaz was adamant: "I'm not going to go on the air unless it's with him. If I can't do a television show with him, I'm going to travel with him." This rather unprecedented devotion was born more of desperation than a desire on Lucy's part to be stubborn. Coming as no great shock to anyone in or out of show business, the Arnazes' marriage, solidified by a Catholic ceremony on June 19, 1949, was crumbling as the 1940s faded.

Lucy and Desi met in May 1940 at the Hollywood studios of RKO Pictures. Arnaz had been summoned to the West Coast to reprise his Broadway role as Manuelito in the movie version of the Richard Rodgers and Lorenz Hart musical *Too Many Girls*. (The New York *Times* said of his stage debut: "As a South American broken field runner, Desi Arnaz is a good wooer of woman.") Director George Abbott introduced Desi to Lucy in the studio commissary one lunchtime.

Lucille Ball and Desi Arnaz posed for this publicity still for RKO's Too Many Girls, *summer 1940, a few months prior to their wedding.*

"I didn't like her at first. She looked awful. Very tough," Desi says. "She was made up like a burlesque queen for a role in *Dance, Girl, Dance.*"

Lucy did look pretty unusual. She was sporting a stage black eye she had received earlier that day in a rough-and-tumble scene with co-star Maureen O'Hara. So when Abbott informed the twenty-three-year-old Desi that Lucille Ball would be playing the part of Consuelo Casey, the ingenue, in the *Too Many Girls* film version, he told the veteran director: "What kind of girl is this? She's no sweet, ingenue type."

Later that day, when the cast was called together for a briefing, the pair "met" again. This time, Lucille was dressed in a yellow skirt and cashmere sweater, and Desi then turned to a studio employee and, in his Cuban accent, observed: "Wot a hunk o' woman!"

"I asked her if she knew how to rumba," Desi recounts, "and when she said no, I offered to teach her."

"Some line he had!" Lucy counters. "We went out all right, but all we did was sit and yak all night. Never got to dance once."

They fell in love almost immediately. "But the studio didn't want us to get married. The gossip columnists kept telling the reasons why we shouldn't

Lucy arrives in New York on November 20, 1940, to help publicize the release of Too Many Girls. *She is met by twenty-three-year-old Desi Arnaz at LaGuardia Airport. The pair would surprise everyone—including Lucy and Desi—by suddenly marrying on November 30.*

get married," Arnaz offers. "We spent the better part of our courtship telling each other it would hurt our careers."

Lucy completes the story: "We talked about marriage, but it seemed impossible. Then, on a personal appearance tour in November of 1940, I flew to New York where Desi happened to be playing with his band at the Roxy Theater."

Lucille was met at the airport by Eleanor Harris, a persistent movie-magazine writer, who was bent on getting an interview to prove the actress and Cuban would never marry. After it was over, Desi surprised both Lucy and the columnist by proposing marriage. At 5 A.M. the next day, November 30, 1940, the couple drove to Greenwich, Connecticut, and at the Byram River Beagle Club at ten o'clock in the morning they were married by a justice of the peace.

As they drove back to Manhattan they heard a radio broadcast describing their marriage. When Desi led his bride onto the Roxy stage to explain why he had missed the first show, thousands of voices roared good wishes—and they were pelted with a barrage of rice, supplied to the crowd by the theater management.

Says Lucille: "I threw away all my conservativeness and took the plunge because I loved him. It was the most daring thing I ever did. Hollywood gave our marriage six months; I gave it six weeks!"

The "daring" redhead was born in Jamestown, New York, on August 6, 1911, to Fred and Desiree (De-De) Ball. He was an engineeer whose job of stringing telephone wires carried him around the country; she was a concert pianist. When Lucille was only four, her father died of typhoid in Wyandotte, Michigan. De-De and Lucy moved back to New York State to the village of Celeron (near Jamestown) to live with Lucy's maternal grandfather, Henry C. Hunt.

From the time she was ten, the little girl took summer jobs: "The first one was to lead a blind man around while both of us sold soap. After that I worked as a soda jerk in a drugstore, as a salesgirl in a dress shop, and I sold hot dogs and popcorn in an amusement park." Lucy even organized the neighborhood children to act out plays, using the family chicken coop for a stage. "I can't remember not wanting to perform."

De-De Ball, now deceased, remembered Lucille's first show business fling: "As a child, she was in the Elks. They always put on little plays, and somehow she got into them. Then I was the producer of the plays in the school where she went. That's how we raised money for the things we wanted, like the senior class trip. Even then, Lucille had a faculty for choosing the part that would stand out. I'd tell her there was nothing to the part, but she'd come back with, 'I don't care. I want that part.' And I swear to God, she was right every time!"

By then, Grandpa Hunt and Lucy's new stepfather, Ed Peterson, had introduced their "Lucyball" (the family nickname) to the world of vaudeville. She loved laughter and fantasy.

"She always had enormous energy, flair, and style," says Lucy's cousin Cleo, once married to Desilu's public relations head Ken Morgan and now the wife of the former Los Angeles *Times* television critic Cecil Smith. "She took us all over, particularly me, who was eight years younger. Always conning us to be in her plays—and *always* in hot water with somebody."

By the time Lucille had quit high school at age fifteen, she had staged virtually a one-man (woman) performance of *Charley's Aunt.* "I played the lead, directed it, cast it, sold the tickets, printed the posters, and hauled furniture to the school for scenery and props."

Jamestown citizens still remember her explosive personality with wide-eyed wonder; it took quite a while for the dust to settle in the little town near Buffalo when "Lucyball" finally left for Manhattan. Neighbors were horrified. Remembers Cousin Cleo, who was raised by De-De Ball and, hence, has a sisterlike relationship with Lucy: "De-De was never bound by the social conventions of the day. She didn't mind the ridicule of the neighbors. She allowed us to express ourselves. She taught us character, values, involvement. She operated on the theory that none of us would ever do anything to disgrace Grandpa Hunt. It was a relationship based on trust. She was the one who decided to let Lucille go to New York City at fifteen."

Lucy enrolled in the John Murray Anderson–Robert Milton Dramatics School (Bette Davis was the star pupil) and at the end of the first year of study, Anderson tactfully told De-De that her daughter should try another line of work.

Determined to make her teacher eat his words, Lucy went out the next morning and landed a job in the chorus of the third road company production of *Rio Rita.* After five weeks of rehearsal, she was canned. The director's opinion was the same as her teacher's. A Ziegfeld aide then told her, "It's no use, Montana [Lucille's preferred nickname then]. You're not meant for show business. Why don't you go home?"

Lucy stayed. Three more chorus jobs followed, and she was fired from them all. Her first job "on Broadway" was as a soda jerk in a West Side drugstore. (For that, she had experience.) In the meantime, she studied modeling, and finally graduated to become a model for Hattie Carnegie, the famous dress designer. As a hat model, Lucy called herself Diane Belmont, choosing the moniker in honor of the Belmont Park Race Track, a nearby Long Island horse arena.

An automobile accident sidetracked her for a few years (she spent eight months in a hospital and the next three years learning how to walk again), but she was back as a model when the ordeal was over. She was once the Chesterfield (cigarettes) poster girl on billboards blanketing New York.

It was now 1933, and Lucille Ball was approaching age twenty-two. She was no closer to an acting career than she had been seven years earlier when she impulsively left high school. One afternoon in July, while strolling up Broadway near Times Square past the Palace Theater, she met agent Sylvia Hahlo coming down from Sam Goldwyn's office. Sylvia grabbed Lucy

Lucille Ball, 1942.

and cried breathlessly: "How would you like to go to California? Goldwyn just picked twelve showgirls for an Eddie Cantor picture. Six weeks' work. One of the girls' mothers has refused to let her go. They're desperate . . ."

At that time, famed musicals director Busby Berkeley was instrumental in selecting the yearly crop of Goldwyn Girls. Before his death, he said: "Goldwyn called me in one day and said, 'I want you to come up to the projection room. I've made some tests of girls from New York and I want to see whether you like them.' We ran them and there were two girls that I liked very much. But Goldwyn didn't like them.

"The next morning I went by his office and asked his secretary, 'Mary, did he send for the two girls that he didn't like but I did?' She smiled and said, 'Yes, he did, Mr. Berkeley.' The two girls I had picked were Barbara Pepper and Lucille Ball."

Within a matter of days Lucy was aboard a westbound express train

Lucille Ball (far right), age twenty-one, arrives at Union Station, Los Angeles, on July 19, 1933.

Lucy (left) appears in the first of several Goldwyn films, Roman Scandals, 1933. That's Eddie Cantor in blackface.

headed for Hollywood. The movie was *Roman Scandals,* and it was six months instead of six weeks in the making. Columbia Pictures soon signed her to a contract (fifty dollars a week) as a stock player where she landed a succession of bit parts in a variety of films and worked with the Three Stooges. Convinced that her luck had finally turned, Lucy wired her family— mother, younger brother Fred, Cousin Cleo, and Grandpa Hunt—to come and live with her. The morning after she'd sent for the family, Columbia decided to dissolve its stock company. By the time the foursome arrived by bus, Lucy was toiling as an extra in the RKO film *Roberta.* The role impressed studio officials, who signed her to a contract. During her seven-year tenure at RKO, Lucy appeared in a series of B pictures, then began making films with comics like Jack Oakie, Joe Penner, and even the Marx Brothers *(Room Service).* Her salary rose to fifteen hundred dollars a week; and the quality of her roles improved, including a plum part in the Katharine Hepburn– Ginger Rogers film *Stage Door.* Other RKO films included *Panama Lady, Five Came Back,* and *Dance, Girl, Dance.* It was while she was finishing photography on this Erich Pommer–directed movie that Lucille Ball, then twenty-eight, met Desi Arnaz, twenty-three.

The only child of a Cuban senator and the *Alcalde Modelo* (model mayor) of Santiago, Cuba, Desiderio Alberto Arnaz y de Acha III, was born March 2, 1917. His mother, Dolores de Acha, was considered among the most beautiful women in Latin America.

Three ranches totaling one hundred thousand acres, a palatial home in the city, a private island in Santiago Bay, an armada of speedboats, a fleet of automobiles, and a stable of racehorses were all at the command of youthful Desi. By the time he was sixteen, he had become, by his own admission, a fathead. His future already had been planned for him by his father: He would attend the University of Notre Dame in Indiana, study law, and then return home to a ready-made practice.

His father's grandiose plans did not include the first Batista revolution in Cuba, which came on August 12, 1933. Papa Arnaz was jailed instantly, his property confiscated. Within twenty-four hours, everything was gone except five hundred dollars that Mrs. Arnaz had socked away. Young Desi and his mother fled to Miami where they devoted the next six months to efforts to free the elder Arnaz from prison. Desi also attended St. Patrick's High School in the beach city where one of his classmates was Sonny Capone, Al's son.

During this difficult period of adjustment, Desi worked at a number of odd jobs to help pay the rent at the dingy rooming house where his family lived. His first job was cleaning out canary cages for a local bird buff bent on selling the warblers in drugstores. Desi was paid twenty-five cents per cage.

He also worked at truck driving, train-yard checking, taxi driving, and bookkeeping. Desi spoke little English at first; once when ordering a meal at a restaurant he mistakenly got five bowls of soup.

In 1937 the show business bug bit. With a borrowed suit, he auditioned at the swanky Roney Plaza Hotel in Miami Beach. The overflow crowd

Desi Arnaz, 1943.

cheered—they were his St. Pat classmates. Fooled, the owner hired Arnaz at a huge salary, fifty dollars per week.

"My first job was with the Siboney Septet. I don't know why it was called a septet since there were only five of us. I guess septet sounded better," Desi claims.

It was during this gig that Xavier Cugat spotted him and hired the handsome twenty-one-year-old as a singer for thirty-five dollars a week. Following a year's apprenticeship with Cugat, Desi decided to strike out on his own. After a few months, he was back in Florida where he bluffed his way into a new club, the swank La Conga Café, at a whopping seven-hundred-and-fifty-dollars-a-week salary.

The local critics agreed on Desi's meager musical gifts. "He was always offbeat," one of his bosses contended. "But he's an awfully nice guy—a clean-cut Latin."

Before too long, his good looks and effervescent humor landed his band in New York. There he was singled out by George Abbott and given a leading role as a Latin football player in the new stage musical *Too Many Girls*. When RKO bought the film rights, they beckoned Desi, along with co-players Richard Kolmar, Eddie Bracken, and Hal LeRoy, to Hollywood to reprise their Broadway roles. Pretty Marcy Wescott, who had the femme lead in the legit musical, did not go West. Her part in the film went to an RKO contract player, Lucille Ball.

Following Lucy and Desi's impromptu 1940 marriage, Desi had parts in

Desi and Lucy play at their ranchette in Chatsworth in the San Fernando Valley of Los Angeles. The couple purchased the property shortly after their marriage and remained there until 1955 when they bought their Beverly Hills home, where Lucy still resides.

a few other pictures (his best was the M-G-M war drama *Bataan,* directed by Tay Garnett), but as he puts it: "I didn't take well with movies and they didn't take well with me."

At the same time, Lucy's movie career was soaring. A needed break came in the form of Damon Runyon's *The Big Street,* in which she portrayed a hard-bitten showgirl who was paralyzed from the hips down. She played the role so convincingly that she soon had every studio bidding for her services. On August 6, 1942 (her thirty-first birthday), Lucille signed with M-G-M, which immediately cast her in the title role in *Du Barry Was a Lady,* with Gene Kelly.

Her proud Cuban husband, not content to loaf at the couple's rambling San Fernando Valley home in Chatsworth and let Lucille be the breadwinner, hit the road again to make nightclub appearances. The enforced separation their respective jobs occasioned put their marriage on an erratic course, headed for divorce.

The crack-up was postponed by World War II. Desi was drafted into the infantry and later transferred, because of a broken kneecap, to Army Special Service where he made sergeant and spent much of the war guiding USO troupes from one California camp to another.

But the war gave their marriage only temporary respite. Lucille sued for divorce in the fall of 1944, although the couple subsequently patched up their differences. But the same old arguments about Desi's out-of-town engagements versus Lucy's movie career began all over again.

Lucy succeeded in keeping Desi home for two years in the late 1940s by approaching Bob Hope and suggesting that Desi and his orchestra replace the departing Stan Kenton on Hope's popular NBC radio show.

By this time Lucy was busy with her own radio show, "My Favorite Husband," which CBS wanted to develop into a TV program. The more the network tried to convince her that audiences would not believe that she and Desi would make a logical married couple on television, the more determined she became, insisting, "What do you mean nobody'll believe it? We *are* married!"

While the network didn't agree, Jess Oppenheimer, Lucy's radio producer and head writer since November 1948, and agent Don Sharpe liked the idea

Lucy and actor Richard Denning receive last-minute instructions from "My Favorite Husband" producer-director Gordon Hughes at CBS Columbia Square, 1948.

The Coopers—Liz and George—of radio's "My Favorite Husband." It was the network's desire to team the pair in a TV version of the popular radio comedy despite Lucy's demand that she co-star with her own husband, Desi.

of a TV show starring Lucy and Desi. But neither of them could convince the broadcasting bigwigs nor the all-important advertising agency men.

The Arnazes finally decided to take themselves—husband and wife—directly to the people. "Let's go out and 'test' it," Lucille suggested. "If no one will give us a job together, we'll give ourselves one." It was April 1950 and the first thing the pair did was form Desilu Productions (their ranchette in Chatsworth already had been christened thusly). In order to hit the road, the couple needed more than enthusiasm—they needed an act.

The Cuban and the redhead put together a series of slapstick routines involving a movie star who tries to join her bandleader husband's act, and decided to join forces during Lucy's summer radio hiatus and Desi's usual band tour. They armed themselves with a wardrobe of eccentric costumes and billed themselves as "Desi Arnaz & Band with Lucille Ball."

"I went to my old fishing friend, Pepito," recounts Desi Arnaz about the famed showman of international repute who was billed as "The Spanish Clown." "He came up with a few routines for us to perform and even taught us how to do the skits in a hotel room near San Diego."

Late spring 1950. Lucy and Desi rehearse "Cuban Pete/Sally Sweet" number for their vaudeville tour, which opened in Chicago on June 2, 1950.

"He built me this incredible cello," Lucille explains. "It was an entire act. Real Rube Goldberg stuff. I pulled a stool out of it, a horn, a toilet plunger, gloves, flowers, a violin bow." It was a duplicate of a prop Pepito had used himself years before, one that was more or less guaranteed to get laughs. With some assist from Lucy's mentors, Buster Keaton and director Eddie Sedgwick, the Arnazes polished their act—a broad satire of a year in the life of Lucille Ball and Desi Arnaz—and set out on a twelve-week vaudeville tour after pretaping several "My Favorite Husband" radio shows and playing a few local California dates.

The act, which featured comedy dialogue by Lucy's radio scribes, Madelyn Pugh and Bob Carroll, Jr., opened at the Chicago Paramount Theater on June 2, 1950. "After the first show, Desi and I looked at each other in wild surprise," Lucy remembers. "Well, I guess we *can* work together after all. We're on our way!"

About their twenty-minute act, *Variety* commented: "One of the best bills to play house in recent months. Most of it revolves around Desi Arnaz and his frau, Lucille Ball, who have developed a sock new act.

"It's a rare day in June when film stars hit this vaudeville stage with proper material and this is a rare day, or week," the review continued. "Lucille Ball and hubby, Desi Arnaz, have come up with funny quips and terrific burlesque situations, which, if film comedienne wishes to continue, would make them one of the top vaudeville comedy teams. If the redheaded gal wants to slide on her tummy for five or six shows a day past the initial five-week booking for this package, her agency, G.A.C., should have no trouble lining up dates.

"Turn really gets hilarious when a Red Skelton-type character in oversized tails and crushed hat comes running down the aisle seeking an audition with the band. It breaks up the audience.

"Leader [Desi] brings on a group of horns, similar to those the seals play in circuses, and Miss Ball makes like a seal burping out the notes, flipping her tails and overlong sleeves, waddling on her tummy across the stage.

"For finale, she joins her Latin friend, dressed as a denizen of lower New York, in a green split skirt with spangles and sequins, and pops the eyes out of the first-row viewers with her hip-slinging activities to hypoed beat of 'Cuban Pete.' Credit must be given to Madelyn Pugh and Bob Carroll, Jr., for some of the earlier material but the situations are supposed to be the brain product of the Arnaz family. Top fare."

Next the pair hit New York's famed Roxy Theater. Following a one-week bill starring TV's Sid Caesar, Imogene Coca, and Faye Emerson, the Arnazes opened on Friday, June 9, 1950, for two full weeks. The New York reviews echoed the earlier Chicago reactions—all excellent. Lucille and Desi decided to celebrate their tenth wedding anniversary early on June 13 in their Roxy dressing room, the same suite where Desi had carried Lucille over the threshold on November 30, 1940, after their Greenwich, Connecticut, ceremony.

Lucy recalls an unsettling incident that took place during the New York run: "I had been taught about props by Buster Keaton. Especially attention to detail, which was the most important thing. He taught me that my prop is my jewel case. Never entrust it to a stage hand or anyone else. Never let it out of your sight when you travel, and rehearse with it all week. 'Honey,' he told me, 'if you noodge it, you've lost the act.'

"Well, wouldn't you know it, it happened at the Roxy. I was supposed to run down that seven-mile aisle when some maniac sprang my cello by leaping up and yelling 'I'm that woman's mother! She's letting me starve!' It scared me to death. I ad-libbed around it, and I am one lousy ad-libber," Miss Ball reveals.

After playing only a few days in New York, Lucy began to feel ill. "Suddenly I feel tired all the time," she confided to Desi one night after the show. At first they believed it was merely the fatigue of performing seven shows daily, including a belly-flop entrance at each performance. But when the illness persisted she went to see a doctor.

"Are you pregnant?" Dr. Sym Newman asked. The thought hadn't entered Lucy's mind. She had had a miscarriage in her first year of marriage, and for nine years after that she had been unable to conceive. She underwent a thorough physical, including the rabbit test for pregnancy. It was a Friday, and the results would not be available until Monday morning at the earliest.

As it turned out, they learned the results sooner than the doctor. Between shows on Sunday night, she and Desi tuned to Walter Winchell's weekly radio broadcast and were dumbfounded when he announced: "Flash! After ten years, Lucille Ball and Desi Arnaz are expecting a bundle from heaven." Listening in their dressing room, they were ecstatic. "It's true! It's true!" Lucy screamed. "If Winchell says so, it must be true."

It was. An overzealous laboratory worker had reported the news to Winchell first. The Arnazes made immediate plans. They canceled the last half of their tour (they were supposed to play the London Palladium) and slightly revised Lucy's acrobatics. "In the seal bit, I no longer wiggled around on my stomach," she said. "But I still did backflips and barked."

In newspaper accounts dated June 27, 1950, Lucy reported that she would be expecting the child in January. She and Desi rested up a few days in New York before heading for their next vaudeville stand, a four-day engagement at the Paramount in Buffalo (June 30–July 3). After that they played the Riverside Theater in Milwaukee, opening July 6. It was the theater's first vaudeville bill in weeks, and it was breaking records with a hefty thirty thousand dollars grossed in a matter of a few days.

After closing in Wisconsin, they flew back to California on an American Airlines flight, and as soon as Lucy reached their home in Chatsworth, she went to bed. She wasn't feeling right. Within two days, she was rushed to Cedars of Lebanon Hospital in Hollywood where a team of doctors tried for a week to save the baby. On July 27, just a month after making the baby announcement in New York, Lucy suffered a miscarriage, her second.

The couple escaped to Del Mar, a favorite seaside resort town just north of San Diego, where they tried to shake off the trauma of the tragedy. But Lucille still had her "My Favorite Husband" commitment, which would start again on September 2, and a few solo TV appearances to fulfill plus a third feature on her three-picture deal with Columbia (*Miss Grant Takes Richmond* and *The Fuller Brush Girl* were the first two). As always she happily plunged back into her work while at the same time she prodded agent Don Sharpe: "Please find a way for Desi and me to do a television show together. *Please.*"

Because CBS still wanted no part of a Lucille Ball-Desi Arnaz show, the pair commissioned scripts and ideas from writers not connected with "My Favorite Husband" in an effort to get as far away from that concept as possible so as not to be accused of plagiarism.

"The first script wasn't about Lucy and Ricky Ricardo at all," says Desi Arnaz. "It was about a successful orchestra leader, Desi Arnaz, and his successful movie star wife, Lucille Ball, and how *Life* magazine loused up their plans for a quiet wedding anniversary celebration. It was a very funny script, very funny. But it wasn't honest."

Lucille Ball agrees: "I didn't want to play a typical Hollywood couple. It would have been a stereotype. Everybody thinks if you're a Hollywood couple, you have no problems. We know it isn't so—just because you have a pool and a couple of cars, it's ridiculous for people to assume you don't have problems. But it's hard to prove that you do, so that was out. Anyway, I didn't want my character to be glamorous. I didn't want her to have beautiful clothes. And I didn't want her to be a wisecracking girl who drops a line and walks out of the room. I'd done all that in pictures and I certainly didn't want to do it over again."

Though the Arnazes themselves weren't satisfied with the concepts dreamed up by various writers, rival NBC did show interest in them as a comedy team. This pleased Lucy and Desi because they were totally convinced, based on the excellent scrapbook of reviews they had collected during their road tour that summer, that audiences would accept them as a married couple on television. And if it wasn't going to be CBS putting them on the air, NBC would do just fine.

In late October 1950, three months after losing her unborn baby, Lucy discovered she was pregnant again. Determined not to take chances this time, she canceled all of her engagements—including a plum role in Cecil B. DeMille's *The Greatest Show on Earth* movie epic—and decided to do only the once-weekly radio show, which was a relatively easy undertaking.

"At that point, I decided," Lucille Ball confirms, "that unless Desi and I could act together in the future, I would never act again."

2 The Pilot

Soon after Christmas 1950, Lucy received a welcome phone call from her agent, Don Sharpe: "I've just finished negotiating a deal with CBS to make a pilot film of a TV series to star you and Desi."

The tenacious Sharpe, once president of the giant GAC talent agency, kept prodding the CBS brass, particularly the West Coast director of network programs, Dartmouth-educated Harry S. Ackerman, warning them that they might lose Lucy to NBC if they didn't act immediately on the proposed television series. Having had to withdraw formally, because of her pregnancy, from the Cecil B. DeMille film that would go into production at the end of January, Lucy was particularly pleased with the news.

"You know what that means?" Sharpe continued. "After the pilot film is made, CBS will try to find a sponsor for the show. If they succeed, by the terms of the contract the show will go on the air next fall."

"What show?" Lucy countered. "We have no show."

"We'll have to have one by February 15—that's when the pilot film has to be done," Sharpe informed her.

"We'll have one," Lucy said evenly.

Although she had vowed not to work much during her pregnancy, Lucy managed to complete *The Magic Carpet,* the last picture under her three-film Columbia contract (she was paid a hefty eighty-five thousand dollars for a six-day shooting hitch). Desi and his orchestra had recently closed at the Chi Chi, a swanky new Palm Springs nightclub, and were booked into Ciro's on Hollywood's famed Sunset Strip. Also he was about to debut (January 21, 1951) in his own CBS radio show, "Your Tropical Trip," a half-music/half-game show mélange that Harry Ackerman put together for him.

"Everybody warned Desi and me that we were committing career suicide by giving up highly paid movie and band commitments to go for broke on TV, but it was either working together or good-bye marriage." It was estimated that the pair kissed away approximately five hundred thousand dollars in order to work together in television. "It was then that I dreamed about Carole," the comedienne says, referring to her late friend Carole Lombard. "She was wearing a very smart suit, and she said, 'Honey, go ahead. Take a chance. Give it a whirl!' "

The first order of business was coming up with a format for the television script. The "My Favorite Husband" premise was still verboten—the network knew audiences wouldn't believe Desi Arnaz as a banker—Midwestern or otherwise. In fact, they were still not overjoyed with the prospect of having him involved at all in the Lucille Ball series. To ensure smooth sailing, Harry

Ackerman of CBS agreed to Lucy's condition that Jess Oppenheimer be assigned to helm the television project. Jess had served his Arnaz apprenticeship for about two years as Lucy's "Husband" producer and head writer. Oppenheimer still had five years to run on his exclusive CBS contract.

Born in 1913 and raised in San Francisco, Oppenheimer began his writing career in radio. After Stanford University and a brief tenure in the fur trade, Jess struck out for Hollywood to get a job in show business. He landed one with the Young & Rubicam advertising agency in 1936 with a starting salary of one hundred and twenty-five dollars per week. He lent his talents in the medium to "The Packard Hour" starring Fred Astaire and Charles Butterworth, "The Jack Benny Program," "The Chase and Sanborn Hour," Fanny Brice's "Baby Snooks Show," the Edgar Bergen programs, and, of course, "My Favorite Husband," which he wrote, produced, and also directed.

CBS had a lot of faith in Jess, whom they originally hired to revamp "Husband" and make the characters more identifiable to the average person. To that end, the Cugats became the more WASP-ish Coopers, and while George—played by Dick Denning—continued to be a banker, the crises in the couple's lives became more domestic and, hence, the characters more sympathetic. The network was well aware that the format changes that Jess had instituted in late 1948 had helped the show's ratings considerably. They now expected him to work some of that "magic" on Lucy and Desi's new TV endeavor. They matched their faith by giving Oppenheimer a whopping 20 percent (of the network's 50 percent) interest he asked for in the eventual program.

"I read the material that had been written by a few outside writers earlier that fall," recalls Oppenheimer, who in recent years has devoted much of his time to inventing, with more than twenty patents to prove his prowess. "I rejected all of it as Lucy and Desi already had. I preferred to stick closer to the flavor of 'My Favorite Husband' because it was working so well for Lucy. So, with a few minor adjustments, I hit upon the idea of a middle-class working stiff who works very hard at his job and who likes nothing better than coming home at night and relaxing with his wife, who doesn't like staying home and wants a career of her own. That was the nucleus. In fact, one of the lines in the pilot had Desi saying, 'I want a wife who's just a wife.' That bit of dialogue pretty much summed up our basic premise. CBS liked it, and, best of all, so did Lucy."

The format *delighted* Mrs. Arnaz. She loved the housewife image. "Of all the thirty or forty films I had made up to that time," she states, "I could find only three or four scenes in those pictures that I cared anything about. When I put them all together, I discovered they were domestic scenes, where I portrayed a housewife."

Because time was of the essence, Jess and the "Husband" writers, Madelyn Pugh and Bob Carroll, Jr., decided to utilize pieces of the Arnazes' vaudeville act in the pilot film. Madelyn had flown up to San Francisco in mid-July to catch the act at the Curran Theater and knew, firsthand, how well the audience received the pair's shenanigans. With Desi's limited acting experience, his role—originally tagged "Larry Lopez"—was modeled closely after his real-life image, that of a Latin bandleader. "Lucy Lopez" was merely an extension of "Liz Cooper," the wacky character Lucille Ball was playing on the CBS Radio Network. In the opening eight-minute scene, set in the Lopez's Manhattan living room, Lucy confronts hubby Larry about his upcoming television audition. Not satisfied with being only a housewife, she yearns for a career in show business. "George Burns uses his wife on his show," she reminds him. But Larry insists, "I don't want my wife in show business." Larry's agent arrives with the news that the TV show audition is that very night. To keep her away from the nightclub, Larry insists that Lucy take their signed wills to the lawyer, which will keep her occupied for most of the afternoon. (This plot device was lifted, practically verbatim, from a "My Favorite Husband" script.) At a rehearsal that day at Larry's nightclub, the clown hired as one of the acts takes ill and Larry sends him to the Lopez apartment to recuperate. Upon Lucy's return from the attorney's office, she finds the ailing comic in her apartment, and decides to take his place at the audition. That was Act One of the pilot script.

Act Two, set in the nightclub, would include Larry's big musical number, "Babalu," and Lucy masquerading as the indisposed clown, doing the "Professor"/cello routine and the seal bit. Hence, the half-hour test film would wind up being more vaudeville than situation comedy.

On February 6, 1951, *Daily Variety* reported that "CBS is now lining up seven new sitcoms to tee off on video next fall, all emanating from Hollywood. . . . New shows which are being lined up include packages to star Joan Davis, Hal Peary, and Desi Arnaz-Lucille Ball." Exactly two weeks later, the rival trade paper, *Hollywood Reporter,* announced: "Lucille Ball and Desi Arnaz will do their first TV show for CBS on March 2 over a closed circuit at the Hollywood studios. Program will be kinescoped for sponsors' viewing in the East. Show is a CBS package, produced by Jess Oppenheimer, producer of Miss Ball's 'My Favorite Husband' radio program, and will be directed by Ralph Levy, doubling from similar chores on CBS's 'Burns and Allen' program."

Levy, the thirty-one-year-old Yale graduate whom CBS had dispatched to Los Angeles from New York in 1949 to set up its TV studios, joined the network as an assistant director in 1946, directing cameras for boxing, basketball, and professional football games. With some college background and interest in musicals—he helped write many of the Yale shows—Levy moved from sports to entertainment, and was soon directing variety shows such as "The 54th Street Revue," which premiered as a summer series in 1949. As an example of his promise as a director, he got the first "Revue" on the air in just four days, working with writers Max Wilk, George Axelrod, and the late' Allen Sherman (Bob Fosse was one of the dancers on the show). With plans underway to star "The Perfect Fool," Ed Wynn, in his own TV show in Hollywood, CBS moved Levy to the Coast in late August

1949 with four engineers and a dictum to get Wynn on the air in six weeks. He did, and quickly became CBS's fair-haired boy on the West Coast. When tapped for the Lucy-Desi assignment, Ralph was busy producing and directing the bi-weekly "Burns and Allen Show," which was in its first season as a live show, and duplicating those chores on Alan Young's weekly variety show (Young subsequently starred in "Mr. Ed").

"I was anxious to direct Lucy's pilot because I had worked with her on 'The Ed Wynn Show,'" Ralph remembers, referring to her TV debut in 1949. "I recall Jess and the writers having a lot of trouble with the script. They couldn't seem to get it just the way they wanted it. I remember that the script called for Lucy to parade around the living room with a lampshade on her head—trying to prove to Desi she could be a Ziegfeld girl. I didn't think she was walking quite the right way so I showed her how it should be done, not knowing that she had been a showgirl for many years. Instead of telling me off, she simply played along with me. She was *so* professional and *so* good. She walked away with the whole show."

According to a revised schedule, the "audition" (the term for "pilot" in those early days) show was done on Friday, March 2, 1951 (Desi's thirty-fourth birthday), in Studio A at Columbia Square, the Hollywood headquarters of CBS Radio and TV, located on Sunset Boulevard at Gower Street. It was the same stage where Lucy had appeared with Ed Wynn a little over a year earlier. "There were only two sets," Levy explains. "One was a living room and the other the nightclub where Desi worked. The show was shot live with a studio audience in attendance, as most TV shows were being done then. There was no tape yet. Later, the images were recorded on film from a TV screen, providing us with the required kinescope."

From Act One of the pilot for "The Lucille Ball–Desi Arnaz TV Show," March 2, 1951. Lucy reacts when husband Larry Lopez asks her to take their signed wills to the attorney. Set in the couple's chic Manhattan apartment.

Nightclub scene from Act Two of pilot. Orchestra leader Lopez confronts his wife, who is posing as a clown playing a cello as "The Professor."

Interestingly, the pilot was practically aborted that very night. Up until that day, CBS and Lucy and Desi had reached only a verbal agreement. Nothing was on paper, signed. There had been a lot of haggling back and forth between the network lawyers and Don Sharpe, and the two parties were still apart in their thinking. Nothing serious, but nothing on paper either. The studio audience was filing into its seats; Lucy was backstage tending to last-minute makeup. Suddenly, Hal Hudson of CBS sought out Desi backstage and told him that unless he signed the contracts—as is, then and there—CBS would shut down the production and send the audience home. The tall, slender CBS executive was attempting a "power play": Sign the agreement the way it stands, or there will be no TV show. Desi was not about to be intimidated by Hudson or anybody else—not after coming this far.

"How much is this pilot costing CBS?" Arnaz asked Hudson, who was several inches taller.

"Nineteen thousand dollars," Hudson replied, referring to some papers he was carrying.

"Fine. Lucy and I will pay for it," Desi announced grandly.

Arnaz had called the executive's bluff, at which point Hudson cleared his

Actor Jerry Hausner meets Pepito the Clown at CBS Columbia Square prior to performing in the pilot. Hausner played Larry Lopez's agent in the sample film while Pepito, a good friend of Lucy and Desi's, played the clown whom Mrs. Lopez replaces.

throat and said, "No, that's all right. We'll pay for everything. Forget it." With that he walked away, and Ralph Levy, anxious to get started with the show, called for "places" for the actors.

To serve as Desi's friend and confidant, Oppenheimer cast Jerry Hausner to play Jerry, the agent. The forty-one-year-old character actor and ex-vaudevillian had played parts on Lucy's "My Favorite Husband" and had become something of a minor celebrity as the voice of Robespierre, Baby Snooks's little brother in the Fanny Brice radio show, which Oppenheimer also wrote. To play the clown who gets sick and can't perform at the audition, the Arnazes paid back a personal debt and hired their dear friend Pepito, who had helped them get their vaudeville act off the ground. (These were the only other characters featured in the pilot; it did not contain two key elements that eventually helped make "I Love Lucy" such a hit—characters Fred and Ethel Mertz.)

By March 7, kinescope copies of "The Lucille Ball–Desi Arnaz TV Show" pilot were available for sponsor consideration. Walter Bunker, who at one time had worked as a director on the "Baby Snooks Show" with Jess and was now heading up the Hollywood offices of the Young & Rubicam ad agency, had been keeping an eye on the Arnaz TV project for some time. It was Young & Rubicam that represented the General Foods product Jell-O, which sponsored "My Favorite Husband." Bunker loved the audition film and gave it a big send-off to the New York home offices on Madison Avenue.

The Arnazes' agent, Don Sharpe, himself packed up the test film and flew to New York the following week in the hopes of nailing a sponsor willing to underwrite its cost as a TV series. The original plan was to air the show on alternate weeks, much like the "Burns and Allen Show."

Contrary to popular belief, the program did not find a firm buyer right away. According to the late ad agency head Milton H. Biow, Sharpe's show got the cold-shoulder treatment all along Madison Avenue. "Don got turned down by six or seven agencies before bringing his film to Biow. He had heard rumors, all true, that our client of long standing [since 1933], Philip Morris, was disenchanted with the results of its first two TV-show-sponsorship ventures—video versions of radio's 'Truth or Consequences' and Horace Heidt's show. I must be candid and say I was not overwhelmed by the pilot, but I thought it had a better than average chance for success," said the adman who created the famous "Call for Philip Morris" campaign.

When asked why other agencies had passed on the Ball-Arnaz outing, Biow once conjectured, "They may have envisioned it merely as it was originally presented—a routine vaudeville show with a comedy couple, a guest star, and a band. We envisioned it differently."

As was the custom in those days, ad agencies tended to become actively involved with the shows they sponsored or were considering sponsoring. In fact, advertisers and their agencies often developed their own shows and brought them to the networks, all packaged. So it wasn't unusual for a theatrical agent like Don Sharpe to deal directly with ad agencies when he had what he considered to be a "hot" property.

Biow, a shrewd and powerful denizen of Madison Avenue, hesitated

Ad agency president Milton H. Biow's stubborn insistence that "I Love Lucy" be done live from New York was the impetus needed to develop a system whereby the shows could be filmed in Hollywood, thereby inventing the rerun.

making an instant decision, despite Sharpe's pressuring. Surely he could not make a major buy like this one involving more than $1 million without consulting the principals of the companies he represented such as Bulova Watch, Pepsi-Cola, Procter & Gamble, and Philip Morris. With a 16-mm print of the pilot in hand, Biow urged Benjamin Sonnenberg—the cigarette company's suave public relations representative—to invite a large group of people to Sonnenberg's sumptuous Gramercy Park townhouse to see the film. Among the people at the gathering was Biow's close friend, lyricist Oscar Hammerstein II, who, after the screening, reportedly commented, "Keep the redhead, but ditch the Cuban."

"But he's her husband," Biow explained. "It's a package deal. To get her, we have to take him."

"Well, for God's sake, don't let him sing," the famed Broadway librettist urged. "No one will understand him." Hammerstein went on to suggest that the format be changed to emphasize the scatterbrained domestic comedy angle not the musical-variety elements: "Make it a warm, human story built around a wholesome, lovable, dizzy couple." Oscar, who knew from much experience what "hit" meant, predicted the show could be a smash, likening it to radio's undefeatable "Fibber McGee and Molly."

By early April, the show still had no takers. Biow continued to have reservations, which he was trying to dispel by keeping a dialogue open with the Arnazes through Don Sharpe. "We want a down-to-earth approach, and guest stars only when they are an integral part of the episode, and the same is true of the band." The guest star featured in the pilot was, of course, Pepito, the Clown, and the band was Desi's own orchestra, which he was trying desperately to keep together.

Desi sweated: "I pay the boys every week, Mr. Biow, and if we only use them now and then, who's going to stand the cost?"

"Don't worry about that," Biow assured the bandleader. "Include the band in the cost of the program. If the show doesn't go, we won't stay with it anyhow. If it's a success, the cost of the band won't matter."

By this time, CBS was getting anxious. They had some dollars invested in the project and there still wasn't a firm offer from an advertiser. Biow knew he was about the only agency in New York who had any interest in the show. Uncomfortable about the price—$26,500 per show for the first year—he decided to sit tight and play it by ear. The sales office at CBS in New York drew up a three-page document for mass circulation to agencies and other interested parties titled "Available for Sponsorship . . . 'I Love Lucy.' " It was dated April 16, 1951, and reflected the hard-sell approach.

"The high-caliber scripts that play such an important part in Lucille Ball's radio success will make 'I Love Lucy' one of television's most popular situation comedies," the sales piece assured.

About Lucy herself, CBS raved, "In the past few years Hollywood has discovered that, besides being one of its most glamorous stars, Lucille Ball is one of its finest comediennes. For her ability to get the most out of comedy lines is matched by her artistry in 'mugging' and 'double-takes.' In the audition recording of 'I Love Lucy,' Lucille hits the screen with a comedy-glamour impact that is unrivaled in television today. As the stage-struck wife of a handsome bandleader (played by her real-life husband, Desi Arnaz), her brilliant comedy is shown to its fullest advantage."

Realizing that the least attractive selling point was Desi Arnaz himself, the CBS pitch gushed, "Playing the part of a bandleader who feels that his wife's place is in their home—and has a hard time keeping her there—Desi Arnaz shows that his newly-discovered aptitude for comedy is on the same high par as his better-known singing ability. His characterization of a harassed husband is far more than a foil for Lucille Ball's zany wife; it's a skillful interpretation by a polished comedian. And his personable vocalizing, backed by his versatile orchestra, comes across with truly dynamic impact."

At the bottom of page two of the brochure, CBS summed up, "With the same basic ingredients that make Lucille Ball's radio program a great success . . . plus her tremendous visual impact . . . plus the considerable versatility of Desi Arnaz . . . 'I Love Lucy' is assured of big television audiences."

Exactly seven days after CBS began circulating their "Lucy" flyer, Biow—fearful that another agency might suddenly grab the Arnaz TV package—said yes. The following day, April 24, both Hollywood trade papers reported that Philip Morris had bought the show to originate live from Hollywood on Monday nights, beginning October 1. The cigarette firm dropped the Horace Heidt show because, as *Daily Variety* wrote, "It failed to roll up a rating satisfactory to the ciggie roller.

"Harry Ackerman, CBS program head here," *Variety* continued, "has assigned Jess Oppenheimer, Madelyn Pugh and Bob Carroll to write the scripts, the same trio having performed the duty on [Lucy's] radio series. No director has been set, although Ralph Levy looms as the final choice."

Philip Morris was reported to be paying "in excess of $20,000 per week" for the new show, but logically not as much as the original asking price of $26,500. This would bring to four the total number of CBS shows to originate in Hollywood, others being "Burns and Allen," Alan Young's show, and the new "Amos 'n' Andy" on film.

When Harry Ackerman relayed the sponsorship news to Don Sharpe, he noted, "There's a catch. We'd planned on a show every other week, but Philip Morris wants a weekly show."

Sharpe was rightfully concerned. "Making a weekly television show means burning all of Lucy's movie bridges behind her," the agent explained. "She'll have no time for anything *but* television."

Sharpe drove out to Chatsworth to see the Arnazes. Lucy, nearly seven months' pregnant, listened carefully to Sharpe, then answered without hesitation: "Desi and I want to work together more than anything in the world. If he's willing to give up traveling with his band, I'm willing to give up my film work."

Desi nodded his agreement. "We'll gamble everything on this show. The answer is yes."

THE PILOT: March 2, 1951

These candid photos were taken the night the pilot was done by Bob Carroll, Jr., one of the three "I Love Lucy" writers, on Stage A at Columbia Square, the then West Coast headquarters of CBS-TV.

"George Burns uses his wife."

"I want a wife who's just a wife."

"I bet if Earl Carroll saw me, he'd snap me up in a minute!"

Larry wants her to take their signed wills to the lawyer . . . way downtown.

Lucy thinks Larry is ready to kick the bucket.

"What are you trying to do—
push me ahead of you in line?"

Above and right:
Pepito rehearses at Larry's nightclub.

Above left and right:
Lucy later takes Pepito's place in the act.

The answer—alas—was not that simple. When Milton Biow returned to his office on May 7 after a short European jaunt, he decided to put through a call to Jess Oppenheimer in Hollywood. "I was thinking about the show all the time I was away," the fifty-eight-year-old adman said excitedly. "I think it's going to be a great program. By the way, when are you and the Arnazes moving to New York?"

Jess was dumbfounded. "Move to New York??? Who's moving to New York? Nobody told me anything about that. As far as I know the deal calls for the show to originate from here—live—with kinnies for the cable, like 'Burns and Allen' and the Alan Young program."

A few days later, Daily Variety confirmed the confusion by running this front-page headline: "SPONSOR BALKS AT CBS-TV PLAN TO KINE-SCOPE LUCILLE BALL–ARNAZ SHOW." Biow dispatched Charles Tyler, his vice-president in charge of the Philip Morris account, to Hollywood to sort out the misunderstanding. Desi was busy building a nursery wing on to the Arnaz ranchette in anticipation of the upcoming blessed event; Lucy was staying close to home, relaxing, determined not to induce another miscarriage. The ad agency representative met with them and CBS's Harry Ackerman, about to be promoted to vice-president of the network. Philip Morris was not satisfied with the quality of kinescopes. The show would have to either be filmed in Hollywood or done "live" in New York. To make matters more complicated, the sponsor wanted at least the first few shows done "live" in New York even if the remainder were done on film on the West Coast. Lucy and Desi made it clear that it was either stay in Hollywood or no show.

At the time, the coast-to-coast coaxial cable had not yet gone through. A "live" show produced in Hollywood could reach the East only by means of blurry kinescopes. And since more potential Philip Morris smokers lived east of Chicago than west, it was essential to the cigarette company that a "live" show originate from Manhattan.

Sometime during the weekend of May 12, the entire matter was ironed out. The sponsor would allow the Arnazes to remain in Hollywood and film their new TV show. CBS would assist by asking for bids from studios already filming for television such as Jerry Fairbanks Productions and Hal Roach Studios (then in production on the first batch of "Amos 'n' Andy" telefilms). But there would be a clause in the contract to the effect that if the quality of the first few "Lucy" shows was not up to the standards of the "Amos 'n' Andy" episodes already screened for network executives and about to go on the air in June, then the Arnazes would have to move to New York and do the show live until the coaxial cable was functioning.

Marty Leeds, the hard-nosed director of business affairs for CBS in Hollywood, and Austin Joscelyn, director of operations, correctly estimated that filming the shows would cost twice as much as making them "live." On Biow's instructions, Chuck Tyler held firm—no more money than the original contract called for. Just as stubborn, CBS retaliated by refusing to put up the difference—five thousand dollars.

Everything came to a grinding halt—while Lucy and Desi sat staring blankly at each other. "*Do* something!" she cried to her husband.

"Lucy and I were to get five-thousand-dollars-a-week salary between us, plus 50 percent of all rights in the show," Desi Arnaz offers, recalling that Waterloo weekend when Don Sharpe worked some of his agent magic. Knowing full well that CBS hated to welsh on its agreement with a major sponsor like Philip Morris, regardless of the new demands, Sharpe suggested that Lucy and Desi take a salary cut to four thousand dollars a week. This would prove to CBS and the sponsor that the Arnazes had enough faith in what they were doing to take less money up front. Desi liked the strategy, adding one cunning and crucial proviso: "We'll have to own 100 percent of the show."

Sharpe was uncertain CBS would agree to that, but he was willing to try anything to cement the deal once and for all. To everybody's shock, not only did CBS and Philip Morris each agree to put up an additional two thousand dollars per show, but the network said fine to Desi's prophetic condition. (That decision would later cost CBS nearly $5 million when they bought back the rights to the 179 episodes of "I Love Lucy" in 1957.) Lucy recalls Don Sharpe saying, "These films may be worth something someday. You should hang onto them."

Once the flack settled, Lucy and Desi began talking about the method they would use to film the show. Would they do it like the "Amos 'n' Andy" folks were—on a movie sound stage with one camera, doing the same scene at least three or four times to get the various, required angles?

But CBS had already gone looking for a movie studio to film "Lucy" and they were turned down by all of the majors, who wanted nothing to do with television, which they considered to be the ultimate competition. Even the Hal Roach Studios, which *was* seriously considering the offer, had to say no eventually. Their Culver City lot was filled to capacity that summer, what with "Amos 'n' Andy," Stu Erwin's "Trouble with Father" series, "Racket Squad," "Beulah," "Frank Merriwell," and the Abbott and Costello film *Jack and the Beanstalk* shooting. Studio manager S. S. Van Keuren explained that their space inadequacies would not get better for a while, although he urged CBS to consider one of their "house" directors, Jean Yarbrough, to helm "Lucy." (Yarbrough was directing the Abbott and Costello film and would soon begin work on their half-hour TV series and, a year later, that same studio's "My Little Margie." Yarbrough had also directed Desi in the 1946 Universal film *Cuban Pete.*)

The turndowns did not discourage Lucy, who, while certainly experienced with the standard motion picture filming technique, was well aware of how valuable the live studio audience was when she was recording her "My Favorite Husband" radio shows. Also, Lucy's run on radio had proved one thing to CBS's Harry Ackerman: "I learned that she was 'dead' without an audience, so I insisted we find a way to film her with one. It was for the performers' benefit to get that audience reaction, but, more than that, I felt the show depended on it."

Brainstorming sessions commenced at Columbia Square where Jess Oppenheimer and the writers had offices. "One of the ideas we had," recalls Jess, "was to rehearse the show all week on CBS's Stage A and then, when we felt we were ready, bring in an audience and carefully time and record every one of their laughs. Then go over to a movie sound stage and film the episode—motion picture style with one camera—leaving the appropriate gaps for the laughs. But it sounded impossibly confusing, so we dropped that idea fast."

The burden of planning this new "method"—whatever it was going to be—fell heavily on Desi's inexperienced shoulders. He had appeared in all of seven motion pictures during his ten years in Hollywood—hardly enough background to enable him to mastermind a brand-new television venture. He was grasping at straws; no one had attempted a situation comedy on film, shot before a live studio audience. He clearly was plowing virginal fields.

To the rescue came a thirty-nine-year-old former radio writer, Al Simon, whom Edward H. (Eddie) Feldman, head of the radio and television departments for the Biow agency on the West Coast, recommended as an innovator. CBS's Hal Hudson, coincidentally Simon's neighbor, agreed that Al might be helpful to the "Lucy" project. He knew Al well from his work on Ralph Edwards' "Truth or Consequences" game show, which premiered on CBS-TV in the fall of 1950 after a successful run on NBC Radio since 1940. It was Simon who had fiddled around with local television for a number of years, and who had developed a system for filming Edwards' game show using three 35-mm cameras shooting from different angles from ramps located atop the audience seats in a radio studio. Hudson had already hired George Fox as Film Operations Manager to oversee the "Lucy" venture. CBS was confident that these two men could help solve the two primary problems—(1) doing the show on film, and (2) having a studio audience in attendance for "live" response. Simon was sure he could work out the necessary plans and signed on as Production Manager in early July of 1951, just after completing the first TV season of "Truth or Consequences."

"I came in at a point when they were really desperate," remembers Al Simon, who, years later, would run the studio responsible for such hits as "The Beverly Hillbillies," "Green Acres," and "Petticoat Junction." "When I was suggested, everyone said, 'He's just a writer. What does he know? But Eddie Feldman knew what I had done for Ralph Edwards' TV show because the Biow agency was involved with that for Philip Morris.

"Desi invited my wife and me to dinner and to meet Lucy at the ranch in Chatsworth. She was pregnant with Little Lucie, I remember. We had a lovely dinner that Desi prepared and then the two of us retired to a makeshift theater where Desi ran the 'Lucy' pilot for me. I loved it, and told him there was no reason why we couldn't successfully come up with a method for filming it with 35-mm cameras, because I had already done it for Ralph Edwards. Desi was relieved and I went right to work."

The big problem then was where to film the show. CBS didn't have available space. Their three TV facilities—Studio A at Columbia Square, Studio D at 1313 Vine Street, and, occasionally, the Earl Carroll Theater on Sunset Boulevard—were not free for the kind of show the "Lucy" writers had in preparation. The Earl Carroll Theater presented the added problem of being too large and, therefore, not intimate enough.

"We searched out every empty movie theater in town, I think," reveals Al Simon. "A lot of them were empty at the time because television had already eroded some of that audience. The picture business was not booming in 1950–51. We were looking at theaters because that's where the networks did their shows, in theaters. But the problem was when we found a good possibility, it was either in a bad neighborhood or too far away from everything, making it difficult to get an audience every week. We looked at every available theater in Los Angeles and came up empty-handed. And without a home for 'I Love Lucy,' we really couldn't develop an exact system with which to film it. We were, in other words, desperate."

3 Fred and Ethel

"I remember saying that if I got a fur collar for my coat, I wanted a whole show written about that. I want the smallest wardrobe possible, maybe five pairs of pants and the same number of housedresses. I'd wear the same clothes often," recollects Lucille Ball about the creation of the Ricardos in June 1951. "We were middle class, we had a typical brownstone apartment in New York, and we had problems with the washing machine and with paying the baby-sitter. We always talked about expenses and the budget. I had to go to work to help pay the bills. That was part of the magic: people could identify with Lucy and Ricky. I wanted her to be an average housewife. A very nosy but very average housewife. And then the writers came up with the older married couple, which made two generations of marrieds—the four of us—and from there we sailed."

Once the show was sold to Philip Morris, and Harry Ackerman had officially assigned the writing team responsible for the pilot and Lucy's radio show—Jess Oppenheimer, Madelyn Pugh, and Bob Carroll, Jr.—the creative development of "I Love Lucy" commenced. At their offices at CBS Columbia Square, the trio got busy. "The first order of business," recalls Madelyn Davis (née Pugh), one of TV's only female comedy writers during the fifties, "was changing the name of Desi's character [Larry Lopez]. Desi wasn't fond of it and we all felt that there might be some confusion with Vincent Lopez, a real-life orchestra leader. We also thought the alliteration was a little too heavy—Lucy and Larry Lopez. It had a phony ring to it. Just exactly who thought up the name Ricky Ricardo is hazy after all these years, but, like most of the creative decisions we made, it probably was a joint effort."

The most critical change made after the pilot was sold was the addition of the Mertzes. "We knew right away," confirms Jess Oppenheimer, "that Lucy needed a girl friend: Someone to talk to, confide in, plot with. A person who could help move the plot along. On 'My Favorite Husband,' Lucy had Katie, the maid, and the Atterburys, who were Lucy's husband's boss and his wife. We toyed with the idea of having interaction between Lucy and Ricky and his nightclub boss, but then the situations would have revolved more around Ricky's job than domestic life. And that was definitely out. For the same reason, we decided to drop the character of Jerry, the agent, from the regular cast."

Jerry Hausner, who played the agent in the pilot, figured he had landed a steady job—any actor's dream—when the pilot sold: "Jess phoned me to say I would not be a regular character in the series, although he assured me of a job when the part of the agent was used. He said they decided to go in a different direction, with different subsidiary characters."

Lucy's first choices for the neighbors—Gale Gordon and Bea Benaderet, both age forty-four—when the "I Love Lucy" show was being developed.

On the radio show, the Atterburys represented the older, more established couple. They obviously had more money than the Coopers (Lucy's and Dick Denning's roles) and, hence, the so-called upper hand. "We decided to reverse roles for the TV show," Oppenheimer confirms. "We wanted the Ricardos to have a few more pennies than the neighbors, but not a lot more. We were very careful to make the couples different in some ways, yet very alike in others. Lucy herself wanted Gale Gordon and Bea Benaderet to be with her on the series as they had on radio."

Gordon, who appeared in Lucille Ball's later two TV series ventures, says, "It sounds a little egotistical for a performer to say something like this, but Lucy did want Bea and me in her show. We had played Iris and Rudolph Atterbury on the radio show, and she wanted us to be in on the TV venture. I had worked with Lucille way back in the early forties in *Look Who's Laughing,* an RKO movie version of the 'Fibber McGee and Molly' series. But when 'I Love Lucy' came along, I was under exclusive contract to CBS Radio to do 'Our Miss Brooks' with Eve Arden, and Bea had already begun playing Blanche Morton on Burns and Allen's television program, so neither of us could do it."

(Ironically, both Gale and Bea made guest appearances on "I Love Lucy" during its first season. Gale played Ricky's Tropicana boss, Alvin Littlefield, in two episodes aired during late spring 1952, and Bea shared the "Lucy" spotlight with Edward Everett Horton in a segment that had her playing Miss Lewis, a shy spinster neighbor of the Ricardos.)

Without Gale and Bea to play subsidiary characters, the writers drew up lists of character actors who could conceivably play the parts of the neighbors.

No one quite recalls precisely who was on these lists, but James Gleason (he had appeared with Lucille Ball in the Columbia picture *Miss Grant Takes Richmond* a few years earlier) and Ruth Perrott (she played Katie, the maid, on "My Favorite Husband") were likely contenders to play the irrepressible Mertzes, who, incidentally, derived their surname from a doctor who lived down the block from Madelyn Pugh in Indianapolis. The writers spent many hours mulling over possible monikers, ruling out truly funny names like Throttlebottom. They knew they needed something that was wryly humorous, something they could "play with." When Madelyn suggested Dr. Mertz, the team echoed, "That's it!" The first names, Fred and Ethel, were the result of "serious" thinking—what sounded good with Mertz? John and Cynthia? William and Mary? The comic ring peeled loudly when someone suggested Fred and Ethel, and the names were adopted immediately, another example of the fine Oppenheimer-Pugh-Carroll teamwork.

Bob and Madelyn had begun working with Oppenheimer in late 1948 when Jess was hired by CBS to fine-tune Lucy's "Husband" radio show. They had a great working relationship—a give-and-take that is essential to successful comedy-writing. Madelyn met Bob in 1944 when she joined CBS as a writer. "I graduated with a degree in journalism from Indiana University. After a brief apprenticeship at WIRE Radio in Indianapolis, I moved to Hollywood in 1942 and joined the staff at NBC Radio. After about a year, I was hired by CBS as a staff writer. A short time later, I met Bob. We were teamed two years later to write a situation comedy, 'The Couple Next Door,' about a man, his wife, and baby, and their neighbors."

Bob's route to a writing career was more circuitous. Born in 1918 (he was thirty-three when "I Love Lucy" debuted), he's been a fife player, usher, butcher's assistant, mailroom chief, publicist, and disc jockey's helper, but insists he owes his interest in script-writing to an infected hip that once kept him confined to a hospital bed for five months during his youth.

While convalescing, he listened regularly to a little theater radio program, and when they announced a radio script contest, Bob entered it. He won ten dollars.

"The script," Carroll remembers, "was titled 'Anthony Drum, Esquire,' and it had something to do with the struggle between self and conscience—'good' and 'bad,' you know. In those days, 'good' won out."

Soon after, Bob turned to comedy-writing, scribing a column called "Wang the Gong" for his St. Petersburg, Florida, high school newspaper. In 1941, he entered the University of California to study cinematography but lasted only two months when, again, his old hip infection began plaguing him.

Bob quit college and searched for a job. He found one at CBS in Hollywood—ushering. "It was a decided improvement over my last job as a butcher's helper," Bob says. He soon went from ushering to the mailroom, later becoming its head, and from there got an assignment in CBS's publicity department. Later, he moved to the transcription section where he played records for a disc jockey, fed the jock comedy chatter, and wrote station breaks. In a short time, Carroll was upped to senior staff status, becoming a full-fledged CBS writer.

"Lucy was doing her radio show," Carroll relates, "and Madelyn and I said, 'Let's see if we can write for it.'"

"We went to Harry Ackerman," says Madelyn, "and said, 'We think we can write that. Can we do a script?' and he said yes. We said, 'Will you pay us for it?' and he said no, and I said, 'Well, we'll write it anyway.'"

The "audition" script obviously passed Ackerman's muster because when Frank Fox and Bill Davenport, the first writers on Lucy's "Husband" series, left after the summer of 1948 season to return to their regular gag writing for Ozzie and Harriet Nelson, Bob and Madelyn got the nod to take over the writing chores. They were still doing the radio show when CBS asked them and Oppenheimer to write a pilot script for a television show to star Lucille Ball and Desi Arnaz. They never dreamed the pilot would sell so fast and when it did Madelyn had to be called home from a Paris vacation to start the creative work on the new show, which included manufacturing the Mertzes.

With the Arnaz baby due on July 4 (but finally delivered by Caesarean section on July 17), Lucy spent all of her time at the ranch preparing for Little Lucie's arrival. Suddenly there was a serendipitous phone call from an old character actor whom Lucy had met briefly during the forties and most recently had seen walking on the Columbia lot while she was filming *Miss Grant Takes Richmond*. The gruff-sounding, self-assured old curmudgeon growled, "I'm wondering if there's a role for me in your TV show."

"Bill Frawley, how are you?" Lucy responded, surprised to hear from the sixty-four-year-old actor whom she barely knew. And there began a close, nine-year association that ended in 1960 when the "Lucy" characters were retired from prime-time television.

Frawley's agent, Walter Meyers, responsible for establishing the Beverly Hills offices of the William Morris Agency before going freelance, had alerted his client to the casting rumor. A film actor since 1931, Frawley had learned the hard way that you have to get out there and hustle for yourself.

Lucy obviously could not make any commitment without consulting Desi and Jess but she did promise the actor that she would discuss it with them as soon as possible. The Arnazes agreed that it would be great to have the old movie veteran, who had acted so brilliantly in *The Lemon Drop Kid, Mother Wore Tights, Miracle on 34th Street,* and nearly a hundred other films, do the Mertz role. However, when Desi mentioned Frawley's name to the network and agency people they warned him of the actor's instability and chronic insobriety.

Bill was living with his sister Mary in a suite at the old Knickerbocker Hotel on Ivar Street, just a few hundred feet north of Hollywood Boulevard. Desi made an appointment to meet him at a mutually convenient location, a popular restaurant/bar right next door to RKO on Melrose Avenue. Seated in a back booth, Desi leveled with Bill immediately, making him privy to

William Frawley, veteran of more than a hundred film roles, asked Lucy for the job—and got it!

CBS's concerns. Claiming moderation in drinking, Frawley called the network and its myriad stable of vice-presidents every name imaginable, interrupting himself only once to order another drink. When the Frawley flak died down, Desi laid it on the line. He would hire him with one provision—if he was late to work or unable to perform except because of legitimate illness more than once, he'd be written out of the show. This was acceptable to Frawley, who, despite the fact that he had a successful picture in release at the time, *Rhubarb* with Ray Milland, was experiencing hard times in the industry.

A steady job for Frawley in a soap opera, "The First Hundred Years," lasted only thirteen weeks beyond its May 1, 1950, premiere. Things got so desperate at one point that Bill went to CBS Columbia Square and pleaded with the producer of a popular TV variety show for a fifty-dollar loan. A soft touch, the producer instead instructed his writers to think up a couple of lines for Bill to say in the next show. They had him play a hot dog vendor at a ball game. Bill didn't need the loan any longer; he had *earned* the fifty bucks.

Frawley was born in Burlington, Iowa, on February 26, 1887. His uncle, Bill Brady, remembered: "Bill had a head of golden curls. His mother prided showing them off, but as Bill grew up he wanted them cut, as his playmates called him a 'sissy.' '' Though he had ambitions to become a newspaperman, Bill's real love was entertaining. Recalls his cousin Tom Dailey, ''The Bradys, Frawleys, and Daileys—all related—used to gather at Grandma Dailey's house on Washington Street for big family sings. Bill had a fine Irish tenor voice and used to sing in the St. Paul's Catholic Church choir.'' He also played small roles at the Burlington Opera House and was in amateur shows at the Garrick Theater.

His mother, a deeply religious woman, scorned her son's show business aspirations and urged him to take a job in Omaha after graduation from high school, as a stenographer for the Union Pacific Railroad. Said a co-worker: ''Bill would walk into the office every morning dressed in a brown derby hat with white eyelets, a shepherd plaid suit, and spats. He looked as though he'd break into a song and dance any minute. While he worked, he'd be humming and singing the latest ragtime tunes and Irish songs.''

The railroad job got him to Chicago and, without his mother's knowledge, he landed a position, at age twenty-one, in the chorus of a musical, *The Flirting Princess*. Bill once explained: ''My mother sent a note with my younger brother Paul saying that she'd rather plant flowers on my grave than see me on the stage. So I quit the show and went to St. Louis, where I got a job as a bookkeeper for another railroad.'' The lure of show business got the better of him and, again without his mother's sanction, he formed a vaudeville act with brother Paul. The act broke up six months later when Mrs. Frawley ordered her younger son home. Bill headed West, stopping off in Denver, where he got his first real professional solo engagement. ''I had gone to a prizefight at the stockyards and afterwards went to the Rex Café. They had an orchestra but no singer—the singer had quit the day before. Someone said, 'There's a man who can sing,' meaning me. The first thing I sang was 'Waitin' for the Robert E. Lee' and I was hired at twenty-three dollars a week.''

After gaining quite a reputation for himself there and later at the Mozart Café, Bill teamed with a piano player, Franz Rath, and on the Orpheum circuit, headed for San Francisco. The name of the act: ''A Man, a Piano and a Nut.'' It was during the four-year stint that he introduced the song ''My Melancholy Baby.''

In 1914, he met and married Edna Louise Broedt and, hence, formed a new act, Frawley and Louise, with his young wife. It was described as ''light comedy with singing, dancing, and patter.'' In the book *Vaudeville*, by Joe Laurie, Jr., and Abel Green, Frawley and Louise is listed among ''the great comedy acts of vaudeville.'' Until their divorce in 1927, they played the Orpheum and Keith circuits, including the Palace Theater in New York. In a 1960 television interview, Frawley's ex-wife recalled: ''Walter Donaldson and Gus Kahn gave Bill the opportunity of introducing a new song they had just written, 'Carolina in the Morning.' ''

Broadway soon beckoned and Bill landed jobs in such shows as *The*

Gingham Girl, Bye, Bye Bonnie, Here's Howe!, She's My Baby (with Bea Lillie, Clifton Webb, and Irene Dunne), and *Sons o' Guns.* Then on December 29, 1932, at the Broadhurst Theater, the curtain went up on his first dramatic role, that of the press agent (Ward O'Malley) in *Twentieth Century,* for which he garnered rave reviews. Six months later, there was another big role on Broadway in *The Ghost Writer,* and then it was off to Hollywood where he was put under a seven-year contract at Paramount Pictures (he stayed eight years).

By the time 1951 had rolled around, Frawley had appeared in more than one hundred films. His face was familiar and that was considered a definite plus for "I Love Lucy."

Casting the role of Frawley's wife, Ethel, was decidedly more difficult. Many actresses read for the part and were rejected. With the signing of Frawley, the requirements were now more stringent. The actress had to look as if she could be married to a William Frawley, and yet not be so old-fashioned and elderly that she could not conceivably and realistically get involved with Lucy Ricardo's wild shenanigans.

"My introduction to 'I Love Lucy' was one of those fortunate happenings that actors only dream about," recalled Vivian Vance in an interview given shortly before her death in 1979. "A friend of mine from New York, Marc Daniels, had signed to direct the new TV series. He, Desi Arnaz, and Jess Oppenheimer were looking for an actress to play Lucy's neighbor and pal. Marc suggested me."

Director Marc Daniels (left) confers with Jess Oppenheimer and his employers, Lucille Ball and Desi Arnaz.

Pittsburgh-born Marc Daniels (real name: Danny Marcus) came out of the University of Michigan during the Depression with the idea of becoming an attorney, but couldn't afford law school. He was working as a doorman at the Brooklyn Fox Theater when someone from a theatrical trade paper suggested he could get a scholarship at the American Academy of Dramatic Arts. "They were always looking for men. Parents sent their girls to acting school to learn poise and style, but there were never enough boys. If you were a male, a scholarship was a cinch," says Daniels.

He studied acting and directing and then wound up with Jane Cowl's legendary stock company. She made him a director. After four years of World War II, during which he served in a Special Service unit under the command of Willard Josephy, assisting Hal Wallis on the Army show that Warner Brothers released as a film *(This Is the Army)* in 1943, he returned to teach at the American Academy and take courses. "A guy named Harvey Marlowe was teaching television, though there wasn't any, in a mock-up studio he built. I was the only one with directing experience so I was the director."

An executive for the Kenyon & Eckhardt advertising agency was impressed with a stage production *(For Love or Money* with Francis Lederer and Janet Blair) Marc had directed in stock and, hearing of the young man's "experience" with TV direction, hired him to launch their client, the Ford Motor Company's first TV venture, a once-monthly dramatic anthology, "Ford Theater." The idea was to trim available three-act Broadway shows down to sixty-minute offerings, with all-star casts, and do them "live."

The company moved into a brand-new CBS television studio, one so new that it hadn't been completed yet, and the carpenters and electricians worked around the cast and technical crew, wiring and hammering. "We did everything," Marc remembers. "A show a month the first year, and then a show on alternating Fridays the second. We did *Twentieth Century* with Freddy March and Lilli Palmer. We did *On Borrowed Time* with Basil Rathbone, Dorothy Stickney, and young Tommy Rettig. Paul Muni did a show for us and we became intimate friends until the day he died. Louie Calhern was going to do one but he took one look at our primitive methods and backed out.

"Remember, those were the days that what you shot was what you got. No isolated cameras, no sweetening. The mistakes, of course, were legend— the scenery that fell, the door that didn't open, the telephone that didn't ring on cue, the corpse that got up and walked off. Ray Massey rose from the table on one show and his head hit the mike boom and it knocked him out cold. There used to be a theory—which I fought, I didn't think it was professional—that the audience looked forward to those mistakes, they delighted in them. And of course, they did mean one thing—it was happening while you watched it, then, immediately. The mistakes didn't happen as often as you'd think because we had wonderful actors."

"Ford Theater" presentations included *Arsenic and Old Lace* with Boris

Karloff and Josephine Hull; *The Man Who Came to Dinner* with Edward Everett Horton as Sheridan Whiteside and Zero Mostel as Banjo; *Uncle Harry* with Joseph Schildkraut; *She Loves Me Not* with Judy Holliday; *One Sunday Afternoon* with Hume Cronyn and Burgess Meredith; and *Light Up the Sky* with Barry Nelson, Sam Levene, and Audrey Christie.

After two seasons with Ford, Daniels switched "makes" to helm Nash's "Airflyte Theatre," a CBS anthology that premiered September 21, 1950, with William Gaxton as host. When that show posted its closing notice and left the air on March 15, 1951, Marc ventured out to Hollywood to work with producers Jerry Wald and Norman Krasna on a few films that would be distributed through RKO.

The first order of business was looking up his old army commanding officer, Willard Josephy, who was partnered with Lucy's film agent, Kurt Frings. Impressed with Marc's credentials (he had won the "Variety Show-manship Award" for his "Ford Theater" work), Josephy hinted to Frings that Daniels be considered as director of "I Love Lucy." The young man had ample experience using multiple cameras and, by this time, a method employing three or four cameras had been decided upon for the new series.

Marc was staying at the Chateau Marmont, a chic hotel tucked into the hills on Sunset Boulevard in West Hollywood, when the phone rang. It was Billy Josephy suggesting that Marc meet with Desi Arnaz, Jess Oppenheimer, and Harry Ackerman at CBS Columbia Square regarding the possible "Lucy" assignment. He did just that and promptly landed the job for five hundred dollars per week (plus an assignment from CBS to direct Marie Wilson's TV pilot of "My Friend Irma" on August 9). During the course of the interview, Jess routinely reminded Desi that no decision had been made regarding an actress to play the Ethel Mertz role. The three men felt that the performer should have stage as well as film credits. The more Marc heard, the more convinced he was that they should consider his pal Vivian Vance, whom he'd met in New York through an instructor at the American Academy of Dramatic Arts.

"Vivian who?" Desi and Jess bellowed.

"Vivian Vance," Marc repeated. "I've known her for ten years. I directed her in *Counselor at Law* with Paul Muni. She just finished her second film, *The Blue Veil*, a drama with Jane Wyman for Jerry Wald and Norman Krasna. She's been in a half-dozen Broadway shows. In fact, she's appearing this very week at the La Jolla Playhouse. Let's go see her."

On Saturday, July 28, 1951, Marc, Desi, and Jess (Lucy had given birth to Lucie eleven days earlier and was unable to accompany them on the two-hour trip) drove down to the 850-seat theater—actually the local high school auditorium—in La Jolla, a quaint oceanfront town north of San Diego. Founded by Gregory Peck, Mel Ferrer, and Dorothy McGuire in 1947 so they and their fellow movie actors could ply their trade before a live audience, the "playhouse" was enjoying moderate success in its fifth summer season. The theater's policy was to produce a different play every seven days during its nine-week schedule.

This particular week, the fourth, it was John van Druten's *The Voice of the Turtle,* in which Vivian portrayed the acid and hateful "other woman," Olive Lashbrooke. Diana Lynn and Ferrer (who also directed) co-starred. A Los Angeles *Times* critic wrote: "Miss Vance is excellent as the thick-skinned but essentially tenderhearted actress."

Apparently, Desi harbored the same opinion because after the first act, he leaned over to his two companions and said, "I think we found our Ethel Mertz." Oppenheimer agreed.

Daniels describes what happened next: "I went backstage during the intermission and told Viv they liked her and wanted her to try out for the show. Then she said to me, 'What do I want to get mixed up in that for? It's only a television show. I'm up for a picture at Universal.' I was furious with her, and said, 'You idiot, take the job if they offer it to you! It's going to be a great show. I've already seen six or seven scripts and the pilot. It's going to be terrific!' "

When she returned to Hollywood the following week, she read a script for them, and then left with husband Phil for their little ranchito in Cubero, New Mexico. The rest of the negotiations were conducted via telephone, and she was informed that rehearsals would begin in about three weeks.

Vivian, who was once advised by a Hollywood agent to go home because her eyes were too close together, remembers all too well that July in La Jolla: "Fate sure is a funny thing. When Mel Ferrer called me in New Mexico to play in *Turtle,* at first I said no. I had a good reason."

It was in Chicago in 1945 while appearing in a road company production of that same play for producer Alfred de Liagre, Jr., that Vivian Vance suffered a nervous breakdown. "One day I was up and around, the next I was lying in bed in my hotel room, my hands shaking helplessly, in a state of violent nausea, weeping hysterically from causes I didn't know.

"A few nights before, on stage, a piece of business called for me to pick up an ashtray. I began to do it and found I couldn't move. The brain ordered, but the arm declined. It was one of the most sickening moments I have ever gone through," Miss Vance once recounted. "My husband was playing in *Dear Ruth* in San Francisco but I didn't want to burden him."

After two more seizures in Chicago, her husband of four years, actor Philip Ober, was summoned to her side, whereupon he accompanied her back to San Francisco. She barely managed to play six extra weeks in *Turtle* in the Bay City before the couple fled to New York, their headquarters. For two years she was incapable of doing anything but following Phil around like a puppy. Then she met a woman psychiatrist at a party in Philadelphia who changed her life.

After four months in analysis, she was on her way to health. Following a brief visit to Phil's parents in Maine in 1949, Vivian retired to a small ranch in Cubero, just outside Albuquerque where she grew up. She had just about shaken off the tag end of the breakdown when an old friend, Mel Ferrer, invited the Obers to Hollywood to appear in a new Claudette Colbert film he was directing, *The Secret Fury.* A second feature, *The Blue Veil,*

With only two films to her credit, thirty-nine-year-old Vivian Vance lands the plum role of Ethel Mertz. Technically, she was young enough to portray William Frawley's daughter.

materialized in May of 1951 because of the Obers' friendship with producer/ screenwriter Norman Krasna.

Back in New Mexico, Vivian again heard from Ferrer, who offered her her old role in *Voice of the Turtle* at the La Jolla Playhouse. Against her initial apprehensions (she still associated the play with her breakdown), she accepted the job, and, hence, got the "Lucy" assignment.

Born Vivian Roberta Jones on July 26, 1912, in Cherryvale, Kansas, Viv was part of a family that included five daughters and one son. After a brief period, her family moved to Independence, Kansas, where as a schoolgirl she studied dramatics under Anna Ingleman and William Inge, author of *Come Back, Little Sheba*. Her father, Robert A. Jones, relocated the family near Albuquerque where her talents continued to flower, now at the Albuquerque Little Theater. Her dramatics teacher, Vance Randolph, helped her not only with her technique, but also with her name. The directors of the little theater group were so impressed by Vivian's talent that they organized a special performance of *The Trial of Mary Dugan,* starring Vivian, the proceeds of which were to send her to New York to study with Eva Le Gallienne.

Upon arriving in Manhattan in 1932, Vivian was disappointed to learn that the enrollment at the school was already greater than it was supposed to be, so she started going to auditions on her own. "New York was a lot tougher to crack than Albuquerque," Vivian once recalled. "I found out I wasn't as good as my friends thought I was, but, of course, I couldn't go back." Although she had collected letters of recommendation from her hometown, no one jumped at the chance to hire the twenty-year-old. While residing at the MacDougal Street Girls' Club (for eleven dollars a week), she was told of an audition being held at the Alvin Theater for a muscial by Jerome Kern and Oscar Hammerstein II. Lo and behold, she was hired—the very first time out—for *Music in the Air,* which ran two years. During her spare time, she sang in such nightclubs as the Biltmore Roof and the Club Simplon, boasting quite a following. (Her two best songs were "Danny Boy" and "Japanese Sandman.")

Vivian's next job was a small role in *Anything Goes* in 1934 (she also understudied Ethel Merman) and *Red, Hot and Blue!* in 1936. Her big break came in *Hooray for What!* in 1937 when Kay Thompson left the cast of the Ed Wynn vehicle before opening night. Vivian stepped in at the last moment and managed to get her name up on the marquee. The following year she played her first dramatic role in Clare Boothe's *Kiss the Boys Goodbye*.

During the summer of 1941, Vivian met her husband, Philip Ober, while opening a theater at Harrison, Maine. Later that year, Vivian appeared at the Imperial Theater on Broadway in *Let's Face It,* sharing the stellar billing with Danny Kaye, Eve Arden, and Nanette Fabray for an eighty-five-week run. During World War II, Vance and her troupe were the first legitimate entertainment to be sent to a combat Theater of War, going from North Africa to Italy. Returning from Europe, she then took over a leading role in

The Voice of the Turtle from June 1945 to June 1946, before retiring for three years to her ranch in New Mexico.

With more than twenty years of stage experience and training behind her, it was clear that Vivian Vance had the credentials necessary for a TV show that was to be filmed like a stage play, "I Love Lucy." Granted she was twenty-five years younger than Frawley, but with the right wardrobe and makeup, she could be made to look a generation older than Lucy.

Once the show became an established hit, Vivian was not pleased with the public's ready acceptance of her as Ethel Mertz. After all, she reasoned, "Ethel is a frump. She's frowsy, blowsy, and talks like a man."

Moreover, Vivian hated the idea of being thought of as Frawley's wife. Not that she had anything against him at the outset. It was just that he was sixty-four and she was thirty-nine. "He should be playing my father," she complained frequently to anyone who would listen. Complicating matters was the clause in her contract that stated that if anything happened to either of them, the other could be written out of the show.

It was this overconcern about being identified with Bill that laid the groundwork for the infamous Frawley-Vance feud that would rage for the full run of "Lucy." Once Bill discovered how Vivian felt, the gloves were off and no one could reconcile their differences.

Many times during the series run, Jess had to be called down to the stage to arbitrate one of their arguments. Usually it was ignited when Vivian suggested some changes in dialogue or additional bits of stage business. Because the ideas were Vivian's, Bill refused to cooperate, often retreating to his dressing room. Not even the director could make him budge. Jess would have to go in and soothe his ruffled feathers. The producer usually got Bill to cooperate by saying, "Do it for me." Frawley would eventually agree, reminding Jess, "I'll do it for you, but not for that bitch!"

After "Lucy" went off prime time, Bill made this remark about Vivian, his TV wife, his so-called "honeybunch": "She's one of the finest gals to come out of Kansas but I often wish she'd go back there. I don't know where she is now and she doesn't know where I am and that's exactly the way I like it."

Throughout the series history, psychiatrists dealt with Vivian's dislike of Ethel by carefully disassociating "the character" from "the actress" in Vivian's subconscious. Lucy helped by building up Ethel, making her larger than life, giving her laughs, and constructing whole scenes around her. Finally, Viv no longer minded when people called her Ethel on the street. She realized that the fans were just being friendly, and came to recognize Ethel as merely a part—though perhaps the best part ever written for a supporting player in television history.

4 Opening Night

The true challenge of that early period was met by the three "Lucy" writers, Jess Oppenheimer, Madelyn Pugh, and Bob Carroll, Jr. They were required to crank out one episode every week—forty to fifty pages of dialogue and stage business. (During the sixties, Carl Reiner and Sidney Sheldon accomplished similar feats on their shows, "The Dick Van Dyke Show" and "I Dream of Jeannie," respectively.) It wasn't easy. When the trio started writing in June 1951, the specific method of filming was still unresolved, so the three were concocting scripts that would play as if done "live," stories that required a minimum of costume changes, sets, and complicated physical business. These restrictions only served to limit the writers' ability to be wildly imaginative.

"Luckily, we had a two-and-a-half-year backlog of scripts from 'My Favorite Husband' or we never would have survived the first season," says Oppenheimer. "Not that we just changed 'Liz' to 'Lucy' and 'Dick' to 'Ricky,' and did them exactly as they had been presented on radio, but we *did* 'steal' many of the basic premises. I would estimate that of the forty shows we did the first year, twenty or twenty-one of them were 'My Favorite Husband' scripts, rewritten to fit our television format."

For example, the "My Favorite Husband" show entitled "Liz on Stage" became "Lucy Writes a Play," the seventeenth show in the series. "Valentine's Day," about an amorous butcher, was rewritten as "Lucy Plays Cupid," the episode that teamed Bea Benaderet and Edward Everett Horton; and the "I Love Lucy" show "The Séance" was the December 25, 1948, edition of "Husband." The "My Favorite Husband" shows titled "Court Case," "Love Letters," and "Time Schedule" became "Lucy" shows named "The Courtroom," "Lucy Changes Her Mind," and "Lucy's Schedule," respectively.

With the writing chores in three very able hands and a director, Marc Daniels, already set, the "Lucy" company shifted into high gear in order to surmount the technical difficulties still unresolved. The month of July 1951 was slipping away and still there was no place to film the show that would have to go into production within a few weeks if it was going to meet its scheduled CBS air date, October 15, 1951. Al Simon, the program's associate producer, was spending his waking hours searching out empty movie theaters that could be converted into a TV playhouse, but his quest was fruitless.

In the meantime, Lucy suggested that Simon contact master cinematographer Karl Freund, who had photographed her in late 1942 in the M-G-M film *Du Barry Was a Lady*. She felt that his contribution could prove to be immeasurably important, especially during these early stages.

"I called Karl," recalled Al Simon. "He listened carefully to what I had to say and then responded, 'I'm not interested in TV; I'm an Academy Award-winner.' "

Known to his friends as Papa, Karl had the distinction of photographing three Greta Garbo films, including *Camille,* and in 1937 had won the Oscar for cinematography for *The Good Earth.* Freund's career began in 1905 in Berlin when, after a brief apprenticeship to a German rubber-stamp manufacturer, he became an assistant projectionist, soon working up to become head projectionist and the first to be granted a license by the Berlin Fire Department. Within two years he talked his way into being hired as a newsreel cameraman for Pathé in Berlin, and was soon commissioned by the King of Yugoslavia to make a documentary, the first of its kind, depicting the national history of the country under his rule.

In 1916, Freund photographed Robert Wiene's *Frau Eva,* his first full-length motion picture, and by 1919 had started his own laboratory for processing the film from motion pictures on which he had served as either cinematographer or camera operator. Five years later, for *The Last Laugh,* a modern classic, he was the first to put a camera on a dolly. (Prior to this innovation, *actors* did most of the moving.) With director Fritz Lang, Freund helped make *Metropolis* in 1926, a landmark film. This futuristic movie, made on a tremendous scale, involved more special effects than any of Karl's previous endeavors; needless to say, they were carried off brilliantly. When he left Germany for America in 1929, he was the head of production for Fox-Europa.

His first assignment in Hollywood was at Technicolor, the mammoth film processing lab, but his contract was soon sold to Universal where he is still credited for creating the stirring "butterfly sequence" at the end of *All Quiet on the Western Front,* one of cinema's most memorable scenes. As a cinematographer, Freund filmed *Dracula* in 1931 and also directed eight films, among them *The Mummy* in 1932. Irving Thalberg later brought him to M-G-M where he photographed *Camille, Pride and Prejudice, Tortilla Flat, The Good Earth,* and *Du Barry Was a Lady.* It was on the latter film that he first worked with Lucille Ball.

To quote one reviewer about the latter work: "Freund concentrates on getting the utmost out of the textures of the costumes and settings. . . . That is especially true where he reproduces the silks and satins, and the wonderful powdered wigs. . . . The portraits of Lucille Ball are similarly delightful in their pink-and-white porcelain style. The picture should be seen by anyone interested in the use of color photography by one of the really great cameramen."

It was common knowledge in the industry that Freund was a genius: He had developed the Norwich light meter and was credited with inventing the "process shot." He had become a wealthy man from these inventions and, having retired from active film work, headed his own Photo Research Corporation headquartered in Burbank, California.

Simon tracked down the sixty-one-year-old German in Washington, D.C.,

Producer–head writer Jess
Oppenheimer (left) and
cinematographer Karl Freund
confront the "moment of truth"
just an hour before the first studio
audience was admitted onto the
sound stage at General Service
Studios to witness the filming of
Episode #1, "Lucy Thinks Ricky
Is Trying to Murder Her."

where he was serving as a consultant to the Film Research and Development
Laboratory. "Karl told me that he was on his way back to Los Angeles in a
few days," Simon continues. "I explained our problem—we wanted to film
with three or four 35-mm cameras, in front of an audience, like a stage play,
without stopping, resorting to retakes only under the most dire circumstances."

Freund responded flatly: "You can't do that. Every shot requires different
lighting. You couldn't photograph three or four angles at the same time and
come up with a decent piece of finished film."

When Simon informed Freund that they could only pay him basic union
scale if he took the job, the ace cameraman responded: "I made fifteen
hundred dollars a week at M-G-M ten years ago. I'm not working for scale."

Upon Karl's return to California, he did agree to meet with Al and Lucy
and Desi. Jess Oppenheimer adds: "I never thought that a man of Freund's
stature would want to do television. He was a giant in the industry and a
brilliant man technically. I think the challenge that our show presented
ultimately led to his decision to come aboard, and, of course, I was very
pleased we had him."

When Lucy explained how much this project meant to her and how much
she respected and admired Freund's talents, the Academy Award-winner
finally said yes. Freund remained with Desilu until the spring of 1956, having
supervised the photography on four hundred television episodes, creating a
filming technique that is still in use today.

If July was hectic, what with Little Lucie's birth and other "minor"
exigencies—like a new TV series—August proved to be twice as bad. With
a little less than four weeks before the first "Lucy" episode had to begin
rehearsals, the company still had not found the proper filming facility. Every
available theater, dance hall, and nightclub had been inspected; none was
suitable. Time was slipping away fast.

On the twenty-fourth of August, just two weeks before the first segment was shot, Frank Falknor, CBS vice-president in charge of operations for the network, and Austin E. Joscelyn, the West Coast director of operations, prompted an immediate decision. As *Daily Variety* reported: "Being given first consideration are the Fox-owned Belmont Theatre at First Street and Vermont Avenue, which has been shut for a month, and the Civic Auditorium on Culver Boulevard in Culver City. If the Belmont is leased it would have to undergo considerable reconstruction due to its small stage. Also scouted for the past few days were independent picture studios."

Production manager Simon explains: "Earl Spicer of the local RCA office phoned me and said that Jimmy Nasser, who owned General Service Studios, heard I was looking for a place to film the 'Lucy' shows. He said, 'As a favor to me, would you go see Jimmy? He's a helluva nice guy.' I said sure."

General Service Studios was a seven-and-a-half-acre lot consisting of eight sound stages built in 1920 at 1040 North Las Palmas Avenue, just south of Santa Monica Boulevard in Hollywood. Purchased in 1947 by the four Nasser brothers—James, George, Henry, and Ted, who had interest in 130 theaters in central and northern California—for $1.5 million, the studio had enjoyed better times. With film production at a perilous low in 1951, the brothers were on the brink of bankruptcy, with the threat of losing the studio that played home in 1946 to the Marx Brothers *Night in Casablanca* romp. In fact, in July of 1950, the brothers had petitioned the Federal District Court for "arrangement of debts." And by the summer of 1951, a conservator was already on the lot to protect the interests of the major creditor, Western Electric. At the beginning of August, the Hollywood trade papers had reported that the studio was involved in a possible sale to the United States Air Force, which would use it to make training films. The price tag: $1.8 million.

The studio had a rich heritage. During its early years, the lot housed many silent film makers, including Mary Pickford and King Vidor. Harold Lloyd made *Safety Last* and other silent comedies at General Service, then named Jasper Hollywood Studio. Howard Hughes shot much of *Hell's Angels* with Jean Harlow there. In the 1930s, the lot housed bungalows and production companies of Mae West, Gary Cooper, and Bing Crosby. Shirley Temple made her first film there. To this day, George Burns, who filmed his and Gracie Allen's TV show there in the fifties, maintains an office there, even though the studio was recently owned by Francis Ford Coppola.

When Al Simon arrived on the lot in mid-August to meet Nasser, Simon really hadn't given much thought to housing the "Lucy" show at a motion picture lot. For one thing, bringing in an audience of two or three hundred people was verboten. It had not been done before to any great extent.

"When I first went on the lot," Simon explains, "what hit me immediately was that if we could knock down a wall and create an entrance for the audience on the side street [Romaine], maybe we *could* use a sound stage. The studio people, operating under rigid and inflexible rules, told me they wouldn't want people on the lot 'wandering around.' They also explained the fire regulations to me. I told Nasser that if I could get permissions for all of that, would he let me break through the outside wall to make an entrance. He said, 'Sure, as long as you agree to put it back the way it was when you leave, because we have no money for reconstruction of any kind right now.' I told him that was no problem.

"As I wandered around Stage 2—the most suitable stage—I was intrigued by the fact that perhaps we could build three or four permanent sets, side by side. In live television, the sets were always flimsy-looking because they had to be 'struck' quickly after the show was over to make way for the next program. I figured if I could rent this stage on a full-time basis, we could simply leave up the sets we built. And those sets could be very realistic. I felt we could also use the stage to rehearse on. At first Nasser was a little reluctant to go along with me, but the court-appointed conservator felt that the thousand-dollars-a-week rental fee I offered was better than nothing. We shook hands and I went off to tell Desi about the studio."

When Arnaz inspected the facilities a few days later, he immediately agreed with Simon that this would be the ideal place to shoot "I Love Lucy." While the sound stage *was* a little small, it did adjoin a dubbing stage, which, if part of the wall was knocked down, would add additional space to produce the show. Nasser agreed. There were also no private homes in the immediate vicinity—across narrow Romaine Street was the Department of Water and Power and the headquarters of both Glen Glenn Sound and Consolidated Films—so there were no neighbors to complain about noise from the production itself or the people waiting on the sidewalk to get in to see the show. Desi also learned quickly that the fire department would require not only a special entrance for the audience, but also a complete overhead sprinkling system.

On August 29, *Daily Variety* reported: "In what is probably the largest studio rental deal ever consummated in West Coast television, CBS and Desilu Corporation have signed a contract with General Service calling for production of 52 half-hour television films in the Desi Arnaz-Lucille Ball series, 'I Love Lucy.' Rehearsals start Saturday [September 1], filming next week. . . . James Nasser, of General Service, said yesterday the deal is probably the largest of its kind and predicted it may set a pattern for the future."

On Harry Ackerman's approval, CBS put up twenty-five thousand dollars overnight to underwrite the cost of renovating the stage, and the "Lucy" company moved onto the lot on Thursday, August 30, only eight days before the show was to be filmed before a live audience. Desilu, a few days before, had signed the final Philip Morris contracts. The stipulations, as reported in the Hollywood trade papers: "Present plan is to initiate the series on film, switching to a live-on-the-relay basis only if the film quality doesn't hold up to the sponsor's satisfaction. . . . The relay-cable link won't be available until sometime in November. The family team insists on doing the show from here and kinescope is not acceptable to sponsor."

Karl Freund had spent the entire month of August engineering a new lighting system for the show. When Al Simon insisted early in the month that Karl run some film tests with Lucy so CBS, Desilu, and the Biow agency could see how the film was going to look on a television screen, Freund hesitated. "I know what I'm doing," he told the young production manager. But when Simon ran the film through a projector and onto a closed circuit TV receiver, it became painfully clear that the quality was lacking. The problem was with the lighting. With some help from CBS's Herb Pangborn, Freund decided on a system of "flat lighting," as opposed to the sort of artistic lighting he was so used to.

"One night," Lucille Ball recalls, "Karl brought us out to his house in the San Fernando Valley, and showed us a model of the system he had devised." An innovator, Freund's true contribution to the so-called Desilu three-camera method was not the use of three cameras—which had been done before on a number of television shows—but the revolutionary overhead lighting system that lit the entire set uniformly.

This system—as well as the future of the entire show—was suddenly in jeopardy because of a misunderstanding. Jess Oppenheimer remembers: "We were just moving over to the lot from CBS Columbia Square, and it came up in a conversation with Desi that I had 20 percent ownership in the series. Desi hit the ceiling. CBS never told him about my contractual arrangement with them dated January 1951. He said, 'This can't be. Lucy and I own the package. How can CBS do this? No way are we going to do the show. Forget the whole thing!'

"Desi stormed off the lot. When he got home to Chatsworth, he told Lucy, 'The show is off.' Lucy was in shock. 'We can't back out now,' she told Desi. She broke into tears and phoned me at home.

"I told her my side of the story, that CBS had promised me 20 percent interest and that's the reason I agreed to work on the TV pilot. When I called Harry Ackerman to straighten out the matter, he claimed he couldn't recall any such arrangement. Naturally, I had to back out if my understanding wasn't lived up to. When I told Lucy that CBS simply forgot to inform Desi and her about my deal, she cried, 'Jess, everyone knows we're doing it. If we don't go through with it, they'll say we failed. My entire career is at stake.'

"I phoned my attorney immediately and he finally negotiated with Desi that I get the 20 percent, although Desi couldn't give anyone else anything. I gave Bob and Madelyn 5 percent of my share," Oppenheimer concludes.

Eight days before the first episode was to go before Karl Freund's cameras in front of a live studio audience, an army of carpenters, plumbers, electricians, and assorted technicians swarmed into the thirty-year-old movie studio, tore out partition walls to make Stage 2 and the adjoining dubbing stage into one, broke through an outside wall to make a proper exit (officially giving the new "Desilu Playhouse" its own address—6633 Romaine Street, Hollywood 38, California, as it was printed on "I Love Lucy" tickets), and began building a more or less permanent four-room set following designs executed by art director Larry Cuneo.

The existing floor was wood—full of holes, camera tracks, and nails, and badly warped—the same inferior surface found in most movie studios. If Karl's system of using three or four mobile cameras was to work at all it had to do so silently and smoothly. "I went to Fred Hepp, head of construction at General Service," recalls Al Simon, "and told him we had to level the floor. He thought I was being impertinent and said, 'You can't do that,' a phrase I began hearing at least ten times a day during that early period. Anyway, we tore out the existing wood floor and replaced it with a special composition, smooth as cement and capable of withstanding heavy weights. On top of that was a layer or two of Masonite.

"I also told Fred I was putting in bleachers, seats to accommodate three hundred people. He looked at me long and hard and pointed to a beat-up sign that read, 'Silence. No Admittance.' I explained we already had permission from the Nassers, who owned the studio, and from the various city departments. He walked away, shaking his head in disbelief. We were going to build those bleachers from wood until our stage manager, Herb Browar, suggested an alternative."

Browar, who had graduated ten years earlier from the Drama Department of the Carnegie Institute of Technology, came to Hollywood after the war to get into the movie business. Although his father had owned a string of motion picture theaters in his native Pittsburgh, Herb started at the bottom, aspiring to become a producer and director. Through some contacts he eventually secured a job under production manager Argyle Nelson at the Selznick Studios in Culver City. A few years later, seeing the potential of the infant TV medium and through a friend of the family—CBS vice-president in charge of operations, Henry Grossman—Herb got a job at station KLAC. The station manager was Don Fedderson, one of the directors was Sam Peckinpah, Betty White was a girl friday. After a few more months of training, he moved to another local station, KTSL, the new CBS television affiliate, gaining more experience, until he was promoted to the network level in late spring 1951 as a floor manager on Alan Young's show and others.

A man at CBS, Leo Pepin, who eventually became production manager for the Ozzie and Harriet TV show, told Herb, "We need a stage manager for a show that's going to be done with Lucille Ball. We're doing it on film. Since you were exposed to film at Selznick, why don't you go and interview?

"But I must tell you, Herb," the CBS staffer warned. "They have a contract for only thirteen shows. And since the show is being done by Lucy's company, Desilu, you'll have to officially resign from CBS. That means if the show doesn't last beyond the first cycle, you'll be out of a job."

Nevertheless, the thirty-three-year-old Browar made an appointment for an interview with Jess Oppenheimer and director Marc Daniels, also a Pittsburgh native, and gladly accepted the position at seventy-five dollars a week. He also recommended a young CBS comrade, Maury Thompson, for the job of script clerk. "I went on the General Service lot on Saturday, September 1," says Herb Browar, now retired after an illustrious career in television ("Burns and Allen," "Life with Father," "The Bob Cummings Show," "The People's Choice," "Mr. Ed," "The Beverly Hillbillies," "Green Acres," etc., etc., etc.). "There was so much to do that first week that for three days I didn't go home. I slept on a couch in Al Simon's office!"

Among Browar's many contributions to the "Lucy" legend was his idea for the audience bleachers. "I remembered back to my college days at Carnegie Tech when the Safeway Steel Scaffolding Company pitched in and helped us with a complicated stage set. I went to the Los Angeles phone book to see if they had a local office or plant, and sure enough, they did. They immediately came out to survey our needs, gave us a price and started putting up the grandstand." (An interesting sidelight is that when Francis Ford Coppola purchased the studio complex in 1979, those bleachers were still standing—twenty-eight years later.)

Early on Saturday morning (September 1), a get-acquainted meeting for the primary staff was held in Jess Oppenheimer's office on the lot. In attendance were Al Simon, Herb Browar, Bob and Madelyn, Desi, and director Marc Daniels. It was a short session but an important one. The group discussed its mutual goals and what needed to be accomplished during that first critical week (everything!). There was a lot of hand-shaking and each went off with a buoyant feeling of anticipation.

Down on the stage, carpenters were frantically constructing the "Lucy" sets. Space was at a premium and it became clear very quickly that there wasn't enough room on the stage to fit side by side all of the permanent sets that the first several scripts required: the Ricardo bedroom, living room, and kitchen, the Tropicana nightclub, and the Mertz living room (the latter was required for Episode #3). Herb Browar remembers: "Larry Cuneo's original plans called for the Mertzes' living room to adjoin the Ricardo living room. Because the Ricardo bedroom wasn't required for that many of the early shows—although it was critical for the first episode—we decided to improvise and create the Ricardo bedroom in front of the Mertz living room set. The guys in the paint department of the studio came up with a brilliant solution: they cut out panels of plywood and wallpapered them, and then hung them in front of the other set wall. Then all we had to do was pull out one set of furniture and replace it with another after putting up the panels. You'll notice that the Mertzes' living room has two windows in the same location as Lucy's bedroom. Sometimes we didn't even take down the curtains."

The actors were due to arrive at noon to begin rehearsals, but it was impossibly noisy on the stage, so Browar laid out masking tape on the floor of the adjoining dubbing stage to simulate the sets. The dubbing stage also housed the makeup area, the portable dressing rooms, and, up a flight of stairs, the projection booth, which served as Bill Frawley's dressing room.

The first reading of the premiere script, "Lucy Thinks Ricky Is Trying to

Murder Her," was held in Desi's office, away from the din of the stage area. Vivian Vance was among the first to arrive: "I was scared to death, so I fortified myself by getting all dressed up in my best clothes. Now I'm the kind of woman who likes to wear blue jeans, slacks, and sloppy shirts. But not this day. It was too important. I was meeting Lucille Ball for the first time!

"She had always been my favorite in the movies in all those splashy Technicolor movies made at M-G-M. As I sat there awaiting the execution, this creature walks in—old sweater, old pair of blue jeans, a thing tied around her head. It was Lucy. She looked me up and down and said, 'Well, you're certainly dressed up!' I breathed a sigh of relief and said, laughing, 'This is the last time you'll see me this way.' "

When Desi wasn't required for rehearsals, he was busy pulling together a staff and crew. Lucy helped. She called her favorite makeup man, Hal King, who happened to be Max Factor's brother-in-law, and said, "I don't care what you do the rest of the week. You just be here every Friday night!" And King was, for the next twenty-three years.

Maury Thompson, who began as script clerk and was later upped to camera coordinator status on "I Love Lucy," looks back on the summer of 1951 when Herb Browar suggested him for the position: "When I took the job, a friend of mine told me I'd have to fit into the family." Thompson remained in the "family" (with Miss Ball, at least) for twenty years, later assuming the prestigious position of director on "Here's Lucy."

To conduct Desi's orchestra, the Arnazes asked Wilbur Hatch to come aboard. The forty-nine-year-old native of Illinois had been responsible for music for "My Favorite Husband" as well as other CBS radio offerings such as "Dr. Christian," "The Whistler," and "Our Miss Brooks." He gladly joined the Desilu camp that summer and remained with Lucy until his death in 1969.

In a few days, a complete staff was assembled. As announced in both daily trade papers on Wednesday, September 5, it was as follows:

Producer: Jess Oppenheimer
Director: Marc Daniels
Writers: Jess Oppenheimer, Madelyn Pugh, and Bob Carroll, Jr.
Director of Photography: Karl Freund
Production Manager: Al Simon
Art Director: Larry Cuneo
Film Operations Manager: George Fox
Musical Director: Wilbur Hatch (Conducting the Desi Arnaz Orchestra)
Casting: Mercedes Manzanares
Sound: Glen Glenn Sound (Cameron McCulloch in charge)
Stage Manager: Herb Browar
Choreography: Lee Scott
Wardrobe: Della Fox

Announcer: Johnny Jacobs
Makeup: Hal King (courtesy Max Factor)
Production Assistant: Emily Daniels
Office Manager: Felice Greene
Script Clerk: Maury Thompson

The first staff was small. It was a dedicated group that didn't complain about overwork. Eventually, ninety-one people were required to put together the average "I Love Lucy" segment, including grips, camera operators, sound technicians, gaffers, and so forth. "We didn't even have a prop man at first," says Herb Browar. "It wasn't until later in the season that we hired someone, and then it was for only two days a week. We had no set decorator, no costume designer. Della Fox, Lucy's wardrobe girl, made the clothing purchases in stores. Our art director, Larry Cuneo, became ill during that first week and never came back. Luckily, I had two years of scene design in college and a little experience in summer stock, so whenever we needed a new set, I would go down to Fred Hepp and say, 'Fred, I need a hotel room' and Fred and I would go down to the scene dock and pull out flats and put a hotel room together or any other set the scripts called for."

Marc Daniels was frantic. The director had had experience using three or four electronic television cameras during his New York days, but working with 35-mm cameras posed quite a different challenge. For one thing, he could not rehearse and see what he was getting. With TV cameras, the images are transmitted to monitors in the control booth and, therefore, the director knows precisely what the shots look like. Using multiple motion picture cameras provided no such proof. The first time you knew what you had shot was when the film came back from the film lab.

"I can remember quite vividly," Daniels says, "that we were working under extreme pressure. The distractions were constant. If Desi wasn't being called away to make a decision, I was. Karl Freund's new lighting system was being installed right up to the last minute, and that was a very intricate process. I recall at one point during the rehearsals for that first episode suggesting to Larry Cuneo to put up those louvre shutters which separated the Ricardo living room from the kitchen. As he had it, it was a 'dead' wall, and I felt I could get a lot of mobility out of being able to shoot through an opening."

By the time Thursday, September 6, rolled around, it became clear that the company would not be ready to shoot "Lucy Thinks Ricky Is Trying to Murder Her" on schedule the next evening, as announced. Harry Ackerman flew back from Las Vegas, where he was in meetings with Frank Sinatra concerning a possible television program, and seeing the problems Desilu was experiencing, especially the lighting dilemma, suggested they simply postpone the filming until the following evening, Saturday. This meant overtime for the crew as well as the construction people, who were now working almost around the clock to complete the renovation. CBS had already invested a small fortune on the Lucy-Desi show—more than a quarter of a million dollars—a lot of money for TV, in those early days.

While the steel bleachers to seat the audience of three hundred people were being installed under a control booth just completed, Marc and his four stars had their first opportunity to rehearse "I Love Lucy" with the cameras. With Freund adjusting his overhead lighting and Emily Daniels, Marc's young wife, marking the floor with masking tape for the cameras, the principals tested Episode #1. To make matters worse, the Oppenheimer-Pugh-Carroll script called for dogs to appear in a scene. It was nothing short of a nightmare.

"What made it impossible was the fact that we were actually using four cameras on that first show, not three," Marc adds. "Because Desi wanted to do the show as if it were live—without ever stopping except where the middle commercial was to be inserted—to give it the genuine look of a stage play, it had to be shot virtually straight through. It was so complicated because each Mitchell camera wasn't capable of holding fifteen or twenty minutes of film—the most we could fit into them was ten minutes' worth. That meant we had to have footage counters in the control booth so my wife, the camera coordinator, could inform each cameraman when to reload. The fourth, the backup camera, would fill in while another was being loaded with new stock.

"It was ridiculously expensive to do it that way because we had to have an extra camera crew on hand. It was a mob scene on that floor. We had four cameras, four camera operators, four dolly grips, four camera assistants, plus two microphone booms with a boom operator and boom pusher for each. And electricians, stagehands, props—you couldn't find the actors.

"The company was also using a new technique known as the Q-Track System developed by our film operations manager, George Fox, which supposedly made the clapstick unnecessary by replacing it with an automatic synchronization of sound and picture tracks via a 'pop' sound. It was ingenious but it drove us a little crazy and we finally abandoned it after the third show, in favor of a long clapstick."

The first dress rehearsal took place Friday night. It was a nerve-wracking affair—everyone knew it would be—so Lucy and Desi invited the key personnel to their studio bungalow for dinner afterward. Desi cooked his favorite dish—*arroz con pollo*—and Lucy acted as bartender, dispensing drinks. When everyone was sated and relaxed, Jess conducted a "critique" of the night's dress rehearsal—a give-and-take discussion of every aspect of the show. Technical problems were ironed out, dialogue changes were discussed, and any other last-minute considerations were dealt with. Future critiques would be held on the dubbing stage. (This procedure is a time-honored tradition still carried on today on three-camera sitcoms.)

On the day of the first filming, Saturday, September 8, 1951, the cast was still in rehearsal, attempting to iron out all the technical problems discussed at the previous night's critique session. The sets had not even been completed, let alone "dressed," and an audience was expected to file in at 7:30 P.M. It was an exhausting day, the end of an exhausting week. The Arnazes were

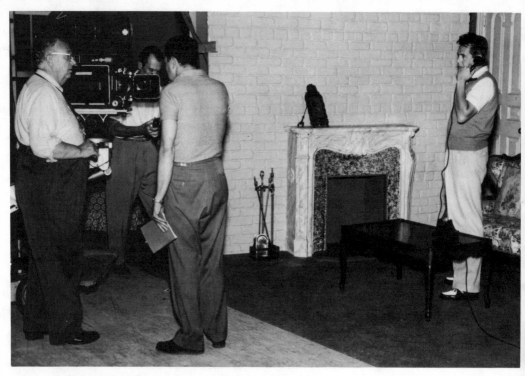

With the cast in street clothes, director Daniels oversees last-minute rehearsals, Saturday, September 8, 1951. Note that sets are not fully "dressed."

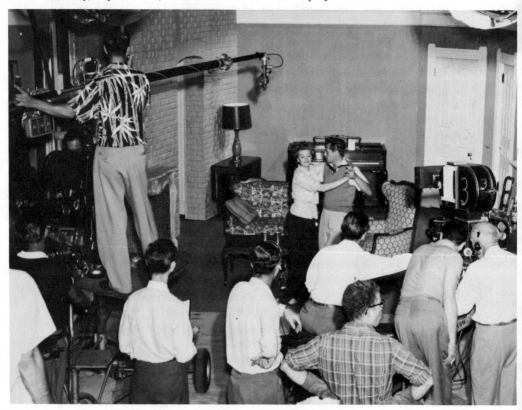

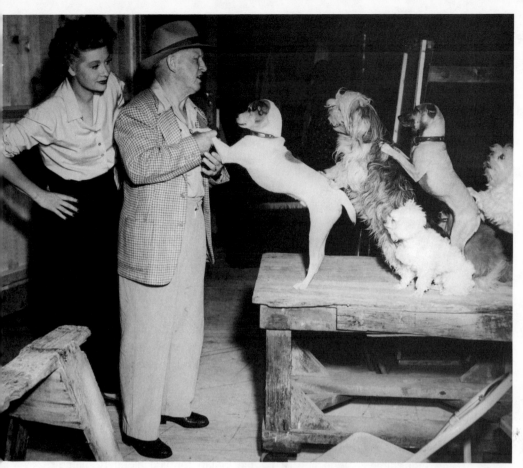

On the dubbing stage, adjacent to Stage 2, Lucy watches as an animal trainer puts his canine troupe—Ann, Mary, Helen, Cynthia, Alice, and Theodore—through their paces.

Saturday, 7:30 P.M. The first studio audience being admitted to Stage 2 via a new entrance just built to herald the Desilu Playhouse, 6633 Romaine Street, Hollywood 38, California.

Desi accepts "opening night" congratulations from Art Linkletter, who would transfer his own "House Party" radio show to TV the following year where it would remain for seventeen years. Looking on are Harry S. Ackerman, vice president of CBS Television, and his actress wife, Mary Shipp.

beginning to wonder whether they had made the right decision in the first place, but it was obviously too late to turn back now.

After dinnertime, a long line of people began forming along Romaine Street. The imposing exterior of Stage 2 now boasted new double doors and a sign overhead that read "Desilu Playhouse."

Inside, CBS executives, Biow agency representatives, Philip Morris big shots, some celebrities, and assorted members of the press inspected the refurbished facilities. Imagine how Philip Morris people reacted upon seeing a barrage of fire department signs ordering, "Positively No Smoking!" Martin N. Leeds, Director of Business Affairs for CBS in Hollywood, said of that evening: "We'd been paying out a hundred and fifty thousand dollars a week for the past two weeks just on Desi's say-so—how did we know this show would be a runaway hit? We'd expected just another domestic situation comedy. To put it mildly, we were quite interested in seeing where our money had gone."

As the last nails were being pounded and the CBS ushers were putting down multicolored cushions on the rising tier of bleachers under the command of Felice Greene, Al Simon's secretary, the cast was receiving last-minute instructions backstage from Daniels. Vivian Vance was particularly nervous. "I was scared to death when we did our first show," Vivian once revealed. "After all, I had done only two movies and wasn't accustomed to working with one camera, much less with four of them. Lucy sensed that I was scared and went out of her way to set me at ease. She got me laughing so hard before my entrance that I didn't have time to remember that I was so frightened."

As the audience filed in, never thinking they were about to witness the birth of a legend, and took places on the bleachers, Desi's orchestra, under Wilbur Hatch's direction, was playing an appropriate Latin number as background music. Urged by Jess to "go out and warm 'em up," Desi reluctantly grabbed a hand mike and started for center stage. He didn't get very far. "His fly was open," Herb Browar recalls. "The zipper on his tuxedo pants was stuck and the more he panicked, the less cooperative his fly was. He was very nervous, so someone else volunteered to get it unstuck."

Once the mechanical difficulty was corrected, Desi strolled onto the set and proceeded to ad-lib his way through yet another obstacle. With surprising deftness, Desi welcomed the audience, explained to them the nature of the new system, told a few corny jokes, and then introduced his co-stars Bill Frawley and Vivian Vance. The pair was greeted warmly, particularly Frawley, whose face was as familiar as an old friend.

Then, as the band segued into Eliot Daniel's new theme song, Desi introduced the star of "I Love Lucy." Her red hair flying, Lucille breezed on stage with all the confidence she could muster, waved to the three hundred people, kissed Viv and Bill, and threw special kisses to the back row of the grandstand where her mother, Desi's mother, and the writers sat nervously.

Suddenly, Marc's booming voice from the overhead control booth inter-

Act 1, Scene 1 from Episode #1.

Desi looks a little worried even though he's just completed the first segment of "I Love Lucy." In the background, leaning against the kitchen counter, is stage manager Herb Browar.

rupted the proceedings. "Please take your places," he announced on the loudspeaker to his cast and crew.

It was now the moment of truth. The Arnazes' careers—particularly Lucy's—were on the line. Harry Ackerman had okayed the expenditure of three hundred thousand dollars on the show.

But, alas, there was no need to worry. For the next hour or so the audience howled as they watched kooky housewife Lucy Ricardo unfoil her first video adventure. "All I remember about that night," says Lucille Ball, "was trying to protect my stomach. Lucie had just been born by Caesarean section and I was wearing a huge bandage over my stomach. I was more concerned with that than anything else. When the laughs started coming, I was very relieved. I remember saying, 'Whew! It's working.'" It should have been obvious to everyone—the show would be a smash hit when it premiered in five weeks, just as Oscar Hammerstein II had predicted back in March. Not so.

For one thing, there were serious technical problems. Marc Daniels explains: "After that first film came back from the lab, we all had a look at it on Monday morning. It was painfully clear that using four cameras and doing the show without stopping was not only ludicrous, but hurt the show's pace. I asked them, 'Why can't we stop between scenes? What's the big deal?' They felt that an audience wouldn't sit still that long. 'They sit two or three hours to see a stage play. What's an extra half-hour?' I argued.

"Then Jess suggested that Desi could talk to the audience during the breaks like he had for the warm-up and have the band entertain them with a few songs. Finally, everyone agreed. Bob and Madelyn were particularly

Surrounded by well-wishers' flowers, the Arnazes give each other a kiss after filming "Lucy Thinks Ricky Is Trying to Murder Her."

pleased because now they could write scripts that didn't require instant costume changes within an act. If we stuck with the original method—running the show straight through, without stopping—we could never have done shows like 'Pioneer Women' [where a huge loaf of bread pops out of the oven], or any theme that required outlandish costuming, bizarre makeup, or a really tricky piece of stage business."

The second week had its difficulties too. The film editor was spending too much time piecing together a rough cut because the standard Moviola was capable of holding only one reel of film at a time. Having film of three different angles of every scene available to choose from, the editing got to be quite a time-consuming headache until George Fox, the film operations manager, built a special, four-headed Moviola, especially for Desilu. It became known in the industry as "the monster."

By some miracle, an edited print of "Lucy Thinks Ricky Is Trying to Murder Her" was available by Friday evening, September 14. Desi was anxious to see the reaction of an audience watching the actual film. That night, after rehearsing the second show, a makeshift audience was gathered on the dubbing stage for a showing of the film. The reaction was hopeful, but not good enough to prevent Desi from taking the first two episodes the next weekend to a theater near Riverside, California, to "sneak" them. Again, the reaction was fair, but the paranoia continued.

A week later, Desi, Jess, Don Sharpe, and Marc Daniels walked into Harry Ackerman's fifth-floor CBS office and sat down. "They were all nervous and worried about the show," Marc says, looking back. "None of them smiled and the only thing on their minds was, 'What are we going to do?'

"I couldn't understand what the hell they were so worried about. I felt it was a marvelous show right from the beginning. The audience killed themselves every week. Days later, the show went on the air and they never looked back."

5 Her Freshman Year

♡

On Monday, October 15, 1951, in the nine-o'clock time slot vacated by Horace Heidt and his "Original Youth Opportunity" show, "I Love Lucy" made its debut on the CBS television network, which then consisted of a few big stations and seventy-four local affiliates. The competition on rival NBC was formidable: "Lights Out," a popular video version of the radio classic with a Top Ten history of its own. "Lucy," so the critics predicted, didn't stand a chance.

For the "I Love Lucy" company, the premiere day was like any other Monday. The cast spent the better part of the day reading the script and rehearsing for the seventh show, "The Séance," to be filmed the following Friday evening. Saturday shootings had been discontinued as the routine and new system became more comfortable and less frantic. In several weeks, they would be able to enjoy a four-day work week, beginning each Tuesday morning and shooting on Friday night, but on this particular fall day, Monday was a workday—and a busy one at that, keeping the regular cast and guest star, Jay Novello, and crew toiling until almost eight o'clock.

Finally it dawned on someone that the premiere "Lucy" episode would be on the air shortly. The Arnazes lived about thirty miles from the Hollywood studio and would barely make it home in time to witness the fruits of their many labors. In the next breath, Emily Daniels, Marc's wife and efficient assistant (also television's first camera coordinator), made a welcomed suggestion.

"We invited everyone to watch the show at our house at the end of Laurel Canyon in Horseshoe Canyon where we had just moved," Emily looks back. "I remember because I made dinner and had the plates in the oven to keep them warm. While we were watching the show, I forgot all about them, so when it was over we had to wait another ten or fifteen minutes for them to cool off before we could eat. When we were finished, it was eleven o'clock."

The first "Lucy" that went out over the CBS network facilities was not "Lucy Thinks Ricky Is Trying to Murder Her," the first segment shot (on September 8). Because of technical problems inherent in it, including the awkward use of four cameras instead of three, Jess and the others chose the second "I Love Lucy" installment as the premiere show. Titled "The Girls Want to Go to a Nightclub," the half-hour was described in the official CBS press release as follows:

"When the curtain rises, Ricky and Fred are plotting to attend the boxing matches despite the announced plans of the wives to go night-clubbing in celebration of Fred and Ethel's wedding anniversary. When the girls refuse to go to the fights, the boys arrange for a pair of blind dates. Later Lucy

and Ethel deck themselves out as a couple of hillbillies to substitute for the blind dates."

The "lead-in" show was the top-rated "Arthur Godfrey's Talent Scouts" and its red-haired host was gracious enough to give "Lucy" a proper send-off, urging his many fans to stay tuned for a new program. At precisely nine o'clock, Philip Morris' official spokesperson, the four-foot-tall Johnny Roventini, came on the screen with his famous "Call for Philip Mor-rees" pitch, followed immediately by the sponsor's theme song, "On the Trail" from *The Grand Canyon Suite* (by Ferde Grofé). And, for the first time, television audiences enjoyed the delightful animated footage of Lucy and Desi frolicking atop a pack of Philip Morris cigarettes. Then the voice-over: "Philip Morris, America's finest cigarette, presents the Lucille Ball–Desi Arnaz show, 'I Love Lucy.' " Next, the strains of a theme song that would become world famous.

Before the episode actually started, John Stevenson, acting as a commercial spokesperson for Philip Morris, presented the first "Lucy" commercial—not from the Philip Morris headquarters in Virginia nor from a special set built

Below left: Philip Morris spokesperson, Johnny Roventini, on hand to view the filming of an "I Love Lucy" episode.

Below right: Using the sponsor's product always played an integral part in early TV shows. Both smokers, Lucy and Desi obliged Philip Morris; smoking was often written into the scripts.

for the occasion, but right from the Ricardo living room! "Good evening and welcome," the handsome actor began. "In a moment we'll look in on Lucille Ball and Desi Arnaz but before we do may I ask a very personal question? The question is simply this—Do you inhale? Well, I do. And chances are you do too. And because you inhale, you're better off—much better off—smoking Philip Morris and for good reason. You see, Philip Morris is the one cigarette proved definitely less irritating, definitely milder than any other leading brand. That's why when you inhale, you're better off smoking Philip Morris. . . . And now, Lucille Ball and Desi Arnaz in 'I Love Lucy.' "

Watching quietly in the Danielses' living room were Lucy and Desi, Vivian Vance and her husband, Phil Ober, Jess Oppenheimer, and their hosts. According to Marc Daniels, "The only one who was laughing a lot was Phil Ober because he hadn't seen it. And he had this deep baritone laugh like 'HO HO HO.' But the rest of us just sat there motionless staring at the set."

Making the half-hour more frustrating for the group—and other Southern California-area viewers—there were projection room problems at local station KTSL, causing reception to be impaired, although the commercials came in crystal clear.

Lucie Desiree Arnaz's christening, October 1951. Left to right: Vivian Vance, Karl Freund, Lucy, Emily Daniels, and husband Marc Daniels.

The following day, the reviews came in. Columnist Dan Jenkins, who had seen the pilot in June and predicted then "the immediate ascendancy of Lucille Ball and Desi Arnaz to TV stardom," wrote glowingly in the *Hollywood Reporter,* calling Lucy's eyes "the brightest, clearest, and bluest in existence" (which was quite an accomplishment for a black-and-white show). Later in the week, Jenkins hailed the series as "situation comedy at its very best, serving the double purpose of giving the TV film industry a tremendous shot in the arm."

Other reports dubbed the series "high-quality slapstick," "refreshingly unpretentious," "sprightly comedy," "entertainment of a high level," "just what the doctor ordered."

Daily Variety was a little more reserved in its enthusiasm: "This initial teevee effort of Lucille Ball and Desi Arnaz should have carried the foreword: not to be taken seriously. As story-line comedies go, it is the better part of appreciation not to ask yourself too many questions and just go along with what transpires on your screen."

Its sister publication, the weekly *Variety,* reported:

"CBS and Philip Morris fell heir Monday night to one of the slickest TV entertainment shows to date. It's costing P-M $30,000 a week (exclusive of time) for the half-hour film series (without enjoying the benefits of residual rights, which revert back to the packagers), but on the basis of this week's preem installment, it should sell a lot of cigarettes.

" 'Lucy' 's emergence as refreshing and big-time video is significant from various angles. It cannot help but strengthen the growing belief that video programming, to save face and sponsors, must of necessity detour into such avenues where the writing and the material, the human equations and comedy formulas inherent in well-produced situation comedies, will take TV out of its present rut of over-produced spectacles from which any element of anticipation has been dissipated.

". . . The new Lucille Ball–Desi Arnaz show establishes film's secure place in video sweepstakes—when introduced into the medium under such handsome and professional auspices as applies to 'Lucy.' For here is a film that has all the Grade A qualities of major studio production, achieving a depth and visual values that pertain to theatre presentation, yet encompassing the desired intimacy for TV. It's a slick blending of Hollywood and TV showmanship, for which much credit belongs to Karl Freund on the camera masterminding and Marc Daniels on the direction."

But as sometimes happens even with a Broadway smash hit, one cardinal critic dissented. Val Adams of the prestigious, all-important New York *Times* decided "Lucy" has "promise of providing a refreshing half hour of video entertainment." Adams liked the first act, commenting that it could be "readily understood and appreciated by any married man or woman," but had serious reservations about what followed: "The play could not stand up under outlandish farcical stress and fell to pieces. . . . When Miss Ball dropped the jug she was carrying, lunged at a frightened Mr. Arnaz and yelled, 'Let's neck,' the audience was asked to believe these absurd shenanigans. . . . It was not her fault that the entire scene was utterly unbelievable."

On Tuesday morning, October 16, just twelve hours after the first show's airing, O. Parker McComas, president of Philip Morris, called Terry Clyne, vice president in charge of television at the Biow agency, to ask, "What would it cost us to cancel the contract for 'Lucy'?"

Clyne, backed up by his able West Coast counterpart, Eddie Feldman, urged the Philip Morris mogul to reconsider and give the series a little time to hit its stride. Good advice: the initial show placed among the Top Ten in the Nielsen ratings.

From all indications, the new filming technique was working well. Following telecasting of the first three films in the series ("The Girls Want to Go to a Nightclub," "Be a Pal," and "The Diet"), Karl Freund was being acclaimed by his American Society of Cinematographers colleagues for his technological excellence. By the end of the first season, the A.S.C. awarded Desilu Productions the society's Scroll of Achievement at an informal ceremony attended by society members and their spouses held right on the "Lucy" set at General Service Studios.

It was just one of the twenty-five awards and plaques that poured in during the 1951–52 season. At the Fourth Annual Emmy Awards dinner held in Los Angeles at the Cocoanut Grove of the Ambassador Hotel on February 2, 1952, after accepting the second of two Emmys for excellence in

Lucy and Desi reenact their "Cuban Pete/Sally Sweet" duet from their 1950 vaudeville tour in this scene from "The Diet."

comedy, Red Skelton remarked: "Ladies and gentlemen, you've given it to the wrong redhead. I don't deserve this. It should go to Lucille Ball." The overflowing audience of industry bigwigs and stars rose to its feet, cheering loudly. The Arnazes, unable to contain their jubilation, broke down and wept.

The so-called multicam system, included and described many years later in the Encyclopedia Americana, meant that the show was not filmed in separate shots but was picked up by three cameras (hence, multicamera) simultaneously in sequences that sometimes ran for ten minutes. Between scenes the program was interrupted to set up the cameras and prepare the next action. A film editor put the program together by selecting the best shots from those made by the various cameras. The method permitted the production of a program before an audience to which the performers played and which, in turn, provided the laughter for the sound track. This made it almost unnecessary to add laughter later by using recordings or a "laugh machine."

The same system, with very few differences, was later used to produce such classic sitcoms as "The Danny Thomas Show," "The Dick Van Dyke Show," "The Mary Tyler Moore Show," "Rhoda," "Happy Days," and "Laverne and Shirley."

"Lucy" was photographed on 35-mm film by three Mitchell BNC cameras mounted on "crab" dollies adapted by Steve Kranlonovitz from standard TV camera operations. Since all three cameras shot the action simultaneously, the camera in the center (#1) made all the long shots with a 40-mm wide-angle lens. The cameras at either side (#2 and #3) recorded the action in close-ups, using three-inch and four-inch lenses.

Cuing of camera operators, grips operating the dollies, and the gaffer handling the light dimmers was a minor miracle. While a segment was being photographed, the camera coordinator in the booth overlooking the stage was in direct contact with key technicians at all times via two-way intercom. (Associate producer Al Simon purchased for Desilu the intercom paraphernalia from Ralph Edwards' company when he left "Truth or Consequences" to join Desilu.) Although each man previously was briefed on the operation and in many cases had floor marks to guide him, the camera coordinator's cues ensured against any possibility of error. It was amazing how quickly the crews were able to change setups and start shooting again; delays averaged a mere ninety seconds.

A major factor making such speed possible was the unique lighting arrangement Freund developed for the production. Since invariably the players were in action over almost the entire set ("intercommunicating"), the light intensity had to be uniform over the total area at all times. There were no light changes, other than those made by dimming. All set illumination, therefore, had to be from overhead. There were none of the usual floor lamps found in most motion picture production units, and the only illumination from a lower level came from portable "fill" lights mounted just above the matte box on each camera. The set lamps were rigged carefully on catwalks

Director of photography, Karl Freund, checks his light meter during rehearsals for Episode #3, "Be a Pal," September 21, 1951.

suspended above the set. This overhead lighting method also kept cables off the floor, making feasible the unobstructed operation of camera dollies as well as the quick movement of equipment to subsequent setups.

Freund once described the unique challenge with which he was faced: "To light a set for three cameras operating simultaneously and from different positions is a problem in itself. We have to light as uniformly as possible, yet watch for opportunities to add highlights whenever we can. This is very important, inasmuch as 'Lucy' is a comedy show requiring high-key illumination.

"Contrast also has to be watched carefully," Freund continued, "since the tube in the film image pickup system of the television station is quite contrasty. Any contrast in the film therefore is compounded if not exaggerated in each step of the transmission of the picture. This makes it necessary to keep the contrast in the original negative down to what we call a 'fine medium.'"

This matter of contrast was further revealed in the decor of the "I Love Lucy" sets. They were painted in various shades of gray. Freund even employed what he called his "standby painter," who would, upon Karl's command, repaint a set wall to get just the right contrast. Props likewise followed the demands of correct contrast, as did the wardrobe of the players. For the first two seasons, Lucy's wardrobe mistress, Della Fox, had to consult Freund when purchasing clothing. Day players who furnished their own wardrobe were required to bring a selection of outfits from home so Freund could select the most appropriate. Likewise, costume designers Elois Jenssen (1953–55) and Edward Stevenson (1955–60) were required to get the director of photography's approval before proceeding with costume construction. Even newspapers used in scenes had to be tinted gray to satisfy the overall uniformity of color and tones required by Freund's illumination formula.

Although each weekly show went before the cameras at eight o'clock Friday evening (from fall 1953 through spring 1957 it was Thursday night) and was photographed entirely in about an hour, the preceding three days were employed by the company in rehearsals, preproduction planning, and script revision.

At ten o'clock sharp on Tuesday morning, the director (during the first season, Marc Daniels; thereafter, William Asher and James V. Kern), actors, and writers gathered around a rehearsal table set up on the dubbing stage for a first reading. "We never saw a script until that first morning," Lucy once told a visiting reporter. "We trusted the writers implicitly."

Until 6 P.M. the cast rehearsed, incorporating changes the writers had made during the day's morning reading. Sometimes a phrase was reworked slightly, and other times an entirely new passage was substituted. Sometimes an entire page or two or three didn't work, so Bob and Madelyn went off to their office and came up with something different. The cast members also made suggestions that were often incorporated into a script.

"Lucy had a marvelous sense of what would work and what wouldn't," offers Jess Oppenheimer. "Hundreds of times she would question certain things. If she was certain a scene wasn't exactly right—even if she couldn't articulate exactly what was wrong with it—we'd take another look at it. After a closer inspection, we would discover she was right and we would rework the scene. Also if Desi didn't like something, we'd change it, because if he didn't like something, he was incapable of doing it. Or sometimes he just didn't understand things that were part of our American culture."

Once a script ("Lucy Tells the Truth") called for Ricky to "cheat" on his income tax return. Being sensitive about his cherished U.S. citizenship, Desi refused to do the scene, which comprised the entire second act, contending that Ricky Ricardo would never cheat the government. No matter how much Jess and the others tried to convince Arnaz it was like "eating apple pie," Desi wouldn't buy it. The scripters had to rewrite the entire second act.

A similar schedule (10 A.M. to 6 P.M.) prevailed for Wednesday, but now the cast rehearsed on the sets, not around a table. Hopefully, over the preceding evening, the lines had been memorized—some forty to forty-five pages of dialogue. By 4:30 P.M. the company was ready to run through the entire show. No cameras were on the set at this time, nor were any members of the camera crews present. During this run-through Karl Freund studied the players in their directed movements about the sets and took note of how and where they entered and exited, and planned his cameras accordingly. Jess describes this critical rehearsal: "The actors tried to put down their scripts for the first time. This would give me a good idea as to what was working and what wasn't. Then we had a 'note session' where we'd discuss everything that I made notes about. I'd give my suggestions about line readings, or whatever wasn't working."

A late "call" for the actors was the order of Thursday as Freund and his electrical crew began the arduous task of lighting the sets, hoping to complete the exacting job by noon. By this time the members of the camera crews came on the set and were briefed on camera movements and other pertinent details. With the various crews and cameras assembled on the stage, camera action with the cast was rehearsed until six. This enabled Freund to make any necessary changes in the lighting or operation of the camera dollies. Cues for the dimmer operator also were worked out at this time. Chalk marks and masking tape were placed on the floor indicating the positions the cameras were to take for the various shots or the range of the dolly action for a given shot.

A full dress rehearsal was held at about 7 P.M. The writers, who had been kept busy the preceding days creating an entirely new script for another episode, were present, as were network and ad agency officials. Freund, his camera operators, gaffers, and grips were on hand—but the cameras were not wheeled on the floor. Immediately thereafter, a meal was served on a trestle table near the set. Sometimes it was a complete spaghetti dinner, other times just sandwiches. While eating, the cast, director, producer, prop men, and assistants discussed the episode. From 8 until 10 (or later— sometimes as late as 1 A.M.), this fine-toothed-comb session was conducted. Lines of dialogue were cut, action shortened or deleted, camera movements analyzed—in short, everything that would tighten up the show, scene by scene, from beginning to end.

"Everyone would stay for this," recalls Jess, "even the stage hands. They were wonderful sessions where we'd even get into the philosophy of the script. We'd have our share of arguments, too. Bill Frawley would get his back up over the way he wanted to read a line or something. But they were very stimulating and fruitful. We really dug into the characters because we took these people very seriously and tried to make everything logical."

On Friday, the cameramen were present at nine o'clock in the morning, blocking out their lines on the floor; the lighting men used stand-ins to mark cue sheets and to crisscross the stage for the regular players (Hazel Pierce and Bennett Green were Lucy and Desi's stand-ins). At 1 P.M., Lucy arrived to have her hair washed and set in pin curlers by Irma Kusely, her hairdresser. All afternoon, with a scarf tied around her head, Lucy would rehearse with the rest of the cast. If any major changes in the action, dialogue, or camera treatment were decided in the previous evening's discussions, these would be integrated into the show.

A final dress rehearsal would take place at about four-thirty with the cameras on the floor. Freund gave his lighting a final check and made any necessary last-minute changes before the company broke for dinner at six. On thirty-foot trestle tables set up on the dubbing stage, sixty people sat down to eat soup, salad, meat, dessert, coffee—actors, grips, cameramen, film editors, electricians, the three writers, Lucy and Desi's mothers, the musicians, agents, representatives from Philip Morris and CBS. Usually the dinners turned into cake-cutting parties, because Lucy liked to commemorate birthdays, anniversaries, or just about any event she could think of.

After dinner, the company and cast returned to the stage, and there followed a general "talk-through" of the show. At this time, further suggestions were considered and immediate decisions made on any remaining problems. At that point, Lucy would be made up by Hal King.

In the meantime, an atmosphere reminiscent of a summer theater took over. The audience filed in, after waiting for up to an hour along Romaine Street, and was seated in the bleachers with an assist from ushers supplied by CBS. As in radio days audience members were supposed to "work" a bit for free admission. An assistant director gave them their cues for laughter, cheers, groans, or applause. Nothing, not even a bum funny bone was left to chance, although an emphasis was put on the importance of natural, spontaneous reaction.

Lucy and Desi take a bow after filming the sixth "Lucy" show, "The Audition," which was a rewritten version of the show's pilot.

At seven-thirty Desi would be brought on. Grabbing a microphone for the "warm-up," he would introduce not only his co-stars, but also Jess, Bob, and Madelyn, Wilbur Hatch, the director, even the stage hands.

Then at eight, for approximately sixty minutes (one first-season show was shot fully in forty-five minutes), the show was filmed. As soon as action was completed for one setup, the cameras, crews, and players moved rapidly to the next setup, and the action was resumed. All scenes were shot in strict chronological order to keep the flow of the story moving for the studio audience.

Due to the meticulous planning and thorough rehearsals, retakes (known as "pickups") were seldom necessary. In this respect, each camera operator had a major responsibility. He had to get each "take" right the first time—every time. Of course, he could hardly miss, considering the careful preparation that went into the filming phase of the production beforehand. Focus was carefully measured and noted for each camera position (there were as many as eighty focus changes per show); chalk marks had been placed conspicuously on the stage floor; there were the numerous rehearsals; and, of course, there was vigilant Emily Daniels (during the first season) overlooking the proceedings from the control booth, relaying instructions over the intercom system.

The three cameras shot an average of 7,500 feet of 35-mm film per show. It was taken across the street to Consolidated Film Industries, Hollywood's largest processing lab, for developing. After Dann Cahn's editing process (using the special Moviola, a "rough cut" could be produced in as little as one day), each episode was turned into a master print at a cost of about twenty-five hundred dollars, which included the negative, plus charges for

Film editor Dann Cahn at work on the four-headed "monster," the special Moviola invented for Desilu by George Fox.

developing, and mixing the optical effects, such as fades and dissolves. Adding a minute each for the opening titles and credits to the twenty-four and a half minutes of actual "I Love Lucy" accounted for a reel of film totaling twenty-six and a half minutes, a print of which cost approximately thirty dollars.

In a *Time* magazine cover story (May 26, 1952), the phenomenon of "I Love Lucy" was analyzed: "In about six months [Lucille Ball's] low-comedy antics, ranging from mild mugging to baggy pants clowning have dethroned such veteran TV headliners as Milton Berle and Arthur Godfrey.

". . . The television industry is not quite sure how it happened. When 'Lucy' went on the air last October, it seemed to be just another series devoted to family comedy, not much better or much worse than 'Burns and Allen,' 'The Goldbergs,' 'The Aldrich Family,' or 'Mama.' Like its competitors, 'Lucy' holds a somewhat grotesque mirror up to middle-class life and finds humor in exaggerating the commonplace incidents of marriage, business, and the home. Lucille's Cuban-born husband, Desi Arnaz, is cast as the vain, easily flattered leader of an obscure rumba band. Lucille plays his ambitious wife, bubbling with elaborate and mostly ineffectual schemes to advance his career. But what televiewers see on their screens is the sort of cheerful rowdiness that had been rare in the U.S. since the days of the silent movies' Keystone Comedies. Lucille submits enthusiastically to being hit with pies; she falls over furniture, gets locked in home freezers, is chased by knife-wielding fanatics. Tricked out as a ballerina, or a Hindu maharanee or a toothless hillbilly, she takes her assorted lumps and pratfalls with unflagging zest and good humor. Her mobile, rubbery face reflects a limitless variety of emotions, from maniacal pleasure to sepulchral gloom. Even on a flickering, pallid TV screen, her wide-set, saucer eyes beam with the massed candlepower of a lighthouse on a dark night."

Attempting to explain Lucy's unprecedented TV triumph, Jess Oppenheimer said about his contribution: "You took the greatest living comedienne and worked from there . . . For every word you write in this business, you figure you're lucky to get back 70 to 80 percent from a performer. With Lucy, you get back 140 percent."

It was no secret that Lucy possessed an unfailing instinct for timing. This was evident in just about every "I Love Lucy" scene ever filmed. Her first television director adds his praise: "To me, Lucy is the most extraordinary innate talent I have ever known. She's a sensational actress. I don't think she knows how she does it. She would have been some 'Anna Christie.' Now it's too late because every time she opens her mouth people expect her to be funny. But the reason her old shows were so great—and still are—was that her basic instincts were so right, her reactions so quick. Not only that, but she was fantastic at handling props."

Lucy credits her old M-G-M pal Buster Keaton, with whom she never had the opportunity to work, with teaching her about props. Keaton and his director, Eddie Sedgwick, were among Lucy's champions who tried to talk Metro bigwigs into starring her in major comedy vehicles for the studio.

Later, when Lucy and Desi were putting together the pre-"I Love Lucy" vaudeville tour, Keaton and Sedgwick were on hand to lend creative support. "You'd be amazed," says Lucy, "at how many people cannot pick up a prop, let alone work with a conveyor belt and do the things that I had to do with a whole kitchen full of props—toast up in the air or pancakes. Viv could never do it. She just died every time she had to touch a prop.

"I haven't had a great many fights with directors but I had a real battle with my first director on television [Marc Daniels]. I guess it's because I was frightened. I had to handle a pop-up toaster and during rehearsals he had me use balsa wood instead of real bread. And it was popping way up in the air. So I said, 'I'm going to have to eat this bread. Don't you think we ought to start working with the real thing?'

"By the second day of rehearsal with the balsa wood, I said, 'Sir, don't you think we should be working with the bread?' 'For what?' he asked. 'Because of the weight,' I explained. 'The balsa's taking off like a Ping-Pong ball.' So he got a little miffed. And I said, 'May I use the bread?' 'No.' So I insisted: 'It's *my* bread, bring it in!' And what a helluva difference."

Lucy's ever-present pursuit of perfection sometimes bordered on the eccentric. Stage manager Herb Browar, who also acted as prop man and assistant director for the first few months of "Lucy," remembers an incident that explains Lucy's perfectionism: "One of the early episodes ["The Amateur Show"] called for a frog. All during rehearsals, Marc Daniels was using a fake frog, the type of thing they used on live TV. Lucy insisted on a real frog. But it was six o'clock in the evening on dress rehearsal night, and no stores were open where you could buy frogs. Tony Montenaro, who was head of the prop department at General Service, suggested a frog farm located way out in the San Fernando Valley. I drove there, found the house, and interrupted the family's dinner. The woman pointed to the backyard, which was pitch black. In my haste to get a frog and get back to the studio, I stepped off her porch and was suddenly knee-deep in mud. Somehow I thought the frogs would be outside hopping around, not living under water. The woman asked me how many I needed and I told her three. She just reached in the mud and pulled them out, and I drove back to Hollywood with Lucy's frogs. I loved that dedication to detail in Lucy and would do *anything* to please her."

One character actor who made several appearances on "I Love Lucy" is Ross Elliott. An old army buddy of Marc Daniels, he was cast in March 1952 as a TV director in a segment ("Lucy Does a TV Commercial") that called for Lucy Ricardo (posing as Lucille McGillicuddy) to act as spokeswoman for a liquid vitamin product, Vitameatavegamin. "Lucy was fantastic," says Ross, who was thirty-five at the time he did his first "I Love Lucy." "An inspired clown in the classic sense. She was always the hardest worker on the set. Everything had to be perfect."

Elliott, who is remembered to this day by fans of that classic episode, made a habit of bringing his dog Chloe, whom he smuggled all through Europe during World War II, with him to the Desilu sound stage each day.

Twins Timmy (left) and Jimmy Hudson (David Stollery and Sammy Ogg) sing "Ragtime Cowboy Joe" in the final scene from "The Amateur Hour," just moments before Elmer, their pet frog, runs amok.

"Lucy loved Chloe, and if I didn't bring her in she would ask me why and insist I bring her the next day," recalls Ross. Years later as a tribute to Miss Ball, the actor named his second pooch Lucy.

His allegiance to "I Love Lucy" was so fervent that Elliott actually postponed his wedding in 1954 because of the show. "Jess wanted me for an episode ["Don Juan and the Starlets"]. It was to shoot the week Sue and I were to be married. We decided to postpone the ceremony until after the show was filmed. We didn't want to disappoint Lucy and the staff."

Ross wasn't the only actor to admire Lucille Ball's stamina and perfectionism. "I can remember a scene in one of the episodes during her pregnancy in 1952 which required her to jump up and down on the bed," explains Jerry Hausner. "Lucy became ill, went off the set, threw up, and was back within minutes doing the scene over again. She was a fantastic trouper."

During one rehearsal the first season, Lucy set fire to her dress with a cigarette but continued the scene. "It was right in the middle of a good rehearsal and I was afraid to stop," she explained. Luckily, Vivian noticed the smoldering fabric and screamed. Another time, the script, "Cuban Pals," called for a running leap toward Desi. Lucy jumped, missed him, and ricocheted fifteen feet. Bruised, she got up and redid the scene.

Her physical stamina notwithstanding, by the close of the first season, Lucy's doctor, Mark Rabwin, insisted that she spend her weekends in the hospital to rest because she was precariously close to exhaustion. To make matters worse, she and Desi had committed themselves to play New York's Roxy Theater (where they appeared two years before on the vandeville tour) for two weeks and the London Palladium for another fourteen days in July. The deal, negotiated by General Amusement Corporation, called for fifty-seven thousand dollars, plus a hefty percentage of the gross over a hundred thousand.

Business was good. As reported in *Newsweek* (February 18, 1952): "Desilu's success has sent a stream of Hollywoodites to tour the Arnazes' soundstages. Among them are Rosalind Russell, Eve Arden, Arlene Dahl

Desi and Lucy play host to Rosalind Russell and Teresa Wright, who were in the audience the night "Be a Pal" was filmed.

and Lex Barker, Laraine Day and Leo Durocher, and Bing Crosby, who told Lucille he would probably use the Desilu technique when he makes his long-awaited television debut. The Durochers were so impressed that they had Desilu film a baseball series for them. Red Skelton uses the facilities for his [Tide] commercials. And last week Eve Arden was making a pilot film of 'Our Miss Brooks.' "

Simultaneously, plans got underway to produce an "I Love Lucy" radio show for CBS. The idea was born quite accidentally one night when CBS's Hal Hudson and his wife were home watching "Lucy"—except that the picture went out on the Hudson set just before the show started. They "watched" the show with sound only. Hal had seen the film in a projection room and was able to fill his wife in on the visual aspects of the story, but they both nevertheless agreed that the sound track alone was pretty entertaining. Hudson phoned Oppenheimer the next day and the pair agreed it was a possibility. After a good deal of effort, it was decided in April that using selected "Lucy" sound tracks as an inexpensive radio package for Philip Morris would not jell. Too many editing, music, and sound effects snags. There exists on the nostalgia market today a long-playing record of a radio version of the "Lucy" episode titled "Breaking the Lease," although it was never broadcast.

By spring, Desi had decided to convert a trio of episodes into a theatrical motion picture. He hired Eddie Sedgwick, the director of countless Buster Keaton films and his and Lucy's dear friend, to transform three half-hours into a ninety-minute feature film for experimental release in the United States and Latin America. At a cost of about twenty-five thousand dollars, Sedgwick directed several days' shooting—opening and closing sequences, and middle bridges, which were written by the "Lucy" writers. Desilu was offered four hundred thousand dollars for the package, although it would never be released after being previewed at a theater in Bakersfield, California. (When the Arnazes made a deal in early 1953 to star in *The Long, Long Trailer* for M-G-M, the studio made them promise not to release their "Lucy" picture. Too much competition, Metro reasoned.)

By May, an estimated 11,055,000 American families were inviting the Ricardos and Mertzes into their living rooms every Monday night, an excellent audience considering there were only 15,000,000 TV sets in operation that year. The April 7 broadcast, "The Marriage License," broke a TV record. On this evening, ARB reported 10,600,000 households tuned to "Lucy," the first TV show to be seen in 10,000,000 U.S. homes.

" 'I Love Lucy' was the top program in the nation in April with a rating of 63.2," ARB director James W. Seiler stated. "And it was the first-ranking show in practically every major city."

With an estimated 2.9 viewers watching each TV set, the April 7, 1952, "I Love Lucy" show was seen by approximately 30,740,000 individuals. Of these, 32 percent, or 9,836,800, were men, 44 percent, or 13,525,600 were women, and 24 percent, or 7,377,600, were children.

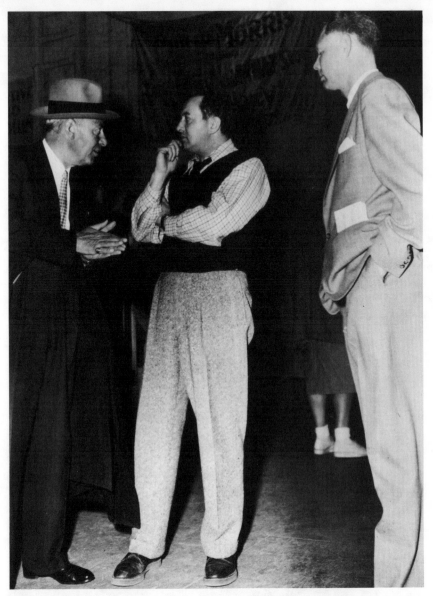

March 1952. Marc Daniels listens to advice from Philip Morris chairman of the board Alfred E. Lyons as assistant director James Paisley looks on.

These "numbers" pleased ad agency mogul Milton Biow and his client, Philip Morris cigarettes, whose chairman, Alfred E. Lyons, made a special trip to Los Angeles on March 6, 1952, to congratulate Lucy and Desi and to watch an episode ("The Kleptomaniac") being filmed. At an intimate dinner party hosted by the Arnazes for the cigarette mogul, Biow announced that the puffery was picking up its option for "Lucy" for a second season.

TV Guide's own endorsement defined "I Love Lucy" as "the season's most popular program—smooth, deft, solidly produced, and funny."

Concerning the classic Vitameatavegamin TV commercial, Ross Elliott

William Frawley—better known as Fred Mertz—in makeup for the episode titled "Pioneer Women." Note in the background the chart with names and foil stars beside them. This was Lucy's idea—rewarding those who "said funny things" during rehearsal.

Bob Carroll and Madelyn Pugh, writers of "I Love Lucy," bestow their award—a silver dollar—on Lucy. The pair gave out shiny dollars to anyone who was responsible for a spontaneous reaction from the studio audience.

confirms: "I chewed the inside of my mouth out to keep from laughing out loud. Lucy would do new stuff that wasn't rehearsed, like an extra-funny face. Then, at one point, she became 'drunk' and started making eyes at me, flirting, and I almost broke up again."

The ability to evoke laughs came easily to the four principals and staff. A backstage bulletin board listed the names of cast and crew with a series of gold stars next to each name. The stars represented off-camera ad-libs.

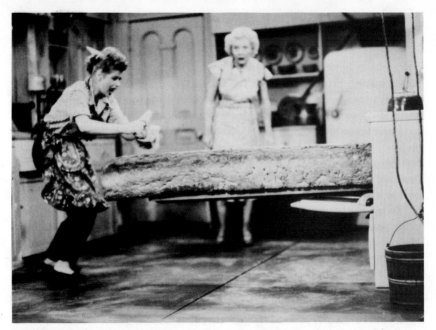

It would have been easy to have a Hollywood prop shop make a papier-mâché loaf of bread for this scene that lasted only a few seconds on screen, but Desilu opted for realism and got it in the form of edible rye bread.

Frawley's stars ran the length of the board, and then some, so quickly that the project was soon abandoned. "Lack of competition," Lucille explained.

Bob Carroll, Jr., and Madelyn Pugh, two of the "Lucy" scribes, instituted their own method of recognizing comedic excellence among the cast and crew. If something caused the studio audience to burst into spontaneous applause, the writers awarded the person responsible a shiny silver dollar. Lucy collected more than sixty dollars that way.

Very rarely did Lucille Ball make a mistake. Rehearsals were too thorough. However, one wag remembers an occasion when she hopelessly stumbled over a speech eight or nine times in succession, until she broke the tension by yelling out into the audience to her mother, seated in the top row of the bleachers, "Don't worry, Mom, I'll get it!"

"Pioneer Women," the twenty-fifth episode filmed, and originally telecast March 31, 1952, created a number of production problems that were nearly insolvable. The basic premise of the script was the men (Ricky and Fred) versus the women (Lucy and Ethel) in a contest (bet: fifty dollars) to determine which sex could withstand better the rigors of the pioneer days (actually the 1890s) when there were no modern conveniences. In one scene, Lucy bakes her own bread, and, having put in too much yeast, an eight-foot loaf explodes from the Ricardo oven, pinning Lucy against the sink.

"When we went to a prop shop to find out what it would cost to have a loaf of bread made that long," says Marc Daniels, the director, "we found out it would be enormously expensive. So someone had the bright idea to go to a regular bakery."

That idea man was none other than Herb Browar, the efficient and dedicated "Lucy" stage manager. "I went to the phone book and looked under 'commercial bakeries,' " says Browar. "I finally found one, the Union

Made Bakery, that would bake the bread. But they didn't have a pan that big so we had to go to a sheet metal shop in Hollywood and have the pan made to order. The baker asked me how long the bread had to last and I told him two or three days. He suggested a rye bread because it stays fresher longer. The bakery baked it, we sent a truck downtown to pick it up, and then rigged the oven with a wooden platform and roller. Our prop man, Nat Thurlow, had the job of shoving the bread through the oven door." When the filming was over, the mammoth loaf was cut up into huge slices and distributed to the crew to take home.

"In another scene in the same episode," Marc Daniels adds, "we had Desi riding a horse, since he wasn't permitted to use modern transportation. We rehearsed the hell out of that horse all week. But came the night of the filming, the horse took one look at the three hundred people in the bleachers laughing at him and refused to cooperate any longer. Desi couldn't get him through the apartment door, as the script called for, so we improvised a scene on the back porch set. It was a mess."

Although three of the thirty-eight "I Love Lucy" episodes that Marc Daniels directed were saved for the early weeks of the series' second year, he resigned after one season. As reported in *Daily Variety* on May 9, 1952: "Parting is amicable, although Daniels's withdrawal was prompted by refusal of Desilu to meet his demands for pay increase." Marc's last episode was "The Operetta," filmed the night of May 23. Recently, Daniels explained, "I left because the show was getting more and more difficult to do. I now admit it was a mistake."

Perhaps his confrontations with Lucille and his occasional disagreements with Jess Oppenheimer were factors that led to his decision to leave Desilu. The producer remembers one such incident clearly: "During rehearsals for one episode ["The Gossip"], I was called down to the stage from my office because Lucy and Marc were arguing about a bit of business that Marc wanted to do that wasn't in the script. This sort of thing happened all of the time and usually the improvisations and suggestions were sound and they became part of the script, but not this time. Marc wanted Bobby Jellison, who was playing a milkman, to enter the Ricardo bedroom and cross on top of the bed. Lucy and Bobby both agreed it was silly, that there was no earthly reason why anyone would jump up on a bed if he could just as easily walk around it. Marc's feeling was that it was funny. But I had to agree with Lucy that it wouldn't be realistic and therefore didn't belong in the show. Marc was very concerned about who was boss and would literally cringe anytime I came on the stage." Several months later, Daniels took over the direction on Joan Davis' sitcom "I Married Joan," a show often likened to "I Love Lucy," which ran for three seasons on NBC.

A few days after Marc's resignation was made public, Desilu announced that William Asher would "run a couple of 'I Love Lucy' shows" since there were two episodes left to be filmed before the summer hiatus, "Job Switching" and "The Saxophone." Asher had directed Desilu's pilot of "Our Miss

Filming a scene for "Pioneer Women" on a special set constructed in front of the Ricardo bedroom caused problems for Desi and the horse.

Principal cast members and assorted clubwomen from the Wednesday Afternoon Fine Arts League perform the drinking song from The Pleasant Peasant, a scene from the classic "Operetta" episode, Marc Daniels' last "Lucy" outing.

Marc Daniels instructs Desi on the proper way to hold the mock Look *magazine used in episode titled "Men Are Messy."*

Brooks" early in February and was comfortable with the three-camera technique. In the very same issue of *Daily Variety*, however, the "Lucy" company announced that Edward Sedgwick had been signed to direct the second season of the sitcom. Sedgwick, of course, was one of the Arnazes' closest friends. The fifty-nine-year-old director of Buster Keaton comedies and a few Laurel and Hardy features was an old hand at slapstick comedy, but was considered by his former studio, M-G-M, as "incurably old-fashioned." His most recent credits included being "comedy consultant" on the Red Skelton film *The Yellow Cab Man*, and director on *Ma and Pa Kettle Back on the Farm*, two run-of-the-mill comedy vehicles.

On May 16, the trade papers reported: "William Asher has been inked to direct 'I Love Lucy' when Marc Daniels bows out of series following May 23 show. Asher will probably direct the remainder of the season . . . Edward Sedgwick, who recently joined Desilu Productions, is assisting Desi Arnaz and acting as production co-ordinator for Desilu." For some reason and despite his close relationship with Lucy and Desi, Sedgwick was not given the plum "Lucy" assignment, but, instead, was tapped to supervise the making of the theatrical film version of "I Love Lucy."

"I knew Lucy and Desi very slightly through my sister Betty, who worked in the M-G-M publicity department," says Bill Asher, one of TV's most prolific triple threats (writer-producer-director). The son of Ephraim M. Asher, a Universal producer *(Magnificent Obsession, Dracula's Daughter, The Black Cat,* etc.), Bill began his career in the Universal mailroom at twelve dollars a week, finally directing (with Richard Quine) his first feature in 1948 at age twenty-nine, *Leather Gloves,* for Columbia Pictures. "CBS hired me to direct the television pilot of 'Our Miss Brooks' [in January 1952] because they were impressed with some of my early TV work. It had been the understanding that if the 'Brooks' pilot sold, I would be the director.

"But Desi approached me one day on the lot where I was shooting an episode of 'Big Town' and said, 'Wouldn't you rather do "I Love Lucy"?' I said, of course, but I have this 'Our Miss Brooks' thing, and he told me not to worry about it because it too was going to be a Desilu show and he could make other arrangements for 'Brooks.' I had also worked as an assistant cutter and Desi wanted a cutter he could control and asked me if I would help cut 'Lucy.' I had already directed a motion picture so I was familiar with using movie cameras. Obviously, it was an incredible opportunity for me—directing the number one show on television—so I happily accepted. It's proof that timing and luck are something."

Asher remembers his first "Lucy" show in May 1952 and how it almost was his last: "I have a street background. If someone bothers me, I tend to bother them back. Lucy is a strong person with a tendency to take over, which she immediately did with me. I was bothered by her behavior and decided to tell her so. I said, 'Look, Lucy, if you want to direct these shows, then you should direct them and save some money—if you're going to tell people where to go and what to do. I mean I'd like to hear your ideas, but . . .' Well, she burst into tears and ran from the stage to her dressing trailer.

"So there I was standing by myself, everyone staring at me. I had no office of my own where I could go while the furor blew over so I retreated to the men's room. I thought about how stupidly I had acted—after all, Lucy was the biggest star on television at the time. I got up my nerve and went back to the set, where Desi was waiting for me, with that look in his eye.

"He asked me what I had done, so I told him that I agreed Lucy knew a lot, but that she started taking over and then what was I supposed to do. Desi agreed—she shouldn't have done that—and told me to go to her dressing room and talk to her. Tentatively, I did. I told her I was sorry and she said she was sorry, and that was that. I must say that after that she was very cautious about suggestions, but her instincts were always incredible. We got along great after that. Hell, that first episode of mine about the candy factory is considered a classic!"

"Job Switching," the thirty-ninth show in the series, was quite a challenge to the "Lucy" company. Aside from rigging up a conveyor belt system directly in front of the Tropicana set (and the Acme Employment Agency office in front of the Ricardo bedroom), Herb Browar was approached by Jess Oppenheimer with an assignment. "I want you to find a professional candy-dipper for next week's show. I don't care if she can act, but she has to be good at chocolate-dipping."

This was Browar's major "swan song" assignment, as he would leave Desilu with associate producer Al Simon during the summer to help mastermind the new Joan Davis show for NBC. "I remembered seeing a See's Candy factory somewhere nearby on Santa Monica Boulevard. It was on the second floor of a building. I dropped by and spoke to the manager, telling him I wanted to hire the best candy maker he had. He introduced me to this lady whose name was Amanda Milligan. She was the best as far as the swirls on top of each chocolate were concerned. A real pro. I made arrangements to get her into the Screen Extras Guild simply because no one already in the union had her particular expertise. Now, remember, all this woman did all day long was put swirls on chocolates. Eight hours a day, for years. So, it's the second day of rehearsals and I notice her sitting by the 'Lucy' set watching the principals rehearse the first scenes. I go up to her and say, 'Well, what do you think about being in the movies?' She looked up at me wearily and said, 'I've never been so bored in my life!' "

Jess recalls the moment Lucy met the professional candy dipper: "Lucy was introduced to the woman on the stage and asked if she liked the show. The woman answered, 'What show?' Lucy replied, ' "I Love Lucy." ' Then the dipper asked, 'When is it on?' and Lucy answered, 'Monday night.' 'Oh,' said the woman, 'I watch wrestling that night.' "

The scene depicting Lucy and the candy maker dipping chocolates was, like the sequence following with Lucy and Vivian wrapping bonbons, a crucial few minutes. Rehearsals were not going well. It was the day of the dress rehearsal and Amanda Milligan was reluctant to slap Lucy in the face, as the script called for her to do. "I'm afraid I'll hurt you, Miss Ball," she said. "Don't worry, I can take it," Lucy responded. "Just haul off and slap me in the face as hard as you can. The scene depends on it." Later that day during the dress rehearsal, Milligan was still being too timid, and Lucy knew this critical bit had to be captured on film the first time—no retakes or "pickup" shots would do.

"Lucy was brilliant," Herb Browar recalls. "Without telling anybody, the night of the actual filming, when she had to hit the candy maker first, she did it really hard, not at all like she had been doing during the countless rehearsals. The woman was so stunned by Lucy's fervor, she hauled off and really slugged Lucy, practically knocking her off the stool. But that was exactly what Lucy was hoping she'd do. It was a perfect take, a prime example of Lucy's impeccable instinct."

The real challenge, especially during the first "Lucy" season, was met by the three writers, who wrote forty-nine scripts in the first eleven months of their Desilu employment. Luckily they were able to capitalize on their knowledge of Lucy and Desi's real-life characteristics, having known the couple since 1948 when Lucy began doing the radio series for CBS. Consequently, they were able to parlay the real-life Lucy and Desi into the family situation comedy Lucy and Ricky. For instance, when Bob and Madelyn sat down together to do their first draft (Bob often clad in Bermuda shorts), their reaction to suggestions was based always upon whether Lucy or Desi—in reality—would or would not do certain things or act in certain ways.

The writers carefully tailored their material. Knowing, for instance, that Lucille Ball superstitiously knocks on wood, they wrote an episode, "The Séance," in which Lucy Ricardo spoiled a business deal for Ricky by

Madelyn Pugh, Bob Carroll, and Jess Oppenheimer exchange thoughts backstage with the stars of their show.

consulting a horoscope. Similarly, because Lucille likes to imitate Tallulah Bankhead, Bob and Madelyn fashioned a sequence in "Lucy Fakes Illness" where Mrs. Ricardo imagined herself to be a famous actress known as "Taloo." Lucy loves bop musicians so the writers dreamed up "The Saxophone," an episode that required Lucille Ball to learn how to play "The Glow Worm" in several days, in order to do it well enough in the segment.

"I never can get cool; Desi is never warm," Lucy once remarked, explaining the inspiration for a scene in "Breaking the Lease" in which each sought to outsmart the other by surreptitiously opening and closing windows after going to bed for the night.

There were more important similarities to the real-life couple. For instance, Lucy and Desi were married in 1940; so were the fictional Ricardos. Lucy Ricardo says she went to high school in Celeron, New York; that's where Lucille Ball attended school. The make-believe pair was married at the Byram River Beagle Club in Greenwich, Connecticut, according to "The Marriage License" segment, in which they repeated their marital vows. The Arnazes too were married at the Byram River Beagle Club in Greenwich and once repeated *their* marriage vows in 1949. Marion Strong was one of Lucy Ricardo's best friends; Marion Strong was also the name of a person from Jamestown, New York. Lucille Ball grew up with her.

So personal a project was "I Love Lucy" that both Lucille and Desi made sure their friends had acting assignments. Barbara Pepper, who got her start in the movies along with Lucy as a Goldwyn Girl in *Roman Scandals,*

Far right in this scene from "Ricky Loses His Voice" is Lucille Ball chum Barbara Pepper, a former Goldwyn Girl (circa 1933).

appeared in countless "Lucy" episodes, usually portraying a matronly woman bystander. This was years before she played the role of Doris Ziffel, Arnold's (the Pig) "mother," in the bucolic sitcom "Green Acres." Eddie Sedgwick's wife, Ebba, once commented: "When Lucy gives a down-and-out friend a job on 'I Love Lucy,' she acts as if the friend is honoring her by taking the job, yet she gets this idea across with a wisecrack." Desi was just as loyal. Besides keeping his entire band on the payroll, he made certain his buddy from the Xavier Cugat days, Louis A. Nicoletti, got acting jobs on the show. He usually played waiters. Years later "Nick" became an assistant director and before his death in 1969 was performing that function on "Here's Lucy," Lucille Ball's third and last TV show. Even Vivian Vance's husband, actor Phil Ober, showed up in a few "Lucy" 's, one as early as November 1951.

Desi's fractured English, which evoked a great deal of laughter throughout the years, was *not* written into the scripts, as one might assume. However, his Cuban accent often made retakes necessary: Once his reading of "recognized talent" came out distinctly as "recognize Stalin." He said "ever thin" for "everything," "mushing peectures" for "motion pictures," "widdout furderadoo" for "without further ado." "Won't" was "wunt," "stage" was "staitch," "apartment" was "apparrmin," "partner" was "parner," and, best of all, "Fred Mertz" was "Frat Mers."

When Arnaz saw a dubbed "Lucy" show in Japan recently, he had what he calls "the eeriest feeling" as he heard himself apparently speaking Japanese. "It sounded so genuine," he says, "that I had to ask how they handled my lousy English. 'It was easy,' said the producer. 'We just hired an actor who speaks lousy Japanese.'"

Desi poses with old pal Louis A. Nicoletti, who played countless minor roles on "I Love Lucy." He later became an assistant director and functioned in that capacity until his death in 1969.

Someone once put a sign on Desi's dressing-room door: "English broken here." Ricky Ricardo's classic Spanish outburst, usually delivered nonstop at Lucy, "*¡Miraquetienecosalamujeresta!*" was merely an extension of the real Desi Arnaz, who generously punctuated his English with peppery *español*.

However, no real-life similarity could possibly have matched the circumstances surrounding Lucille Ball's pregnancy in 1952 when it was decided that Lucy Ricardo would also have a baby on "I Love Lucy."

6 We're Having a Baby ♡

"One day Desi walked me off the set so we could be alone," recalls Jess Oppenheimer about an afternoon in May 1952 just prior to filming one of the last "I Love Lucy" shows of the first season. "I could see that, whatever the news, it could only be bad. Swallowing hard, Desi said, 'We just came from the doctor. Lucy's going to have a baby.'

"He looked to me for answers: What could we do? How long would we have to be off the air? How much would it hurt the show? Without thinking twice, I said, 'Congratulations! This is wonderful. It's just what we needed to give us excitement in our second season. Lucy Ricardo will have a baby too.' As Desi rushed off to tell Lucy, I started wondering whether I shouldn't have thought twice before making that decision." Never before had a pregnant actress portrayed a pregnant woman on television.

"We could have filmed enough shows in advance to tide us through until the baby came," Arnaz states, "but I wanted to talk about my child. I didn't want to put Lucille in a closet for nine months. Having a baby is a perfectly natural happening."

While Desi went about trying to get permission from CBS, the Biow agency, and Philip Morris to carry out these new plans, other problems arose. Associate producer Al Simon decided to leave the company. Simon was among the first people aboard when the TV production company was formed the previous summer. He was instrumental in developing the three-camera technique, finding the studio, and solving a myriad number of production problems that arose during the first critical year of operation. When he announced his resignation in early June, Desi was not overly concerned. "Desi was a fast study," recalls Herb Browar, who left Desilu with Simon that summer. "He absorbed an enormous amount of information that first season. He really didn't need us anymore." Desi had, in fact, been given the title "Executive Producer" by Jess Oppenheimer at mid-season (actually for Desi's thirty-fifth birthday on March 2, 1952) because he had become so active behind the cameras.

Despite Arnaz's growing expertise, he hired away from RKO Pictures Argyle Nelson to serve as general manager in charge of production. Nelson, who stayed with Desilu and eventually Lucille Ball Productions for many years, was general manager in charge of production at Selznick Productions for five years during the 1940s. He was an experienced professional. Many of the departing Browar's duties were taken over by James Paisley, an assistant director hired in early 1952.

As soon as production on the first season's shows was completed on June 6 (with the filming of "The Saxophone"), the "I Love Lucy" sets were transferred to Stage 1, right next door. Sets for the new Desilu production, "Our Miss Brooks," slated to begin production on June 26, were installed permanently on Stage 2.

Already having proved to the Hollywood community that he was more than just a bongo-beater, Desi continued to show his mettle as a businessman. "Desi had a mathematical mind, but he never used it much up to that point," Lucille Ball points out. "Then CBS sent over a new budget for the second season and he began to study it. He said to me, 'They've made a million-dollar mistake.' I said, 'That's impossible.' 'No,' he said, 'I know there's a million dollars more in here for us to spend on production. They've got their figures wrong.' The next day he took the papers to Harry Ackerman at CBS and said, 'You've made a million-dollar error.'

"Ackerman said, 'That's impossible. Look, Desi, stick to your acting. We'll handle the business details.' So Desi spread the papers out all over the office. He proved to Ackerman that the network was wrong: There *was* an extra million in there to be used for production. From then on, when he talked, CBS listened. That gave him a boost of self-confidence."

With the baby on the way, Lucy and Desi decided to cancel the four-week personal appearance tour they were set to do in New York and London in July. The May 23, 1952, issue of *TV Guide* carried this explanation: "Lucille Ball and Desi Arnaz have cancelled two weeks of personal appearances at the Roxy and another at the London Palladium. They don't want to leave their nine-month-old daughter, Lucie Desiree, and their San Fernando Valley home. They are turning down an estimated $200,000." No mention was made of Lucy's pregnancy since it had not been made public as yet and since plans regarding the second season were still unresolved.

CBS, having been approached by Desi about writing Lucy's pregnancy into the series, didn't like the idea. There were conventions to consider, and matters of "taste." Years later, Harry Ackerman commented in *TV Guide,* "We had every intention of keeping 'I Love Lucy' right where it was—Lucy always trying to get into show business. When Lucille Ball announced that she was going to have a baby, all we could think of at first was complete disaster. As it turned out, it was the best thing that ever happened to 'I Love Lucy.' It gave the show a change of pace, a change of perspective.

"After the first season of any show, it becomes necessary to find new things for the characters to do and talk about, new places for them to go, and even new characters for them to bounce off."

Hindsight is fascinating, but Arnaz kept running into brick walls with his "baby" plans. Philip Morris and its ad agency, run by strong-willed Milton Biow, issued statements urging Desi to consider one or two shows about Lucy's pregnancy, but no more. They advised him to "hide" Lucy behind chairs, or not feature her at all during her pregnant period. Desi's temper flared quickly, and he fired off a letter to the Philip Morris mogul, Alfred E. Lyons, who was away in England on business. After all, it was Lyons who essentially controlled the company and it would be his decision that would be final.

Carefully worded, the letter said, in effect, that if Philip Morris was satisfied with Desilu's track record—having produced the nation's most popular television program—then the cigarette company would have to relinquish any and all creative control it had or might have had during this period, if their association was to continue amicably. Lyons' immediate reply came in the form of a transatlantic cable addressed to his New York office and the Biow agency. It warned all concerned not to (expletive deleted) with Arnaz.

The Arnazes managed a two-week vacation at Sun Valley, Idaho, with Little Lucie. Lucy was exhausted after that grueling forty-episode first season. She desperately needed a rest. While they were away, and despite fervent efforts to keep her pregnancy a secret (Bill Asher claims everyone was sworn to secrecy, with the threat of being fired if the news leaked) until the propitious moment, Lucy's friend Louella Parsons broke the news in her "Louella O. Parsons in Hollywood" column on June 18, 1952. She apologized in the piece to Lucy and Desi for revealing the news without their permission, but said it would be a "disservice" to her many readers to withhold such "important information."

The June 23 edition of *Daily Variety* carried this blurb: "Scheduled resumption of lensing of 'I Love Lucy' was pushed up a month when doctors confirmed over the weekend that Lucille Ball and Desi Arnaz are expecting a second child, sometime in January. Show is slated to return to CBS September 8. Five shows have already been filmed as a head start. New episodes to begin production August 8 at General Service Studios."

The planned thirteen-week hiatus for cast and crew was, by necessity, shortened. In order to film enough episodes and still leave Lucy with sufficient time to rest before the baby was due, production had to begin almost immediately. Frantic telephone calls were placed and telegrams fired off, informing people to come back to work six weeks earlier.

Jess, Bob, and Madelyn were called back from their well-deserved holidays to produce a new batch of teleplays. Vivian and Phil Ober were vacationing at their little ranch in Cubero, New Mexico. They were contacted and advised of the new start date, Tuesday, July 29. Jess, Bob, and Madelyn came in early. They had no time to waste. Writing the "baby" shows was a new challenge. "We finally decided that although it had never been done before, we could tackle the job of a pregnancy on TV," Oppenheimer recalls. "We felt certain we could extract all the inherent humor from the situation while staying within the bounds of good taste. To further ensure that we offended no one, we arranged for a Catholic priest, a Protestant minister, and a rabbi to approve the scripts and see the shows being filmed."

Hastily, Desilu, through its PR man, Kenneth Morgan, issued this statement, which appeared in the July 18, 1952, edition of *TV Guide:* "Lucille Ball's

Vivian Vance with her real-life "Fred Mertz," husband-actor Phil Ober.

pregnancy won't keep her off TV. The approach of the stork will be written into 'I Love Lucy.' "

In the meantime, a new situation comedy produced by the Hal Roach Studios, "My Little Margie" starring Charles Farrell and Gale Storm (in the role originally meant for Mona Freeman), took over the "I Love Lucy" time period for thirteen weeks beginning June 16, 1952. Although it became a popular hit, it was a critical disaster, dubbed "unfunny," "pointless," "pathetic," "tired," "trite," "dreary," "hackneyed," "dismal," and so forth. Where Walter Winchell decided he "loved Lucy," he was just "mild about Marge." Lucy had set a precedent difficult to challenge or even come close to. In fact, when the 1952–53 season blossomed, there were fourteen new sitcoms—from "Leave It to Larry" to "Doc Corkle" to "I Married Joan"—all trying to copy the basic "I Love Lucy" formula.

With only Labor Day off for the next sixteen weeks, Desilu commenced production for the second season on Tuesday, July 29, with Episode #41, titled "Vacation from Marriage," which had been written prior to the writers' brief summer break. The episode featured only the four principals, but required three new sets—the Mertzes' bedroom, the hallway outside the Ricardo apartment, and the rooftop of the building. In her fourth month of pregnancy now, Lucy delighted in getting back to work, despite the pressures of getting so many new shows done before her maternity leave scheduled for mid-November. Eight additional episodes were filmed, five of which would later serve as the "post-birth" shows with the addition of a brief flashback sequence.

Lucy rehearses scene from "Ricky Loses His Voice," filmed August 22, 1952. She is four months pregnant although no hint is made of this fact within the context of the story line. Backstage, Lucy, Vivian, and Bill confer with producer Oppenheimer before being introduced to the studio audience by Desi, who did the warm-ups.

During this same period, Jess, Bob, and Madelyn were busy preparing the seven episodes that constituted Lucy Ricardo's entire pregnancy. "We didn't want to do anything that would upset the public," Desi Arnaz admits. "There was nothing we had to throw out except the word 'pregnant.' CBS didn't like that, so we used 'expectant.' CBS thought it was a nicer word."

Philip Morris put its two cents in. They requested that during Lucille's pregnant state, she should not be viewed smoking cigarettes.

In the meantime, "Lucy" 's second season got underway on September 15 with the airing of the now-classic "Job Switching" show. Jack Gould wrote this review in his New York *Times* column:

" 'I Love Lucy' is back in fine fettle. The top program of last season . . . once again proved a delightful slapstick romp for Lucille Ball. The success of 'Lucy' is proof of the old adage of show business that what you do often is far less important than how you do it. Incorporated in Miss Ball's weekly endeavor is probably every pat comic situation ever devised, yet withal her program consistently achieves a hilarious level. It is a triumph of familiar nonsense beautifully turned.

"The basic situation . . . antedated television by a few generations. The Ricardos . . . have words about a few beauty parlor bills, and in no time . . . Fred and Ethel Mertz are drawn into the argument. The upshot is that the men will do the housework and the women will go out and be the

Lucille Ball's favorite impersonation—Tallulah Bankhead—gets the Ricardo treatment in "Lucy Fakes Illness." Six years later, "Taloo" herself appeared in an hour-long "Lucy-Desi" special titled "The Celebrity Next Door."

breadwinners. [Then] followed the predictable course: The husbands made a mess of the cooking; their cake didn't rise, the rice boiled all over the kitchen, and they washed the chickens in cleansing powder. The girls had trouble finding jobs and finally landed in a candy-making plant where, in a superb scene, they found they couldn't keep up with a conveyor belt.

"The loose conglomeration of serviceable ideas would have added up to little but for the talents of Miss Ball, whose comic artistry can easily be missed because she has a way of making it appear deceptively easy. Desi Arnaz . . . has improved remarkably as a performer since the debut of 'I Love Lucy' a year ago. He's much more at ease now and an engaging foil. Vivian Vance and Bill Frawley . . . are fine in rounding out the main quartet of players. The scripts . . . are consistently polished jobs."

The first "pregnancy" episode was scheduled for filming on Friday, October 3. Titled "Lucy Is Enceinte" (a French word meaning pregnant), it was the crucial script that had to set the tone for the series and the tone had to be just right. The night before filming, a special dress rehearsal was given for the three local religious leaders—Monsignor Joseph Devlin, head of the Catholic Legion of Decency, Rabbi Alfred Wolfe of the Wilshire Temple, and the Reverend Clifton Moore of the Hollywood Presbyterian Church. Scripts had been sent to them in advance, but they watched the performance with anticipation. When they were asked for their opinions—"Was there anything objectionable?"—the three said in unison, "What's questionable about having a baby?"

From then on every script in the baby series was submitted to the three men for their opinion. They never changed a word of Bob, Madelyn, and Jess's scripts:

Important scene from "Lucy Is Enceinte." Hidden by the three 35-mm cameras, Lucy Ricardo tries to break the news of the impending birth to Ricky.

ETHEL: Good morning, Lucy.

LUCY: Oh, hi, Ethel.

ETHEL: Where are you going so early?

LUCY: Oh, I thought I'd go down to see the doctor.

ETHEL: What's the matter, honey? Are you sick?

LUCY: No, I just want to get a checkup. I need a tonic or something. I've been feeling dauncey.

ETHEL: Dauncey?

LUCY: Yeah, that's a word my grandmother made up for when you're not really sick but you feel lousy.

ETHEL: Oh.

LUCY: I don't know what's the matter with me. I've been getting a lot of rest and then I wake up feeling all dragged out in the morning. I don't have much energy and yet I've been putting on a lot of weight. I just feel blah.

ETHEL: Well, maybe you need some vitamin pills or a liver shot or something.

Next Lucy swears Ethel to secrecy because she doesn't want Ricky to worry needlessly over what might prove to be nothing. Then Lucy reveals something that causes Ethel to speculate in amazement.

LUCY: Gee, I'm gonna have to go on a diet. You know I could hardly get into my dress this morning.

ETHEL: Hey, Lucy, wait a minute. You don't suppose . . .

LUCY: I don't suppose what?

ETHEL: You don't suppose you're gonna have a baby?

LUCY: Of course not. [Long pause] *A baby??*

ETHEL: Yeah, baby. That's a word *my* grandmother made up for tiny little people.

Lucy goes off to the doctor and returns in a dreamy trance. She tells Ethel the good news, then again makes her promise not to tell anyone else until she has had the opportunity to break the news to Ricky. Ricky comes home for lunch and Lucy is determined to tell him, despite his bad mood. After a number of telephone and doorbell interruptions . . .

RICKY: Oh, what a business. Sometimes I think I go back to Cuba and work in a sugar plantation. Just the two of us.

LUCY: Just the two of us?

RICKY: Yeah. I don't mean to get you all involved in my affairs, but you should be happy you're a woman.

LUCY: Oh, I am, I am!

RICKY: You think you know how tough my job is, but believe me, if you traded places with me . . . you'd be surprised.

LUCY: Believe me, if I traded places with you, *you'd* be surprised!

The crucial scene.

Ricky has to return to the Tropicana before Lucy has the chance to tell him about the baby, so she decides to go to the club herself and tell him there. With musicians and stage hands everywhere, Lucy can't bring herself to reveal such personal news. After a long silence, Ricky asks her what she wants. Looking back at the two-dozen staring faces, Lucy asks: "Do you have the right time?" Foiled again, she decides to return to the nightclub that evening, even if she has to tell Ricky during the middle of the show.

In the last scene, Lucy manages to relay the news to Ricky. The script called for Desi to become excited and bellow with joy. Instead, as the three cameras rolled under Bill Asher's direction, he unexpectedly broke down and cried. So did Lucy. Many members of the audience cried right along with them.

"Lucy and Desi got to this point in acting out the script," recalls Oppenheimer, "and then this strange thing happened: suddenly they remembered their own real emotions when they discovered that at last they were going to be parents, and both of them began crying and couldn't finish the song. It was one of the most moving things I've ever seen."

Believing that the film and sound track had been ruined by all the tears, Bill Asher halted the cameras and ordered a retake. "We were all crying in the booth," the director remembers. "It was a very emotional thing. Lucy and Desi were really overwhelmed because it meant so much to them."

After viewing the rushes on Monday, October 6, Jess and the others agreed that the crying scene had more of a dramatic impact than the funnier, more upbeat version. Desi and Lucy agreed, and when "Lucy Is Enceinte" aired for the first time two months later on December 8, the nation shed a tear, too.

By the time this first "baby" episode was shot, Desilu had already begun a major publicity campaign. At first they had decided to have the Ricardo baby the same sex as the Arnaz offspring, who was expected to be delivered via cesarean section on January 19, 1953. (The original due date had been January 12, but upon closer examination by Lucy's physician, Dr. Joseph Harris, the later date was pinpointed.) It happened to be a Monday, the same day "I Love Lucy" aired, only because Harris performed all his cesarean operations at Cedars of Lebanon Hospital on that day. On October 13, a magazine reported that the "Lucy" producers were "leaving the sound track open and later will insert whether it's a boy or girl." That was a short-lived idea, as a little child psychology prevailed.

It was for Little Lucie's sake that they decided to make the baby in the script a boy. The Arnazes were concerned that when their young daughter saw the films she would wonder why she had been left out. If it had been a girl on the show, she would have reasoned that this was her sister, not herself. Not to be overlooked was the fact that Desi wanted a boy.

At a solemn conference with a battery of press agents was born a five-part, five-page memo titled "Various Aspects of the Ricardo Baby in the 'I Love Lucy' Publicity and Promotional Campaign." All present swore "that there must be absolutely no word about the baby released out of any office before December 8." Only then were 40 million televiewers to be let in on the secret of Lucy's pregnancy, although it had been written about in the press as far back as July *(TV Guide)*.

Plans were developed to tie in the show with a new Columbia record of "There's a Brand New Baby at Our House" (which Desi had written the night Lucie was born) and the series' theme song. All the PR men promised to bombard newspapers, magazines, and wire services with feature stories. Regarding the Ricardo baby's sex, the memo contained this clause, titled "The Secret Gimmick About the Baby's Sex." It required an inviolate pledge of secrecy until January 19. "The Ricardo baby will be a boy regardless of the sex of the actual Arnaz baby. Of course, if the Arnaz baby does happen to be a boy, then all writers and editors can assume that the producers of 'I Love Lucy' are clairvoyant and possessed of sheer genius. If it happens to be a girl, the story (and the truth) is that Desi was so set on having a boy . . . that he went ahead and filmed the Ricardo baby as if it were, regardless."

What to do about notifying Hollywood's competitive gossip columnists: "Walter Winchell should be alerted to be given the first news of the Arnaz baby. We will phone the news to him since he will be expecting the phone call. When he is alerted, he is to be told nothing of the gimmick, but when he receives the phone call, and not before, he will be given the story of Desi's thinking concerning the Ricardo baby. Of course, the news of the Arnaz baby will be given out simultaneously to Louella, Hedda, Johnson, Graham, all the wire services and all the local dailies. But the story of the gimmick as released to the other outlets will be a follow-up . . . to give Walter the edge."

On October 17, the cast rehearsed and filmed "Lucy's Show Biz Swan Song," the third episode in the "baby" series. The script, like several before it, called for musical numbers to be performed by the entire cast. By this time, the writers were familiar with the varied talents of their four stars. Not so when "Lucy" made its debut the year before. "When we first started," Oppenheimer claims, "no one knew very much about Viv and Bill. When we decided to introduce the fact that the Mertzes were once vaudevillians, we sheepishly asked Viv and Bill if they *could* sing and dance. They were both highly insulted that we had to ask since both had had successful careers on the Broadway musical stage. But we didn't know that. I knew Vivian through *Voice of the Turtle*, a dramatic play, and Frawley through his character roles in movies. Of course, we were thrilled when we discovered that they enjoyed doing the musical numbers because it made our job so much easier."

Frawley, who had a long and illustrious career in vaudeville as a singer and dancer, was particularly pleased that "Lucy's Show Biz Swan Song" contained a barbershop quartet number. He had been involved with them since his youth back in Iowa. He considered barbershop singing an art and, after a dismal rehearsal on Stage 1, sought out Lucy in a darkened corner. "It's terrible," he growled, referring to their rendition of "Sweet Adeline" called for in the script.

A walking expert on the subject, Bill continued his gruff assault on the six months' pregnant Lucy: "You amateurs are lousing up this whole thing! If we let that song go out on the air the way it is now, we'll be laughed off every TV set in the country."

Lucy smiled, amused, "What are you complaining to me for?" she asked. "I've only got one lousy note in the whole arrangement. What do you want from me?"

"And that damn Vivian Vance," Frawley foamed. "That Galli-Curci!"

"Look, Bill, I've got only one note to sing. Go ahead and complain to Desi."

"Desi?" Frawley groaned. "That Cuban square? What does *he* know about good old American music? All right, all right. I'll go see Desi."

He stalked across the long sound stage, muttering to himself. When he got to the other end, he suddenly turned around and bellowed back at la Ball: "And as for that one note of yours, it sounds like a barrel of gravel on a baked Alaska!"

Other prebirth episodes included "Lucy Hires an English Tutor," filmed the night of October 24. Thirty-five-year-old Hans Conried guest-starred (his second "Lucy" in two months) as Percy Livermore, a highfalutin teacher of the king's English who had a bent for songwriting. Lucy Ricardo was concerned that she, Ricky, and the Mertzes were not smart enough to raise a child. Lucy even wanted Ricky to promise her he wouldn't talk to their child until he was at least nineteen or twenty, sure that the tyke would acquire his father's speech patterns.

In another "baby show," "Ricky Has Labor Pains," Ricky developed sympathetic "morning sickness." The goateed doctor, played by Lou Merrill, pinpointed his problem: With all the attention centered around Lucy and the baby, Ricky was beginning to feel neglected and unloved. The physician prescribed some treatment that Lucy and Ethel turned into the world's first "daddy shower." (It eventually turned into a stag party.) A funny show. In the segment filmed November 7, "Lucy Becomes a Sculptress," Lucy took up sculpting so her unborn child would have artistic leanings. A fair show.

It was on the evening of November 14 that Lucille Ball appeared in her last segment before going on a four-month hiatus. Scores of personal friends were invited that night; they enjoyed a catered dinner prior to the actual filming. The episode, "Lucy Goes to the Hospital," climaxing with the birth of Little Ricky Ricardo, played in this initial half-hour by eighteen-day-old James John Ganzer, who had blue eyes and reddish-black hair (coincidentally the same as Desi Arnaz, Jr.'s features at birth). Because of her condition, Lucy's role in the segment was minimal (she barely appeared in the second act), causing a reviewer in *Broadcasting* magazine to speculate: "Until Lucy left for the hospital, the . . . production was up to the quality of any other in the series. It descended to routine levels, however, the moment she was out of sight. . . . Mr. Arnaz and his writers exerted every effort, perhaps too much effort, to keep the comedy going while he was awaiting the delivery of his child, but at best 'I Love Lucy' was mediocre in those sequences."

Before Lucy went into temporary retirement, she and her three co-stars participated in a gala, one-hour televised dedication ceremony, "Stars in the Eye," on the occasion of the opening of CBS's Television City in Hollywood.

No, you're not seeing things. Jack Benny did not appear in an "I Love Lucy" segment. It's from the CBS special "Stars in the Eye," telecast November 15, 1952, on the occasion of the inauguration of CBS's massive West Coast production headquarters, Television City. Benny appeared in a skit featuring the "I Love Lucy" cast.

During the live broadcast hosted by Jack Benny, twenty-five CBS stars performed in sketches, including Eve Arden, Gale Gordon, George Burns and Gracie Allen, and the casts of "Amos 'n' Andy," "My Friend Irma," and "Meet Millie"—all Hollywood-based comedies.

After that, Lucy spent all of her time at the couple's Chatsworth ranch. Caring for Little Lucie and preparing for an addition to the family, Lucy rarely ventured off the San Fernando Valley property, except one night in late December to accept the *TV Guide* award as "Best Comedienne of the Year." She deserved it.

As for the rest of the company—Desi, Viv, and Bill—it was back to work in order to film the various short flashback sequences that would introduce all the episodes that would air from January 26 through mid-April. These included not only the five shows filmed the previous summer ("Sales Resistance," "The Inferiority Complex," "The Club Election," "The Black Eye," and "Lucy Changes Her Mind") but also seven repeats from the first season. In each bit of flashback footage, the Ricardo baby was mentioned. For instance, to introduce the episode "The Diet," Ethel offers to bake some cookies so Ricky can take them to Lucy in the hospital. Ricky insists that Lucy wouldn't want them, that she is watching her weight. Ricky: "She says she's going to go on a diet." Fred: "She was always going to go on a diet." Ricky: "Well, she did . . . once. Remember?"

For the next six weeks, newspapers were responding en masse to the PR workings of the Desilu and CBS organizations. Writing in *Reader's Digest,* Eleanor Harris reported: "On January 14, 1953, when reporters discovered that the Ricardo baby . . . would be 'born' the following Monday, the excitement began. An electric current seemed to race through newspaper offices all over the country: Perhaps [although the Arnazes already knew] Lucille Ball's real baby would make its appearance on the same day. Reporters everywhere picked up the telephone; hundreds of calls began flooding the Arnaz home, office, studio. Voice after voice said, 'It's the greatest human-interest story of our time—when is she going to the hospital?' Newspapers published hourly bulletins and ran pools betting on the baby's sex."

Jack Gould's January 16 New York *Times* TV column carried this reaction: "Both CBS and Philip Morris have received letters from a number of viewers who for several reasons have taken exception to the subject of pregnancy as the main point of interest for a comedy series. As the matter has been handled on the screen there seems [to be] no grounds for valid objections. Rather, there should be applause. Miss Ball and Mr. Arnaz not only handled the topic of their approaching baby with a great deal of taste and skill but also have been thoroughly amusing in the process. Far from ridiculing motherhood, 'I Love Lucy' has made it appear one of the most natural things in the world."

Without meaning to be crusaders, the Arnazes did manage to lift from the shoulders of all expectant mothers a load of embarrassment and gaucherie.

Where a few newspaper readers wrote in protesting the frankness (by 1952 standards) of the dramatization, the papers were subsequently flooded with irate answers in reply: "I feel sorry for the lady who protests Lucy's expectancy. Has she heard of the story of Mary, Joseph, and the Christ Child?"; "I believe that TV with this program is bringing to the children of America true facts that many parents neglect to teach in their homes"; "Did it ever occur to you that if a whole family was watching one of the recent shows, it might make it easier for parents to explain to children and would eliminate embarrassment on both sides?"

Mail that reached Desilu was more pro than con. Only 207 letters arrived disapproving of pregnancy on television. "Hundreds of thousands of women all over the country who were pregnant along with me," Lucille Ball explains, "wrote me encouraging notes, and after our baby was born, I received thirty thousand congratulatory telegrams and letters."

One woman whose life was devoted to charitable work for American GIs in Korea had planned to forego her position because she was pregnant and embarrassed to meet the public. Inspired by the show's treatment of Lucy's pregnancy, she wrote that she would continue until her baby arrived.

Quietly, on Sunday night, January 18, Desi drove Lucy to Cedars of Lebanon Hospital, where Little Lucie had been born eighteen months before. That same night Vivian Vance had a dream: "Lucy came into my room clad in a beautiful white dress and said, 'Vivian, I had a boy.'"

The following morning at six o'clock, Lucy was wheeled into surgery, and given a spinal anesthetic so she could remain conscious during the operation. "We really don't care what it is, but as long as we already have a girl, it would be nice to have a boy," she said just moments before the surgery began. "I'll have a son on television tonight anyway."

Talking to James Bacon of the Associated Press, the only reporter allowed in the fathers' waiting room with Desi, the proud papa-to-be speculated, "If it's a boy—swell, but if it's a girl, the producers of 'I Love Lucy' will just have to write it off to artistic license."

In the operating room, Lucy badgered her doctor, Joe Harris: "What is it? What is it? Can't you give me at least a hint?"

"Relax, honey," Dr. Harris replied, trying to calm his impatient patient. "A few more minutes and we'll know."

At 8:15 A.M., PST, Dr. Harris announced, "It's a boy!" The attending staff of nurses reacted with glee. Murmuring "Desi will be so happy," Lucy fell instantly asleep, quite unaware of the worldwide hysteria that started one minute after Desiderio Alberto Arnaz y de Acha IV entered the world. (Had it been a girl, she would have been named Victoria Dolores.)

Grinning from ear to ear upon hearing the news of his new eight-pound, nine-ounce son, Desi burst into the hallway outside the waiting area, waving wildly. "It's a boy! It's a boy!" he shouted. "That's Lucy for you. Always does her best to cooperate. Now we have everything!"

Next he grabbed a nearby telephone receiver and blurted out to Jess

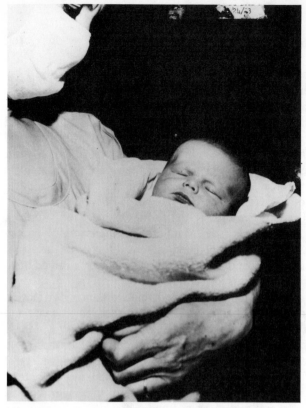

Nurse Evelyn St. Leo holds Desiderio Alberto Arnaz y de Acha IV, five days old.

Oppenheimer, who had been holding on the phone for nearly thirty minutes, "Lucy followed your script! Ain't she something?"

"Terrific!" exploded Oppenheimer. "That makes me the greatest writer in the world. Tell Lucy she can take the rest of the day off!"

Next Desi phoned his father in Miami. "I'm entering him in Notre Dame, class of seventy-four," Desi shouted in Spanish. The news of a grandson particularly pleased the senior Arnaz. Desi III was his only son; his two brothers each had girls. If Lucy and Desi had had no son, it would have spelled the end of the Arnaz clan.

Newspapers went wild. Headlines all over the world carried the news. Seven minutes after the baby's birth, it was broadcast in Japan. Los Angeles school officials went around to classrooms to announce the blessed event to the students. A spokesman for the Associated Press claimed, "We covered the birth on a wartime basis, with hourly bulletins."

Lucy and Desi received 1 million indications of public interest, including letters, telegrams, gifts, and telephone calls. Gifts of baby booties, bonnets, sweaters, and blankets arrived in such quantities that they were sent by truckload to state institutions. The day following the baby's arrival, General Dwight D. Eisenhower was inaugurated as the thirty-fourth President of the United States, and on his ABC Sunday (January 25) broadcast, Walter Winchell reported, "This was a banner week—the nation got a man and Lucy got a boy."

While 29 million people witnessed Ike's swearing-in ceremony on American television, 44 million tuned in to watch Little Ricky's birth. This audience figure represented a television first. The fifty-sixth episode of "I Love Lucy," "Lucy Goes to the Hospital," boasted an unbelievable 71.7 Nielsen rating.

"How about that?" beamed Desi, as he perused a newspaper. "She's as important as Ike. I wonder if we could run her for President in fifty-six?"

Exactly eight days after Lucy came home from the hospital, she and Desi checked into a suite at the Statler Hotel in Los Angeles. That night, February 5, 1953, on a makeshift stage at the downtown hotel, Lucy, shaking like a leaf, stepped up to accept from Art Linkletter her first of two Emmy Awards— one for "Best Situation Comedy" and the other for "Best Comedienne," prompting Linkletter to crack, "It looks like Lucy and Desi get something every month."

The "I Love Lucy" furor did not stop there. By the start of February, Lucille and Desi had signed to star in M-G-M's *The Long, Long Trailer,* a comedy about a couple making a cross-country tour in an auto trailer, based on a Clinton Twiss novel published by Thomas Y. Crowell. The Arnazes' price: two hundred and fifty thousand dollars for six weeks' work; filming to begin when production on "I Love Lucy" shut down for the season in June. They almost agreed to appear in a different film—their first since *Too Many Girls,* the RKO musical where Lucy and Desi first met—a Universal flick called *Policewoman* in which Lucille would have played a lady law guardian and Desi her long-suffering police captain.

On February 5, the Hollywood trade papers reported that Philip Morris chairman of the board, Al Lyons, was "disturbed because 'Lucy' doesn't supply the sales surge expected of their high rating. Philip Morris sales dropped to fifth place recently, behind Pall Mall." Indeed, there *was* speculation that the cigarette company would drop the show, according to *Advertising Age,* which reported "the company's sales had dropped from $234,346,380 to $232,559,372 in 1952, with the net profits down $2,371,990."

But on February 18, CBS announced that Philip Morris would sign a new $8 million contract with Lucy and Desi, the biggest ever written for television to that time. This would guarantee the series run for the next thirty months— through the 1954–55 season (ninety-eight episodes). About half of the amount was paid to Desilu to produce the shows, the other half to CBS to cover air-time charges. The weekly budget was pegged at between $40,000 and $50,000, a far cry from the original $19,500 figure proposed in the spring of 1951.

At a gala Hollywood signing, Lucy said happily: "It couldn't happen to a nicer pair of kids—I mean our two children, of course."

Several weeks later Philip Morris president, O. Parker McComas, addressed the membership of Financial Analysts of Philadelphia, during which he gave a rave endorsement for "I Love Lucy":

"This show is the all-time phenomenon of the entertainment business. On a strictly dollars-and-cents basis, it is twice as efficient as the average nighttime

Lucy and Desi sign the historic $8 million Philip Morris contract on February 18, 1953. Seated next to Lucy is Harry W. Chesley, Jr., of the Philip Morris company. Looking over Desi's shoulder is CBS vice-president Harry Ackerman.

television show in conveying our advertising message to the public. It is nearly three times more efficient dollarwise in reaching adults than *Life* [magazine] or your own Philadelphia newspapers. Three times more people see every Monday night's 'I Love Lucy' show than watched all the major-league baseball games last year. . . . Although the entire sum [$8 million] sounds huge, it is probably one of, if not the most efficient advertising buys in the entire country. In addition, we derive many supplementary merchandising and publicity benefits from the show. As you can see, we love 'Lucy.' ''

The arrival of Little Desi sent the popularity of the series to an all-time high and opened the door to lucrative merchandising deals. Experts referred to the new Arnaz offspring as ''Lucy's $50 Million Baby,'' because revenues from certain tie-in commitments were expected to top that mark, an amazing figure for a field in which Hopalong Cassidy promotions were considered a smashing success when they passed the $3 million-a-year mark.

At one time you could purchase official ''I Love Lucy'' aprons and genuine ''I Love Lucy'' dolls. Thirty-two thousand white, heart-bedecked aprons and eighty-five thousand dolls were grabbed up in one thirty-day period in late 1952. One year later, a Ricky, Jr., doll made its appearance in department and toy stores, and their maker couldn't keep up with the reorders. Neither could a furniture manufacturer who sold a whopping five hundred thousand dollars' worth of bedroom suites in just two days! Years later, a Connecticut real estate agent chose as a selling point ''a cocktail table that is the replica of the one on 'I Love Lucy' '' in trying to rent a summer cottage.

Three thousand retail outlets carried Lucille Ball dresses, sweaters, and blouses; ditto for Desi Arnaz robes and smoking jackets (which had gone

Following the signing, everyone gets in the act. Left to right Desi, Terry Clyne (from the Biow agency), Harry Chesley, Madelyn Pugh, Bob Carroll, Lucy, and Jess Oppenheimer.

out of style, but because of "Lucy" had a resurgence in popularity); He and She pajamas, which the Arnazes were obliged to wear on the show according to merchandising agreements, Desi Denims, Lucy Lingerie, costume jewelry, desk and chair sets, three-dimensional picture magazines with Polaroid eyeglasses, nursery furniture (after Little Ricky was born) and compatible training chairs, insulated diaper bags, dressing gowns, toys, and games.

A comic strip that began running on December 8, 1952, was the work of artist Bob Oskner and writer Lawrence Nadler and ran in 132 newspapers through King Features Syndicate. Thirty-five "I Love Lucy" comic books were released from 1954 to 1962 by Dell Comics.

These and other commercial tie-ins were the work of A. E. (Ed) Hamilton, Desilu vice-president, who was in charge of their New York office, located in the Fred F. French building at 551 Fifth Avenue. He handled the royalty arrangements (5 percent of the gross) on promotions that reached into every corner of the country.

As Jack Gould wrote in the New York *Times* in February 1953: " 'I Love Lucy' is probably the most misleading title imaginable. For once, all available statistics are in agreement: Millions love Lucy." And they kept on loving her when she returned to the screen on April 20 in "No Children Allowed," the first episode filmed since November 14, 1952.

Since California law limited the posing time under lights of an actor less than six months of age to just thirty-second intervals, Desilu sought out the services of a pair of undersized, six-month-old twins who, by state child labor laws, could pose two hours each per day and spell each other in the Little Ricky role. Jess Oppenheimer sent James Paisley, the "Lucy" assistant director, to Los Angeles City Hall to examine the birth records of twins. Paisley found nine sets and, on the basis of coloring, finally narrowed the

"I Love Lucy" MEMORABILIA

Left: *This 1947 RCA Victor record album featured four 78 rpm discs with such Desi Arnaz favorites as "Babalu," "Brazil," "Tabu," "La Comparsita," "Tico-Tico," "Peanut Vendor," "Green Eyes," and "Siboney."*

Above: *These paper dolls, complete with Lucy and Ricky outfits, were mass-produced by Whitman Publishing Company in 1953.*

Left: *Sheet music of the 1953 song "There's a Brand New Baby [at Our House]," which was featured in an "I Love Lucy" episode.*

Left: Philip Morris introduced a premium item, "Lucy's Notebook," a how-to cook and party booklet containing forty-eight pages of hints and tips, via TV commercials and coupon order blanks in various cities in June 1954.

Below: Dell produced this coloring book in the mid-1950s as well as thirty-five comic books from 1954 to 1962.

Above: Magazine advertisement featuring baby-related items merchandised under the "I Love Lucy" name. Other items available included an "I Love Lucy" hobby horse, a toy baby carriage, toy kiddie baths, training chairs, insulated diaper bags, mattresses, and a complete set of bedroom furniture. In fact, any home could be furnished with "I Love Lucy" living room and bedroom furniture sets, with floors covered with "Lucy" linoleum.

Left: This fourteen-inch, stuffed vinyl Ricky, Jr., doll was produced by American Character Doll company. Over eighty-five thousand units were sold in one thirty-day period in 1953.

Above and below: *The Desilu Sales organization used these items as gifts for clients—a cigarette lighter featuring the Lucy animated figure, and a set of cuff links with both Lucy and Desi characters on them.* The most valuable TV Guide in existence—Vol. I, No. 1 (April 3–9, 1953)—featured Desi, Jr., and Lucy on its cover. It is valued today at two hundred dollars. (Lucille Ball has been featured on the cover of TV Guide more often than any other performer—twenty-five times.)

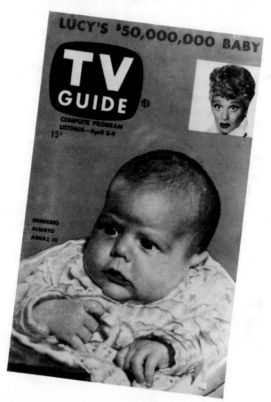

choice to Richard Lee and Ronald Lee Simmons, the identical twin sons of Mr. and Mrs. Arthur L. Simmons, a Los Angeles department store shoe buyer. Born on September 7, 1952, the infants were paid 25 dollars each per show and were attended on the set by a nurse and Department of Welfare social worker. Stand-in dolls were used during rehearsals so that the boys had to show up only for the Friday filmings.

The Simmons twins were not the only new actors to begin recurring roles with the "No Children Allowed" installment of "Lucy." Having guest-starred in "The Marriage License" episode the preceding season, seventy-eight-year-old actress Elizabeth ("Patty") Patterson was tapped to portray Mrs. Mathilda Trumbull, an elderly neighbor of the Ricardos. She brought with her a long list of movie credits, over one hundred, the first of which was *The Boy Friend* in 1926. Born in Savannah, Tennessee, a small town on the Tennessee River, Miss Patterson never married and lived alone at the Hollywood Roosevelt Hotel during her thirty-year motion picture career. She died of complications from pneumonia on January 31, 1966.

Martin Lewis, a *TV Guide* staffer, was there for the March 20 filming. He recalls: "Before the filming, Desi explained to the three hundred people in the audience that Ricky, Jr., would be featured in the show, and that a doll wrapped in a blanket would be used in the long shots and a real baby in the close-ups.

"In the doll scenes, the crying was done on cue from backstage by Jerry Hausner, who had years of experience as a "crybaby" on radio. This was particularly important since the episode was centered around the baby's incessant crying. However, the real baby proved to be a ham. He cried during the scenes as per the script, and when the scene was finished and Lucy picked him up out of the crib, he stopped crying as though on cue and stared at the applauding audience.

"Lucy fluffed her lines only once. Jokingly, she blamed Desi because the scene had to be done over. He said it was all her fault, at which point Lucy playfully threw a roundhouse right that landed on Desi's back.

"Eight setups were required, with five-minute intermissions between scenes for costume changes. A five-piece Latin American musical group entertained during the breaks. When Lucy and Desi returned from a costume change before the camera crew was ready for the next scene, they did a rumba for the studio audience that would have made professional dancers jealous."

The remainder of the 1952–53 season was hectic. The staff and crew had become accustomed to a certain production pace before the baby boom began. There was usually a six-to-eight-week postproduction schedule for an average "I Love Lucy" segment. For instance, an episode filmed January 1 was not likely to air until late February or early March. Miss Ball's period of convalescence following Little Desi's birth prohibited the luxury of such a time span. Instead, the eleven episodes filmed upon her return to work were broadcast about a month after they were put on 35-mm celluloid, requiring the staff to maintain a vigorous pace.

Lucy poses with Richard Lee Simmons, one of the twins who portrayed Little Ricky during the spring of 1953. The boys were born September 7, 1952, and subsequently featured in an issue of Life magazine (February 2, 1953). Director Bill Asher gives some last-minute instructions to Lucy before filming "No Children Allowed" on March 20, 1953, the first episode after Lucy's four-month maternity leave.

On the "Lucy" set of "The Camping Trip," the Arnazes welcome pal Danny Thomas, who had recently signed a deal with ABC-TV to headline his own comedy series to be filmed by Desilu (using the three-camera method).

Desilu's business was burgeoning. When Danny Thomas was signed to a contract by ABC to headline his own sitcom (originally to be titled "Here Comes Daddy") in March, he chose Desilu to film it. Similarly, Ray Bolger's series and Loretta Young's anthology, "A Letter to Loretta," were to become shows "filmed in association with Desilu Productions." Jack Benny decided to film some of his shows for the fall 1953 season, alternating them with the live half-hours. He opted for the Desilu technique. Even Frank Sinatra was toying with the idea of headlining a dramatic human interest series about a musician to be titled "Blues in the Night." It was to be a Desilu show.

With this increase in production, Desi needed a key executive to carry the bulk of the load. There was just so many hours in a day and he was still playing Ricky Ricardo every week. Instinctively, he went to the one man at CBS who, in the long negotiations for the original "I Love Lucy" deal, had given him the most trouble. "It figured," Arnaz said simply. "There was this one guy who kept costing me money and saving it for CBS. I figured I had better get him on my side where he could start saving me money for a change." This is how Martin Leeds, a six-year veteran of CBS where he was in charge of business affairs in Hollywood, joined Desilu Productions as executive vice-president in charge of production on March 15, 1953.

From March 20 through May 29, when the last episode of the current season ("Never Do Business with Friends") was shot at General Service Studios (the last at that filming facility), eleven half-hours were filmed, including other classics such as "Lucy Hires a Maid," "Lucy's Last Birthday," and "The Camping Trip." A fourteen-week hiatus was called, during which time "Racket Squad" filled in for the vacationing "Lucy," but not before an event that would wrack the "Lucy" company: The death of a dear friend.

Director Eddie Sedgwick chats with Bill Frawley during a break in filming "Lucy Goes to the Hospital," November 14, 1952.

Early in the morning of Wednesday, May 7, Eddie Sedgwick, Lucy and Desi's friend of many years, died of a heart attack. The director and senior officer of Desilu Productions—and godfather to both Arnaz children—was sixty years old. He had just completed the editing on the full-length movie version of "I Love Lucy" and was preparing other projects for Desilu, including a possible situation comedy for movie comedian Eddie Quillan. Sedgwick's passing came three weeks after the movie veteran celebrated his fortieth year in the movie industry.

In Sedgwick's obituary, the Los Angeles *Times* wrote about his first meeting with Lucille Ball, quoting his own words: "I saw this beautiful girl walking around the Goldwyn lot. She was one of the Goldwyn Girls. I'd see her tell a story and watch her facial expressions change. She'd illustrate it with everything she had. I got up my nerve to talk to her and said, 'Young lady, if you play your cards right, you can be the greatest comedienne in show business.' "

7 Seeing Red

While most of the Desilu people enjoyed a summer of rest and relaxation, Lucille and Desi plunged into production on *The Long, Long Trailer* feature after only nine days' vacation. (Vivian interrupted her summer break by appearing with Mel Ferrer in a stock version of *Pal Joey* at the La Jolla Playhouse, the site of her discovery by Desi for the Ethel Mertz role two summers before.)

Trailer, not so incidentally, became M-G-M's most successful film comedy despite a large sampling of lukewarm reviews, one of which accused the ninety-six-minute movie of being "a long, long 'I Love Lucy' decked out in CinemaScope."

Metro wanted no part of it at first. They subscribed to the theory that the audience wouldn't pay to see actors they could get at home free. But Pandro S. Berman, the film's producer, insisted that these were different parts, and Lucille Ball and Desi Arnaz could make the picture hilarious. If the picture were funny enough, he had no worries about whether people would pay to see it.

Berman had plunked down a lot of money to buy the film rights to the "Buddy" Twiss book and an even heftier sum to Frances Goodrich and Albert Hackett to adapt it into screenplay form. Ironically, Desi himself had made inquiries into securing the rights a year earlier, after reading a condensed version of the tome in the January 1952 issue of *Reader's Digest.*

The Arnazes enjoyed the six-week assignment, especially after the grueling week-in-week-out pace of "I Love Lucy." In fact, they had got so used to producing a half-hour "mini movie" (sixty-seven "Lucy" episodes thus far) in less than a week that after the first day of shooting *Trailer* (June 8, 1953), they were flabbergasted at the meager results—they had managed to film only a single line: "Okay, I'll buy the trailer."

Vincente Minnelli, who had directed Lucille in the M-G-M musical *Ziegfeld Follies* in 1944, was director of *The Long, Long Trailer.* "She and Desi were at the height of their television popularity. I thought the story was perfect for them," contends Minnelli in his autobiography. "There were times when the action was broad and those were the opportunities Lucy grabbed hold of and ran away with.

"It was an inexpensive picture to make, and a painless one. All the film editor had to do was clip off the end slates of the film to make this a smoothly flowing picture. Lucy is one of the few comedic talents who can be broad and uniquely human at the same time. She can get away with things that less talented people wouldn't even presume to handle. On television, week after week, she's handled manufactured situations and passed them off as real."

At times the film came precariously close to resembling "I Love Lucy," especially in the slapstick sequences. The roles Lucy and Desi played were Tacy and Nicky Collini, which even sounded like Lucy-and-Ricky if you said it fast enough (the names were changed just prior to the start of filming.)

After six weeks of *Trailer* photography, which ended on July 16, Lucy and Desi bundled up their two children and escaped to a rented house in Del Mar. They had intended to do personal appearances for "I Love Lucy" that had been postponed from the previous summer, but they were too exhausted to travel. Instead, they planned to enjoy the four or five weeks at the beach.

As president of Desilu, Arnaz initiated some important changes that summer. Because General Service Studios did not have enough sound stages that could be converted into Desilu "playhouses" (each had to have access to a public street), he sought suitable space elsewhere. He found it several blocks east at Motion Picture Center, a seven-acre lot that boasted nine stages, six of which could be converted into "summer theaters" to accommodate the growing number of situation comedies that Desilu was producing, co-producing, or about to produce. As soon as Desi put his signature on the ten-year lease, major reconstruction at the studio, located at 846 North Cahuenga Boulevard in Hollywood, commenced. Four sound stages were converted into audience theaters (at a cost of thirty-five thousand dollars

Posing in his office at Motion Picture Center, Desi Arnaz observes the many awards bestowed on "I Love Lucy" since its debut two years earlier.

each) and hundreds of offices were fashioned for the invasion of Desilu staffers. Work had to start immediately if Danny Thomas was to film his first episode on August 7, as scheduled. "I Love Lucy" was scheduled to start up again right after Labor Day as was the "Our Miss Brooks" company. By the end of 1953, Desi correctly estimated that Desilu would have totaled ninety hours of film production and would do a gross business of $6 million.

Lucy, resting up in Del Mar, was delighted with the move: she gained a four-room apartment only a few steps from the "Lucy" stage: two large dressing rooms, a bathroom, a living-dining room, and a kitchen . . . complete with a cook. Willie May Barker, who spent ten years cooking for Lucy and Desi at their ranch, would now spend her days at the studio, serving her bosses hot lunches in their apartment, and carrying trays of cheese and coffee to the entire cast every afternoon. Thanks to Lucy's touch, the main room looked as if it belonged in a permanent home. It contained silver-framed pictures of the children, lamps, a TV set, and convertible sofas. (At first, the Arnazes intended to spend dress-rehearsal night at the studio apartment, but discovered it was too noisy. Instead, they spent Wednesdays at a suite at the Beverly Hills Hotel.)

In addition to the physical changes, Desi implemented a number of personnel changes. He promoted assistant director James Paisley to the status of assistant production manager and hired Jerry Thorpe to replace him as first A.D. on "Lucy." Son of veteran M-G-M director Richard Thorpe (*Night Must Fall, Three Little Words, Ivanhoe,* etc.), Jerry had been Vincente Minnelli's assistant on *The Long, Long Trailer.* Desi was so impressed by young Thorpe's dedication to detail (the number one requirement of an assistant director), he hired him for "I Love Lucy" halfway through *Trailer* photography. Thorpe's only stipulation was that Desi also hire his assistant Jack Aldworth as second A.D. Since they had worked so well together on the M-G-M comedy, Arnaz agreed.

However, Thorpe's first assignment in August of 1953 was to find a new set of twins to portray Ricky Ricardo, Jr., during the third "Lucy" season. Child labor restrictions prevented the company from fully utilizing the "talents" of the Simmons twins, who were not yet one year old. Arnaz had a good lead—he had seen what he thought was an ideal pair pictured in a newspaper layout, so he instructed Thorpe to contact the boys' parents and offer the fourteen-month-old twins the role.

Eva June Mayer, mother of Michael Leo and Joseph David Mayer, and member of the nationwide Mothers of Twins Club, was skeptical when Jerry called. There had been many news accounts of fraudulent talent agencies bilking parents of so-called talented kiddies.

"I thought this was phony, too," she said, "because we'd never given a thought to placing our children in TV. I told Jerry I'd bring them in for an audition, but emphasized that the minute it cost me a penny, he could count us out."

Thorpe was amused. "I've got a whole corridor full of doting mothers with their kids, looking for this job," he told Mrs. Mayer. "I give you first whack at it and you call me a crook!"

Mrs. Mayer dressed the twins simply in seersucker playsuits, quite a contrast to the sartorial splendor of some of the other applicants. One look at the boys and Desi signed them to a contract (starting at a combined salary of a hundred and fifty dollars per week and rising to seven hundred dollars over the next five years). They remained in the role for three full seasons, amassing an educational trust fund and, as a gift from Lucy, all the clothes they wore on the show.

"It's an unnatural life for children, especially after they reach school age," Mrs. Mayer now confides. She promptly retired them from show business at age four. One of them, Michael, now works in the accounting department of a major Southern California drugstore chain.

Another key figure who joined the "I Love Lucy" staff that summer was Academy Award-winner (in 1950 for "Color Costume Design," *Samson and Delilah)* Elois Jenssen. "Lucille first came to me in 1951, asking if I'd design her clothes for a new TV series she was starting," relates Elois, a lovely and articulate lady who's pretty enough to be a movie star herself. "At the time, I was under exclusive contract to 20th Century-Fox and couldn't do it. When my three-year hitch was up, I decided to free-lance.

"Jack Chertok, who had produced Lucy's film *Lured,* for which I designed the costumes, was starting a new TV series starring Ann Sothern, 'Private Secretary,' and he asked me to design Ann's clothes. That became my first designing assignment in television.

"After a season of 'Secretary,' I decided to get together again with Lucille to see if she still wanted me to design clothes for her. I knew I could handle both TV assignments at the same time. Up to that point," Elois reveals, "all of her dresses for 'I Love Lucy' were either cut out of one or two dress patterns with details changed slightly and sewed up by a dressmaker, or purchased at Orbach's.

"I drove out to M-G-M where Lucy and Desi were filming *The Long, Long Trailer,* and told her some of my ideas. She thought they were great, and then asked me about salary. I told her that Jack Chertok was giving me a flat rate of two hundred dollars per episode on 'Private Secretary.' Lucy said that she couldn't afford that much right now, but could pay about half of that."

The salary matter wasn't the first account of Desilu's thriftiness. Academy Award-winning cinematographer Karl Freund started out during the first season at scale. He was an independently wealthy man—due to his inventions and patents—and took the Desilu assignment because it presented a challenge. Director Marc Daniels earned five hundred dollars per week during his thirty-eight-episode tenure in 1951–52. Vivian Vance and William Frawley started out at three hundred and fifty dollars per week each (by 1956 they were earning two thousand dollars each per episode). One veteran character actor offers: "It was supposed to be a privilege to appear on 'I Love Lucy.' It *was* nice—don't get me wrong—but they were awful cheapskates. We got paid the absolute minimums. If your part was small, they just hired you for one day—the day of the actual filming—which gave you just one or two rehearsals. The company didn't want to pop for a full week's pay, which was pretty standard."

Because "I Love Lucy" was a *filmed* TV series, it came under the Screen Actors Guild jurisdiction. SAG minimums, until the summer of 1955, were as follows: a "day player" received seventy dollars; for three days' work, a hundred and seventy-five dollars; and for a five-day, or weekly, assignment, two hundred and fifty. For example, Verna Felton, the veteran character actress who played Lucy's unflappable customer in "Sales Resistance," earned two hundred and fifty dollars for her week's work, although Sheldon Leonard, who appeared in the same segment as salesman Harry Martin, pocketed four hundred dollars for the assignment. Doris Singleton's first appearance in the series also netted her four hundred dollars. When Jerry Hausner appeared in the minor role of Ricky's agent, he usually earned seventy dollars (for his announcing chores from 1952–54, he earned an additional seventy dollars for the day's work).

Typically then, Elois Jenssen—Paris-educated at Parson's School of Fine and Applied Art, Oscar-winner, designer of costumes for over twenty-five films and still under the age of thirty—waited more than a month for a decision to be made on the "Lucy" assignment.

"Marty Leeds had to okay my being hired," recalls Miss Jenssen, who designed all of Lucy's clothes for sixty episodes (Vivian was receiving a weekly clothing allowance). "Because they didn't have a designer for the first two seasons, I had to set up an entire wardrobe department from scratch. This meant purchasing sewing machines, cutting tables, dummies, needles, thread, everything."

Elois was hired shortly before the start of the third season. "I immediately sat down and started sketching designs for Lucy. On the Saturday of Labor Day weekend, I took my sketches and drove out to the Valley, first to see Karl Freund. Because of Papa's involved lighting system, he was very concerned about colors and, in fact, always had to approve my sketches. Papa liked what I was doing, and then I stopped off at Lucy's house in Chatsworth. She had just come back from her summer vacation in Del Mar. Desi wasn't due back until Tuesday morning, when rehearsals were set to begin.

"We spent hours going over my ideas. Lucy was very concerned that the character be dressed appropriately, emphasizing that each outfit would be worn often. She didn't want 'high style' or anything that didn't typify an all-American housewife. When we concluded our meeting, she walked me to my car. I'll never forget what happened next," Elois shudders. "As we walked across the lawn, we suddenly spotted Little Lucie, about two years of age, floating face down in the swimming pool. She had apparently fallen in. Lucy immediately froze—panic-stricken—and couldn't move, she was in

Costume designer Elois Jenssen adds the finishing touches to a sketch of an outfit to be worn by Lucy on an upcoming "Lucy" episode.

An Elois Jenssen design.

One of the many "trick" outfits created for Lucy by Jenssen. Note the finished product in this scene from "Bonus Bucks," 1954.

a state of shock. I kicked off my shoes as I ran toward the pool, dove in with all my clothes on, and pulled her out. Thank God she was all right."

Something else that happened that Labor Day weekend caused Lucille some added anguish. Several weeks before in Del Mar, she had received a phone call from a member of the House Un-American Activities Committee, asking if she would volunteer to appear at a closed meeting on Friday, September 4, in Hollywood. "We simply want to go over the statements made at your previous appearance before our committee last year," explained an aide of Representative Donald L. Jackson, chairman of the committee, referring to an April 3, 1952, closed meeting at which time Lucy had been questioned concerning her intention to vote on the Communist Party ticket in 1936. She had explained fully her grandpa Hunt's role in her political activities that year, and when the hearing ended she shook hands with the various committee members and left, completely cleared. No word of the interview went beyond the committee room.

Having returned early from Del Mar especially to make a second appearance before the group, Lucy again testified that she had registered her intention to vote the Communist ticket only to placate her aging grandfather. After two hours of intense questioning, the hearing ended. Investigator William

Wheeler concluded by telling Miss Ball, "I have no further questions. Thank you for your cooperation." When the hand-shaking ended, Lucy was assured by committee members that she was completely cleared, again. She was also assured that her testimony would remain secret.

Two days later, with Desi still in Del Mar playing poker at movie producer Irving Briskin's ocean-view home, Lucy put the children to bed and settled down in a comfortable rocking chair in the den of their Chatsworth home to read over the next "Lucy" script and catch Walter Winchell's weekly Sunday-night broadcast. Toward the end of Winchell's infamous "Mr.-and-Mrs.-America-and-all-the-ships-at-sea" program, he punched across a "blind" item: "The top television comedienne has been confronted with her membership in the Communist Party."

Winchell's emphasis on the word "top" left little doubt that he was referring to Lucille Ball. Instantly in Del Mar, Desi's poker game was interrupted by an urgent phone call from Desilu PR representative Ken Morgan. "Desi," Morgan began, "did you hear Winchell's broadcast?" Desi had not, but after being told the details, he immediately phoned Lucy. "I'll be right home," he explained, slamming down the receiver.

Within an hour Howard Strickling, M-G-M's publicity director and an old friend, arrived at Chatsworth with Kenny Morgan. Lucy was puzzled. She had not yet realized the impact of Winchell's cryptic statement. Strickling, whose studio had just shelled out $2 million to film *The Long, Long Trailer,* knew what the consequences could be. The era of Joe McCarthy and of the infamous Senate hearings was in full swing, and an accusation such as Winchell's could spell the end not only of the *Trailer* film but also the entire Desilu empire—including "I Love Lucy," the nation's number one television show. Following on the heels of Strickling and Morgan, the Arnazes' neighbor, columnist Bill Henry of the Los Angeles *Times,* knocked on their front door, offering his help. Suddenly Lucy began to realize the full impact; she was in a panic, wishing desperately that her husband were home.

Sometime around 1 A.M. Desi arrived, having sped the 125 miles from Del Mar. He found Lucy in a chain-smoking state. "You're making too big a fuss over this," he said, trying to calm her. "Don't get so excited."

"But why are you so cool?" she asked.

"Because I've known about it for two weeks."

"You have?"

"Yes. J. Edgar Hoover told me about it at the racetrack. He said there was nothing he could do about it."

Strickling agreed. He advised the Arnazes to ignore Walter's broadcast, play dumb, and the whole affair would be forgotten in a day or two. Dismissing his urge to fight back, Desi decided to follow Strickling's recommendation, mainly to spare Lucy and her family further embarrassment.

However, the next day, Monday, September 7, Winchell's widely syndicated newspaper column carried the same accusation. Still, Lucy and Desi intended to start rehearsing the first new "I Love Lucy" segment, "The Girls

Go Into Business," the following morning as if nothing was wrong. On Wednesday, amid a run-through on Stage 9 of Motion Picture Center, their new "Lucy" headquarters, someone alerted Desi to columnist Jack O'Brian's barb in the New York *Journal-American:* "Lucille Ball has announced that she intends to retire in two years. It may be a lot sooner than she thinks." He tore up the newspaper, hoping Lucy wouldn't see the item.

On Friday, the day of the first "Lucy" filming, he and Lucy drove in the back gates at Motion Picture Center for a 1 P.M. "call." The front offices were jammed with reporters; the Desilu telephone (HOllywood 9-5981) had clocked several hundred calls. At noon the Los Angeles *Herald-Express* (which was also Winchell's local outlet) broke the story; in huge four-inch-high red letters the front-page banner headline proclaimed, "LUCILLE BALL NAMED RED." The evidence, printed: a photostated copy of the 1936 registration card on which Lucy had indicated her intention to vote for the Communist Party candidates in that year's election.

While the subject of all the furor, Lucy, went about her business preparing for the evening's filming, under Bill Asher's able direction, Desi picked up the telephone and called CBS in New York. He told network president Dr. Frank Stanton about the headlines and confessed that he had had no word yet from Philip Morris, the sponsor. Desi was scared—the cigarette company, fearing bad publicity, had every right to cancel its contract with Desilu. If it did, or threatened to do so, Desi was prepared to cough up about thirty thousand dollars to buy the half-hour time slot "Lucy" usually occupied, although "Racket Squad" was currently running as its summer replacement. Stanton agreed to sell Desi and Lucy the time so they could explain their side of the story to the American public.

Meanwhile, Lucy followed Desi's strict orders not to speak with any reporters if they managed to sneak onto the lot. Instead, she continued rehearsing. Around her the other actors and crewmen tried to pretend it was an average day, although everyone knew the empire was in danger of collapsing. Nobody discussed the crisis with her.

In New York, an executive of Philip Morris put in an urgent call to the firm's independent public relations consultant, Benjamin Sonnenberg. "What should we do?" asked the cigarette man.

Sonnenberg, who had been in on the "I Love Lucy" negotiations from the start in 1951, knew strong-willed Desi. His advice to the client: "Let *them* handle it."

At 3 P.M. the call came from New York. Desi grabbed the telephone, listening to the sponsor's verdict: "If all the facts are as they now are, we're behind you 100 percent."

Relieved and choking back tears, Desi hung up and raced fifty feet across the studio courtyard that separated his office from Stage 9, to inform Lucy. He approached her slowly from behind a camera, caught her eye, and then smiled at her knowingly. Tears quickly filled her eyes. Then in a carefully controlled voice she said, "Well, that's fine. I'll get back to work."

Sponsor's faith or not, Lucy was still upset. The headlines of the day caused her to conjure up visions of the entire American public hating her. Desi decided to get Donald Jackson on the phone and insist he hold an immediate press conference exonerating Lucille of any Communist suspicion. Lucy's only concern was the night's filming—she was scared to death that she would be booed off the stage by the studio audience. Desi tried to allay her fears even though he was thinking the same thoughts. He even considered canceling the live audience that night (it had been done only once before), but later reasoned it would be almost an admission of guilt.

Jackson grudgingly agreed to hold a press conference at the Statler Hotel at 6 P.M., if he could get together a quorum of committee members. Desi insisted he try very hard, and then arranged to have favored newsman Jim Bacon of the Associated Press personally cover the conference for him. It most likely would be concluded just moments before the "Lucy" filming that evening. Arnaz *had* to know that Lucille had been publicly cleared before he went out to face three hundred people seated in the bleachers.

The call finally came, and Bacon relayed the news that Jackson had cleared Lucy and there would be beautiful headlines in all the morning papers. Lucy, chalk-faced and near collapse, smiled weakly. A doctor was in attendance all day just in case. Quietly, the group, which included Harry Ackerman, Marty Leeds, *TV Guide* writer Dan Jenkins and his wife, and Lucy's mother, made its way across the narrow courtyard that led to the rear of the sound stage.

At a few minutes past eight, Desi stepped through the living room door on the set and faced the throng of people seated in bleachers extending the entire width of the building. He had a little trouble with the door and laughed nervously about it. However, instead of the usual warm-up, which always included a few planned jokes, he gave an impromptu speech to the unnaturally silent crowd.

"Welcome to the first 'I Love Lucy' show of the season," he began. "We are glad to have you back and we are glad to be back ourselves. But before I go on, I want to talk to you about something serious. Something very serious. You all know what it is. The papers have been full of it all day."

He paused briefly to switch the mike to his other hand. Suddenly his lower lip began to quiver and his voice broke. "Lucille is no Communist!" he blurted out fiercely. "Lucy has never been a Communist, not now and never will be. I was kicked out of Cuba because of communism. We both despise the Communists and everything they stand for."

An emotional Latin, Desi was angry. His eyes had now filled with tears and his voice was shaking uncontrollably. "Lucille is 100 percent an American. She is as American as Barney Baruch and Ike Eisenhower. Last November we both voted for Ike. Tomorrow morning the complete transcript of Lucille's testimony will be released to the papers and you can read it for yourself. Then you will know this is all a pack of lies. Please, ladies and gentlemen, don't believe every piece of bunk you've read in today's papers!"

On September 11, 1953—the night of the infamous "red scare"—the studio audience awaits Desi Arnaz's emotional speech.

He had to stop. The audience had risen to its feet in roaring approval. One man shouted, "We're with you, boy!" and Desi turned, looking over in the man's direction, and said, "Thank you."

Glancing into the wings where the staff was huddled, Arnaz spotted his wife. She was sobbing.

Then, as was the usual preshow custom, Desi introduced Bill Frawley and Vivian Vance. They received warm, hearty welcomes from the crowd. Desi was pleased, but now he was approaching the really difficult moment— introducing Lucy, who was quickly trying to regain her composure and repair her makeup.

"And now," Desi began, his voice calmer, "I want you to meet my favorite wife—my favorite redhead—in fact, that's the only thing red about her, and even *that's* not legitimate—Lucille Ball!"

Getting hold of herself, Lucille took a deep breath and quietly stepped out from behind a door at the rear of the set. The heavy makeup for the show concealed the lines of worry and strain. Following the last dress rehearsal, she had been in seclusion in her dressing room and had spoken to no one but Desi, her mother, and close friend Barbara Pepper. Suddenly

"The Girls Go Into Business," the first episode to be filmed at Motion Picture Center and the one shot on the night of the "red scare." Guest star Mabel Paige as Mrs. Hansen haggles with Lucy and Ethel over the price of the dress shop.

Bill Hatch's band was playing the "I Love Lucy" theme song, and the audience gave Lucy a standing ovation. She tried to smile, but was unable to speak. Instead, she punched the air lightly with both hands as if to say, "We'll fight this thing out." Grimacing with emotion, she bowed briefly and humbly, and walked backstage through the set door.

Then came Bill Asher's voice from the overhead control booth: "Please take your places for the first scene. . . . Cameras ready? . . . Roll the sound, . . . roll the film. . . . Action!" And "The Girls Go Into Business"—Episode #68—was on its way.

When it was over a little more than an hour later, Lucy and Desi came out arm in arm and asked each of the supporting players—Mabel Paige, Emory Parnell, Kay Wiley, Barbara Pepper, and, of course, Vivian Vance and Bill Frawley—to take a bow. Then Lucy stood alone with Desi for a moment, looked at the audience, and said, "Good night, God bless you for being so kind—and thank you." It was a long walk offstage, clear across the width of the studio. She received an ovation every step of the way. When she reached her dressing room, she broke down and cried her heart out. It had been a very long Friday.

On Saturday, the Arnazes held an informal press conference at their ranch home at 19700 Devonshire Street in Chatsworth. An army of reporters fired questions at Lucy, who was now capable of answering them calmly. The Los Angeles *Times* already had printed this banner headline for all to read: "LUCILLE BALL NOT RED, REP. JACKSON DECLARES." At the end of the two-hour session, held in a garden setting, a reporter faced his colleagues. "I think," he said, "we owe both of them a vote of thanks. And I think a lot of people owe them an apology."

The apology that counted most came the following night on Winchell's broadcast: "During the past week, Donald Jackson, chairman of the House Un-American Activities Committee, and all its members, cleared Lucy a hundred percent, and so did J. Edgar Hoover and the FBI, plus every newspaper in America, and tonight, Mr. Lincoln is drying his eyes for making her go through this." After seven long days, the ordeal was finally over.

Thousands of fans wired their support to Lucy. Harry Ackerman issued a simple statement that appeared in *Variety:* "People seem to feel this thing is silly, not serious, and they all love Lucy." Ed Sullivan expressed his support in his nationwide column: "It's a singularly fortunate thing for Lucille Ball that she's been a weekly visitor to millions of American living rooms. In those Monday night visits, people have come to know her well. TV cameras being as revealing as they are, so the jury of Public Opinion is an informed jury as it renders its verdict on a silly thing she did seventeen years ago."

As further confirmation of her innocence, on November 25, 1953, the B'nai B'rith named Lucille Ball "Woman of the Year," the first time the award had been bestowed on an actress. The next day, Lucy, Desi, Vivian, and Bill were invited to the White House to dine with President Eisenhower and Mrs. Eisenhower, who were staunch "I Love Lucy" fans; guests included Eddie Fisher and Jackie Robinson. After performing for his hosts, Desi approached Ike: "They said a foreigner with an accent wouldn't be believable playing an average American husband." The President replied: "Out in Kansas they said I'd never be President. You know what we are? A couple of walking miracles!"

The premiere episode of the third season, telecast October 5, 1953— "Ricky's *Life* Story" (actually filmed the previous May and saved)—managed to maintain the high ratings (62.6, according to Nielsen) the series had become noted for. The "red scare" apparently had little effect on the popularity of "I Love Lucy." The public still adored the antics of the Ricardos and Mertzes.

The critics, however, thought otherwise. One wrote: "The opening show was pretty funny. Just pretty funny. Last year's opener ["Job Switching"], as I recall, was a riot. This one wasn't. . . . The 'Lucy' shows, let's face it, are beginning to sound an awful lot alike. Miss Ball is always trying to bust out of the house; Arnaz is trying to keep her in apron strings. The variations on this theme are infinite, but it's the same and I'm a mite tired of it."

"Happy Birthday to . . . The Brains" reads the inscription on the cake in celebration of Jess Oppenheimer's fortieth birthday on November 11, 1953, the night of the dress rehearsal for "Lucy Has Her Eyes Examined."

In November, "Dragnet," Jack Webb's series about the Los Angeles Police Department co-starring Ben Alexander, achieved the impossible—it momentarily passed "I Love Lucy" in the Nielsen race and the two series began a neck-and-neck race for supremacy. For the week of November 15, with a 61.3 rating, "Dragnet" nosed out Lucy with an even 60.

Karl Freund was hospitalized in early November with pneumonia, and his "Lucy" chores were taken over by one of his cohorts, Nick Musuraca. Freund returned to work for the episode ["Ricky Minds the Baby"] shot on December 3. Unfortunately, he missed the surprise thirteenth wedding anniversary party that Desi threw for Lucille at the Mocambo nightclub on November 30. Lucy had expected only a quiet dinner with Desi and their longtime friend Vincente Minnelli. When they arrived at the posh Sunset Strip club, Desi escorted Lucille to a private back room.

"We can't go in there," she insisted. "Someone's having a party."

Someone was—Lucy. Forty guests helped the Arnazes celebrate their anniversary. At nine o'clock, nightclub owner Charley Morrison wheeled in a television set. It was a Monday night, and no one wanted to miss "I Love Lucy." The crowd watched the "Too Many Crooks" episode, as did an estimated 46 million devotees of Lucy's televised high jinks.

"As the show became more and more popular, so did the theme song," says Eliot Daniel, composer of the catchy melody. "In writing a theme for the show I tried to get an opening musical phrase that would say, 'I love Lucy.' Having settled on the first four notes, the rest of the song practically wrote itself. I played it for Jess, Desi, and a few others, and we had a theme song. Not a note was changed and no other tune was submitted.

"When Ricky had to sing a song to Lucy on her birthday ["Lucy's Last

The Arnazes celebrate the Christmas holidays at their ranch in the San Fernando Valley, 1953.

Birthday," telecast May 11, 1953] we decided to use the theme song, but we needed lyrics," recalls Mr. Daniel. "I was most pleased when Harold Adamson came up with lyrics that I feel are just right for the song and the show.

"Throughout the series, there were several shows that included musical numbers. In a few cases they were popular songs, but for the most part they were special material, with lyrics by Madelyn Pugh and Bob Carroll, and music by me. One show was a complete operetta ["The Operetta"], and on this one we had the help of an outside lyricist. One original song that seemed to do very well was in a baseball skit with Bob Hope ["Lucy and Bob Hope"]—'Nobody Loves the Ump' [Music by Eliot Daniel, Lyrics by Larry Orenstein].

"In these musical numbers the principals would rehearse with piano during the week, either with me or with Desi's pianist, Marco Rizo, and do it with the full orchestra during the filming. We were fortunate in that our four principals all handled musical numbers very well and seemed to get a genuine kick out of doing them."

Daniel describes the procedure he followed to furnish his original music for each "Lucy" installment: "After the show was edited, they would run it in the projection room for the music editor and me, and I would tell him the footages I wanted—sometimes just a ten-second bridge, sometimes three minutes of underscoring, catching various accents and moods. The editor would then send me a cue sheet with all the timings and descriptions of action, and I would go ahead with composition and orchestration.

"We recorded the music for the early shows done at General Service Studios at Glen Glenn studios, which were right across Romaine Street; but when we moved to Motion Picture Center, they ran cable to the Glenn complex and we were able to record in a room right next to where the show was being filmed. Bill Hatch would conduct the orchestra from my score, and I would be in the control room with the engineer. Everything was done to stopwatch so we didn't waste time for rollback starts with the projector. I would check the balance, and Bill and I would check each other on the timings, so we soon had a pretty efficient setup.

"When all the various tracks were ready—dialogue, sound effects, music, et cetera—we had a rerecording session where all the tracks were run with the picture, balanced, and then reduced to one master track. This session was usually attended by all concerned: producer, director, film editor, music editor, ad agency representative, and myself."

Members of the versatile Desi Arnaz Orchestra, conducted by Wilbur Hatch, included Marco Rizo, pianist; Alberto Calderón, drums; José Betancourt, Latin percussion; Nick Escalante, bass; Tony Terran, trumpet; Vince de Bari, trumpet; Felipe Hernández, trumpet; José Gutiérrez, trombone; Jack Pickering, trombone; Joe Miller, flute and sax; Jack Baker, sax; Jack Echols, sax; and Nancy Youngman, harp.

Most familiar of all musicians was pianist Marco Rizo. He was featured in dozens of episodes and referred to in many others. "My association with Desi started long before 'I Love Lucy.' I was Desi's pianist-arranger when he appeared at the Copacabana in New York in the forties, then continued in the same capacity when his orchestra headlined the Bob Hope NBC radio show in Hollywood for two years. Then we did 'Your Tropical Trip' for CBS Radio in 1951, which featured music from South America and the Caribbean. Then came the 'I Love Lucy' pilot and there I remained until the very end in 1960," Rizo points out, adding that on his worldwide concert tours he plays his own special arrangement of the "I Love Lucy" theme song. "It meets with instant approval all over the world."

Lovely Doris Singleton, who played Caroline Appleby, Lucy Ricardo's friendly nemesis, once was approached in a shoe store in Italy by an "I Love Lucy" fan. "The woman greeted me like we were old-time friends," says Doris, who is prettier today than she was during her Caroline Appleby days in the fifties. "Once a man came to my table at Prunier [a bistro in Paris] and asked me if I was from San Francisco. He said his wife was sure she knew me. I told him that while I had visited San Francisco a few times, I didn't have any friends there. A few minutes later he came back, insisting his wife knew me. Finally it dawned on me, so I told him to ask her if she ever watched 'I Love Lucy.' He went off and, a few seconds later, came back grinning. 'Of course,' he said, 'you're Caroline Appleby!' "

Doris Singleton as Caroline Appleby in "Baby Pictures," originally telecast November 2, 1953.

Like many "I Love Lucy" alumni, Miss Singleton had worked with Lucille before the television series came along: She did a few parts on "My Favorite Husband." When the TV show was underway, Jess Oppenheimer hired her to play one of the girls in the women's club.

Doris explains how her character became Caroline Appleby: "Lucy liked to use real persons' names. As you know, Marion Strong, which Shirley Mitchell played on the show, was actually one of Lucy's girl friends from Jamestown, New York. When we were trying to come up with a name for me, Lucy suggested that I use my own name, but I didn't want to. So she said, 'Okay then, Doris, you'll be Caroline Appleby.' I told her that would be fine. Later I discovered that Caroline Appleby was one of Lucy's schoolteachers." Caroline's husband was Charley Appleby. He ran a TV station. Doris Singleton's husband is Charley Isaacs. He's a TV writer. "Lucy" was just one big, happy family.

The 1953–54 season saw one member of the "happy family" depart. It was Jerry Hausner, the actor who had appeared in the original "Lucy" pilot, and for two and a half years had played Ricky's agent Jerry. It was not a happy parting. "Desi and I had a scene in which I was to call him from a pay phone," recounts the actor about an incident that took place during the "Fan Magazine Interview" episode. "The set with the pay phone was on the opposite end of the sound stage and, during rehearsals, the phones were not connected. In other words, it was impossible for us to hear each other without cues. I told Desi I didn't think it was going to work out, but he assured me the phones would be connected by Thursday night when the show would be filmed in front of a live audience.

"The night of the show we did the scene, but the phones still were not connected. It did not go very well, as I had expected. The audience was laughing in the wrong places. When the scene was over, Desi stormed across the sound stage and cursed me out in front of the entire cast and crew and audience—about four hundred people. I couldn't believe it—in all my professional career I had never been treated so badly. I was so upset that I walked over to Jess Oppenheimer and told him I would never again do the show. He understood. It was terrible when Desi and I had to do another scene together in the last act. I found it very difficult looking him in the face."

Midway through the season, Lucy and Desi flew to New York for the February 18, 1954, premiere of *The Long, Long Trailer* at Radio City Music Hall. The highlight of their Gotham visit came when Lucy was honored on the Radio City stage. She recalled for the SRO audience the days she sat in the darkened theater dreaming that one day she would be on that stage. Another thrill came when she and Desi discovered a woman in the lobby of their hotel who wanted them to baptize her baby. The pair went from one party to another. . . . Billy Reed's Little Club, the Waldorf, the Astor . . . and mobs of "I Love Lucy" fans thronged each affair to pay homage to TV's number one team.

When Lucille was asked what she thought was the main reason for the excellence of her TV show, she unflappingly replied, "Desi does it all."

"I found that bringing 'I Love Lucy' to home screens," Desi once admitted, "was 90 percent desk work, 10 percent acting. From the overwork, I soon developed an eye twitch and headaches. I was worrying myself sick trying to be everywhere at once. Then one day Bill Frawley remarked, 'Remember when you led a band? You just waved a stick and the boys took it from there. Why don't you develop faith in others?' That took some of the air out of me. Once I tried delegating authority, making each of the five hundred workers feel pride through accomplishing a task unassisted, everything went twice as smoothly."

Desi's entrepreneurial leanings blossomed again during the spring of 1954 when he announced plans to film four pilots. With a $1 million loan from CBS (as collateral, the network retained 24 percent interest in Desilu), Desi teamed with writer-producer Parke Levy to turn the CBS radio hit "December Bride" into a television series. In February, while Lucy and Desi were busy promoting their new movie, Desilu shot the thirty-minute pilot starring Spring Byington, which eventually sold to CBS in June for a fall start. Also in production were pilots for "Mr. Tutt" to star Walter Brennan (it did not sell), "Country Doctor," a drama with Charles Coburn in the title role (it did not sell), and "Willy" starring June Havoc (it sold but lasted only one season on CBS). These disappointments did not faze Desi; he immediately plunged into preproduction on pilot ideas for the next TV season.

Emmy Awards night,
February 11, 1954, the
Hollywood Palladium. "I
Love Lucy" wins as "Best
Situation Comedy" and
Vivian Vance wins as "Best
Supporting Actress in a
Comedy." Frawley was
nominated but did not win;
Desi was never nominated.

There was not a person interviewed for this book who did not agree, however, that most of the credit for the show's superiority goes to Lucy herself. Her dedication, hard work, and incredible drive for perfection were what made "I Love Lucy" a hit.

"It was a demanding week when I worked on 'I Love Lucy,'" offers Doris Singleton. "It was one constant rehearsal. Everything had to be absolutely perfected. It was definitely not fun-and-games time on that set.

"I was lucky to have been in the Harpo Marx episode. He was absolutely fantastic to work with and was about the sweetest man I've ever met. He wasn't a bit funny offstage, but a very warm, lovely gentle man. When the fright wig was off, he was just Harpo. After the show was filmed, he gathered us all around and did a concert on the harp; Vivian sang.

"Every time there was a lull during rehearsals, Lucy would drag Harpo off to the other side of the stage to rehearse that incredible mirror bit. She refused to do it unless it was absolutely perfect."

Evidently the perfection paid off. On February 11, 1954, at the Sixth Annual Emmy Awards ceremony of the National Academy of Television Arts and Sciences, held at the Hollywood Palladium, "I Love Lucy" walked off with "Best Situation Comedy" honors, the second year in a row, and Vivian Vance won as "Best Supporting Actress." Lucy was nominated but lost to pal Eve Arden for her role as Connie Brooks in "Our Miss Brooks," a Desilu show. Bill Frawley also received a nomination—the first of five for his Fred Mertz characterization—but he lost to Art Carney.

Years later, when asked about his numerous Emmy losses, Frawley

cracked, "It didn't surprise me. I knew they didn't know what they were doing when Vivian Vance got one!" A loner, Frawley rarely socialized with anyone connected with "I Love Lucy." "Mostly my friends are in baseball or they're golfers. I just don't go to dinner at people's houses. I don't even know the names of the people next door at the Knickerbocker Hotel where I live. I don't mix easily, and mostly I mind my own business."

Frawley, who was associated with "Lucy" for nine years, was well liked by his friends, among them baseball great Joe DiMaggio. One buddy comments: "He was an able performer and probably came pretty close to being Fred Mertz in real life. He was well-meaning, but obstreperous, at times vaguely ridiculous. He was moral and responsible, likable and uncompetitive. He fussed and fumed, but his bark was much worse than his bite."

Another Frawley aficionado observes, "If he didn't like you, he was just awful. He was a completely prejudiced man. Couldn't stand any ethnic group. But, in general, he was a warm, wonderful, hearty old guy with a great sense of humor."

Doris Singleton remembers Frawley: "He would come on the set with the *Racing Form* under his arm. He never had an entire script with him—just his scenes. As I recall, he usually spent most of his time in his dressing room."

Lucille Ball adds a footnote: "Bill was something else. You couldn't rely on him to know where he was going or what he was doing because he just tore out what he was supposed to do, and when he came in he never knew what the story was about. But he was a funny, irascible, wonderful man for whom our writers wrote perfectly."

By the close of the season, Desi had reached the thinking-out-loud stage on plans to expand "I Love Lucy" to a full hour for the 1955–56 season after the $8 million Philip Morris contract had run its course. This, despite some poor mid-season reviews.

Jack Gould, in his March 31, 1954, New York *Times* television column wrote: "What's happened to 'I Love Lucy'? At the rate the . . . program has been going in the last few weeks [episodes like "Oil Wells," "Ricky Loses His Temper," "Home Movies," "Lucy Is Envious"] it's surely jeopardizing its exalted place in the popularity charts. Where once the show was a recognizable and hilarious farce on married life, it currently seems bent on succumbing to the most pedestrian and sophomoric slapstick . . .

"What's gone wrong is not easy of analysis, but an offhand guess is that in their search for things to do every week the producers and writers have taken refuge in the sight gag. The integrated situation built on sound and witty dialogue and plausibility, which was the heart of 'Lucy' 's appeal, has been sacrificed in the process . . .

"Perhaps 'Lucy' has run its course and has no choice but to press too hard. Or perhaps Gresham's Law has taken its inevitable toll: 'Lucy' has been reduced to the level of its competitors. But it must be hoped that a further try will be made to bring 'Lucy' back into perspective."

In spite of poor reviews, lower ratings, the Communist scare, and a handful of mediocre episodes, "I Love Lucy" did manage to take top honors as the "most-viewed show in the 1953–54 season," according to ARB. In May, an estimated 50,840,000 persons watched a single "I Love Lucy." Not bad, considering there were only 23 million television homes by the close of the season.

8 *Hooray for Hollywood*

"The first 100 shows are the hardest," read the inscription on the icing of the mammoth twelve-layer cake that was wheeled onto Stage 9 by two Desilu stage hands on the evening of June 17, 1954, after an overflow audience of more than three hundred people witnessed the filming of "The Business Manager," the one hundredth episode in the "Lucy" series.

As scores of "I Love Lucy" staff and crew members looked on, Lucille Ball paid homage to the three people most responsible for keeping the show on top of the heap. "I love them dearly," she said sincerely, "I appreciate them daily, I praise them hourly, and I thank God for them every night." Every person in the studio, from janitor to network vice-president, knew to whom Lucy was referring: producer and head writer Jess Oppenheimer, and writers Bob Carroll, Jr., and Madelyn Pugh.

Earlier that year, while accepting a Los Angeles Press Club award, Lucy had said, "Without my writers, I'm dead," repeating it several times for emphasis.

From the start, the "Lucy" writers were held in an esteem at Desilu uncommon in television. Lucille bombarded Jess Oppenheimer with photographs inscribed to "The Bossman," and early on Desi presented the producer with a statuette of a baseball player, inscribed with the punning tribute, "To the man behind the ball."

The "ball"—*Lucille* Ball, that is—said, "We had the same writers for three years on radio, before going into TV. We concentrated on our characters and what we wanted them to do, and never vacillated. Desi had one or two story ideas a year, and the writers took them and developed them. I didn't get involved with that. I'm not an idea girl; I'm a doer.

"My type of comedy had a lot of props, and what we call 'block pages,' " Lucy maintains. "Literally, my directions were a whole page, sometimes two, of what to do and how to do it. Bob and Madelyn—we called them 'the kids'—were sensational. They would actually do it themselves before asking me to do it. If I read a script and said, 'I don't know if I can do this,' Madelyn would jump up and reply, 'Yes, you can. We did it. We acted it out. You can do it.' I learned an awful lot from doing what they wrote. They were great."

The pair often toiled more than seventy hours a week talking, testing, and dreaming, then putting their ideas and jokes on paper. Every Monday morning, they would start plotting an "I Love Lucy" episode with Oppenheimer, often spending the entire day outlining the story scene by scene, laugh by laugh.

"Our schedule demanded that we write a script every single week because we didn't use outside writers," Oppenheimer insists. "It was just Bob and Madelyn and I for four years, and then we added Bob Schiller and Bob Weiskopf. We'd begin each weekly story conference with 'Does anybody have any ideas?' Then we'd kick around a few of them, finally latching onto one and start developing it. I think in the five years I was on the show, there might have been three times that we didn't finish the story we started on the same day because if it had taken two or three days to get and develop an idea, there would have been no way to do the series. Of course, it also helped that we had that two-and-a-half-year backlog of scripts from 'My Favorite Husband,' and we used a lot of them. Each one had a good solid basis for a story, whether we used any of the particulars or not.

"We would spend many hours on that Monday afternoon taking all the information necessary to the plot and lacing it into the story while other things were happening so it would flow naturally. We usually worked on this outlining until five o'clock, but sometimes until seven. We'd just kick the story back and forth, and, when we finally felt we had it, I'd dictate the entire thing into a machine while it was fresh. In fact, we'd often get other ideas when we heard it being talked aloud. By the following morning, we all had a typed draft of that outline," Jess explains.

During the next two days, Bob and Pug would go off to their boxlike office in a far corner of the studio complex and write a first draft, which they delivered to Jess on Wednesday night: "I'd go over it carefully on Thursday, amid my other responsibilities on the show, and return it to them with comments and suggestions for changes, and they'd give me another draft by the following Monday when we'd all sit down again to work on a new script. At that point, the script never went back to them. I'd do a 'polish' [rewrite it] and would redictate the entire script from start to finish into my dictation machine.

"I made it a point, no matter how good their draft was," Oppenheimer reveals about his writers' handiwork, "to redictate the entire thing, from beginning to end, because that way each of the characters consistently spoke the same way. It didn't have to be *me*, necessarily, but as long as it was filtered through one person's senses. . . . There was another reason for this. The fact that I knew every aspect of every script meant that if a question arose at any time during the production of that episode, I knew the reason why something was in there—a line, a piece of business, whatever. So if they wanted to make a change, I would immediately know if we couldn't do it because of something that preceded the proposed change. There has to be one person with that sort of overview.

"I remember one time that Bob and Madelyn gave me their draft and I felt it was *so* good, and I was so tired, that I said, 'That's just the way I would do it; I'm going to turn it into mimeograph without any changes.' So at the first reading with the actors, questions naturally arose and I was completely lost because I didn't have any of the answers. I had no idea why a certain line was in there, or a bit of business. It scared me half to death, and I never did it again. So, rightly or wrongly, the show sounded the same each time because it funneled through me. I knew best the mood and feel of our previous shows; I could bring it all into line so that nothing sounded too different or out of character.

"Even though we always got along great, they thought I loused up all their scripts. One time, after they complained bitterly to me, I said, 'There's a good and logical reason for everything I do, everything I change. So, on the next script, I'm going to keep a journal of all my changes and the reasons why.' I told them, 'Now you're going to know why I make alterations.' So I did it, and it took a lot of time, but I felt it was worth it. The next time we sat down to talk, I asked them if they had read my revision. Figuring that I had done a pretty masterful job, I told them that I would show them line by line the reasons for every change. Frankly, I thought they would throw themselves at my feet when I finished. But when I got through, I asked them whether they agreed. They said, 'No. We still think you screwed up the whole thing!' " Jess recalls with a nostalgic smile.

Madelyn—short, cute, and utterly feminine—and Bob, whose bushy eyebrows remind one of a friendly Svengali and John L. Lewis all rolled into one, sat before facing typewriters behind a closed door marked "Writer's Room." There they would not only create the situations, but also write the lines and, most importantly, test the gags to see if they would work.

"That was Madelyn's job," says Carroll. "It was up to her to see if it was physically possible for a woman to do all the things we dreamed up for Lucy."

"You see," adds Madelyn, "if I could do it, Lucy could. The situations not only had to be funny, but believable." During her writing days for "I Love Lucy," Madelyn had been locked in a steamer trunk and stuck in a loving cup. She had also glued icicles to her face, filled her blouse with eggs, and tried wrapping chocolate bonbons at breakneck speed. "We got our ideas from real life, or at least things that *could* happen in real life."

Jess, particularly, was concerned that even the most absurd slapstick be rooted in reality: "I always insisted that everything in an 'I Love Lucy' story have a logical foundation. I wanted there to be a sound reason for everything in the script, because I knew from experience that if you take viewers one step at a time, and they know *why* they're being taken there, you can go to the heights of slapstick comedy and outlandish situations. An audience lives in a cause-and-effect world: nothing happens without a reason and you cannot give them things that don't make sense.

"Let's consider the candy factory scene in 'Job Switching.' The assembly-line concept is an old one, done dozens of times on other shows. But I don't think I've ever seen another show that didn't violate the logic of the moment. They'd have the conveyor belt speeding up and slowing down just for comedic effect, but without regard to logic. And that's the kind of thing that turns off an audience. It suddenly reminds them that this is just for fun,

Although comedy-writing is a serious business, "Lucy" scribes, Bob Carroll, Jr., and Madelyn Pugh, "cut up" in their office as well as on the set with Desi.

rather than allowing them to be comfortable and go with it," Oppenheimer reasons. "Even the bread scene in 'Pioneer Women' is a logical extension of what *could* happen if one put in too much yeast. And 'The Freezer' episode—it was merely an imaginative extension, having Lucy come out with icicles on her face. It's not *completely* illogical. But had we had her come out of the freezer frozen in a giant block of ice, then we would have lost everyone. Don't forget, we didn't always *try* to get the laugh. We took time to develop a situation that would eventually pay off with a bigger laugh."

Oppenheimer, a onetime "gifted child," whose career had been closely watched by psychologists ever since he was in the second grade, held one of the toughest jobs in television. As producer of "I Love Lucy" (he was thirty-eight when the series began), he was required to keep track of thirteen separate episodes at all times. In a given week, he would discuss with Bob and Madelyn the show to be shot nine weeks in the future, and edit the finished script for the show eight weeks away. The same day, he had to check on costumes (his initials, like Lucille's and Papa Freund's, were required on all costume sketches before they were given the green light for "construction") and casting for episodes three and four weeks in the future, while taking care of production details for the show in production that week. After that he supervised the cutting, editing, and dubbing of episodes filmed two, three, and four weeks earlier. So valuable was Oppenheimer that when he resigned at the close of the 1955–56 season to accept a lucrative and prestigious network post with NBC, industry insiders predicted the immediate demise of "I Love Lucy."

"There is no question about the fact that Jess was the creative force behind the 'Lucy' show," director Bill Asher confirms. "He was the field general, as it were. Jess presided over all the meetings, and ran the whole show. He was very sharp. Unfortunately, Jess was never treated right and this caused a lot of ego clashes on the set. Desi and Jess had their differences, not so much Lucy. Even Bob and Madelyn were at odds on occasion—everyone worrying about who was doing what and who got the credit. As the success of the show grew, so did the clashing of egos. It got to be terrible.

"I never got involved with that," Asher continues, "I was just 'The Kid' and I sided with no one. What little I offered to Jess or Desi, or Bob and Madelyn, was for everyone not to forget one thing: If Lucille Ball wasn't out there, we'd all go down the drain."

Oppenheimer was an idea man—one of the best in the business. It was he who, as early as February 1954, decided to make some changes. He called Pugh and Carroll to an important story conference meant to decide the fate of the approaching 1954–55 season. He said, "We've got to do something new. When we started out, Desi is in show business and Lucy tries to get into the act. Later, we did more about the husband-and-wife angle, and when that got heavy, we were lucky and Lucy had her baby. Now we've got to think of something else."

It was fairly evident that Jess, too, had read some of the less-than-rave reviews "Lucy" had garnered during the previous season, the series' third. The competition, particularly NBC's "Dragnet," was encroaching on the Desilu comedy, and "Lucy" was suffering. The show needed a shot of creative adrenalin if it was going to stay on top much longer.

"Let's take the Ricardos from New York to Hollywood," Oppenheimer put in suddenly. "Desi could get a studio offer."

"Let Desi take a screen test," Bob Carroll added excitedly. "That would give us a couple of funny scenes with Lucy."

Madelyn added the womanly touch: "Suppose Hollywood was shooting *Don Juan* and they thought Desi would be perfect for the part. This opens up all kinds of scenes. Lucy trying to play femme fatale, Lucy getting jealous of the women Desi must make love to in the show . . ."

The concept was perfect. It would give the show a logical reason to use real stars playing themselves—a surefire ratings' booster. Oppenheimer instructed "the kids" to start brainstorming episodes during their upcoming summer break. The three of them would resume the critical task of writing the new spate of episodes in August, six months away.

While the stars themselves found summer solace at Del Mar, Bill Frawley began work on a new radio show, "Great Scott." He didn't need the extra money but the role, that of a major-league baseball scout, was right up his alley. Such a baseball fanatic was Frawley that his agent, Walter Meyers, demanded and got from Desilu a contract that stipulated that if the New York Yankees (Frawley's favorite ball club) copped the American League pennant, his client would be free to attend the World Series. And sure enough, seven out of "I Love Lucy"'s nine seasons, that seemingly minor clause caused Desilu Productions a good deal of grief over schedule juggling.

Desi's passion had turned from boats (the Arnazes owned a thirty-four-foot cabin cruiser, *Desilu)* to golf and skeet-shooting. In fact in September 1954 he was privileged to play golf with President Eisenhower. And while vacationing in Del Mar, Desi spent a good deal of time (and money) at the racetrack. *TV Guide* reported: "For $18,000—the cost of approximately 15 minutes of one 'I Love Lucy' film—Lucille Ball and Desi Arnaz have bought a brown colt by Count Speed out of Nursery School and have thus started Desilu Stables."

Desi's summer vacation was not all fun and games. There appeared in print in July a story quoting Lucille Ball as saying she would retire after the 1955–56 season: "Upon completion of Desilu Productions' current contract with Philip Morris in 1956, there will be no more 'I Love Lucy' television films made, according to present plans, star Lucille Ball revealed. She has always wanted to direct, the comedienne declared, adding there is a possibility she might do 'an hour-long show, in color, every three months or so.' Miss Ball said the desire to spend more time with her children was the reason behind her decision."

Although Desi himself was mulling the possibility of doing monthly one-hour "Lucy" shows in the future, he was incensed by the newspaper article: "This whole thing is ridiculous. Now it's possible that Lucy might have made such remarks in a very offhand way. Everybody would like to quit work and loaf for a while. It's the kind of thing everybody tosses off a dozen times a week in casual conversation. Only with Lucy, the casual remark got picked up off the floor and blown right up to the ceiling.

"In the first place, Lucy can't quit . . . even if she wanted to, which she

Desilu's president takes care of business between rehearsals on the Motion Picture Center lot.

doesn't. Our contract with Philip Morris runs until the end of the coming [1954–55] season. After that, CBS has the right to ask us to do two more years of the show, which would carry us through the end of the 1956–57 season . . .

"And I want to make one more thing crystal clear. Some people have been speculating in print about the possibility of 'I Love Lucy' continuing with someone else taking Lucille's place. That is the one thing we are absolutely dead sure about: There will never be an 'I Love Lucy' without Lucille Ball. Period. Exclamation Point!"

The use of guest stars on the show helped to drive up the slightly faltering "Lucy" ratings. The two Tennessee Ernie Ford episodes, aired May 3 and 10, 1954, were among the higher-rated of the season's shows. After the careful analysis by Oppenheimer in February, *Daily Variety* reported: "There is a geographical shift in the works for 'I Love Lucy,' with Desi Arnaz [getting] a job in filmland." Additional guest stars for the "Hollywood shows" certainly would be easy to come by—most of them were Lucille and Desi's personal friends and acquaintances. But in order to bear the extra costs and pay for other amenities, Desi called the CBS brass to a meeting that summer. He and Lucy wished to "renegotiate" their contract. The network would have to "come across" with something to make the couple "happier."

Spencer Harrison, a young [thirty-seven] but powerful CBS attorney who was vice-president in charge of business affairs on the West Coast, and J. J. Van Volkenburg, the network president, agreed to sit down with Desi and talk. Arnaz drove up from Del Mar in early August and ensconced himself in Bungalow 5 of the secluded Beverly Hills Hotel. Ken Morgan, the Desilu

PR head and Desi's "brother-in-law" (actually at that time he was married to Lucy's first cousin Cleo) joined him. Shrewd and demanding, Desi refused to budge on forty separate issues. Harrison and Van Volkenburg were getting nowhere fast. Their only hope was to call William S. Paley in New York and see if he could help. Paley, the head of CBS, flew to the Coast.

"Paley called me and asked me to meet him for breakfast at the hotel," Harrison recalled in an interview a few years before his death in 1983. "After breakfast we drove to the bungalow where the negotiations were taking place. It was hot and the air conditioning was barely working. We started at 9 A.M. and worked until 7:30 in the evening when we finally closed the deal." Paley came to terms with all forty points on which Desi had been unyielding. "He very seldom got involved like that."

It was back to work on Monday, September 13, 1954. Lucille, Desi, Vivian, Bill, and guest players Frank Nelson (he had played Freddie Fillmore and other characters in six previous "Lucy" episodes) and Elizabeth Patterson exchanged niceties before sitting down to read through the one hundred and third "I Love Lucy" episode, which would be broadcast eight weeks away on November 8. Entitled "Ricky's Movie Offer," it was the first of many shows incorporating Jess, Bob, and Madelyn's original ideas on the Hollywood trip concocted the previous February and developed during the summer months.

Nelson played Ben Benjamin (Bob and Madelyn's literary agent was a man named Ben Benjamin), a talent scout whose studio, M-G-M, was looking for a new face to portray classic lover Don Juan. When the news of Ricky's impending stardom leaked out (Lucy: "I didn't tell a soul, and they all promised to keep it a secret!"), what seemed to be all of New York wanted to audition for parts: Mrs. Sawyer and her French poodle; Pete, the grocery boy-cum-trumpet player; songbird Mrs. Trumbull; Ethel, wearing the garb of a Spanish *señorita*, complete with a rose between her teeth; Fred, the matador; and, of course, Lucy, who, upon reading the *Don Juan* screen-test script, discovered a part for "a Marilyn Monroe type." It took her little time to deck herself out in the appropriate, tight-fitting dress (designed by Elois Jenssen) to impress Benjamin.

Before the first dress rehearsal on Wednesday, Lucille poured herself into the Monroe gown and strolled casually around the Motion Picture Center lot. She went from one office to another—hip-swaggling all the way—staring insolently but saying nothing. One electrician quipped, "Marilyn Monroe can look like that, too. But can Marilyn manage to look like Lucille Ball?"

The next filmed episode in the Hollywood vein was "Ricky's Screen Test," shot the following Thursday evening. It turned out to be twice as funny as the "Ricky's Movie Offer" segment, especially the hilarious scenes featuring Lucy feeding Ricky his lines during the *Don Juan* screen test.

Two non-Hollywood-theme shows followed, the first of which, "Lucy's Mother-in-Law," introduced us to Ricky's Cuban mother, beautifully played by lovely Mary Emery (a Spanish actress whose real name is Maria Francisco

Cavazos). On the night of October 7, the company filmed "Ethel's Birthday," a funny show that spotlighted the marvelous comic talents of Vivian Vance.

Just prior to that, the new fall season got off to a grand start with the airing of "The Business Manager," the one hundredth episode, shot the previous June and saved. To ballyhoo "Lucy" 's fourth year, Ed Sullivan devoted his entire "Toast of the Town" hour on October 3, 1954, to Lucille and Desi. It was a hectic weekend that saw the four principals board a night-flight to New York after filming "Lucy's Mother-in-Law." Desi traveled on the "red-eye" with a 101° temperature, suffering from a virus, but he refused to cancel his appearance on Sullivan's show.

Daily Variety reviewed the hour: ". . . Couple made a very good impression and at an emotion-packed climax the tears flowed like wine. First Lucy had trouble keeping the tears back as she thanked all who helped make her show a hit; then Arnaz became so choked up as he said, 'Thank you, America.' . . . He had told how his first job in this country was cleaning canary cages, and said of his rise, 'Nowhere else in the world could this happen.'

"Highlights of 'Lucy' vidpix of the past were shown and Arnaz was revealed as an [actor] of no mean dramatic ability in a clip from Metro's *Bataan*.

"Fast-moving show was enlivened by sketches featuring the team, Arnaz vocalizing his trademark, 'Babalu,' and a song-and-dance specialty by Vivian Vance and William Frawley. . . ."

Ed Sullivan pays tribute to Lucille Ball and Desi Arnaz on the October 3 (1954) installment of "Toast of the Town," the day before the start of "I Love Lucy" 's fourth season.

During the televised salute, Sullivan presented the Arnazes with the "Champions of Show Business" plaque to pay tribute to their phenomenal TV success. Following the live telecast, the principals flew back to Los Angeles, arriving early Monday morning, just in time to start rehearsing another episode, "Ethel's Birthday."

From that point on, "I Love Lucy" concentrated solely on the Hollywood trip. In all, twenty-seven episodes, six of which aired during the 1955–56 season, were shot using the Ricardos-go-to-Hollywood theme. Except for a few clinkers, they were pure gold.

Who could forget the time Fred Mertz bought an antique Cadillac roadster for three hundred dollars for the cross-country trip? Or the time Lucy learned to drive the new 1955 Pontiac convertible Ricky purchased to replace Fred's old clunker (Lucy to Ethel: "Oh, he makes me so mad! . . . How was I supposed to know we didn't have enough room to make a U-turn in the Holland Tunnel?")? How about the episode ("California, Here We Come!") in which Lucy's mother, Mrs. McGillicuddy, arrived in New York, insisting on going along too (Kathryn Card's debut as Ricky's mother-in-law)? Or the brilliant half-hour titled "First Stop," which found the Ricardos and Mertzes holed up in a rickety motel outside Cincinnati?

Because of Tennessee Ernie Ford's good showing in the two back-to-back "Lucy" 's of the past season, the writers created another episode employing his talents. Titled "Tennessee Bound," it was set in the small (population: 54) fictional town of Bent Fork, Ernie's hometown (his real birthplace is Ford

Tennessee Ernie Ford's first of three appearances on "I Love Lucy" featured him getting "vamped" by wicked city woman Lucy Ricardo.

Town, Tennessee). Again, he played Lucy's Cousin Ernie; and the actor loved every minute of it. About his first "Lucy" stint, Ford once commented: "What really amazed me is the way those writers came up with a script full of genuine mountain expressions I hadn't heard in a passel of years. When I read that 'hitch in his gitalong' bit, I just lay down thar on the floor and liked to die laughin', it was so natural-like."

"Ethel's Home Town," the last episode before the foursome arrived in Hollywood, also made use of an "I Love Lucy" alumnus: Irving Bacon, who portrayed Ethel's father, Will Potter, had appeared in the first-season installment, "The Marriage License." Having arrived in Albuquerque, New Mexico, the group expected simply to enjoy a visit to Ethel's birthplace. Instead, they quickly learned that the town was under the impression that it was Ethel, not Ricky, who was going to Hollywood to be in the movies. A theater marquee even read, "Ethel Mae Potter. We Never Forgot Her."

Late fall 1954 proved to be a hectic season business-wise. Luckily, Marty Leeds, executive vice-president of Desilu, hired Bernard Weitzman away from CBS to serve as his assistant. Already, Desilu had initiated construction over the past summer of three new theaters at Motion Picture Center, at a cost of thirty-five thousand dollars each. Desilu was shooting "Lucy," "December Bride," June Havoc's "Willy" series, "Our Miss Brooks," "Make Room for Daddy," and "The Ray Bolger Show" at the Cahuenga Boulevard location.

As early as June, Desilu had been trying to purchase the studio complex, but negotiations were not going well. Six months later, Desi learned, quite by accident, that Joe Justman, owner, was about to accept an offer from none other than Harry Cohn, Columbia Pictures' head and Lucille's nemesis. Rumor had it that Columbia would agree to rent space to Desilu, but Desi did not want to take a chance of losing this important real estate on a Cohn whim.

Without wasting a moment, Desi summoned his tax attorney and told him the problem. The two devised a scheme: Justman would be invited the next day to Chatsworth for lunch along with the tax man. "I want you to stay," Desi told the accountant, "until Desilu owns controlling interest in Motion Picture Center." After more than eight hours of negotiation, it was all arranged. On January 17, 1955, it was announced: "Lucille Ball and Desi Arnaz, as individuals, have assumed voting control of Motion Picture Center studios, Hollywood, under a new corporate set-up whereby Joseph Justman continues as President. . . . Board members are Mssrs. Arnaz, Justman, [Martin] Leeds, [Andrew] Hickox, and Al Pracca, who represents the Lutheran Aid Society, which has renewed its mortgage on the property under a refinancing set-up. Desilu continues to rent space for its film properties."

Another interesting financial negotiation took place that fourth season. It was no idle choice that resulted in the use of a spanking new 1955 Pontiac convertible in seven "I Love Lucy" episodes. For the inherent promotional consideration, General Motors agreed to pay Desilu fifty thousand dollars cash to cover the added production costs of some exterior shooting involving the automobile. GM also tossed in five Pontiacs, three of which went to the series' writers.

In order to stifle the persistent rumors about Lucille and Desi's retirement, CBS signed the pair to a new contract right before Christmas, despite the fact that the current agreement still had nearly a year to run. The multimillion-dollar deal, which also called for Philip Morris to share sponsorship with Procter & Gamble (both Biow accounts), ensured the continuation of "I Love Lucy" as a half-hour comedy, through the 1955–56 season, with an option for one more year (1956–57).

The first "Lucy" actually set in Hollywood, "L.A. at Last!" began rehearsals on Monday, November 29, right after the Thanksgiving holiday weekend. William Holden, who had appeared with Lucy in the 1949 Columbia movie *Miss Grant Takes Richmond*, would not take a dime for his guest shot. His studio, Paramount, agreed to "loan him out" on the proviso that he plug his current release, the movie *The Country Girl*. As a favor to Lucy and Desi, Eve Arden agreed to a cameo appearance. Her "Our Miss Brooks" show was shot next door on Stage 8. Even director Bill Asher's wife, actress Dani Sue Nolan, played a role in the show, Dayton Lummis' M-G-M secretary.

The episode—a classic in everybody's book, including Lucy's and Jess Oppenheimer's—depicted Lucy Ricardo's first adventure in Tinseltown. Having lunch at the Brown Derby on Vine Street with the Mertzes, Lucy spies handsome Holden dining alone in the adjoining booth. One thing leads to another, with the scene climaxing as Lucy causes a tray carrying desserts (actually a piecrust filled with applesauce) to fall on the movie star. Later, back at their Beverly Palms Hotel suite, Ricky surprises Lucy by bringing Holden home with him after having met the actor at M-G-M that afternoon. In order to disguise herself so Holden will not recognize her, Lucy dons a long putty nose and eyeglasses, and puts her hair up in a kerchief. What follows is sheer comedic brilliance that includes Lucy igniting her nose with a cigarette lighter, then nonchalantly extinguishing the flaming, putty proboscis in a cup of coffee.

Makeup man Hal King had a terrible time getting the right proportion of cement, plastic, and putty for the false nose. "It took me all week," recalls Jess Oppenheimer, "to convince Lucy that her real nose wouldn't catch on fire! We actually placed a candle wick in the nose to ensure Lucy's safety. Still she was nervous all through rehearsals and the final shooting. We all held our breath until the scene was over and in the can."

When the episode aired on February 7, 1955, *Daily Variety* wrote: "The experting gentry that ordained 'they've had it' had best change their thinking. . . . Lucy and Desi . . . will be on long after most of their apers have wondered what hit them." The episode, nominated the following year for an Emmy as "Best Written Comedy Material" resulted in a flood of congratulations from outsiders. The morning after the show aired, Jack

William Holden and Desi Arnaz look alarmed as Lucy's putty nose goes up in flames. Makeup artist Hal King used a candle wick to prevent Lucy's real nose from igniting. This comedy bit is one of Lucille Ball's favorites.

Benny (who would soon become the Arnazes' next-door neighbor after their move to Beverly Hills in May) called to congratulate the couple who, in turn, offered him a guest shot on the show.

Even Sam Goldwyn, Lucy's first Hollywood boss, called to say he had missed the show and could he please have a print to run that night for his house guests. Colleen Moore sent Lucy a telegram: "Your program last night was the funniest I have ever seen anyplace, anywhere, and your scene with the putty nose was so great that it should go down in history. My children, my husband, and I send congratulations to our favorite comedienne and her husband."

M-G-M executives, so pleased with the first Hollywood show, even suggested that Lucy and Desi team with William Holden for their next full-length motion picture, due to start filming in May (although there was no script set).

At first, a filmed tour of Metro was to be featured in a "Lucy" episode. All phases of filmmaking were to be depicted—as well as massive plugs for M-G-M product. *Daily Variety* reported: "Everything Lucy and Ricky do in Hollywood will now involve Metro." A few weeks later, it was reported that Desilu would shoot two episodes on the Culver City lot, "a teaser for the Desi Arnaz–Lucille Ball film to be made for M-G-M. Metro's advertising-publicity chief, Howard Dietz, is trying to get a relaxation of studio dictum

The "I Love Lucy" episode in which fashion designer Don Loper appeared also featured (l. to r.) Mrs. William Holden, Mrs. Richard Carlson, Mrs. Van Heflin, Mrs. Gordon MacRae, Mrs. Dean Martin, and Mrs. Forrest Tucker.

against any of its stars being in telefilms. He'd like to have them included in the 'Lucy' episodes at Metro. Desi's hopeful, but admits that when he tried recently to get some M-G-M starlets for a 'Lucy' he was turned down."

Dore Schary, the M-G-M production chief, was set to play himself in *"Don Juan* Is Shelved," but at the last minute he developed an acute kidney infection and was admitted to Cedars of Lebanon Hospital. Vivian's husband, Phil Ober, stepped into the role. Schary said, "Phil will do a lot better job playing me."

Lucy's longtime friend Hedda Hopper also made a guest appearance that season in "The Hedda Hopper Story." She would also appear in the first hour-long "Lucy" show in 1957. Such bosom buddies were they that upon her death in 1966, Miss Hopper bequeathed her black-and-blue Rolls-Royce to Lucille Ball.

Other big names who guested on the series were Cornel Wilde in "The Star Upstairs." This role was originally written for Van Johnson, but the Warner Brothers star had to back out at the very last minute because he had an endorsement deal with Lucky Strike cigarettes—a rival sponsor—and couldn't do anything in any media for the year's period of his deal. Wilde stepped into Johnson's spot, and worked in a healthy plug for his film *The Big Combo.*

Desi also wanted Ray Bolger, his neighbor at Motion Picture Center, to

appear in "The Dancing Star," but this show was later rewritten for Van Johnson. Desilu asked another studio neighbor, Danny Thomas, to play himself on "Lucy," but, again, sponsor conflict created an impasse (Thomas' show was sponsored by Pall Mall cigarettes). Lucy and Desi successfully arranged to have Harpo Marx play himself in an episode (now considered among the show's top ten episodes).

Also signed to play themselves that season were Richard Widmark and a young (twenty-nine) Universal contract player, Rock Hudson. For Universal, it was the first time they loaned one of their players to a filmed TV series. In the past, they had allowed their stars to do only *live* TV. Desilu's Marty Leeds negotiated the deal for Hudson—which included a generous plug for a Universal film—with Robert Rains, head of the TV-Radio Promotion department at the giant studio.

By April 1955, Nielsen again hailed "Lucy" as the number one television show in the nation, a rank it had enjoyed almost without interruption for three consecutive years. The series also had the longest waiting list for tickets. And if it is true that "imitation is the sincerest form of flattery," then "I Love Lucy" had registered yet another plus: In Puerto Rico, a TV comedy series blossomed that resembled "Lucy" right down to the next-door neighbors.

Entitled "Mapi and Papi," it starred another husband-and-wife acting team, Fernando Cortes and Maria de Pilar Cortes. (Coincidentally, the former appeared with Lucille in the film *Seven Days' Leave.*)

Unfortunately, on March 7, 1955, at the Seventh Annual Emmy Awards ceremony (telecast for the first time by NBC from the Moulin Rouge in Hollywood) "I Love Lucy" won no awards. This was particularly disappointing since the show had garnered a record five nominations. "I Love Lucy" lost to "Make Room for Daddy"; Lucille Ball lost to Loretta Young ("The Loretta Young Show"); Vivian Vance lost to Audrey Meadows ("The Honeymooners"); Bill Frawley lost to Art Carney ("The Honeymooners"); and Jess Oppenheimer, Robert G. Carroll, Jr., and Madelyn Pugh lost to George Gobel's comedy-writing staff.

The following day, Philip Morris announced that it was dropping "I Love Lucy" after the June 27, 1955, telecast. The published reason: "We want to try new concepts in program patterns at lesser cost." Since the beginning of the year, the puffery had been sharing the "Lucy" load with Procter & Gamble, which was hawking its Cheer detergent. Now that the cigarette manufacturer, which had sponsored the series since its inception in the fall of 1951, wanted out, the giant General Foods wanted in.

Roger Greene, then Philip Morris advertising director, said his company was "happy to have had the privilege of bringing to the American public the fine entertainment of the 'I Love Lucy' program these past four years. This program reached the highest audiences ever achieved by any single entertainment vehicle over a sustained period. We wish to thank the stars of the show—Lucille Ball, Desi Arnaz, Vivian Vance, and Bill Frawley. . . ."

Conversely, top admen who were polled claimed that "Lucy" was never considered a smart "buy" for a cigarette company. For General Foods, it was considered a "natural" because women buy food staples out of loyalty, but the same doesn't hold true, according to surveys, for cigarettes.

Just why did Philip Morris pull out when "Lucy" was still the nation's most popular TV show? Some people were quick to point to demographics as the major factor—"Lucy" viewers were not cigarette smokers.

"For some strange reason, no one seems to want to admit the real reasons," says Edward H. Feldman, who was head of Biow's radio and TV departments on the West Coast during that period. " 'Lucy' was selling Philip Morris cigarettes all right, until the Federal Trade Commission forced us to stop using the slogan 'Philip Morris is recognized as being less irritating to the nose and throat by eminent nose and throat doctors.' On top of that, *Reader's Digest* published a 'scare' story in its July 1954 issue warning the public of possible cancer from smoking. This, more than anything, hurt our sales.

"The people that heeded the *Digest* warning switched to Winston, which was one of the first filter-tipped cigarettes on the market," continues Feldman, who joined Desilu in 1955 as vice-president in charge of film commercials. "Then Pall Mall came out with the first king-size cigarette, which also didn't help matters too much. Competition was very strong and it hurt Philip Morris sales to a large extent."

Maurine Christopher, the astute radio and television editor of *Advertising Age,* has her own theories: "My guess is that [Philip Morris] fell down at the merchandising level—that they did not effectively achieve a natural association of the product with the show. Remember how everybody thought of Texaco when they thought of Milton Berle? Or Jack Benny and Jell-O? Or, then again, perhaps the program had its greatest appeal to non- or light-smokers. Hindsight is a great thing but I doubt if I would have signed for two and a half more years of such a 'high ticket' show in 1953. I would have preferred a variety show with an on-screen smoking host—Jackie Gleason, Dean Martin, for example."

When asked how he explained the fact that Philip Morris sales were lagging at a time when it was sponsoring the country's most popular television program, Thomas Christensen, assistant to the advertising director for the cigarette company, said: "I don't believe the show didn't sell. Nobody knows where we would have been if we hadn't had 'I Love Lucy.' And if we had changed our copy story, we might have done better."

Accordingly, in December 1955, Philip Morris, a client of the Biow agency since 1933, moved its $8 million-a-year advertising account to N. W. Ayer and Sons. A few months later, Milton H. Biow, the man who was instrumental in the formulation of "I Love Lucy," announced the closing of his agency.

As for "I Love Lucy," the cancellation by Philip Morris did not hurt in the least. CBS had already ensured the continuation of the series through at least the 1955–56 season. The Hollywood segments were among the highest-rated in the show's history (a rating of 51 was not uncommon). Desi was making plans to star Jack Benny, Bing Crosby, and Burns and Allen in the final Hollywood episodes to be shot and aired in the fall. And by April, Oppenheimer had decided to expand the Ricardos' horizon for the following season—this time taking them to Europe. New scenery, more guest stars, and, it was hoped, a million laughs.

Beginning on Sunday, April 17, 1955, the series had the distinction of being on twice a week. Desi had leased the first fifty-two "I Love Lucy" episodes to the Lehn and Fink Corporation, makers of Dorothy Gray Beauty Preparations, and Hinds, Etiquet, Lysol, for thirty thousand dollars each (six thousand dollars more than each episode originally cost to produce). Retitled "The Lucy Show" (not to be confused with Lucille Ball's 1962 sitcom), the show was slotted in the 6–6:30 P.M. (EST) time period. The deal had particular significance: Since the episodes, starting off with "The Ballet," were first shown during the 1951–52 season; more than twenty-seven new territories had opened to television service and an estimated 23 million new TV sets were in operation. The scheduling on Sunday afternoons also made it possible for every member of the family, particularly youngsters, to see the original programs.

This unique move especially pleased Marion Oring, who was president of

Lucy-Desi Fan Club president Marion Oring presents Mrs. Arnaz with one of the club's bulletins.

the original Lucy-Desi Fan Club. The official organization, sanctioned by Desilu Productions, had only a hundred and fifty members, but they were a loyal crowd. Fan mail continued at a staggering rate—ten thousand letters monthly. Sometimes the mail proved a giant headache. In one batch, for instance, Lucille and Desi received letters from a woman who wanted to sell them her home to finance a major operation; a man who wanted them to adopt his dog's puppies; a mother whose son invented a clothespin for them to manufacture; a maid with stage experience who wanted to be an actress; and several strangers seeking financial assistance. "To get to the point," one such person wrote, "could you lend me ten thousand dollars and write it off your taxes?"

How did Lucy memorize one script per week? "Doing 'Lucy,' we read the script once and we were on our feet," recalls Miss Ball, who never saw a script until the first day of rehearsal, Monday. "We had to learn from forty-five to fifty pages of dialogue in two days, and because we were on our feet with the props, it came easily. The next two days would be camera rehearsals, doing refinements, and getting angles set—then on Thursday night we'd be off like opening night.

"Over the weekend, the whole thing had to be erased mentally because on Monday we'd start with a new one in the same surroundings. I'll admit I've been known to walk on the set and start right in with last week's dialogue. Same set, same people—and the director would yell, 'Cut! That's last week's show.'

" 'I Love Lucy' completely changed my methods of memorizing; as a movie actress, I used to have great trouble remembering lines. Now I have a quicker way, worked out with cooperation from the writers. Everything is cut down to the nub before I get a script," Lucille explained. (Lucy used to be kidded for using what she calls an "alphabetical system" to remember her lines, concentrating on the order of the key verbs.)

One actress who appeared occasionally on the show had a more difficult time with the memorization process. "There were no cue cards used, so a lot of us would write parts of our dialogue on the palms of our hands," she remembers. "One time I recall Lucy and Vivian having a terrible time with a scene in the living room. It ended up that they wrote the difficult parts all over the coffee table. But before the filming began, and while Lucy was in her dressing room getting ready, a stage hand came on the set and sprayed the coffee table with something to cut down the glare from the overhead lights. Naturally, the dialogue was wiped out in the process. But, like all of us, they managed to pull it off all right."

Did Lucy collaborate with her writers on the scripts? "We never really saw them. We never discussed anything with them. We trusted them first and always," Miss Ball says. "All I ever contributed to the lines was what I call 'naturalizing'—twisting a phrase here and there to the way I'd say it—but very seldom. The writers used very graphic descriptions of what they wanted me to do. Some of their names for these expressions were in code. I'd know what they meant when they asked me for the 'Umlaut' look," she says, referring to the German punctuation mark found over certain vowels.

There were code words for each of Lucy's familiar mugs. There was the "Credentials" look (first seen in "The Audition"), where Lucy's mouth would open wide as if to say, "How dare you?" Then there was the often-used "Puddling Up," when Lucy's eyes would fill with tears before breaking into one of her classic wails. "Foiled again" was a popular countenance used when one of her cockamamie schemes went awry; "Light Bulb" referred to an expression that enveloped her face when she had a brainstorm; and then there was the "Spider" look.

Hardly a week went by without "Spider" creeping into a "Lucy" script. That was the writers' way of asking her to re-create a gawkish frown she invented years ago while playing the role of spider in a "My Favorite Husband" radio commercial based on "Little Miss Muffet." To effect it, Lucy's upper lip would raise up and she would make a strange guttural sound. Sometimes it was called "Spider-Combined-with-the-Gobloots-Voice." This was developed in "Lucy Fakes Illness," a first-season show starring Hal March as a phony doctor who tells Lucy she is suffering from "a severe case of the gobloots . . . brought into the country on the hind legs of the boo-shoo bird." After being told of her condition, Lucy stares back at March and says, "I got the gobloots from a boo-shoo bird?" What followed was Lucy's infamous "Spider-Combined-with-the-Gobloots-Voice" look.

"What our key words did," says Jess Oppenheimer, "was remind Lucy to duplicate something she had invented in the past."

Too bad the writers did not remind themselves of what *they* had invented in the past. "I Love Lucy" was filled with factual errors and oversights, points

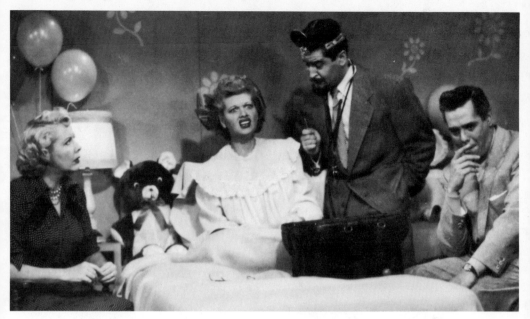

Actor Hal March appeared in this scene from "Lucy Fakes Illness," a 1952 episode where Lucy demonstrates her "Spider" expression, which became an "I Love Lucy" trademark.

that easily could have been corrected. Ethel Mertz's middle name, for example, was Louise in the 1953 episode "Lucy and Ethel Buy the Same Dress," but three months later, on "The Million-Dollar Idea," it had become Roberta (Vivian's real middle name). A year after that, she was Ethel Mae (Vivian's mother's name) in "Ethel's Home Town." (Fred's middle name was always Hobart.)

Similarly, Fred's ex-vaudeville partner was named Ted Kurtz in "The Ballet" and two and a half years later he had become Barney Kurtz. In episodes originally broadcast only a month apart in 1952, Ricky mentioned that he and Lucy had lived in the Mertzes' apartment building for five years, then nine years; and then a few segments later, he gave the exact move-in date, August 6, 1948! By 1954, it had suddenly leaped to twelve years. The longevity of Fred and Ethel's marriage bounced from eighteen to twenty-five years in twelve short months. Then, three years later, while on the *Constitution* sailing to Europe, the pair was celebrating their twenty-fifth wedding anniversary, again.

Amusingly, Ethel Mertz seemed to lose her skills as time went on. In the 1953 episode "The Camping Trip" she was able to drive a car; a year and a half later, she asked Lucy to teach her how to drive. In another instance, Ethel was a fine piano player—she displayed her talent on a number of segments. Suddenly, in 1957, she could hardly get through eight bars of "She'll Be Coming 'Round the Mountain."

The Ricardos' telephone number vacillated back and forth during their five and a half years of living at 623 East Sixty-eighth Street. At one point it was MUrray Hill 5-9975; six months later, CIrcle 7-2099; and two years after that—MUrray Hill 5-9099. (Oppenheimer recalls that the phone company told them what numbers to use to ensure there would be no answer if fans tried calling them, and that's why the numbers changed frequently.)

The one unchanged fact: at the close of the show's fourth year, "I Love Lucy" was again at the top of the Nielsen heap with a 49.3 rating for the season, a full seven points ahead of number two, "The Jackie Gleason Show."

9 Europe or Bust!

"When we wrote our first 'Lucy' show, we worked like the devil on it," recounts the writing team of Bob Schiller and Bob Weiskopf, who joined the "I Love Lucy" staff during the summer of 1955. "We did it so well that when it was filmed, it sounded as if it were unrehearsed. There were laughs everywhere. We surely thought everybody would hail the new writers."

But, alas, critical praise for the writers, as usual, just was not to be, and it didn't help any that this time the jokes appeared to be spontaneous. After the episode in question, "Lucy Visits Grauman's," was aired on October 3, the first review that Schiller and Weiskopf read went as follows: ". . . As always, Miss Ball carried the show. In this one she did a particularly outstanding job, because the writing was so poor. But she saved everything by making up wonderfully funny ad-libs—right on the spot."

Despite the disappointing press, the two Bobs were grateful to be a part of the writing staff of TV's number one show. Although they had teamed two years earlier to write an episode of Danny Thomas' new sitcom, "Make Room for Daddy," their first *multiple* script assignment together was the Eddie Mayehoff vehicle "That's My Boy!" for George Burns's MacCadden Productions and CBS (April 1954 to January 1955). When it was canceled, the pair moved over to "Professional Father," logging a six-month stint. And then the pivotal assignment that led directly to their "Lucy" job. During the spring of 1955, the boys signed to write the first six episodes of CBS's new Janis Paige series, "It's Always Jan," shooting at Motion Picture Center. They soon became disenchanted by the producer's reluctance to sign a full-season commitment. One day in early April while strolling along a studio street, they ran into Jess Oppenheimer, who had been a friend since before the war (at one time, Oppenheimer and Weiskopf had been roommates).

The pair indicated their growing dissatisfaction with the Paige deal, and Jess volunteered that he was looking to bring in some "new blood" to help with "I Love Lucy." The job would start in late summer, giving Schiller and Weiskopf time to complete their Paige assignments.

While the new blood was about to enter the inner sanctum, one key staffer was about to leave the fold: Bill Asher, who directed Episodes #39 to #127, including such classics as "Job Switching," the baby shows, "L.A. at Last!" and the Harpo Marx episode. "I left the show because I felt I had no creative growth anymore. I was very frustrated, even though all the 'Hollywood shows' were fun to do. Also there was enough dissension on the stage that I just didn't enjoy coming to work. The company had me under contract, of course, but I went to Desi, who was always so fair, and told him the show

was running great and that I had to go away and do something for me."
On April 18—just four days after Asher finished his last "Lucy" episode,
"The Tour" with Richard Widmark—he joined actress Jane Wyman as co-
producer of her "Fireside Theatre," which would debut on NBC in August.

Before Asher departed, however, he acted as instructor to writer-director
James V. Kern, a forty-six-year-old Fordham University law school graduate
who had once been a member of the Yacht Club Boys, a singing group. A
screenwriter with twenty-five movie scripts to his credit, Kern had been
signed that spring by Desilu to direct its new series, "Those Whiting Girls,"
which was created by Bob Carroll, Jr., and Madelyn Pugh to replace "I Love
Lucy" for the summer months. While Kern had a good deal of directorial
experience both in film and television, he was not familiar with the unique
Desilu three-camera technique. Despite the success of the method, still only
Desilu Productions was using it. Asher taught Kern the basics before relocating
to Republic Studios in Studio City to helm the Wyman dramatic series. Bill
would not be the only staffer to leave Desilu.

"I had just returned from my vacation in Hawaii," says costume designer
Elois Jenssen. "Earlier that summer, as we went on hiatus, I put in for a
raise. So I phoned Andy Hickox, who was Lucy and Desi's business manager
and one of the vice-presidents of Desilu Productions. I asked if my increase
had been approved. He said no. I asked Andy, in whom I had a great deal
of faith—he helped me establish the first Desilu wardrobe department—what
I should do.

"He suggested I hold out for the two-hundred-dollars-a-week salary. He
said, 'Don't worry, they'll call you at the last minute.' Well, Tuesday rolled
around and Lucy didn't call. Instead, Madame Sara, who executed my
designs with her two seamstresses, phoned, and in a perturbed voice, said:
'Guess who's here? Eddie Stevenson.' Stevenson was another costume
designer and a close personal friend.

"I drove over to the studio and sure enough—Eddie was already on the
scene. I sought out Lucy on Stage 9 and she said, 'What happened?' I told
her that Marty Leeds [executive vice-president of Desilu Productions] wouldn't
okay my raise. Lucy and I both started crying, and to this day I still can't
understand why I was dismissed because Eddie started out with the same
salary that I had requested," Elois confirms.

By 1955, Desilu had become a complex operation with many officers
responsible for the day-to-day operations of a studio that was producing as
much film as one of the town's major motion picture studios. Where Lucy
had personally sought out some staffers when the show started (Hal King,
her personal makeup man; Della Fox, her wardrobe mistress; and Elois
Jenssen), by now the hiring and firing were the responsibilities of others in
her and Desi's employ. So it wasn't surprising that despite Elois Jenssen's
conscientiousness, she suddenly found herself out of a job. Besides designing
and supervising the construction of Lucy's clothes for "I Love Lucy," she
had also designed much of the redhead's personal wardrobe, including the

clothes she wore for publicity pictures shot in connection with the many product endorsements the Arnazes made. She even designed Desi's racing silks when he bought his first racehorse.

That summer, she dutifully saved Desilu almost fifteen thousand dollars on the costume budget of Lucy and Desi's second comedy film for M-G-M, *Forever, Darling*. "Because I had ample time to plan the wardrobe for that movie, I was able to order exclusive fabrics directly from European sources. We also worked on the costumes all spring if our weekly 'I Love Lucy' costume load was light," confirms Miss Jenssen, who was nominated in 1983 for an Oscar for the Disney film *Tron* and is currently writing a much-needed textbook on costume design.

The Arnazes did appear in *Forever, Darling*, but unlike *The Long, Long Trailer*, which was produced *and* distributed by Metro-Goldwyn-Mayer, *Darling* was produced by Zanra (Arnaz spelled backward) Productions at the Motion Picture Center lot—home since the fall of 1953 of Desilu and "I Love Lucy."

Production on the $1.4 million feature began June 14, 1955, with a staff made up principally of "Lucy" workers. Desi himself produced the film with an able assist from Jerry Thorpe (on summer vacation from his "December Bride" chores); Jack Aldworth was the assistant director; Dann Cahn and Bud Molin handled the film editing assignment; Ralph Berger was art director; and Cameron McCulloch took care of sound. And, of course, Elois Jenssen designed the film's many beautiful costumes, including a lavish wedding gown, although these would be the last clothes she would create for Miss Ball.

Jenssen's replacement, Eddie Stevenson, was Lucy's old friend. He had designed costumes for fourteen of the redhead's RKO pictures, including *Too Many Girls, Five Came Back,* and *Dance, Girl, Dance.* She was not aware, however, when she went to look for him to take over the designing chores on "Lucy" that he had been forced into semi-retirement two years earlier (at age forty-seven) because of failing eyesight. Stevenson was anxious to work again and happily accepted the Desilu post at a starting salary of two hundred dollars per week. He would remain in Miss Ball's employ until his sudden death in 1968.

It was back to work on Tuesday, September 6, 1955, to begin rehearsals on Episode #128, "Lucy Visits Grauman's." Although Desi toyed with the idea of directing "I Love Lucy" in its fifth season, he rightfully decided he had enough to do—running Desilu, co-starring in "Lucy," etc.—so he appointed Jim Kern (at a starting salary of seven hundred and fifty dollars per week) to take over where Bill Asher left off in April. Kern spent the summer directing thirteen episodes of "Those Whiting Girls" sitcom starring Barbara and Margaret Whiting, Mabel Albertson, and a young actor named Jerry Paris.

But it was the next episode that cast and crew would remember for a long time. A few months earlier, John Wayne had agreed to appear in a "Lucy"

Lucy and Vivian pose backstage with John Wayne, September 15, 1955.

show, and Jess and the writers decided to make it a two-parter, although Wayne would appear only in Part Two, to be titled appropriately "Lucy and John Wayne." Wayne's fee for appearing—scale (two hundred and eighty dollars)—but the true value was tied up in incessant plugs for his new film, *Blood Alley.* The filming on the night of September 15 went smoothly except for one short scene.

The sequence called for Ricky, Jr., played by Mike Mayer, to get on his hands and knees and obliterate John Wayne's autograph and cowboy-boot prints in a slab of fresh cement. The three-year-old refused to do it.

"I couldn't understand it," said an assistant director. "I thought all kids loved to dabble in wet cement. Have you ever seen a new sidewalk that doesn't have some child's trademark in it someplace?

"But Mike stubbornly refused to do it. Lucy and I got on our hands and knees, trying to cajole him, even bribing him with candy. But he wouldn't budge."

Mrs. Mayer came to the rescue. With a mother's knack for deciphering the mutterings of her own child, she discovered that Mike didn't want to spoil his new red shoes. "They were the first pair of low shoes he'd ever had and he was proud of them," she said. Miss Ball promised to buy Mike another pair. Finally the boy was convinced. But it took an hour and a half of expensive overtime to get a shot that lasted only five seconds on the screen.

Mike's twin brother Joe had his moments too. One night he started to cry in the middle of a scene, a joyous party sequence. There was a big cake. Joe was supposed to be led off to bed. But he balked, struggled, and began to wail. "He was having fun and didn't want to leave the 'party,'" said Lucy. "So we let him stay and ad-libbed around the situation."

Desi recalls, "Whether we used Mike or Joe on the show depended entirely on the boys' dispositions at the moment. If, for instance, Mike started to fret and cry, then Joe, wearing similar wardrobe, was brought from an adjoining sound stage to play the part."

Lucy always had a hard time telling the pair apart. After filming "The Great Train Robbery," in which Ricky, Jr., appeared in two separate scenes aboard a train carrying the Ricardos and Mertzes home to New York from Hollywood, Lucy turned to the twins' mother: "Mike did a wonderful job tonight."

"That wasn't only Mike," smiled Mrs. Mayer. "It was Joe, too. They each did one sequence."

Just before the new season got underway, a bombshell announcement: Jess Oppenheimer had signed a five-year contract with NBC. Although his resignation would not take effect until the following spring, reaction was immediate. Jess was earning about twenty-five hundred dollars a week as "Lucy" producer and head writer as his seven-year contract with CBS came to a close. Renegotiating his deal with Desilu and the network proved fruitless, so the multitalented Oppenheimer decided to take a plum position in the rival network's West Coast programming department. Because Jess's contract stipulated that he had created the character of Lucy, he received a royalty for whatever she did using that character. This, of course, included three seasons of the hour-long shows and even guest appearances Lucy made with Danny Thomas and Ann Sothern because, on them, she played Lucy Ricardo. (Jess was the only person not to sell his percentage when CBS negotiated with Desilu for the purchase of the 179 "Lucy" episodes in 1957; in the intervening years, he has earned additional royalties in seven figures.)

As soon as the Oppenheimer decision was made public on September 26, 1955, rumors abounded about the demise of "I Love Lucy." These were firmly spiked in print by Desi: "I hate to see Jess go, but his leaving won't interfere in the slightest with whatever plans we make for the show. Personally, I would like to expand 'Lucy' to a full hour every week, maybe even in color, using big-name guest stars—say, three weeks out of four—to help Lucy and me carry the load. But we'd still appear in every show. Of course, this is just my own plan and will have to be concurred in by both CBS and the sponsors. We are working on that right now. CBS, you see, has an option on 'Lucy' for 1956–57. Sure, we'll miss Jess," Desi concluded. "But who knows? By next spring Desilu might buy NBC, and we'd be back together again!"

In the meantime, NBC was the competition. And the competition was trying desperately to displace "I Love Lucy" from its lofty perch in the

Nielsens. Bucking the October 3, 1955, fifth-season premiere episode of "Lucy" ("Lucy Visits Grauman's") was NBC's "Medic," a powerfully dramatic half-hour series starring Richard Boone as Dr. Konrad Styner. NBC pitted the second part of "And There Was Darkness and There Was Light," the "Medic" show about childbirth, against the perennial winner, "I Love Lucy," hoping that viewers who caught the first part on September 26 would not want to miss the climax the following Monday night at nine o'clock. It was a good and valiant try on NBC's part, but it didn't work. "I Love Lucy" was still number one, racking up a Nielsen rating of 42.7, which translated into a 61 percent share of the viewing audience.

Overseas, the British in 1955 loved "Lucy" second only to their favorite BBC broadcast. "Lucy" had a phenomenal rating of 94 in England by the end of the year. The show had become a way of life all over the world.

Jerry N. Jordan said in 1954 in an annual report of the sports committee of the Radio-Electronics Manufacturers Association: "The novelty effect of TV is over, and although television does compete with other forms of entertainment and recreation, it does so because it is good entertainment, not because it is free. Fifty million people staying home to watch 'I Love Lucy' is tougher competition for any sport than the telecast of the sport itself."

Following filming of "Ricky Sells the Car" on September 29, Desi took the "red eye" to New York for meetings with the CBS brass. William S. Paley, chairman of the board, played host to Arnaz and key network officials like corporate president Frank Stanton, CBS-TV president Jack Van Volkenburg, and CBS-TV vice-president Hubbell Robinson at a two-day session that included an important discussion of Desilu's future. Ironically, it was Desi who assured Paley and company that Jess Oppenheimer's anticipated departure would have no negative effects on "I Love Lucy." Just four years earlier—as "Lucy" was being prepared for production in 1951—Paley had made no bones about his feelings that Desi should not be involved in Lucille Ball's television program.

As president of Desilu Productions, Arnaz briefed the network bigwigs on the company's various CBS projects, which included "Our Miss Brooks," "December Bride," "Lineup," "It's Always Jan," and, of course, "I Love Lucy." Desi dutifully described how the season would begin with a smashing two-parter set in Hollywood ("Grauman's" and "John Wayne" episodes), then continue as the Ricardos and Mertzes train back to New York and get ready for their big trip to Europe. He explained that plans to star Jack Benny, Burns and Allen, and Bing Crosby in fall "Lucy" episodes had not panned out, but he was hoping to line up some major celebrities like Maurice Chevalier for the European segments.

The summer months had found Bob Carroll, Jr., Madelyn Pugh, Jess Oppenheimer, Bob Schiller, and Bob Weiskopf busy writing a new batch of scripts. Veteran world-travelers, Bob (Carroll) and Madelyn were able to draw upon their own experiences as they helped concoct this new theme. Ricky would be booked with his Latin band in various European cities like London, Paris, and Rome. The expanded craft departments at Desilu (costume, sets, property, etc.) could surely provide the many trappings necessary to simulate Europe.

Jerry Miggins, who joined Desilu's prop department in 1955, was a twenty-three-year veteran of M-G-M's halcyon days, having worked with such stars as Joan Crawford, Mickey Rooney, young Jackie Cooper, Norma Shearer, and Lucille Ball. Jerry Thorpe, another M-G-M alumnus and now resident director on "December Bride," brought over property master Dick Henrickson a year earlier. It was Henrickson who talked Miggins into leaving his Culver City job for Desilu.

"If the script called for, say, outdoor French café furniture," Miggins explains, "I would go to the prop and furniture suppliers like Cinema Mercantile or First Street Furniture and select the stuff we needed. We had weekly contracts with these dealers, paying them several hundred dollars a week [seven hundred and fifty dollars] for everything necessary to the script. They had enormous selections, so very rarely would you see the same things twice. Doing the European shows was a lot more challenging, of course, than the episodes set in the New York apartment. One of my favorite assignments was putting together the wine vat and surroundings for Lucy's grape fight."

Desi's September trip to New York included a brief session with Desilu's New York chieftain Ed Hamilton. Desi wanted him to explore the possibility of getting a steamship company to help underwrite the added expense of set construction in connection with the make-believe transatlantic voyage the Ricardos and Mertzes would be taking. In return, of course, the name of a specific ship would be mentioned and depicted on "I Love Lucy." A year earlier, General Motors (Pontiac division) had jumped at the chance to tie in with the nation's number one television show at a promotional cost of fifty thousand dollars and five new Pontiac convertibles.

Hamilton approached several lines, both domestic and foreign, with the notion. The tie-in would cost the consenting firm thirty thousand dollars. That deal found no takers. Then, with a new twenty-thousand-dollar price tag, the proposal moved on to American Export Lines, operator of luxury liners to the Mediterranean, including the 23,750-ton *Constitution*.

"I had a heck of a time selling the idea to my company," maintains Allison S. Graham, one-time publicity director of American Export Lines. "The people in the shipping business are traditionally conservative in their approach to public relations, thinking in terms of pennies where many large-scale enterprises plan with dollars. What really surprised us most of all was the idea of rich Hollywood seeking financial aid from a steamship line."

The following are excerpts from Allison Graham's diary [A.E.L.-American Export Lines; A.S.G.-Allison S. Graham]:

American Export Lines dispatched Allison S. Graham, director of publicity, to Hollywood to oversee production on two "I Love Lucy" episodes set aboard the Constitution.

Friday, Oct. 28, 1955: Mr. Ed Hamilton (Desilu Productions, 551 Fifth Avenue, N.Y.C.) submitted proposal calling for two show tie-ins with A.E.L., *Independence* or *Constitution*. Cost to A.E.L.—$20,000 toward set cost. No passage on ships requested in addition . . . A.S.G. checked with William H. McConnell, vice-president of A.E.L. Passenger Traffic, for opinion. Told him I liked it. McConnell called later to say his conferees voted no.

Monday, Oct. 31, 1955: McConnell said further discussion of subject with his staff rendered negative decision on Desilu for $20,000, but will consider $12,000 for two shows.

Tuesday, Nov. 1, 1955: McConnell reaction again unfavorable upon viewing last night's "I Love Lucy" show ["The Great Train Robbery"]. I told him that Hamilton had now proposed four shows for $12,000 and I favored more strongly than ever, because of enormous national audience exposure. McConnell did not close off definitely but suggested his top assistants meet with me to prepare a list of "musts" that A.E.L. would want to be included.

Monday, Nov. 7, 1955: Hamilton requested immediate decision. Said Desilu-Hollywood had advised first mention in program would be Dec. 19 and that program would continue through mid-January 1956. McConnell did not render decision, so I went to John Gehan, executive vice-president

. . . He requested McConnell to meet with him and me at once in his office. Gehan acted at once:

a. Authorized $12,000 tie-in with Desilu
b. Authorized sending necessary support to Hollywood
   to guide construction of ship sets
c. Travel expenses for A.S.G. to Hollywood
d. Charge all to PR Institutional Advertising

I passed this news to Hamilton and sent him the same day an assortment of about 50 color transparencies and 50 B&W prints to illustrate various features of the ship of possible interest to set designer.

Tuesday, Nov. 22, 1955: Dann Cahn, Desilu's film editor, flew from L.A. to N.Y.C. to visit and inspect Pier 84 with Port Captain, Pier Superintendent, and me . . . Hamilton phoned to request we send ten deck chairs, steward's sleeve insignia, officer's cap insignia, dinner menus, "Boat 'n' Bottle Bar" napkins and drink stirrers, blankets with special *Constitution* logo, life preservers, mess jackets, etc., air express, as soon as possible, to Jack Aldworth, Desilu Productions, 846 No. Cahuenga Blvd., Hollywood 38, California.

Lucy and Desi celebrate their fifteenth wedding anniversary on November 30, 1955, on the set of "Bon Voyage," Episode #140 of "I Love Lucy."

It took ninety-three people to put on the average "I Love Lucy" episode. Here many of them pose for a cast-and-crew photo after filming "Bon Voyage" on December 1, 1955.

Wednesday, Nov. 30, 1955: Hamilton says studio anxious to have me check sets for authenticity. Told him I was boarding American Airlines Mercury this afternoon . . . Arrived in L.A., checked into Hollywood Roosevelt Hotel opposite Grauman's Chinese Theatre.

Thursday, Dec. 1, 1955: On set 9 A.M. Aldworth requested I stay all day through shooting and at least until Dec. 8 [date of "Second Honeymoon" episode filming]. Said this was "the most complicated technical production in five years of shooting the series" . . . I was impressed with the cooperative spirit evident among the entire staff and found all very professional and very pleasant.

After telecast of the two "Lucy" episodes set aboard the *Constitution*—January 16 and 23, 1956—the series was the subject of wide comment at downtown New York maritime clubs, the India House, and the Whitehall Club. "The heads of American Export were very surprised at the unbelievable response to the show," recalls Al Graham, a company employee since 1940, now retired. "I attended a luncheon meeting of the American Merchant Marine Institute public relations committee on February 7 of that year. My industry colleagues were high in praise of the shows, although several reported certain executives of their respective companies were not enthused."

Lucille Ball rehearses on the mock-up of the Constitution *gangplank built on Stage 9 at Motion Picture Center. American Export Lines contributed twelve thousand dollars toward the cost of set construction.*

The New York *Times* reported: "American Export Lines voted itself the brightest steamship company of the year for doing a promotional job that was worth several times what it cost. . . .

"Other ship line officials either munched tart grapes or said the whole thing was silly. They pointed out that by law no one can land on a ship by helicopter [a scene from "Bon Voyage"]. And, in any case, no one ever gets halfway through a porthole, finding the shoulders too large to go back and the hips unable to continue through [sequence from "Second Honeymoon"]."

So authentic were these two "Lucy" episodes that a British company, after viewing "Bon Voyage," cabled Desilu asking when the *Constitution* was arriving in Southampton. (The *Constitution* sailed nowhere near England, Lucy's fictional destination.) In Washington, Federal Maritime Board officials liked the shows so well they asked for and got copies of the films to help promote the Merchant Marine.

As 1955 came to a close, it was clear that business at Desilu was burgeoning, with no sign of slowing down. During the year, its various corporations paid out $5 million in salaries alone to 3,300 people. The product: 295 half-hour TV shows (of which 26 were "I Love Lucy" 's), 1 ninety-minute television "spectacular" ("High Tor"), and 1 theatrical feature, *Forever, Darling*. Desi

Arnaz already had clearly developed into a top-flight executive, a television tycoon.

A CBS lawyer describes the tycoon's big plan when trying to make his first capital-gains deal: "Lucy and Desi would sell five years of 'I Love Lucy' episodes to CBS and buy back a 25 percent interest in Desilu Productions, which they already had sold to CBS in 1952 for $1 million.

"Desi was asking $4 million plus for the 'Lucy' shows in the can [153 of them]—and other less important properties [like "December Bride"]—but he was unwilling to pay more than $1 million to buy back the 25 percent CBS interest in Desilu. He kept raising the price on the reruns and each time he did we escalated the price he would have to pay to buy back the 25 percent. He was determined to keep CBS from profiting on its Desilu investment. Paley wouldn't let him get away with it. But Desi was always in there plugging away and he generally got most of what he wanted."

In the meantime, Desi and his business associates had to deal with the increasing salary demands of Vivian Vance and William Frawley. Their respective agents made it clear—always at negotiation time—that their clients were responsible to a large degree for the continuing success of the television series. Vivian's agent always threatened that his client would have another nervous breakdown or retire from show business completely if she didn't receive more money. At the start of the 1956–57 season, each was earning two thousand dollars per week, six times more than either received when they started in 1951.

Vivian Vance as Ethel Mertz.

Truth is, Vivian Vance spent a considerable part of her nine "I Love Lucy" years in psychoanalysis. She once said, "I'd go from the couch to the studio every morning." According to those who worked with her, she was never visibly upset, nor did her personal dilemma affect her performance. In fact, Vivian credits the years in "Lucy" with a therapeutic effect second only to the analysis itself.

If Bill Frawley had personal problems, he managed to conceal them successfully from his "Lucy" cohorts, except perhaps his penchant for betting on the horses. He was highly regarded by the "Lucy" crew, especially for his easygoing manner. He bothered no one, did his job—although he would fall asleep during rehearsals frequently—and, in his own words, "took the money and ran."

A senior member of the sound crew remembers Frawley's outspokenness: "When he was around young ladies, he was like Lord Chesterfield, courtly to his fingertips. In the presence of men, he was a no-holds-barred critic of whatever he didn't happen to like, which was just about everything and everybody. He would say anything to anyone, in language as colorful as it was profane, and the general rule on the 'Lucy' set was that he never be allowed near a newspaperman without a chaperone. If Bill's off-the-record stories had ever gotten on the record, half of Hollywood would've quietly committed suicide."

Frawley was a familiar figure at Hollywood sporting events. He was a racehorse owner, a stockholder in the old Hollywood Stars baseball team in the Pacific Coast League, and a member of the advisory board of the American League California Angels.

Of the twenty-six new "Lucy" segments produced during the fifth season, seventeen half-hours were devoted to the European trip (the season opened with the Ricardos and Mertzes still in Hollywood and that required five episodes to conclude the story line).

Among the most difficult to produce (assistant director Jack Aldworth called it "the most complicated technical production in five years of shooting the series") was "Bon Voyage," in which Lucy missed the ship, tried unsuccessfully to catch a "pilot boat" to overtake the swift liner, donned a descent harness, then finally was lowered from a helicopter onto the deck of the *Constitution*. Aside from the elaborate sets installed on Stage 9 at Motion Picture Center that duplicated certain parts of the *Constitution* (the deck, a stateroom, and the "Boat 'n' Bottle Bar," plus the dock and gangplank areas), a "second unit" film crew (film editor Dann Cahn, a Desilu cameraman, and others) was dispatched to New York on November 22 to capture actual footage of Pier 84 where the *Constitution* was set to dock on November 28. Arrangements were even made to have the ship dock on the north side of the pier instead of its usual berth on the south side. This was to accommodate Desilu's scenic-design department, which had already built the sets in Hollywood based on a north-side docking. Special permission from the Civil Aeronautics Board also was required to allow Desilu to photograph the *Constitution* close up from an overhead helicopter. These film sequences were later integrated into the "I Love Lucy" footage shot the night of December 1, 1955, by film editor Bud Molin. It was a complicated thirty-minute episode that took a great deal longer to shoot that evening than the usual one hour. However, it was not the first time that problems "beyond our control" caused upsets.

"One night, while our studio audience was waiting out on the sidewalk to come in," recalls Jess Oppenheimer, "a ham radio operator's unfiltered signal was being picked up loud and clear on our audio system. We didn't know what to do. And even if the operator stopped briefly, there was no guarantee that he would not begin again before our show finished filming, and any radio interference would have wrecked the show.

"Our music composer, Eliot Daniel, happened also to be a licensed ham radio operator and had a printed log of his compatriots handy. We traced the man's call letters to an address in New Jersey. We got the telephone number from Information and called. The person who answered explained that the radio aficionado was on vacation in Los Angeles and supplied us with the phone number of the traveler's local friend. We put in a frantic call and finally reached the radio operator, who promised he would cease broadcasting for the rest of the night so we could film 'I Love Lucy.' "

A European episode that would require four entirely new sets—a hotel room, an outdoor café, a Parisian street, and the inside of a French police station—was "Paris at Last." The large cast of supporting characters included three familiar faces: Larry Dobkin, who played the French counterfeiter; Shepard Menken, who played the artist; and Maurice Marsac, who played the waiter. Each actor had appeared in previous "I Love Lucy" episodes and was familiar with the demanding work schedule. The scenic-design and prop departments also worked overtime to create the proper Parisian atmosphere.

Desi and Lucy pose backstage before filming a scene from "The Fox Hunt" on December 22, 1955.

For the Charles Boyer show, propman Jerry Miggins recalls: "The script called for a 'rigged' pen, one that would squirt ink on Mr. Boyer's shirt. To get the effect the writers wanted, I knew that an ordinary fountain pen would not do. The best it could do was send out one stream of ink, not the quantity that Lucy was supposed to spray on him. So I went to the Bert Wheeler Magic Shop on Hollywood Boulevard and bought a trick pen with a rubber bulb at the end. At first, everyone said it wouldn't work because you couldn't hide the bulb. But I showed Lucy how it could be done and she did fine.

"The pen bit caused another problem. Mr. Boyer refused to have his own suit and shirt ruined, and Desilu wasn't supplying the wardrobe. In fact, the rumpled raincoat that gets ripped to shreds later in the scene was actually one of Desi's old coats. I went back to the magic shop and purchased a bottle of disappearing ink. Boyer didn't think it really worked, so I had to prove it by spraying my own shirt with the phony ink. Only after he was totally convinced the ink would not damage his shirt, did he agree to do the scene as written. That was a hectic show for me. I even had to supply the sound of the raincoat tearing and the sound of Boyer's head hitting the door as he exits."

A cute half-hour set in Switzerland followed. The Ricardos and Mertzes take refuge from a snowstorm in a tiny Alp-top cabin when suddenly there's an avalanche. They are hopelessly trapped; there's no food, except for a cheese sandwich Lucy squirreled away earlier. "People used to ask me," remembers Jess Oppenheimer, "whether Lucille Ball was funny in 'real life.' And I had to tell them no. However, she could come up with things that were remarkable in their ability to evoke laughs. For instance, in the 'Swiss Alps' show, there was a little moment where she gingerly picks up crumbs from her sandwich with her index finger. It was a short bit, but truly inspired— and all Lucy's. She was good about her own character; she had the ability to throw in little, universally humorous things. She was right on the taproots of humanness, if I can coin a phrase."

"Lucy in the Swiss Alps" was not one of the stronger "Lucy" shows. It had its moments but it isn't likely to appear on anyone's list of Ten Favorite Episodes of "I Love Lucy." There were other European-based shows that would not exactly have won awards—shows like "Lucy's Bicycle Trip" and "Lucy Goes to Monte Carlo," to name two. Although there were now five writers turning out "Lucy" scripts, it was still a yeoman's task coming up with good material week after week, especially after the show had been on the air four years. Oppenheimer recalls one script that just didn't work after a Monday-morning reading. "We decided the basic premise was still good, but that the material was lacking. So we stayed up all night and rewrote the entire show, every scene. We were always prepared to do anything necessary, including working all night, for the good of the show."

One episode set in Europe that needed no fixing, or "punching up" as it's known in the comedy business, was "Lucy's Italian Movie." Set in Rome, the tale dealt with Lucy's foreign-movie fling when she was offered a part in *Bitter Grapes*, the new Vittorio Fellipi film. In order to get in the right mood for her role, Lucy visits Turo, a fictional town renowned for its wine vineyards and old-fashioned wine-making methods on the outskirts of Rome. There, while "soaking up local color," she becomes embroiled in the ancient art of wine making in a huge, grape-filled vat.

"We made that vat out of metal," says Jerry Miggins, Desilu propman *extraordinaire*. "But our biggest concern was that Lucy not get hurt during the fight scene with Teresa Tirelli, the real grape-stomper from the Napa Valley in Northern California. At first someone suggested lining the bottom of the vat with mattresses to cushion her fall, but then we reasoned that a soaked-through mattress would eventually become as hard as a rock. We finally decided on a rubberized form of horsehair, which worked fine."

The scene in which Lucy climbs into the giant bin with the seasoned wine crusher was nothing short of side-splitting. In fact, the show remains one of Lucille Ball's favorite "Lucy" episodes. Just how did the five writers dream up this classic show? Did they start their brainstorming session with the statement, "Let's do a show where Lucy winds up in a vat of grapes"?

"Absolutely not," producer and head writer Jess Oppenheimer claims. "It was a logical development of the basic premise. We knew that the Ricardos and Mertzes were going through Italy. When we got to the subject of Italian movies—how 'earthy' they were—we thought it might be funny to have

Lucy be in one. [At one point, Desi wanted Anna Magnani for the proposed episode.] But, of course, how do we get her into an Italian movie? Then we got the idea that an Italian movie producer sees her on the train; he offers her a role.

"Then we had to figure out how Lucy could get in the 'mood' for an Italian movie role, get some experience. I think there was a discussion about wine making, too. Then one of us suggested it would be funny if Lucy was stomping grapes with her feet. I remember also that we had a large problem with the fact that she'd be unable to understand Italian, and vice versa, and we made a couple of attempts based on her inability to understand, but then we decided to use the subtitles.

"Then we thought about those things which are stereotypically Italian and tried to work them in. I recall one thing we wrote which Lucy couldn't do. She was standing on the hot pavement and she couldn't do the natural thing of standing on one foot as long as you can stand it, then switching over to the other foot and hopping back and forth. She tried this bit, but, for some reason, couldn't cut it, which was very unusual for her. She always did everything we wrote, without question."

Even the wine industry, when asked to supply the grapes (which they did, by the truckload), got into the act. They insisted the writers put in something about the fact that wine wasn't made in such a primitive fashion any longer. So the writers dutifully wrote dialogue between the Ricardos and the bellboy at the Rome hotel which explained that Turo was the only place where wine was still being made the "old way."

Propman Miggins recalls another problem that week: "Because Lucy's hair was so sensitive to dye, we had to find something to make her hair and face purple for the tag scene in the hotel room when she comes back from 'soaking up' the 'local color.' We tried everything, but Lucy was allergic to most everything. At the last minute, we came up with a pale orchid, water-soluble makeup—one gallon of it to five gallons of water."

Interestingly, the most hilarious scene in the show—Lucy's fight with Teresa Tirelli—was not in the original script, which read as follows:

LUCY FOLLOWS HER TO THE VAT. LUCY LOOKS OVER THE EDGE AND SEES WHAT SHE'S DOING AND LOOKS SQUEAMISH. THE WOMAN INDICATES WITH A WAVE OF HER ARM TO COME ON. LUCY CAUTIOUSLY CLIMBS IN AND GINGERLY PUTS HER FOOT ON THE GRAPES. HER FACE REFLECTS THAT THIS IS A VERY WEIRD SENSATION. THE ITALIAN WOMAN IS STOMPING VIGOROUSLY, AND LUCY LOOKS LIKE SHE IS WALKING ON EGGS. THE WOMAN REACTS TO LUCY'S DELICATE AIR, STOPS AND ILLUSTRATES FOR LUCY BY STOMPING HARD. LUCY, GETTING THE IDEA, GOES AT IT WITH FULLER ENTHUSIASM, LIKE A RUNNER RUNNING IN PLACE. SHE BEGINS TO ENJOY THIS, AND STARTS RUNNING AROUND THE VAT, THEN TRIES TRICK STEPS LIKE A BALLET DANCER OR PERHAPS LIKE A PERSON WITH ONE LEG SHORTER THAN

THE OTHER, ETC. LUCY REACHES UP TO CHECK HER EARRING, WHICH
IS LOOSE, TIGHTENS IT, THEN CHECKS THE OTHER EAR AND FINDS
THAT HER EARRING IS MISSING. SHE LOOKS ALARMED AND REALIZES
IT'S DOWN IN THE GRAPES. SHE STARTS FEELING AROUND WITH ONE
FOOT TRYING TO FIND THE EARRING. THE OTHER WOMAN NOTICES
THAT SHE ISN'T WORKING, COMES OVER AND NUDGES HER AND
INDICATES THAT SHE SHOULD KEEP STOMPING. THE WOMAN STARTS
STOMPING TO SHOW LUCY. SHE SUDDENLY GETS A PAINED EXPRES-
SION AS SHE STEPS ON THE EARRING. SHE HOPS UP AND DOWN
HOLDING HER FOOT. LUCY QUICKLY TAKES OFF THE OTHER EARRING
AND THROWS IT AWAY. SHE STARTS STOMPING AWAY AS WE FADE
OUT.

"What was actually done," reveals Jess Oppenheimer, "was probably
developed on the set during rehearsals with director Jim Kern. I really can't
recall at what point the new business about the fight was created. It may
have been that the writers and I saw the first dress rehearsal and felt that
the scene needed more, that it didn't quite build up to a big enough height,
comedically, or it may have been that the actors just improvised that
wonderfully marvelous scene. The actors were absolutely free to do whatever
they wanted and then if I came down to the stage and agreed, it stayed in.
If I didn't agree, then we had a long discussion about it."

Like the episode "Job Switching," shot nearly four years earlier, this
segment employed the services of a non-professional actor. Teresa Tirelli,
the Italian grape-stomper, was not an actress and spoke little English.
Therefore, it was not always easy to explain direction. Lucy, as always,
wanted the fight scene to be as realistic as possible, but, on the night of the
filming, March 8, 1956, she had no idea that Miss Tirelli would suddenly
become a "Method" actress, determined to make the fight scene a brawling
classic. Lucille Ball explains: "I didn't want the scene to be a little tug-of-
war. I wanted it to look as real as possible. But since we hadn't worked with
the grapes in the vat during rehearsals, I had no idea what I was in store
for. Once the fight started, the lady was bent on drowning me. At one point,
she literally held my head under water, and I had to fight to get my breath
back. A lot of that was edited out of the final print. Looking back, of course,
I'm glad it happened that way because the scene was so good."

At the Eighth Annual Emmy Awards ceremony on March 17, 1956, held
at the Pan Pacific Auditorium on Beverly Boulevard near CBS Television
City (telecast over NBC), Lucille Ball copped the statuette for "Best Actress—
Continuing Performance," beating out the likes of Gracie Allen, Eve Arden,
Jean Hagen, and Ann Sothern. She and Desi were out of town so Madelyn
Pugh accepted the award in her behalf. It was the first year since the series
debuted that "I Love Lucy" was not nominated as "Best Comedy Series."
However, William Frawley received his third nomination for the Fred Mertz
supporting role, while his TV wife, Vivian Vance, was not nominated at all.

In another category, Lucille Ball lost as "Best Comedienne" to Nanette Fabray ("Caesar's Hour"); and the "Lucy" writers, hailed for their "L.A. at Last!" teleplay (aka "Bill Holden") lost to the "You'll Never Get Rich" (aka "Bilko") writing group.

The last show in the European vein was the season's closing episode, "Return Home from Europe," filmed Thursday, April 5, 1956, and aired May 14, 1956, set aboard a Pan American Airlines flight (No. 155). In an effort to smuggle a twenty-five-pound hunk of cheese on the plane without being charged an excess-baggage fee, Lucy disguises the bundle as a baby, thinking tykes travel gratis. The ensuing scenes, with actress Mary Jane Croft playing the mother of a four-month-old infant girl, were brilliant—a true tribute to writers Bob Carroll, Jr., Bob Schiller, Bob Weiskopf, Madelyn Pugh (*Look* magazine once tagged the quartet "Three Bobs and a Babe"), and Jess Oppenheimer. Jess left the week after this show was filmed to take an NBC executive post, but those close to "I Love Lucy" claimed "irreconcilable differences" with Desi Arnaz as the primary reason for the exit.

And after supervising the photography on more than four hundred telefilms for Desilu, sixty-six-year-old Karl Freund resigned to return to motion pictures. In a 1963 article in *Films in Review* magazine, Freund "found television a stimulating challenge, but he eventually wearied of the commercial restrictions involved and of the Desilu slapstick itself." Papa's contribution to "I Love Lucy" could not be minimized: had it not been for his supreme talent as a cinematographer and inventor, the quality of the half-hour films would never

Cinematographer Karl Freund kept in constant contact with the director and camera coordinator via a two-way intercom system developed in 1951 by Al Simon.

have come up to the standards CBS demanded when the show first started. Had they fallen short of expectations, "Lucy" would have been converted to a "live on the relay" basis, and these 179 films would not have continued to find an eager audience for years to come.

Although the series did not place number one in the Nielsen chart for the entire season, its fifth (it was beaten out by "The $64,000 Question" by 1.4 rating points), CBS nonetheless was anxious for Lucy and Desi to continue producing the half-hour "Lucy" shows, despite Desi's insistence on a once-monthly, hour-long version.

10 *The Longest Laugh* ♡

"Desi and I were driving in from Palm Springs one Monday morning, headed for another hectic week at the studio, after a weekend that had brought him no rest," Lucille Ball told an interviewer in early 1956. "His problems had come along, crowding me out. Worried about his overwork and inability to relax, I could sense a cloud over his head. His eyes were intent on the road and his hands were gripping the wheel until they showed white. Suddenly he reminded me that five years of doing 'I Love Lucy' were winding up, we had only a few shows to go, and it was time to renew our contract with CBS. We were still on top. How did I feel about it, he wanted to know.

"I spoke as if I had memorized my lines from a script, I knew them so well. Five years before, when 'I Love Lucy' was just starting, we had agreed that if the show were a success, we would begin to taper off after the first five years. Not to retire, but to live graciously and work when and where we pleased, provided it didn't interfere with the pleasures we wanted to enjoy together. Desi always wanted to own a ranch, not just the five acres we had had, but one large enough so the horses he loved so much wouldn't have to crowd together like commuters on a train. We had talked of trips we would take and the adventures we would have with the children.

" 'What do *you* think, Desi?' I asked.

"All he said was, 'We have several hundred people working for us now. It doesn't seem right to let that many people down because we've done what we set out to do.' "

The fact was that once again "I Love Lucy" had shot to the number one position in the Nielsen ratings for the four weeks of March 1956, the fifth time the series had achieved this height. And although the show did not come in at the top spot for the entire season (it was number two), CBS still was anxious to sign the Cuban and his redhead to another year of shows. But Desi was still pumping for an hour-long "Lucy" show. As early as November of the preceding year, Arnaz was quoted in *Daily Variety* as saying, "We would be able to do many things and have far more scope. I want to keep Vivian and Bill with us in the new show. I like working with them." Desi went on to speculate that half-hour shows were slowly but definitely being replaced in popularity by the sixty- and ninety-minute shows. Two months later, the same trade paper reported: "Desi Arnaz, who a couple of months ago said he wants to see his 'I Love Lucy' go on a monthly hour-long basis next year, admits his arguments with CBS have been thoroughly dissipated by the rapid comeback of 'Lucy' in the ratings."

By mid-April, the Arnazes finally had decided to return as the Ricardos in the half-hour version, their sixth season of thirty-minute films. This was precisely what Hubbell Robinson, CBS-TV vice-president in charge of programming in New York, wanted all along. On May 3, the Hollywood trade papers announced that "I Love Lucy" would be back after a thirteen-week summer hiatus (during which "The Charlie Farrell Show" ran) with twenty-six new episodes and thirteen repeats, the originals carrying a price tag of fifty thousand dollars each and the reruns half that.

As if he didn't have enough responsibilities, Desi Arnaz assumed the role of producer for the sixth season, taking over Jess Oppenheimer's key role (although Desi would not become involved in the writing of the show). With an able assist from Jack Aldworth, who was promoted from assistant director to associate producer, Desi commenced preproduction for the upcoming 1956–57 season. Some major changes were in store. Lucille Ball talked to a reporter about them: "The principal change will be to shoot many locations. We'll go outdoors more often than in previous times, although you must remember we shot a lot of footage in Europe and across the country. There will be a shift of emphasis to our son, Ricky, who is now old enough to be included in many situations. . . . We'll travel some, too. Mainly the Ricardos will continue to develop and grow. To be truthful, that's all I know. The rest is up to the writers. They tell us what to do and we take it from there."

In order to benefit from the Little Ricky character, his age was jumped to five, the age of a kindergartener. The Mayer twins—Joe and Mike—who had played the role since 1953, were not old enough, and their mother Eva had already decided to retire them from show business. Therefore, a new actor would be needed. During the month of May 1956, nearly two hundred boys were interviewed. None filled the Little Ricky bill.

At about this time, bandleader Horace Heidt brought his "Youth Opportunity" show to town (you will recall that "I Love Lucy" replaced Heidt in the 9–9:30 P.M. Monday-night time slot in October 1951). One of the acts, featured under the billing "The World's Tiniest Professional Drummer," was little five-year-old Keith Thibodeaux, a native of Lafayette, Louisiana. Heidt called his prodigy "pound for pound, the greatest drummer around."

A friend of Keith's father happened to mention that Desilu was searching for a little boy for one of its television shows. The elder Thibodeaux, an insurance agent, took his drummer boy to the casting department at Motion Picture Center, not really expecting a job to materialize, but anxious to get a firsthand look at the lot where his favorite TV show, "I Love Lucy," was made.

Desi took one look at young Keith and signed him to a seven-year contract at a starting salary of $461 a week, saying: "He's a remarkably talented youngster, and there will be plenty for him to do besides 'Lucy'—if the show doesn't last that long." Aside from his incredible drumming facility, Keith actually looked like a miniature Desi Arnaz. Arnaz immediately ordered basic Spanish lessons for the young boy of French extraction, whose name was

Keith Thibodeaux joins the cast of "I Love Lucy," spring 1956.

then Americanized to Richard (Ricky) Keith, which he adopted as a stage name.

Born December 1, 1950, Keith's musical career happened almost by accident. At the age of ten months, after his father brought him home from his first festival parade in downtown Lafayette, he began accompanying the music he heard on the radio by playing a knife and fork against the floor.

"I thought he was turning in a pretty good performance at the time," Mr. Thibodeaux recalls, "but we thought it was just a phase that would pass quickly."

The phase—alas—did not pass, but grew steadily. On the youngster's second Christmas, he received a toy drum. After a short time he was able to detect the inferior quality of the toy and was quick to inform his father of this. A real drum set followed, and, by 1954, Keith was the talk of Lafayette, Louisiana.

The Beaux Bridge (Louisiana) High School band invited the boy to make a guest appearance at a school benefit, his first public performance. Television appearances at Lake Charles, Baton Rouge, and New Orleans followed in quick succession, and then the Kiwanis Club of Keith's home town chose him to represent the area on the Horace Heidt amateur show, which the fraternal organization was sponsoring.

Heidt was so impressed he hired the four-year-old to make three coast-to-coast appearances in Durham, North Carolina, Washington, D.C., and New York City. Heidt then decided to make the boy a "regular" on his show and thus began a one-year tour that ended in Los Angeles in 1956. On May 23 Keith's agent, Edith Jackson, negotiated the Desilu deal. Within a week, he would become Little Ricky Ricardo.

With Keith set, Desi continued negotiations in an effort to sign big-name guest stars for the new season. He wanted Lucy's old pal, Ann Sothern, for a show to be shot in September, but plans never materialized. Neither did "Lucy" shows featuring Jack Benny and Maurice Chevalier pan out. The latter two stars were "firmed" for early 1957 episodes, according to industry trade papers, but these guest shots never happened. (Arrangements were even discussed for the Arnazes to "trade off" by appearing on Benny's sitcom.) The star who did fulfill the promise was Bob Hope, with whom Lucy had appeared in two Paramount films *(Sorrowful Jones* and *Fancy Pants)* several years earlier.

Hope's schedule, as always, was tight, so Desilu earmarked the month of June to film his episode and three others, to get a head start on the upcoming fall season. The comedian checked into Motion Picture Center on Tuesday, May 29, 1956, to start rehearsals on "Lucy and Bob Hope," the one hundred and fifty-fourth installment of the "Lucy" show. With Jim Kern continuing his role as director from the last season, the company assigned two new staffers to help mount the quartet of June shows: Ed Hillie, assistant director (replacing Jack Aldworth), and Robert de Grasse, director of photography (replacing Karl Freund). For the four continuing writers (Jess had already begun his job at NBC), there was a slight shift in responsibilities. Bob and Madelyn were now the head writers and polished scripts by Bob Schiller and Bob Weiskopf (each earning $1,250 per week). Of course, the four of them would together brainstorm each of the twenty-six episodes ordered for the season. Among their creative changes was having Ricky Ricardo buy the Tropicana and rename it the Club Babalu. The signing of five-and-a-half-year-old Keith proved to be an additional story line gold mine.

The youngster was used sparingly at first. His appearance in the Bob Hope show, for instance, was confined to a short sequence set in the Yankee Stadium bleachers. A large cast of actors and extras was assembled for the episode, including "Lucy" alumni like Lou Krugman, Peter Leeds, and Dick Elliott, all of whom had appeared in earlier shows. Composer Eliot Daniel and lyricist Larry Orenstein (the latter wrote the songs for the episode "set" in Scotland) were called upon to write a special-material number for Lucy, Desi, and Hope and came up with an appropriate baseball-themed song

Lucy, Desi, and Keith Thibodeaux clown with guest star Bob Hope, June 1956.

titled "Nobody Loves the Ump." Jack Baker's choreography called for Desi and Bob to lift Lucy in the air and swing her back and forth. During a critical rehearsal of the scene on Stage 9, Lucy came down hard, leaning on Desi too heavily for support, tearing the ligaments in his back. They made jokes about it, but Desi was immediately admitted to the hospital on the advice of his doctor, Dr. Mark Rabwin, who called in an orthopedic specialist to strap up the Cuban. The filming was delayed until Tuesday, June 5 (Hope had to be in Washington, D.C., on June 7 to emcee a press photographers' dinner for Eisenhower).

The next episode featured the multi-faceted Orson Welles, who received a record amount for his guest stint: fifteen thousand dollars. Two months earlier, in April, Welles and Arnaz had teamed up to produce a one-hour television series, in which the Academy Award-winner would also star. This arrangement never resulted in a series, but Welles did manage to complete a half-hour pilot titled "The Fountain of Youth" that is still shown at film festivals. The Welles "Lucy" show also featured "The Waltons' " Ellen Corby as Lucy Ricardo's high school drama teacher. The show originally contained scenes of Vivian Vance playing Cleopatra to Welles's Julius Caesar, and Lucy sparring with the Shakespearean master as Juliet and Lady Macbeth, but for some unknown reason these sequences did not make their way into the final print of "Lucy Meets Orson Welles" that was shot the evening of June 14, 1956.

The next episode that was filmed, "Little Ricky Gets Stage Fright," would be the last time audiences would see the nightclub. In fact, the episodes that would be produced later, in the fall, would rarely feature Desi in more than a subsidiary role as Ricky. Much of this had to do with Desi's concern over a burgeoning workload, ostensibly heightened as Desilu grew in size and importance. With the filming of Episode #157, "Little Ricky Learns to Play the Drums," on June 28, the "I Love Lucy" company began a ten-week vacation.

The "Lucy" company was set to return to work on Monday, September 10. By this time, the four writers had put the finishing touches on most of the scripts that would eventually air during the fall. Firmed up over the summer was a plan to move the Ricardos and eventually the Mertzes to suburbia—Westport, Connecticut—after the first of the year (1957). In the meantime, a trip to Florida and Cuba was in the works, plus a number of shows set in the New York apartment. Writer Bob Carroll, Jr., joked at the time: "Ricky . . . makes about twenty thousand clams a year now. If he wasn't any better off than he was six years ago, people would say, 'What kind of a no-talent bandleader is this—never gets a raise?' "

Aside from the creative changes, there were personnel additions as the company returned to work after Labor Day. Sid Hickox was installed as the permanent director of photography for the remaining twenty-two half-hour segments, as was twenty-four-year-old Jay Sandrich, who assumed the responsible position of assistant director under Jim Kern. One of the most sought-after directors in the television industry today, Jay is the son of the late Mark Sandrich, who directed such musical classics as *The Gay Divorcee*, *Top Hat*, and *Follow the Fleet* (the latter two featured, in minor roles, a young blond ingenue, Lucille Ball, age twenty-six).

"I was hired as a second assistant [director] during the spring of 1956 right out of the Army Signal Corps by Argyle Nelson, who was head of production at Desilu," explains Jay Sandrich, who has won two Emmys for the "Mary Tyler Moore Show" episodes, "Toulouse Lautrec Is One of My Favorite Artists" and "It's Whether You Win or Lose." "Those were the days when we worked six days a week, so I worked two days each on 'Lucy,' 'Our Miss Brooks,' and 'December Bride' doing mostly paperwork—time cards and the like, working with the extras, et cetera.

"When I got the chance to become a first assistant [director] at another studio, I took it, but that lasted only six weeks. That's when Jack Aldworth called me. He had just been promoted to associate producer under Desi. He asked me if I'd like to be the first assistant on 'Lucy.' Of course, I said yes. It was one of my favorite shows—even before I came to work at Desilu. I think Lucy herself had a lot to do with my being hired as first assistant. I really had very little experience and that job is very demanding, with a lot of responsibility attached to it. Lucy felt very close to my late father. It must have been that for them to put up with a rampant incompetent like me!

"If it hadn't been for Jack Aldworth—who 'wet-nursed' me through that first season—I don't think I ever could have cut it. Some of the 'Lucy' shows were very complicated. In fact, my very first day we were doing process shots."

Sandrich is speaking of the driving scenes in "Off to Florida," the show that featured Elsa Lanchester as Mrs. Grundy, a health-food fanatic who gives Lucy and Ethel a ride to Florida in her convertible. (Lanchester received two thousand dollars for her role.) This show was filmed on September 13 and aired, out of sequence, on November 12. But it was the next show filmed that would demand a great deal of Lucille Ball herself.

For the "Visitor from Italy" show that featured "Lucy" veteran Jay Novello as Mario Orsatti, a Venetian gondolier whom the Ricardos and Mertzes supposedly encountered while in Italy the year before, the writers dreamed up the ultimate Lucille Ball schtick—she would be featured twirling pizza dough in the air. Like the time she was called upon to play the saxophone, Lucille Ball plunged in where most actors would fear to tread. For three evenings, after regular rehearsals were over, Lucy drove over to Micelli's Pizza Parlor on LaCienega Boulevard in West Hollywood and worked with their pizza chefs—among them Aldo Formica—who taught her how to make a pizza. "She got so good at it," recalls property master Jerry Miggins, "that after we filmed the show, we all went over to Micelli's, where Lucy made pizza for everyone. It was delicious!"

Miggins also remembers well the next episode, "Deep Sea Fishing," set in Miami, Florida: "The script called for two giant tunas, each about sixty pounds. I called up Bryant Taxidermy and they came over with one of the fish to show us. Desi felt it wasn't long enough. The man said it would be no problem to make it longer. In the meantime, while the show was being rehearsed, Jack Aldworth called me and said, 'Desi wants *real* tunas.'

"Finding real fish that big was not easy, but I remembered an M-G-M film I worked on that starred Red Skelton in the forties. It was shot partially on location down at the docks in San Pedro. I phoned one of the fishing companies there and told them my problem. I needed two identical tunas, each about sixty pounds, and I needed them fast, the next morning, the day of the filming. The man told me it would be no problem; he was expecting a boat loaded with tunas the next day. So I sent one of our station wagons down there with a check for twenty-five dollars and in a couple of hours we had two large tunas still a bit frozen from the ice-packing. I found a corner in the prop room and hung them up to defrost.

"When I returned later, I discovered much to my horror that they were bleeding from the mouth and gills, and the blood just wouldn't stop. I spent the entire afternoon wiping them down with towels to remove the moisture. Desi kept calling me, 'Are they still bleeding? Are they still bleeding?' We didn't know what to do. This was the crucial scene in the show," explains Miggins, who is reluctant to continue the story because it contradicts the one told about the incident in Desi Arnaz's 1976 autobiography.

Assistant director Jay Sandrich picks up the behind-the-scenes "fish story": "Someone in the prop department got hold of a box of sanitary napkins and stuffed the fish with them. When Lucy heard about it, she stopped by the prop room and asked if it was true that the fish were filled with Kotex. Laughing, she said, 'If one of those things falls out in the middle of the stage, I'll die!' "

To launch the sixth season on October 1, 1956, Lucy and Desi hosted a huge dinner party—with the help of CBS and sponsors General Foods and Procter & Gamble—that very night on Stage 9 at Motion Picture Center. Two hundred and fifty guests helped the Arnazes celebrate at the luau catered by Steve Crane held right on the sets built to simulate Florida for Episode #161, "Desert Island." The festivities were interrupted for thirty minutes while the happy throng enjoyed "Lucy and Bob Hope," the episode shot nearly four months earlier.

Daily Variety called the show "as durable as ever," complimenting the cast, but not the writing, by saying, "True, some of the plot gags are familiar, but the combined talents of Lucille Ball, Desi Arnaz, and Bob Hope are such that they compensated for the feeling of familiarity. Why Miss Ball is one of the top TV comediennes is obvious by her excellent timing, her skilled miming . . . the three actually transcend their material. The battery of four scribes apparently rely on the tried-and-true rather than any attempt at originality."

A few days later, despite that and other less-than-glowing reviews, Madelyn Pugh Martin (she had married Quinn Martin) and Bob Carroll, Jr., were signed to a new, exclusive three-year deal by Desi that provided them with not only the "Lucy" assignment, but also the opportunity to create new shows, TV specials, and possibly theatrical features.

In the meantime, Keith Thibodeaux was really coming into his own as a performer. In "The Ricardos Visit Cuba," shot on October 18, the youngster had the opportunity to do a conga drum duet with his TV dad, Desi, a fantastic rendition of "Babalu." Keith had once again proved himself to be a real trouper.

Desi Arnaz, Jr., whom, in a way, Keith was portraying, reacts to his past "competition": "I can still remember watching the show when I was about three and wondering who was the baby with Mommy and Daddy. When my parents said it was me, I was confused because I knew it wasn't.

"So I had this identity problem, and it wasn't helped any by people calling me Little Ricky, a name I learned to despise. I remember wanting rather desperately to be better at something—anything—than the boy who played Little Ricky. For a while, it seemed as if everything in *my* life was connected to Little Ricky's. I started playing the drums because Little Ricky played the drums. The fact that Keith really played them was what really got me interested in music. I studied percussion because I wanted to drum better than Keith did—and I'll always be grateful to him for that."

Before filming "The Ricardos Visit Cuba," Desi straightens the bow tie on his TV son. It is Keith's seventh "Lucy" appearance.

While two early fall episodes focused on Little Ricky's musical talents, it wasn't until the episode aired December 24, 1956, that the Ricardo youngster got his very own professional drum set, as a gift. Filmed on November 22 and directed by the departing James V. Kern, the segment—known as " 'I Love Lucy' Christmas Show"—was sandwiched between "Little Ricky's School Pageant" and "Lucy and the Loving Cup." It would air only once and not find its way into the eventual syndication package of 179 "I Love Lucy" shows. (Portions of it aired on Rona Barrett's "TV: Inside and Out" in December 1981.)

Written by Bob and Madelyn, the special was Desilu's Christmas gift to faithful viewers who yearned to see the famous "baby shows" again. Many repeat programs had been presented on "Lucy" over the intervening years, but the seven pregnancy stories had not been unreeled for Monday-night audiences since Little Ricky's birth in 1953. Rather than repeat the shows en toto, Desilu decided to present key scenes as flashbacks within a current story line.

The Christmas show was never really considered by Desilu to be part of the series. It was conceived solely as a holiday special, not to be repeated. No one today remembers exactly what considerations went into that decision, but Lucy and Bob Carroll agree that the show was probably withheld because of its Christmas theme. Unlike today, when viewers are liable to catch a Christmas-themed show being repeated in July, "we used to be very sensitive to things like that," remembers Carroll.

The show opens, like so many other "Lucy" episodes, in the Ricardo living room, where Ricky is hanging his son's stocking on the mantel. Lucy supervises: "A little more to the left, Ricky. . . . No, a little more to the right." Little Ricky, watching in his pajamas, wants to stay up until Santa arrives, but Ricky, Sr., quickly explains that old St. Nick will not come down the chimney until the Sandman signals from the roof that all the children inside are asleep. Convinced, the child heads for his bedroom, with one last question: "There aren't any steps. How does Santa Claus get down the chimney?" Momentarily stymied, Lucy offers, "Well . . . How, huh? I'll tell you, Little Ricky. . . . Santa Claus doesn't need steps. He brings the North Pole with him and slides down it—like a fireman."

Once the boy is tucked in his bed, Fred and Ethel arrive with a Christmas tree, their gift to Little Ricky. As a huge box of ornaments is taken from the closet, Lucy notices that one bottom branch makes the tree lopsided, and Fred surprises everyone by pulling from his pocket a tiny saw. "I've been putting up trees with this kid [indicating Lucy] for fifteen years." From then on it is a trip down memory lane for the four principals.

Ricky comments on how much their lives have changed since the day they learned Lucy was going to have a baby. "I almost never got to tell you," Lucy recalls, and there is a flashback to the final nightclub sequence from "Lucy Is Enceinte," wherein Lucy sends Ricky an anonymous note during his act, and he has to guess which lady in the audience is expecting.

Once the good news is determined, Ricky sings "We're Having a Baby." The Ricardos are crying in the final happy moments of that scene, and, as the flashback ends, Lucy, Ricky, Fred, and Ethel have gotten misty-eyed all over again. Fred, as a matter of fact, has gotten so carried away that he has trimmed almost all the branches off the Christmas tree. Disgusted, Ethel orders him out of the apartment to buy another fir.

While he is gone, the others continue to unpack the lights and tinsel. Ricky starts to sing "Jingle Bells" in Spanish and Ethel joins in in English. Then Lucy chimes in—hitting all the wrong notes (as usual). Lucy: "I don't know what's happened to my voice lately. I don't seem to sing well anymore." Ricky and Ethel: "Lately? Anymore?" Lucy: "I don't think that's very nice. I grant you my voice isn't quite what it used to be." Ricky: "It's exactly what it used to be, and that's what's wrong with it."

To illustrate, Ricky recalls, via flashback again, the night Lucy interfered in his barbershop quartet and managed to sing "Sweet Adeline" totally off-key, despite his and the Mertzes' efforts to keep her quiet (by stuffing her mouth with a "loaded" shaving brush).

Back in the present, Fred arrives with a second tree, and the two couples busy themselves with stringing the lights and trying to guess what they have given each other for Christmas. At one point, Ethel holds a cluster of mistletoe over her head: "You know what this means, don't you?" Fred: "Yeah, it means you're an incurable optimist!"

Conversation again turns to Little Ricky, and the gang recalls the night he was born. A flashback of "Lucy Goes to the Hospital" recounts the chaos the ensued once Ricky decided to rehearse Lucy's trip to the maternity ward.

The final scene of the Christmas show, lifted almost verbatim from the special "tag" that aired December 24, 1951, opens with a chubby fellow dressed up as Santa putting presents under the Ricardos' trimmed tree. The man looks suspiciously like Fred Mertz. Suddenly, another Santa tiptoes in from the bedroom, packages in hand. This one is Lucy. Just then the front door opens and Ricky, also dressed as Santa, rolls in a scooter. The kitchen door swings open and Santa number four, Ethel, arrives with a box of games. "For heaven's sake," laughs Lucy, "why didn't we get together on this?"

The sound of Little Ricky stirring in his bedroom sends the four Santas off to the kitchen, where a fifth Santa—Fred—comes through the back door. Lucy counts noses and arrives at five. She pulls down Fred's beard, then Ricky's and Ethel's. Ricky pulls on hers. Confused, Lucy pulls on the fifth set of whiskers. "Ouch," cries the "real" Santa (played by Cameron Grant), who turns and quickly exits. The Ricardos and Mertzes are stunned. They look quizzically at each other, then directly at the audience: "Merry Christmas, everybody."

With the first half of the sixth season (thirteen episodés, plus the Christmas special) in the can, the company broke for a ten-day holiday, although the four principals set out for a seven-day personal appearance tour to Miami, New Orleans, and Houston on November 25. They were due back to start rehearsals on the first episode of the next thirteen-week cycle on Monday, December 3. These new shows would revolve around the Ricardos' move to Connecticut and subsequent residence there.

The first order of business was finding a replacement for director Jim Kern, who was departing "Lucy" to helm the new Betty White sitcom, "A Date with the Angels," on the Desilu-Cahuenga lot. They did not have to look far. Desi made arrangements to "borrow" from Columbia a contract director responsible for a pair of that studio's 1956 output (The Shadow on the Window and The 27th Day). For a thousand dollars per week, Bill Asher returned to the fold.

"Apparently, Lucy came on a bit too strong with Jim," Asher speculates, "and he couldn't take it. Desi called me and asked if I'd come back and finish up the last season. I told him I'd do it if it would make him happy. He said, 'Lucy needs you,' which was funny because on that first show ["Lucy Wants to Move to the Country"], Lucy started in again, saying, 'Okay, Vivian, you come over here and you say so-and-so.' I said, 'Hey, Lucy, let's not start this again.' But we never really had any problem.

"In fact, the whole show was a breeze to do. The people were so talented that if there were difficulties, they were insignificant. Sometimes to get Bill Frawley to understand what the story was about was a chore, or he'd fall asleep in the middle of rehearsals. Getting Desi on the set was sometimes tough. He was so busy with the business end of Desilu that he had little time to devote to playing Ricky Ricardo. There was a time, in fact, when I played Desi's part, at least during rehearsal days. I'd 'block' for him so he wouldn't have to be there. But he was so fantastic that he'd be able to watch a run-through with me doing his role and step right in and do it letter-perfect. He was that quick. As a matter of fact, we did the show that way while I was there that last season," says Asher, who then went on to direct a season of TV's "The Thin Man" starring Peter Lawford and Phyllis Kirk.

Assistant director Jay Sandrich was Asher's aide for the last half of the sixth season. He has the greatest admiration for Asher and feels that he owes a great debt of gratitude to him. With Asher, Sandrich cut his teeth on the "Desilu method" and went on to use it on such shows as "The Mary Tyler Moore Show," "He and She," "Soap," etc. "The basic thing in comedy for three cameras is that you have much more flexibility in finding ways to work the comedy," explains Sandrich. "You have, in essence, five days to make a show work and you're constantly aware that you're going to do it for an audience—not for a laugh machine and not for three people sitting at home. You're really going to do it for people out there, and it had better work; you can't fool yourself. You don't ever get a chance to become complacent, because maybe last week's show was wonderful but you've got a trouble show this week, or you read a script for two weeks from now and that needs work. So you're never able to sit back and relax."

For midseason, the writers had decided to take the Ricardos out of the city and move them to the country. They had, by their own admission, used up every conceivable story line that could be set in the tiny New York apartment. It was time again to broaden horizons, as the show had done with the Hollywood and Europe trips. In other words, make the show different, but not *too* different. The so-called Connecticut shows of 1957 featured two "Lucy" veterans in new supporting roles. Frank Nelson and Mary Jane Croft (both seen most recently in the "Return Home from Europe" episode) signed on as Mr. and Mrs. Ralph Ramsey, the Ricardos' next-door neighbors in Westport. Ramsey was a partner in a New York advertising agency while his wife, Betty, busied herself with civic functions and the like. Young Ray Ferrell rounded out the Ramsey clan as son Bruce. The four "Lucy" writers capitalized on the living-in-suburbia syndrome that had become so widespread in the mid-fifties. They wrestled with such weighty matters as barbecues, Elvis Presley, Grace Kelly, and intercoms. They even built a show around Broadway's *The Most Happy Fella,* a Frank Loesser musical partially bankrolled by Desilu.

It was during this story period, which ran from January 28 to May 6, 1957, that "I Love Lucy" recorded the longest laugh in its six-year history. The show was "Lucy Does the Tango," and it involved Lucy's attempt to hide from Ricky the fact that she had bought five dozen eggs to make it appear their new laying hens were laying . . . when they really weren't.

The Arnazes "relax" backstage between scenes of "Lucy Raises Chickens," filmed on January 17, 1957.

"The block comedy scene, where Lucy hides all the eggs in her shirt," recalls Jay Sandrich, "resulted in the biggest laugh I've ever heard. It went on so long that the editor had to cut the sound track in half. Once the eggs cracked in her blouse, after Lucy and Desi's big tango number, she kept milking the bit for laughs. She would do one funny thing after another and then when the audience's laughter started dying down, she'd do more. She was brilliant. So was Desi.

"The man was a very talented editor. When Lucy would do something in rehearsal and he thought she was overdoing the scene, he would say so, and she always listened to him. He also had the uncanny ability to edit dialogue. He knew instinctively if an unnecessary or wrong word was in a line of dialogue. He had a marvelous ear for comedy, on a par with Neil Simon."

Desi acted as host of the Ninth Annual Emmy Awards ceremony, telecast over NBC from its Burbank studios on Saturday, March 16, 1957. Although "I Love Lucy" was not nominated, three of its four stars garnered nominations, but did not win. (Desi was never nominated.) Lucille lost to Nanette Fabray in the "Best Continuing Performance by a Comedienne in a Series" category, Bill Frawley lost to Carl Reiner, and Vivian Vance lost to Pat Carroll.

Shortly before the awards ceremony, Desilu had decided to discontinue the production of half-hour episodes of "I Love Lucy" at the conclusion of the 1956–57 season. CBS was disappointed but was left with no alternative but to consider Desi's "new" idea: a once-monthly, hour-long comedy show that the Cuban determined would cost $250,000 per program (that figure soon jumped to $350,000). "Lucy" 's present sponsors, Procter & Gamble and General Foods, were not interested in continuing their bankrolling, favoring a weekly exposure for their products. Arnaz subsequently hauled out the big guns and invited a passel of powerful media executives, including his hard-nosed vice-president, Marty Leeds, to Palm Springs for the February 23 weekend. Such people as Ed Ebel, advertising chief of General Foods, Gail Smith, program manager for Procter & Gamble, Rod Erickson, vice-president of Young & Rubicam, and Tom McDermott, TV head of Benton & Bowles, attended. After hours of discussion, no decision had been made regarding the continued sponsorship by P & G and/or General Foods. Both companies wanted to know what shows would fill the nine to ten o'clock Monday-night slot on the weeks "Lucy" wasn't airing. CBS had not yet firmed up its fall 1957 schedule. Desi's idea was to rotate the hour-long "Lucy" with "December Bride" and his new "Adventures of a Model" (starring Joanne Dru), both Desilu products. No decisions were about to be made by any parties, not yet.

But on April 8, at the Conrad Hilton Hotel headquarters of the National Association of Radio and Television Broadcasters, Hubbell Robinson, Jr., executive vice-president in charge of CBS television programs, made this announcement to a gathering of network affiliates: "Lucille Ball and Desi Arnaz have decided to discontinue 'I Love Lucy' after this season. As you all know, they had threatened some time ago not to make any more half-

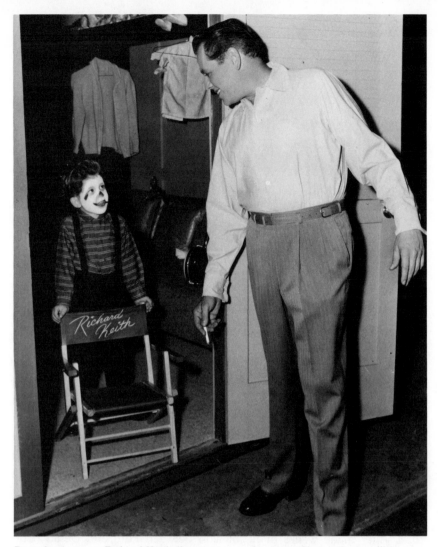

Desi checks in on Richard Keith (his stage name) prior to filming the last "I Love Lucy" episode, "The Ricardos Dedicate a Statue," telecast May 6, 1957.

hour 'Lucy' films. They want to do a one-hour program once a month next season, but we have not made a commitment on this show as yet."

As you can imagine, the Arnazes were flooded with mail from admiring "Lucy" fans who did not want the series discontinued in its present form. These outraged cries sent newspaper and magazine reporters to Desilu's Cahuenga Boulevard headquarters for answers.

"We've loved our work and we've loved being pioneers," said Lucille Ball after completing her last "I Love Lucy" segment on April 4, "but the time has come to let somebody else 'enjoy' it. We're a little brain-weary, you know. How do you make people understand that? In letters, viewers tell us they're sad because of our plans, but I don't think they understand. We're not exactly quitting. There will be as much of 'Lucy' around next season as they'll want to see."

11 Thirteen Hours

"For three years now, I wanted to turn 'I Love Lucy' into an hour-long show on maybe a once-a-month basis," said Desi Arnaz in the spring of 1957 after firming up a deal with the Ford Motor Company to sponsor five Lucy-Desi specials. "Two years ago, when I first suggested it, CBS wouldn't listen. Last year again, they talked me into continuing with the weekly half-hour. But this time I made up my mind."

It was not an easy decision to make. When Arnaz revealed his plan to Paley, CBS made the Cuban an unprecedented offer: They proposed to pay Desilu $80,000 per "Lucy" half-hour and $30,000 for each repeat. (The average cost of a top-quality half-hour sitcom in 1957 was $48,000.)

"When I turned that down," Desi continues, "they finally realized I wasn't kidding."

The original plan called for eight one-hour Lucy-Desi specials, each budgeted at $350,000, for the 1957–58 season. With a $4-million price tag, the proposal found no takers among prospective sponsors. Finally Desi took his idea to Ford; he had done business with the automobile manufacturer earlier in the season when he agreed to preview the first retractable hardtop on the March 4, 1957, "I Love Lucy" installment ("The newest kind of Ford. It's the bright new star of 'I Love Lucy,' " read the ads). At first the giant firm was reserved in its enthusiasm. Four million dollars was a lot to spend in 1957 on one advertising vehicle, even a proven one like "Lucy." But Ford was looking for a means of introducing its new car that fall, the Edsel. After many weeks of negotiation between Ford and Desilu (Don Sharpe was in charge of the dealings), a deal was struck in early May for the auto maker to sponsor five Lucille Ball-Desi Arnaz specials at a reported cost of $2.5 million.

The $350,000-budget specials were a far cry from the original "Lucy" films, which were brought in for less than $25,000 each six years before. "They not only have to be good," Arnaz confided to one of his staffers when the deal was being finalized, "they have to be great. We're going to be in an awful spot with these shows; they've *got* to be good."

Why did Desi want to abandon the reliable "I Love Lucy" half-hour format in favor of the untried, the untested? "You've got to change in this business. You can't stand still," he once said incisively. "I would rather make a big change while we are still ahead. It would be ridiculous for us to wait until people got sick and tired of the regular half-hour every Monday night. We have been the luckiest show on the air, but we've worked for it. I have never worked so hard in my life. And while I suppose it's not really for me to say, I think I can honestly say that we have never done a really bad show in six years. We threw out only two scripts that whole time and started over again. What other program ever had writers with a record like that?"

The general form of the hour specials placed guest stars into the old "I Love Lucy" format. For the first show, Desi and producer Bert Granet lined up Ann Sothern (she received a whopping twenty-five thousand dollars for her services), Hedda Hopper, Cesar Romero, and Rudy Vallee. The writers— the "Three Bobs and a Babe"—dreamed up an excellent tale that they titled "Lucy Takes a Cruise to Havana," a story that told, in flashback, how Lucy McGillicuddy met and married Ricky Ricardo.

The opening scene is set in the Ricardos' Westport, Connecticut, living room where the Hollywood gossip columnist Hedda Hopper is querying the couple on how their romance started sixteen years ago. A flashback transports us on a cruise to Cuba where Lucy and Susie MacNamara (Ann Sothern's "Private Secretary" role) are two stenographers on vacation. Aboard the ship, they meet newlyweds Fred and Ethel Mertz (he with hair) and Rudy Vallee. On arrival in Havana, the girls encounter two local gentlemen who run a taxi-sightseeing service—Ricky Ricardo and his buddy Carlos Garcia (Cesar Romero). They soon discover that Ricky's real wish is to become a musical entertainer. The story goes on to relate Lucy's madcap escapades and whirlwind romance. Songwriter Arthur Hamilton wrote two original songs for the hour special—"Our Ship Is Coming In," sung by Ricky and Carlos, and "That Means I Love You," with Ricky singing to Lucy's drum accompaniment. It was a terrific writing job, all agreed.

Shot before a live audience on Stage 9 at Motion Picture Center in June 1957, with Jerry Thorpe directing and Sid Hickox in charge of the four cameras (a fourth was added because the show was so complicated), "Lucy Takes a Cruise to Havana" was a perfect show to start off the new series. The enlarged budget was obvious—the sets were sumptuous and the costumes were a period delight. The latter element particularly pleased Vivian Vance. Remembers one observer: "Viv had no desire to continue in the hour shows. She had gotten pretty fed up with her treatment in the old 'I Love Lucy,' particularly having to wear all those frumpy clothes. Her contract with Desilu for the Lucy-Desi specials included a clause calling for better costumes. This, more than anything, pleased her. She was always very conscious of how she looked."

That initial segment was a first in many ways—it was TV's first hour show that ran seventy-five minutes. Lucy explains: "In the middle of rehearsals, everything went like this," she indicated, snapping her fingers in rhythm. "But suddenly Desi slowed down. I thought, 'This man has finally forgotten a line after six years.' [Arnaz was well known for memorizing his lines after only one reading.] But, no, he had suddenly gotten the idea the script was so good it had to be extended another fifteen minutes!"

CBS refused to run a segment of seventy-five minutes, demanding that Desilu either shorten it by fifteen minutes or pad it with an additional fifteen minutes of material. Desi balked on both counts, claiming it would spoil and weaken the total effect.

Bill Paley told Arnaz that CBS did half-hour shows, hour shows, and hour-and-a-half shows. There was, he said, no such thing as an hour-and-fifteen-minute show!

Desi suggested to the CBS head that "The United States Steel Hour," which would follow the Lucy-Desi special come Wednesday, November 6, 1957, be shortened fifteen minutes, just that one week. Paley flatly refused.

Well known in the industry for solving problems his *own* way, Arnaz went over Paley's head and called the head of U.S. Steel. He assured the magnate that with the Lucy-Desi special as a lead-in, "The United States Steel Hour," which wasn't doing that well at the time, would probably double its rating. U.S. Steel gave Desi permission to use the first fifteen minutes of its weekly hour, provided, of course, that the Ford Motor Company picked up the tab for the extra quarter hour.

The result, when the ratings were issued in late November, was a high rating for the first Lucy-Desi effort and the *highest* rating "The United States Steel Hour" ever garnered.

"We're trying to get Gary Cooper for another show," Desi hinted, following filming of the first "Lucille Ball–Desi Arnaz Show." "Maybe Bill Holden for another. He was so wonderful that first time he worked with us ["L.A. at Last!"]. We'll be able to move around more and won't have to keep with that weekly continuity. We hope to do location stuff, too. Each show can be a complete and different story without having to worry about being in that apartment every week or in a home or all that."

Planning the second Lucy-Desi show proved a problem. Desi signed Bette Davis in early June 1957 to guest in "The Celebrity Next Door," which would air in the fall in a yet undisclosed time slot (the first season of Lucy-Desi specials had no regular time period) sometime in December. Miss Davis was once a classmate of Lucille's when the two were students at the John Murray Anderson–Robert Milton Dramatics School in New York City in the mid-1920s.

Davis was not easy to deal with. She demanded a salary of twenty thousand dollars for a twelve-day rehearsal and shooting stint *and* equal billing with Lucy and Desi. The Arnazes graciously agreed on both counts. She also wanted a clause added to her contract that stipulated that Desilu pay her plane fare home to Maine if she left within ten days after her assignment.

As most readers probably know, Bette Davis never did "The Celebrity Next Door." On June 23, 1957, she suffered a fall in a rented Los Angeles house at 641 Bundy Drive and cracked her vertebra. This was only two weeks after she filed for divorce after seven years of marriage to Gary Merrill in Santa Monica Superior Court. By month's end, she was thrown from a horse and broke her arm. Obviously, she was in no shape to be a "Celebrity Next Door."

The search for her replacement, which also required a rewrite over the summer of the Martin-Carroll-Schiller-Weiskopf teleplay, got underway almost at once. A half-dozen famous movie actresses were considered until, finally, Desi decided on Tallulah Bankhead. One of Lucy's idols (Ball often amused her friends with a Bankhead impression), Tallulah agreed to fly in from the East to begin rehearsals on September 15, 1957.

The next ten days were a nightmare. "Tallulah was half bombed every day," remembers one senior staffer. "She wouldn't cooperate with Jerry Thorpe, the director, and this infuriated Lucy, who's a stickler for rehearsals. There were a lot of battles on the set, let me tell you. Lucy and Desi were sorry they ever hired her."

When Miss Bankhead was questioned about the rumors that "fur flew" during her "Lucy" stint, she bristled. "Never. Unequivocally never! I've got not even one picayune derogatory thing to say about those wonderful people," Tallulah began.

"Of course, I *did* have pneumonia at the time. And someone nearly blinded me one day at rehearsals with hair spray. But Lucy? She's *divine* to work with! And Desi? He's brilliant! He *has* a temper, however. But that's because he's fat. It worries him.

"I rehearsed ten days for them. I was there every morning at ten. We left at five, and I returned to my bungalow at the Beverly Hills Hotel exhausted. I broke a tooth. I broke the cap they put on the tooth. I broke my nails. I had pneumonia," Tallulah lamented.

About "The Celebrity Next Door" script, Bankhead explained foggily, "They had this plot, darling. They were living in Connecticut, or somewhere, and rehearsing a play for the PTA, whatever *that* is. In one scene I sat down in wet paint. In another, I said to Lucy, 'Remove yourself before I pull out that pink hair and expose the black roots underneath!' Then I locked her inside an iron maiden [a suit of armor] while she was smoking a cigarette. But when they wanted to paint a moustache on me, I drew the line!"

Desi confirms the disagreements with Miss Bankhead. "She would arrive on the set at 9:30 in the morning. But she really wouldn't wake up until 11. Between 11 and 12, she was fine. But at 1 P.M., right after lunch, we'd lose her again. Regarding the moustache incident, I finally had to drop the good manners and lay it on the line to her. I told her we were paying her good money and we expected her to do her best.

"The night we did the actual filming [September 27, 1957], I was terrified. I kissed her quickly, wished her luck, and walked away, hoping against hope. What happened? She came through and was nothing short of magnificent," Arnaz recalled.

Unfortunately, Desilu had not yet adjusted to the requirements of an hour format. It was a challenge for the writers to switch gears and not think in terms of thirty-minute episodes anymore. Because of this, "The Celebrity Next Door" was basically two half-hour "Lucy" adventures sewn together. Each of the parts was well written, and only a few critics took offense.

The first "segment" of the farce featured Tallulah as an unsuspecting celebrity who innocently moves into the neighborhood. Lucy Ricardo, anxious to impress the great star, enlists the Mertzes to pose as the Ricardos' maid and butler. Vivian Vance and William Frawley, reduced to bit parts in the first hour special, literally stole the show in their roles as Lucy's disgruntled domestics.

The second portion had Lucy involving Tallulah in the local PTA benefit show. When Miss Bankhead steals the redhead's thunder at rehearsals, Lucy plots to ruin the actress's performance.

In addition to these dominant plots, the writers threw in a random assortment of gags and sketches reminiscent of early "I Love Lucy": Lucy and Ethel using field glasses to watch the movers unload Tallulah's furniture; Lucy inadvertently spray-painting Tallulah—head to toe; Bankhead, in turn, unknowingly inviting Lucy to sit in a freshly painted chair.

Later that fall, in November, the company filmed its first Lucy-Desi show on location; guest-starring Fred MacMurray and his wife, June Haver, it was titled "Lucy Hunts Uranium." Only a handful of "I Love Lucy" shows had been done away from the studio, and these usually consisted of short scenes, *sans* sound. The first time had been for "First Stop," an episode in the 1954–55 season. A second-unit team shot footage of the Ricardos and Mertzes riding in the 1955 Pontiac convertible, but the major portion of the episode, of course, was filmed at Motion Picture Center. A few other fourth-season shows used location footage ("The Tour," for example), but that was about the extent of away-from-studio filming. Costs were too prohibitive.

Now with three hundred and fifty thousand dollars being spent on each Lucy-Desi special, location filming became more feasible. The Fred Mac-Murray hour was set in Las Vegas at the Sands Hotel, and that's where the Desilu cast and crew went to film a number of outdoor scenes. In one of those sequences, the script called for a stunt man, doubling for MacMurray, to drive a Thunderbird down a hill at top speed and plow into a newly black-topped road, skidding sideways. Every time the stunt was performed, the sports car careened out of camera range, making expensive retakes necessary.

"This is costing us money," complained Desi, who, as producer, had to pay the bills. "Besides, it don't look so damned hard to do."

With that, Desi pushed the stunt man aside and climbed into the driver's seat. Gunning the motor, he barreled down the Las Vegas hill toward the grimy blacktop. The car finally came to a perfect stop directly in front of the camera. It was a flawless take, except for one small problem. The cameras weren't rolling.

Told by director Jerry Thorpe that it was a wasted effort, Arnaz cursed out the camera crew and walked away fuming. Standing on the sidelines were Lucy, Vivian, Bill, and several dozen members of the crew—dissolved in laughter.

When the company returned to the studio to complete the filming of the remaining scenes on Stages 8 and 9 (requiring the studio audience to move en masse from one building to the next), Desi was in the throes of negotiating a deal to buy RKO studios from General Tire & Rubber Company, which had bought the movie-making property two years before from Howard Hughes for $25 million.

After many days of haggling, Desi made an offer: $6,150,000 for RKO's fifteen-stage, fourteen-acre lot in Hollywood (where Lucy and Desi met in 1940), its Culver City complex (RKO-Pathé, formerly David Selznick's studio, where *Gone With the Wind* was made) with eleven sound stages and a twenty-nine-acre back lot, and its valuable library of stock film footage. This would give the Ball-Arnaz TV empire, with its already owned Motion Picture Center, a total of thirty-three sound stages—four more than M-G-M and eleven more than 20th Century-Fox boasted in 1957.

Such major decisions sent violent shivers up the spine of Arnaz's more conservative wife, but for all practical purposes, they can be regarded as "typically Desi." Desilu itself could not afford to pay that kind of money. The corporation was still comparatively small and privately owned; its assets were not on a par with a major studio.

It was now that Desi's original strategy paid off. He knew that CBS was eager to acquire the lucrative rerun rights to the 179 "I Love Lucy" films and some less valuable properties. He was now ready to sell; the price tag—$5 million. CBS readily accepted, and Arnaz borrowed the rest of the money to buy RKO from the Bank of America.

"When Desi decided to buy the RKO studios for Desilu's expanding business, I knew this would mean more pressure on him than ever before," Lucy notes. "Some columnists wrote that both of us had been fired from RKO in years past and we were now taking revenge. That was ridiculous. Neither of us was fired from RKO; our association had been peaceful. I, for one, certainly never thought of buying the studio. In fact, I never dreamed of owning anything. I never had such high aspirations.

"Desi had high aspirations, but I can't believe they included *buying* RKO. It just happened. We needed more space and it was available there. Someone asked, 'Why don't you buy RKO?' and he said, as usual, 'Well, why not? How much do they want for it?' He went to the bank and said, 'Can I buy a studio for $6 million?' and they said, 'Yes. You have excellent credit.' Neither of us decided many years ago, 'Someday we'll own this place!' "

Before 1957 came to a close, Desilu shot the fourth of five Lucy-Desi specials contracted for with Ford Motor Company. This one starred Betty Grable and her husband, Harry James. Titled "Lucy Wins a Racehorse," the hour centered around the fact that Little Ricky, played for a second season by Keith Thibodeaux, wanted a horse. For the one hundred eighty-fourth time, it was Ricky *vs.* Lucy; he was against the idea and Lucy was for it. She entered a "Name the Horse" contest being sponsored by a breakfast cereal company, and won Whirling Jet, a horse described as "love-starved."

The animal, Tony, one of the best-trained horses in Hollywood, had been taught to do his tricks whenever he heard the word *action*. The horse was trained so meticulously that he would respond even if the command was whispered.

In one scene involving Lucy and Betty Grable, the horse stood in the wings waiting for his cue. Each time Jerry Thorpe called for action, Tony jerked to attention, playfully bared his teeth, and pranced before the cameras. He would perform his bits perfectly, including planting a big kiss on Lucy's cheek.

To break the monotony, Thorpe huddled with cast and crew and mapped out a plan to spell the word *action* rather than speak it. Everyone returned to his or her place, and orders for silence were issued by Jay Sandrich, the assistant director. Then Jerry carefully enunciated each letter of the word. As he finished, Tony trotted into the scene, reared up on his hind legs, did a dance step or two, and gave Lucy another kiss.

"My God," Thorpe gasped seriously. "The horse is a genius. He can spell!"

What Thorpe didn't know was that when he had finished mouthing the word, Bill Frawley had whispered "action" into Tony's ear, starting him off again.

On January 6, 1958, less than a month before the Grable/James episode was to be aired (February 3), Jerry Thorpe and the producer of the thirteen hour Lucy-Desi specials, Bert Granet, drove out to Palm Springs in an official Desilu station wagon with a few assistants to show the Arnazes, who were enjoying the holidays in their sprawling desert ranch house, a "rough cut" of "Lucy Wins a Racehorse."

"We carried a projector, screen, and several cans of film into the house," remembers one of the assistants, "and set it up in Lucy and Desi's bedroom. When we were ready to show the film, in came Lucy, Desi, the two kids, and three poodles. Lucy pulled her chair next to a lamp table and put a bottle of red nail polish on it. Desi took his place on a chair near the screen. He had just returned from a round of golf at the Tropicana Country Club. The kids sat on the floor close to their father, and the rest of us sat on the beds or on the long bench in front of the windows.

"The projector was stopped whenever Desi, Jerry, or Bert disagreed over the best way to sharpen a scene, rerunning the parts in dispute so that one or the other, but mostly Desi, could demonstrate the rightness of his solution. Lucy was busy painting her fingernails, seemingly uninterested in the various arguments. Sometimes without even looking up from her nails, she'd say something and the contradicting would stop because the others all said that was just what they meant."

The finished product aired on Monday, February 3, 1958, from eight to nine o'clock. An estimated 50 million watched the special, which placed fifth in the ARB race for the month behind "Perry Mason," "Person to Person," "Gunsmoke," and "Playhouse 90."

Almost a year before, Desi had begun speculating on what would eventually become the basis of the upcoming 1958–59 season. "I would like to do a series of hour shows I'd call 'Desilu Playhouse,'" Arnaz told a reporter. "It would be 'I Love Lucy' alternating with three others, all of them comedies. Maybe Lucy herself would play opposite somebody else in a one-shot. Maybe I would play opposite some young blonde or something. I don't know."

By February 1958 the plan was in the works. It called for thirty-seven hour-long shows to be aired under the "umbrella" title "Desilu Playhouse"; Lucille and Desi would "appear in five or six of them." The production budget: a cool $7.5 million.

Ford had decided to withdraw as sponsor after the five Lucy-Desi shows of the 1957–58 season. Disappointing sales of their new Edsel automobile might have encouraged that decision. Desi didn't care. "This time we're going to do the shows first and then go looking for a sponsor."

It wasn't that easy. Amid the problem-plagued production of the fifth Lucy-Desi special with guest star Fernando Lamas, Desi and his creative staff put together a lengthy proposal. He suggested a series of weekly dramas, comedies and musicals, plus a few undisclosed specials and six additional Lucy-Desi shows. "No violence, no psychopaths, no dirtiness. [Arnaz had made no plans to produce "The Untouchables" when he made the above statement.] There will never be any need to send the kids to bed when we come on."

The Fernando Lamas show—"Lucy Goes to Sun Valley"—required location filming in that resort area, so cast and crew were dispatched via train to Idaho. Lucy and Desi stayed at the Sun Valley Lodge where they rehearsed their scenes in the hotel's banquet room. Much of the action, however, took place right on the ski slopes, and this necessitated meticulous planning. "We had to get to the ski lift by five-thirty in the morning, recalls Jay Sandrich, who assisted director Jerry Thorpe. "We had to haul up our heavy camera and sound equipment before the lift officially opened for skiers. We sent the exposed film back to the studio on the Union Pacific. After two days of shooting on the mountain, we got a frantic call from the editing department in Hollywood, asking where the film was. We told them it had been sent; it should be there by now. They couldn't find it anywhere, so we had to reshoot the entire thing all over again. Three months later, someone found the unprocessed film in the back seat of one of the Desilu station wagons!"

With production finally over on the Lamas outing in early March, Desi flew to Pittsburgh to meet with the president of Westinghouse, Mark Cresap, Jr., to present his "Playhouse" proposal. At the time, Westinghouse was sponsoring the distinguished "Studio One," a CBS anthology series, with an advertising price tag of about $6 million.

"Desi came into town feeling pretty confident," recalls an aide to Cresap. "He was very flashy and very persuasive. Mr. Cresap liked him and was a fan of 'I Love Lucy.' But when Desi revealed the proposed budget of his venture—$12 million for production and air-time charges—Mark was taken aback. This was a lot of money then, and business wasn't that hot. In fact, it was lousy."

That's all Desi had to hear. Using his charm and powers of persuasion, he promised the Westinghouse mogul that business would double within a year if the company agreed to underwrite "Desilu Playhouse."

"Mark took the idea to the board of directors," the company aide continues, "and they approved the $12 million outlay just like that."

Upon Arnaz's return to Hollywood to oversee Desilu's *official* takeover of the RKO facilities, *TV Guide* reported in its May 24, 1958, edition: "Desi Arnaz swung his record-breaking $12 million Westinghouse 'Desilu Playhouse' deal which calls for forty-eight hour-long films, including seven new Lucy-Desi shows, thirty-six dramas, comedies, and musicals, five repeats of this season's Lucy-Desi hours—all without a single test film, no scripts, no guest stars—just the Desilu track record."

With the first batch of hour-long "Lucy" specials behind him, Desi concentrated on the challenge facing him. He thrived on adventures like this one, as much as he had during that frantic summer of 1951—seven years earlier—when he was trying to get "I Love Lucy" off the ground. Like most successful businessmen, he now depended on his staff to see to it that the studio was running efficiently. Desi's forte—well known in industry circles— was hiring the right people to do their respective jobs. The two people on whom he had depended from the very beginning, in 1951 and even earlier, decided to leave after completing "Lucy Goes to Sun Valley": Bob Carroll, Jr., and Madelyn Martin wanted to quit.

Though they had each signed three-year contracts in the fall of 1956, Bob and Madelyn felt that they had run dry, had exhausted every imaginable "Lucy" premise. They were brain-weary.

Desi knew he couldn't force them to write. Perhaps you can coax a bricklayer to lay another row of bricks, but you can't needle the creative process in the same way. As an incentive to remain, Desi offered to pay for a European vacation Bob wanted to take, and build a nursery onto Madelyn and Quinn Martin's house for their newborn son. Despite these gestures of good faith and friendship, Bob and Madelyn took leaves of absence for what would be an undetermined length of time.

That left the writing chores for the first "Lucy" hour under the Westinghouse banner in the able hands of Bob Schiller and Bob Weiskopf, who were about to start their fourth year with Desilu and the "Lucy" show. The first outing starred Maurice Chevalier and getting him was considered Desi's big coup. The Cuban had tried unsuccessfully for three years to get the Frenchman to appear on a "Lucy" show. Desi had met Chevalier in San Francisco in 1947 and was a great admirer of his talents and charm.

Schiller and Weiskopf devised this plot for "Lucy Goes to Mexico": Lucy gets involved with U.S. Customs officials in Tijuana, Mexico, while Ricky is rehearsing with Chevalier for a show aboard a navy aircraft carrier in San

Seven-and-a-half-year-old Keith Thibodeaux gets a rare opportunity to perform with the legendary Maurice Chevalier in "Lucy Goes to Mexico," filmed in June 1958.

Diego harbor. The script was put into production in early June 1958 and it was a complicated one from a production standpoint.

"The Maurice Chevalier show proved to me just how complex a director's job was," recalls Jay Sandrich, at that time an assistant director on "Lucy." "Jerry Thorpe had that show all mapped out like he was going into battle. We were doing process shots, second-unit filming, live action with doubles . . . it was very complicated. Plus there was no audience to use to play off when we were on location. When we did shows that were shot partially on location, we used to process that film and actually show it to the studio audience for their laughter to be recorded. This way they knew what the continuity of the story was. The bullfight scene, of course, was done at Desilu-Cahuenga studios."

The bullfight sequence called for Lucy to work with a live bull that had foot-long horns. Trained carefully, the animal was guaranteed to be docile. Lucy was, nevertheless, dubious, especially since she had to approach the snorting bull and wave a perfume-soaked handkerchief at him. The smell was supposed to stop the bull in his tracks.

During the rehearsal break, a prop man asked Lucy, "What kind of perfume have you got on that hankie?"

Miss Ball, always the kidder, cracked, "Eau de hamburger. That oughta keep him in line."

The wisecrack broke up everyone within earshot and was so hilariously appropriate it was written into the Schiller-Weiskopf script and used.

One of the bullfight scenes, however, caused Lucille some less than hilarious moments. "They had mounted a bull's head on the camera and rolled straight toward me at high speed. And would you believe, I was gored . . . just as if it had been a real bull!"

Even before the premiere on October 6, 1958, at 10 P.M., N. W. Ayer & Company, a leading ad agency known for its TV-ratings predictions, speculated that "Desilu Playhouse" would be among the top shows of the new season, ranking high with Danny Thomas, "Gunsmoke," "Wagon Train," and "Restless Gun." Desi admitted that "Playhouse" was his most important concern that year. "It's my number one baby," he said. "We've planned preview parties in twenty-two cities. A helicopter will fly over, showing our three studios, and we'll tell about our various activities and two thousand employees."

A Lucy-Desi special featuring Danny Thomas and his TV family, the Williamses, followed the Chevalier show on December 1, 1958. The script by Schiller and Weiskopf was story-edited by Bob Carroll, Jr., and Madelyn Martin, who had returned with a lessened workload to their writing posts at Desilu. The breakneck schedule they had pursued during the preceding seven years (writing as many as sixty pages of "Lucy" script a week) was a thing of the past. For Madelyn, Desi built a nursery adjacent to her office at the old RKO Studios on Gower Street in Hollywood, so she could bring her infant son to work and care for him at the same time.

After five years of sharing studio facilities on Cahuenga Boulevard, the "Lucy" and "Danny Thomas" programs were finally "wed"—if for only this one occasion. In the story line, the Ricardos rent their Connecticut house to Danny Williams, then find themselves homeless when Ricky's film commitment is canceled. Danny Thomas, Marjorie Lord, Rusty Hamer, and Angela Cartwright guest-starred in their accustomed roles of the Williamses. Gale Gordon appeared as the local judge who tried to iron out the domestic foul-up.

For the third Westinghouse Lucy-Desi hour, the company went on location to Lake Arrowhead, a mile-high resort area two hours from Los Angeles, to film a sequence simulating the frozen wastelands of Alaska, about to become our forty-ninth state. Guest-starring Red Skelton, the show aired February 9, 1959. The highlight: a ten-minute pantomime sketch, "Dining at the Waldorf," featuring Skelton's Freddie the Freeloader and Lucy as his hapless companion. Composer Arthur Hamilton wrote a delightful comedy song for the production, "Poor Everybody Else." Like the Lucy/Harpo pairing in 1955, "Dining at the Waldorf" was an all-too-rare example of two equally qualified comedians merging their talents and creating extraordinary TV entertainment.

Jay Sandrich remembers well how the two clowns worked together: "The sketch presented a problem for Red. When Lucy asked him how he did it, so she could duplicate his actions, he said he didn't know how he did it. He just did it. Lucy insisted that she learn the act perfectly or it would not work. Lucy studied Skelton the first day, and then the second day she was doing it with him step-by-step, and by the third day, she had it down perfect."

In late 1958 Vivian Vance, who had achieved an enormous popularity due to her hundreds of "Lucy" appearances, was tapped to play the lead role in an ABC-Desilu pilot based on the Patrick *(Auntie Mame)* Dennis novel *Guestward Ho!* Ralph Levy, the director of the original "I Love Lucy" pilot, was signed to supervise the production as well as direct the test film.

"On the first take, I yelled 'action' and Vivian just stood there frozen," Levy points out. "On the second take, the same thing happened. And again with the third. I went up to her to find out if she was all right and Viv said, 'This is the first time in eight years I've been in my own light,' meaning, of course, that after being in the shadow of Lucille all that time, she was finding it a little difficult going it alone. It was a big change for her."

The pilot did not sell, which meant that Miss Vance would remain with Lucy and Desi for an upcoming ninth season. To make matters worse for the Kansas-born actress, she was sued for divorce on March 30, 1959. In the divorce action, Philip N. Ober, then fifty (Vivian was forty-six), said that his wife was "cruel" to him. She said in rebuttal that they "could never agree on how to handle my success." She also revealed that he was "extravagant and did not believe in savings."

They divided property valued at more than a hundred and sixty thousand dollars, which included their California home at 629 Frontera Drive in Pacific Palisades; the Cubero, New Mexico, property; and some stocks and bonds.

Vivian's divorce was not the only example of marital difficulties on the "Lucy" set. By the beginning of 1959, Ed Sullivan, in a blind item in his syndicated newspaper column, hinted of the divorce of "TV's famous husband and wife team." There weren't that many such teams, but, coincidentally, one of them made a guest appearance on the last Lucy-Desi special of the 1958–59 season. Howard Duff and Ida Lupino, then starring in their own CBS sitcom, "Mr. Adams and Eve," appeared in the June 8, 1959, telecast of "Lucy's Summer Vacation." Jerry Thorpe directed the script by Schiller and Weiskopf in mid-April. The result was a delightful romp, set in a mountain lodge in Vermont, although filmed on Stage 9 at Desilu-Cahuenga.

Following filming, Lucille and Desi escaped the rigors of their studio existence. It had been a busy and demanding year that saw Desilu go public and offer half of its stock, or 565,600 shares, on the American Stock Exchange on December 3, 1958. To save her faltering marriage, Lucy planned a trip to Europe aboard the French ocean liner the *Liberté.* Despite the warning of close friends, she decided to bring the children along.

While in Europe, they visited Maurice Chevalier at his home, about twenty minutes outside Paris. It was a wonderful reunion, which took the edge off the negative aspects of the holiday: When the Arnazes returned to the States they were scarcely speaking to each other. Desi was weary from overwork and also resented the presence of his children, even though he was a doting Daddy. The pair's hostilities toward each other touched off one quarrel after another.

In July 1959, Desilu announced that its gross for the year just ended was $20,470,361 in contrast to the 1954 gross of $4,668,660. Its profit for 1959 was $249,566; the net for 1958 was only $92,336. Business was good, even though the marriage—from which Desilu was created—wasn't. Tensions built steadily. In fact, Desi was no longer sleeping in the master bedroom of the couple's mansion on Roxbury Drive in Beverly Hills.

At the studio, they had to put up a front. In late June, upon their return from the European cruise, Lucy and Desi started production on the eleventh one-hour "Lucy" special, which would open the 1959–60 season of "Desilu Playhouse" on September 25. Their guest star was Mr. Television himself, Milton Berle. He agreed to appear only if the Arnazes reciprocated by co-starring with him in an NBC special the next season.

Because Jerry Thorpe was busy directing another Desilu show that would premiere in the fall, Desi himself took on the added burden of directing the "Milton Berle Hides Out at the Ricardos'" show. By this time, the company had all but totally abandoned its technique of filming before a live audience. Production problems and Desi's own erratic schedule precluded bringing in guests. The system of using multiple cameras shooting simultaneously was, however, retained.

On and off the set, and despite persistent rumors in the press, Lucy and Desi tried desperately to maintain a friendly relationship, especially around Milton Berle. A number of times during rehearsal, tempers—particularly Desi's—flared.

"What do I say here?" Lucy asked director Desi, interrupting a run-through.

"You say, 'I can't.' "

Desi's accent is as thick off camera as it is on. "Can?" queried Lucy.

"Can't!" replied Desi brusquely.

"Are you saying, 'can' or 'can't'?"

"I'm saying *can't*, dammit! Can't!" Desi shouted.

Arnaz was boss. "Nothing goes out of this shop without Desi putting his fine Cuban hand into it," said Howard McClay, once a Desilu executive and later PR director of Lucille Ball Productions, Inc., until his death in 1980. Someone once remarked that if Desi had learned to type in Spanish, he would have *written* "Lucy" too.

Even Milton Berle, whom some associates have called a tyrant, was in awe of Desi's ability behind the camera: "I was so struck by the way he handled everything on his own show that I asked him to direct a show for me. He's got a tremendous flair for comedy; there's almost nobody like him around. He's a driver, a perfectionist, and he usually knows 95 percent of what he wants. I think he can do more serious stuff as well. I have great

Desi directed the Milton Berle special but due to Arnaz's heavy Desilu schedule, shooting was done without a studio audience in attendance. Laughs were added artificially later.

respect for his ability to handle people and for his knowledge of what plays and what doesn't.

"Look what he did for Lucy," Uncle Milton continued. "She's the greatest comedienne in the world because she's one of the greatest actresses. He saw that in her and helped to bring it out." That's quite a testimonial coming from a man who once demonstrated to an Irish tenor the proper way to sing "The Wearin' of the Green."

During rehearsals for "Milton Berle Hides Out at the Ricardos'," Desi had the pair play one piece of business five times. It was a bit that would last no more than thirty seconds on the screen, but the rehearsals alone took a half-hour. At the end of the repetitive session, Desi told Lucy and Milton, "Now we go through it one more time."

"Aw, come on, Des," Berle whined.

"No," Lucy said flatly. "We will *not* do it again!"

"Come on," Desi insisted. "We do it one more time."

They did it one more time.

If Desi was manic in rehearsal, he became downright frantic when it came time to shoot. He used the usual three cameras, but sometimes ordered a fourth and even a fifth. His day was one solid block of work. When the cast and crew knocked off for lunch, Desi raced back to his office to dispose of other business demands.

"You want to eat, dear?" Lucy asked him.

"No. No time." There was almost hostility in his voice. He flung himself away and went back to work.

Inside of fifteen minutes, he had consulted with a script editor, looked

After eight years' experience as a television producer, Desi got involved in every aspect of the production of the Berle episode as well as countless others. Here he checks camera angles and directs Lucy's stand-in, Hazel Pierce, in an important scene set at a Manhattan high-rise.

through a catalogue of performers with a casting director, talked to a prop man about props, conversed with a set designer about sets, and listened to a man who was trying to sell him a new electric golf cart.

Back at Stage 9 after lunch, Desi picked up where he left off. One person who was present during the Milton Berle show preparations recalls, "Desi was all over the set like an unruly school kid, squinting through his viewer, shouting orders at everyone, conferring with the lighting men and other technicians. One instant he was up a ladder; the next, he was on the floor on his hands and knees, showing where he wanted a gravel walkway laid.

"Sometimes he was like a human windmill, his arms flailing wildly. Once, while spreading his arms to show an actor how to do a scene, he accidentally rammed his hand into a running electric fan and shaved the flesh off three fingers.

"Working with the actors, he hopped in and out of the field of action, placing them forcibly in position, showing them where to walk, sometimes even twisting his face into the expressions he wanted theirs to assume," the observer concludes.

Westinghouse had requested in late spring that the "Desilu Playhouse" be moved for the new season to Friday night's nine-to-ten time period on CBS. Request granted. The only other second-season change in the show involved Betty Furness, who opened the Westinghouse refrigerator doors ("You can be *sure* if it's Westinghouse.") during the 1958–59 season commercials; she was replaced by a younger woman.

Desi also directed the next Lucy-Desi special, which co-starred Robert Cummings. Titled "The Ricardos Go to Japan," it was the seventh of a total of eight "I Love Lucy"-type hours contracted with Westinghouse. It was filmed in late September 1959, following a three-month hiatus that Lucy spent working with a new group of young acting hopefuls in her Desilu Workshop.

"I also spent as much time as possible with our children," Lucy confided to a close friend. "I took them to Del Mar a couple of times, to Disneyland, Marineland, and helped them with their French lessons."

Desi went back to Europe after the Bob Cummings show, this time alone. Rumors of Lucy and Desi's separation abounded in Hollywood. Lucy tried to explain them away to inquisitive reporters. "Some people live on rumors," she said. "Desi and I have been in this whole thing long enough to be accustomed to them. We've gotten through the thing before, and we'll get through it again. Maybe it's good for some couples to be separated for a time—maybe it can renew and refresh a relationship."

But the rumors began affecting business on the three Desilu lots. When reporters asked Howard McClay if he thought there was a possibility that Lucy and Desi might split up, he answered, "I don't believe there is. Don't forget, they've got a big vested interest in each other—not just the family, the kids, but this whole thing." His sweeping gesture indicated the huge plant. "No. I don't think so."

Their mutual differences did not escape their own two children, then eight and six and a half. "One night, as I stopped by Little Desi's room to tuck him in, I heard him whimpering," recalls Lucille Ball. "Lucie, who was normally a sound sleeper, was tossing and turning in her bed when I looked in on her."

Lucy knew then that she had to tell the children the truth. Daddy was no longer living at home, and there was no use in making excuses for him.

"I took Lucie aside first, because she was older. 'Lucie,' I said, 'I have to tell you that Mommy and Daddy are not getting along and I know that the unhappiness you see is affecting you. And I want you to know that it has nothing to do with you. We love you very much. I want you also to know that we are trying to work things out.'

"She said, 'You wouldn't get a divorce, would you?' "

Lucy was dumbfounded by her daughter's naïve frankness. "What do you know about divorce?" she asked the eight-year-old. "What is a divorce?"

Little Lucie stammered, "Well, it's . . . well, you wouldn't get one, would you?"

In reply, Lucy told the child, "I am only planning on being separated from Daddy, and I just want you to know that it has nothing to do with you. We will probably see much more of Daddy, actually."

"I learned pretty early," says Desi Arnaz, Jr., today, "to relate to 'I Love Lucy' as a TV show and to my parents as actors in it. There wasn't much relationship between what I saw on TV and what was really going on at home. Those were difficult years—all those funny things happening each week on television to people who looked like my parents, then the same people agonizing through some terrible, unhappy times at home, and each of them trying to convince my sister and me separately that the other was in the wrong."

The fall of 1959 was also a low period for Desi Arnaz, Sr. Problems plaguing a motion picture production in Europe were constant, sometimes necessitating fifteen-hour workdays. One night in September, he was picked up by Hollywood police on a drunk-driving charge.

What did the people who worked with Desi think of him?

"I'd like to tell you one story about Desi Arnaz which really points up the kind of guy he is," begins one loyal script girl. "In 1957 when he sold the rerun rights of 'I Love Lucy' to CBS, he was advised to quit television. He was told that he could pay the government $1 million in capital gains tax, take the rest free and clear, and live a life of ease and relaxation. You know the answer? He said, 'That's great, but how do I tell all the people who've worked with us in Desilu? How do I tell them, "I've got mine. I'm gonna quit"?'

"Desi couldn't do it," the lady continued. "He went to the Bank of America, borrowed a few more million, and bought RKO so he could expand and put *more* people to work. That's the kind of guy Desi Arnaz is."

Not everyone thought this way. Once, an actor was called in to redo a scene, which under his Desilu contract the studio would have to pay for. The producer asked him to waive the extra payment because of a tight budget problem and, to press home the point, added, "After all, you're one of the regulars here and we're all one big happy family on this lot."

"Some family," the actor cracked. "Daddy's never home."

Daddy, of course, was Desi and he signed the checks. And, of late, Daddy had been neglecting his professional family as well as his real one. Yet the studio and its many projects continued to move forward, thanks to the strange devotion both Desi and Lucy seemed to have generated among their professional "family."

Such dedication is difficult to decipher. With one of the regular actors, now deceased, the reason was simple: He and Desi once worked together in a band many years ago; subsequently, the actor fell on hard times and when Desi hit it big he took him in.

"Desi liked to play the part of Big Daddy," says one former member of the family. "And Lucy, God bless her, liked to play Baby Snooks."

Lucy and Desi differed in their attitudes toward the huge complex of studios they owned. To Desi, contends one associate, it was an opportunity for a former bandleader and actor to show what "a shrewd cookie he was as an executive." To Lucy, it was the "world's biggest sand pile."

One insider privy to the many Desilu machinations points out: "Success went to his pocketbook. Desi had made so much money that success became very dull and monotonous."

But despite the so-called monotony, Desilu continued to flourish as a multimillion-dollar business enterprise. In early October 1959, after the Bob Cummings show, Desi had gone off to Europe, leaving Lucy alone. Since they were no longer living in the same house, she hardly missed him. Professionally, Lucille was keeping busy with her acting workshop, getting ready to stage a revue that would constitute the Christmas Day "Desilu Playhouse" installment. Without her Cuban compass, Lucy found the going rough.

"Lucy asked me to appear on the Christmas show," Hedda Hopper once wrote. "She was making her bow as director, coaching a dozen or so young players she had been training in her school for over a year. Desi had just returned from the solo trip to Europe.

"During rehearsals, Vivian Vance and Bill Frawley wanted to take cover with me to avoid the storms between Lucy and Desi. It was dreadful. 'You can't insult him before the entire company,' I warned her in her dressing room. 'You're partly responsible for this show, too, you know.'

"It seemed we were doomed to have a flop on our hands. As director, Lucy was lost without Desi, too mad to see straight, and the show was going to pieces. In dress rehearsal Desi said, 'Lucy, dear, will you let me see if I can pull this thing together for you?'

"Lucy snapped back at him with blood in her eye, 'Okay, try it!' In ten minutes, he had the revue ticking like a fine clock," Hedda concluded.

Besides Miss Hopper, Vivian, and Bill, the show, which was called "The Desilu Revue," featured cameo appearances by Ann Sothern, Hugh O'Brian, Spring Byington, and Lassie—all Desilu performers. With a script by Bob Schiller and Bob Weiskopf, the hour-long special spotlighted twenty-two talented newcomers who were personally selected by Lucy from the total enrollment of her Desilu Workshop Theater.

With the revue behind her, Lucy decided to abandon the workshop completely. "Sure, I'll miss it," she said. "It's a satisfying thing. But I've given two years of my time and my heart to the kids, and you can't do everything for them. The objective of the workshop was to provide a stepping-stone for young, talented performers. I think I achieved this. However, I found myself caring about each one. They took two years out of my life as a lay psychiatrist. That's over now, because they drained me dry. I figured if I ever wanted to work again I'd better conclude it."

The workshop was not the only venture Lucille wanted to discontinue. Before the year (1959) was out, she wanted to sue Desi for divorce.

"You can't," a close confidante told her. "You and Desi both signed the Westinghouse contract as partners. If you walk out now, they could cancel and sue you."

The Westinghouse deal did have several months to run, so Lucy decided to wait until the propitious moment before making her long-awaited move. Desi was already aware of her intentions. In fact, they had worked out the details some time ago.

Their most difficult task during the final few months of their stormy marriage was telling the children of their plans.

"We drove to our home in Palm Springs, specifically for that purpose," Miss Ball recounts. "And Desi told them while I just sat there."

He began by telling them that Mommy and Daddy weren't getting along. That's when Little Lucie looked up, "But you won't get a divorce?"

Lucy continues: "Desi explained that perhaps we would. The kids got very quiet, put their heads down, and didn't want to look at us. Desi told them he loved them very much.

"Finally, Little Desi looked up and said, 'But, Daddy, a divorce? Isn't there some way you can take it all back?' That was almost more than we could take," says Lucille retrospectively.

It now came time to perform as Mr. and Mrs. Ricky Ricardo for the last time. It was their most difficult assignment in the eight and a half years playing the roles.

The atmosphere around the set was different. "There was no sign of unpleasantness," one witness maintains. "At the studio they acted with deference and courtesy to each other. In the old days, their relationship had been marked by an easy give and take. They used to kid each other unmercifully. Now they were being too nice to each other. We all knew something was really wrong."

The last Lucy-Desi outing was titled "Lucy Meets the Moustache" and co-

Lucille Ball chats with the late comedian Ernie Kovacs before filming the last Lucy-Desi special, March 2, 1960 (Desi's forty-third birthday).

starred the late comedian Ernie Kovacs and his wife, Edie Adams. It was the thirteenth hour-long special in the three-year period. It was the one hundred and ninety-third Lucy/Ricky/Fred/Ethel plot since 1951.

"Every time they wanted to film a funny scene," Miss Adams recalls, "Lucy would break down and cry. Nobody could stand to watch it."

Ironically, the last scene Lucy and Desi ever played together seemed to explain their marital problems in just a few Schiller-Weiskopf lines:

LUCY: Honest, honey, I just wanted to help.
RICKY: From now on, you can help me by not trying to help me. But thanks, anyway.

As per the script, they embraced and kissed. But before the kiss, Lucy removed the moustache she was wearing to impersonate Kovacs' chauffeur. The sound track "laughed" appropriately . . . for the last time.

Backstage, there was no laughter, nor were there any smiles. A heavy air of melancholy invaded the huge sound stage as good-byes were said, kisses exchanged. Vivian Vance was teary-eyed, and so was gruff old Bill Frawley. They, more than anyone else, had labored the longest with Lucy and Desi.

"I filed for divorce the day after I finished my last piece of film under the Westinghouse contract," Lucille Ball says. On Thursday, March 3, 1960—a

*Lucy poses as Ernie Kovacs'
chauffeur in "Lucy Meets the
Moustache," the very last
Lucy-Ricky-Fred-Ethel
encounter.*

day after Desi's forty-third birthday—Lucy filed papers in Santa Monica Superior Court, claiming married life to Desi was "a nightmare," nothing at all like it appeared on "I Love Lucy."

By the time the public saw the last "Lucy" episode on April 1, 1960, their divorce was already old news, and Lucy and Desi's nine-year reign as "TV's favorite couple" had officially ended.

12 Lucy After "Lucy"

"It wasn't the industry and our working together that broke us up," claims Lucille Ball of her nineteen-year marriage to Desi Arnaz. "The pressure had a lot to do with it. He was a very sick man. I was living with hope for many years.

"When the children got to an age when they were noticing the unhappiness, it was time to move away. That helped me make up my mind . . . that, and the end of our performing commitments together.

"For years and years I wore blinders where he was concerned. I saw only his good points. But somehow I couldn't help myself. I'm very sensitive," the redhead continued. "I stored up all the hurts and humiliations, not the hurts of a day or a week, but the hurts of years. Then some little thing comes along. It opens up the dam; all the resentment rushes out."

When Lucy won her default divorce from Desi on May 4, 1960—a little more than a month after CBS canceled "Desilu Playhouse," the last vestige of the "I Love Lucy" legend—she admitted to the press, "It's very difficult to work the way he worked for the last nine years. Mostly, I think it's bad for the children. It's much better for us to be apart."

In truth, the marriage shattered five years before it was officially terminated by divorce. "Those last five years were sheer, unadulterated hell," Lucy confirms today. "I'm afraid I didn't cope too well. We both knew it was over. But we had commitments to fill. So we stayed together, I was hoping in my heart that maybe everything might change, a miracle might happen, maybe, maybe, maybe. But people don't really change.

"Desi drank and I knew he went out with other women, but I didn't worry about it soon enough. The last five years were the same old booze and broads, the only change being that he was rarely at home anymore. And that was a blessing, because we didn't yell at each other when we didn't see each other."

Superior Court Judge Orlando H. Rhodes listened to Lucy's emotional testimony, then awarded her an uncontested divorce. She was awarded half of the $20 million television empire built on the success of their TV marriage as the happy-go-lucky Ricky Ricardos, as well as the Beverly Hills mansion, two station wagons, and a cemetery plot at Forest Lawn. Desi retained the other half of the Desilu fortune, a golf cart, a membership in the Thunderbird Country Club in Palm Springs, a truck, eleven racehorses, and the ranch at Riverside.

Desi issued a formal statement soon after: "We deeply regret that after long and serious consideration we have not been able to work out our problems. . . . Our divorce will be completely amicable and there will be no contest. Lucy will pursue her career on television and I will continue my work as head of Desilu Productions."

Following the divorce proceedings, Lucy did not pursue her television career. Instead, she immediately plunged into a motion picture with Bob Hope, *The Facts of Life.* When production ended, she packed up the kids and went off to New York, ensconced herself in a twenty-third-floor luxury apartment in the East Sixties, and began rehearsals for her first Broadway play. This was something that was in the offing for over a year; in fact, the previous summer, she had made a verbal commitment to producers Kermit Bloomgarten and Morton DaCosta to star in a stage play adaptation of a Dorothy Parker short story, *Big Blonde.* The deal never came off (the play was too maudlin for Lucy), so Miss Ball jumped at the chance to headline a new musical, *Wildcat!,* which had music by Cy Coleman *(Sweet Charity)* and a book by N. Richard Nash *(The Rainmaker).* The play, bankrolled by Desilu Productions (for four hundred thousand dollars in exchange for all TV rights to the musical numbers), opened on December 16, 1960, at the Alvin Theater. It was a standing-room-only hit because Lucille Ball was the star; when she withdrew some months later because of "ill health," the show posted its closing notice.

Desi flew to New York regularly to visit his two children, whom he missed immensely. His workload, running the massive Desilu operation, was still a formidable situation. Desi, Jr., contends that his father aged ten years because of the pressure of the television industry. "The major operations he underwent in the 1970s didn't help either," the young actor adds.

Bill Frawley wasted no time in securing another acting assignment when the nine-year "Lucy" stint folded. Even though his Desilu contract ran until June 1, 1960, Frawley accepted an offer in the spring from TV producer Don Fedderson to co-star with Fred MacMurray in a new situation comedy that would premiere on the ABC Television Network in the fall, "My Three Sons."

"Desi was a little irate about my accepting another job while I was under contract to him," Frawley once admitted.

His "My Three Sons" role, that of Michael Francis O'Casey, or "Bub" as he was more commonly called, was similar in attitude to the Fred Mertz character he portrayed for so long—goodhearted but cantankerous. "While doing 'My Three Sons,' I've been getting residual checks from the reruns of 'Lucy,' " said Frawley. "And, I must say, they look beautiful."

When "Lucy" ended its first-run engagement on April 1, 1960, the half-hour episodes were still enjoying enormous popularity in the daytime. Since January 5, 1959, the original thirty-minute films were being broadcast on the CBS network Monday through Friday at eleven o'clock in the morning (EST). And beginning July 13, 1960, CBS—which now owned the 179 films outright—retitled the last thirteen episodes "Lucy in Connecticut" and beamed it every Sunday night in prime time for the duration of the summer.

At first, network bigwigs were worried that the Arnaz divorce would dissipate the value of the "I Love Lucy" films for which they had paid millions. Would the public still accept the pair as a married couple? Today, twenty-five years later, that seems like a silly question.

Frawley continued in his "My Three Sons" role for five years before poor health forced him to retire. A short time later, while strolling down Hollywood Boulevard after seeing a movie one night, he died suddenly of a heart attack on March 3, 1966, just a week after his seventy-ninth birthday. He collapsed near the Hollywood Knickerbocker Hotel where he had lived for many years before moving to an apartment at 450 North Rossmore in Hollywood. His male nurse, a constant companion since Frawley's prostate surgery in 1965, dragged him into the hotel lobby to try to revive him. It was too late. The actor was rushed to nearby Hollywood Receiving Hospital where he was pronounced dead.

Upon hearing of his passing, Lucille Ball said, "Oh, I'm terribly sorry. I've lost one of my dearest friends and show business has lost one of the greatest character actors of all time. Those of us who knew him and loved him will miss him."

Ironically, Bill's last video appearance was in a segment of "The Lucy Show," telecast October 25, 1965. "I love that girl," Frawley told a reporter before his death. "I've loved her since she was a star-struck kid at RKO. I get along all right with Desi, too."

Arnaz's affection for the crusty old curmudgeon was demonstrated the day of Frawley's burial at San Fernando Mission Cemetery. Besides acting as one of the pallbearers, Desi took out and paid for a full-page ad in the *Hollywood Reporter.* The layout featured a photograph of Frawley with the dates of his life (February 26, 1887, to March 3, 1966) underneath and the inscription *"¡Buenas Noches, Amigo!"*

What happened to Frawley's TV wife after the demise of "I Love Lucy"? Vivian Vance did not go back to work like Frawley. When her "Guestward Ho!" pilot failed to sell in 1959, Desilu decided to film a new version for possible airing in 1960. Director Ralph Levy wanted Vivian to reprise her role as Babs Hooten in the second attempt, but not everyone agreed. When the revamped version went before the cameras in March 1960, Joanne Dru had inherited Vivian's part. ("Guestward Ho!" premiered September 29, 1960, on ABC and lasted only one season.)

This didn't bother the forty-eight-year-old actress in the least. She had successfully shaken off the trauma of her 1959 divorce from Phil Ober and had met a charming man that same summer at a Santa Fe, New Mexico, party. Seven years her junior, John Dodds, a successful literary agent from the East, proposed to Vivian shortly thereafter. They were married on Monday, January 16, 1961, at the site of their first encounter, the home of author Babs Hooten and her husband. Vivian was given away by actor John Emery, Tallulah Bankhead's ex-husband, who himself had made a number of "I Love Lucy" appearances. The Doddses set up residence in Stamford, Connecticut, an easy commute to Manhattan where John maintained offices. Vivian became active in the Connecticut Association for Mental Health and received a well-deserved award for her dedication. She was a happy lady, satisfied with her new life.

Lucille, too, met a new man and married him that year. "I didn't want to get married again," said Lucy. "I didn't think I would find a mature, adult person like Gary [Morton], a really understanding guy who is wonderful to be around and uncomplicated. He has none of the worrisome characteristics I lived with. I learned from experience. I wasn't going to walk into the same trap.

"One night when I was in *Wildcat!,* Jack Carter and his wife, Paula, said they wanted me to meet a friend. I put it off two or three times . . . I was too tired, I said. Finally one night I was hungry and I said, 'Well, I'll go for something to eat,' and I met Gary. We had fun. He was going away for a couple of weeks. When he came back we started seeing each other after the theater.

"I found out he was, as I said, uncomplicated, good, sweet, hip, funny, and he appreciated a home, not just the trappings. He knew how to enjoy himself in a home. I got sick during the run of *Wildcat!* Maybe it was emotional, I don't know. I came to the Coast to sell my house and go to Switzerland or somewhere, and he followed me. My friends met him. He knew more people than I did.

"By the time he was here for a while everybody was saying, 'My lord, why don't you marry this guy?' Finally I said, 'Yes.' "

Lucille Ball and Gary Morton were married November 19, 1961. She credits him with gently coaxing her back into television the following year.

"In early 1962, Lucy came East for a visit," said Vivian Vance Dodds in an interview before her death. "She told me she had a script for a new TV series in her purse. I said, 'Lucy, don't take it out. I won't read it.' "

Six months later, Vivian Vance was in Hollywood making the first episodes of a new sitcom, to be titled "The Lucy Show."

"I don't believe I'd have started the show without Vivian," contends Lucy. "And I really didn't know how I could start it *with* her. After all, she had settled into a new way of life since we last worked together. She'd gotten married, she had a home in Connecticut, her garden, her pets, her new interests—all the things she loved. She was willing to come back if it was okay with John, and even though it would involve five years of long-distance commuting, he agreed. John felt it was doing him a favor because it made Vivian happy."

Desi Arnaz produced "The Lucy Show" for Desilu Productions. When rehearsals for the first show, "Lucy Waits Up for Chris," commenced on July 12, 1962, Desi was present on the set. He gave Lucy a kiss on the cheek and a good luck emblem, a tiny four-leaf clover made out of antique emerald jade.

"Lucy, dear," he said, "I wish you all the luck in the whole ever-loving world. You really deserve it, kid."

"Oh, Desi," she said, smiling. "How thoughtful."

She returned a sincere embrace, then went back to her rehearsing. Desi made his way up a few steps to one of the catwalks that serviced the overhead lighting. Leaning on the wooden guardrail, he gazed down at Lucy as she practiced a complicated telephone scene. Suddenly his eyes filled with tears and he broke down crying.

As he dried his face with a handkerchief, he turned and discovered that Vivian Vance had climbed to the catwalk and was standing beside him. She, too, was crying. He put his arm around the actress, the same girl whom eleven years ago he had discovered at the La Jolla Playhouse and cast as Ethel Mertz.

"Oh, Desi," Vivian cried. "It isn't the same, is it?"

Vivian knew exactly why Desi was crying. "Like me, he was thinking back to when we all started in on 'I Love Lucy'—him and Lucy and William Frawley and me, and how it was then. All the newness . . . all the anticipation and the hope . . . and the fun. And here we were, starting again, only this time he was on the outside looking in and it wasn't fun anymore. He wasn't acting. He was divorced. I'd been divorced, but I was married again. And Lucy was married again. So much had happened to so many people, but most of all to Desi, leaving him alone and a little sad, although he tried to hide it," Miss Vance explained.

"The Lucy Show" debuted October 1, 1962. Critic Edith Efron wrote: "Encountering America's favorite zany in a new habitat, with a new last name (Carmichael), with unknown young children, and without her dashing Desi, is an odd experience. A decade of 'I Love Lucy' shows has so indissolubly wedded the images of Lucy and Desi Arnaz that to discover a Desi-less Lucy on the screen is like finding a revised edition of *Gone with the Wind* in which Scarlett O'Hara appears without Rhett Butler."

Bob Carroll, Jr., and Madelyn Pugh Martin were back as head writers on the new show, along with their "I Love Lucy" cronies, Bob Schiller and Bob Weiskopf. After "The Lucille Ball–Desi Arnaz Show" went off the air in the spring of 1960, Bob and Madelyn created "The Tom Ewell Show," a CBS sitcom from the Four-Star Entertainment factory. Though it had a clever premise—a man surrounded by women: wife, three daughters, and mother-in-law—it lasted only one season. Schiller and Weiskopf spent the two Lucy-less seasons writing for the Cara Williams–Harry Morgan show, "Pete and Gladys," prompting Lucy to chide, "You gave some of your best material to that *other* redhead!"

After spending two seasons with Schiller and Weiskopf churning out new "Lucy" adventures—decidedly the best of the series' 156 episodes—Bob and Madelyn "quit" television. Each decided to explore new areas. Bob wanted to try his hand at writing movies and Madelyn, now divorced from Quinn Martin, had accepted a marriage proposal.

Lucille Ball contends, "They got a little too rich for a while and they quit. Seriously. You see, outside of my show, all my money goes back into my business. The big thing in this business is residuals, and Bob and Madelyn became millionaires very quickly."

The writing team soon became bored with their "retirement" and returned to their respective facing typewriters (the female half as Madelyn Davis) to pen sitcom scripts for other series like "The Cara Williams Show" and "The Debbie Reynolds Show," which Jess Oppenheimer created and produced for NBC in 1969.

Vivian Vance left the cast after three seasons. Commuting from one coast to another for more than six months a year grew to be a burden on her and her marriage. Every year or so thereafter, she returned to California to guest-star in Lucy's sitcoms, ostensibly for old times' sake. Despite her Hollywood "roots," Vivian said she never felt at home there. In the sixties, while living in a 125-year-old white colonial house in Stamford, Connecticut, she told a reporter, "Even after all the years in Hollywood, I feel now that home is in Connecticut and I'm a visitor out there. So even if it is my house, when I'm out there working, I live like a visitor."

Vivian's husband, John Dodds, closed his literary agency and became a successful publishing executive at such houses as G. P. Putnam's Sons, Simon & Schuster, and New American Library (he was Gloria Swanson's editor when she published her autobiography). During the late sixties and early seventies, Vivian took to the lecture circuit, especially enjoying her talks with college students. She was persuaded to write her autobiography, but later, after completing it, decided to put it in a desk drawer, telling her husband, "Johnny, I want to pay back the advance. I don't want to lose my privacy."

In 1974, the Doddses moved to Belvedere, California, an island in San Francisco Bay, to be close to Vivian's sister. It was there that Vivian lost her long battle against cancer on August 17, 1979, at age sixty-seven.

Commenting on her death, Desi Arnaz said, "It's bad enough to lose one of the great artists we had the honor and pleasure to work with, but it's even harder to reconcile the loss of one of your best friends."

Shortly after the premiere of "The Lucy Show" in 1962, Desi Arnaz asked his ex-wife if she was interested in buying him out—his half-interest in Desilu Productions, Inc., that is. With a little help from the City National Bank of Beverly Hills, Lucille Ball paid her ex-husband $2,552,975, the price for purchasing his 300,350 shares of Desilu stock, pegged at the time at $8.50 per share.

Arnaz retired to his horse-breeding ranch in nearby Corona. The following year, he married Edith Mack Hirsch, the redheaded ex-wife of a millionaire sportsman, in Las Vegas. He returned to the business he once called a "monster"—television—several years later as an independent producer. Doing business as Desi Arnaz Productions, he bankrolled a number of promising TV pilots. The one that sold, "The Mothers-in-Law" in 1967, was created by Bob and Madelyn and ran two seasons on NBC with Eve Arden and Kaye Ballard as the stars.

In 1974, William Morrow and Company, publishers, advanced him a hefty sum to write his memoirs, which were published in 1976 under the title *A Book*. It appeared briefly on best-seller lists and was later issued as a mass market paperback by Warner Books. Desi's plans to write a sequel, to be titled *Another Book*, have not materialized as yet. Now the doting grandparents of two little boys by daughter Lucie, Desi and Edie Arnaz live in their Del Mar, California, home, which overlooks the Pacific Ocean.

Lucy completed a six-year run of "The Lucy Show" in 1968, selling off the rerun rights to it and all of Desilu Productions to the giant Gulf & Western conglomerate for $17 million worth of G&W stock. One of the conditions of the sale required her to abandon "The Lucy Show" format and come up with a new series, if she intended to continue her weekly TV antics. In March 1968, she formed Lucille Productions and, headquartered at Paramount Studios, began a brand new sitcom—her third—"Here's Lucy," which co-starred Gale Gordon and the Arnaz children, Lucie and Desi, Jr.

The half-hour program premiered on September 23, 1968, and, like its predecessors, was an immediate hit. The show ran six seasons, through the spring of 1974, at which time Lucy decided to call it quits after twenty-three years on the tube. Why did she decide to throw in the towel when she was still on top?

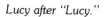

Lucy after "Lucy."

"I think it was the fact that we were all tired of having to lean on the same formula over and over. My writers were tired of having to repeat themselves. Gale Gordon had other, fresher things he wanted to do. And, frankly, I couldn't figure out why, at my age [sixty-two], I was still kicking up my heels and hanging from chandeliers. And besides, I wasn't making that much money, being in such a high income tax bracket," says Lucy, who also bemoaned the fact that she had to dismiss a large and loyal staff, many of whom had been with her since the beginning in 1951.

But now Lucy had to face a new challenge. Since her arrival in Hollywood in July 1933 as a young Goldwyn Girl, she had never been out of work. She went directly from her movie commitments into television in 1951, and this was the first time in her professional life she was idle. "It was one of the most traumatic events in my life," she reveals about the first several months of 1974. "It was a terrible thing for me. It was the loss of my creative arena. I lost not only the pleasure of being with my friends every day on the set, but also the loss of an identity."

She spent much of her time, as she puts it, "just staring. I not only didn't know which way to go—there just wasn't any place I *wanted* to go. Poor Gary, it was really rough on him. No matter what he suggested to get me out of the dumps, I'd mope and say, 'I don't wanna . . .' Then I started to clean. And I mean *clean*. Every corner of the house. And when I finished with my place, I went over and cleaned Desi, Jr.'s, place. And you know something? It was great therapy!

"My main involvement for so many years had been with television. For me, working on 'Lucy' was better than going to a party—more fun, more interesting. It was far and away the most rewarding of all my theatrical experiences. But also there was the fact that being Lucy gave me a built-in intimacy with my public. I *loved* being her. I loved the antics and the gags. I enjoyed my work. People think it has to do with a lot of money or power and all that nonsense, but I never wanted to be a big businesswoman," Lucy confirms once and for all.

Her semi-retirement called for two specials per year for CBS. In 1976, on the occasion of her twenty-fifth anniversary on TV, CBS saluted the redhead with a star-studded two-hour special featuring clips from her various TV outings and testimonials by the various superstars with whom she had worked over the years. Then in 1979, at an NBC press conference, then-network president Fred Silverman announced that Lucy was joining NBC, ending her long association with CBS. The move shocked the industry but Lucy explained that she was tired of doing nothing, and was anxious to get back to work. She headlined a major special for the network that aired in January 1980, and today, headquartered at the Westwood lot of 20th Century-Fox, she and Gary Morton are involved in both television and film production (*All the Right Moves*, starring Tom Cruise, was one of their projects).

Today, Miss Ball donates much of her free time to charities, especially those benefiting children, like the Association for Troubled Children and the Orthopedic Division of the Los Angeles Children's Hospital. When she isn't helping others, or playing backgammon (her passion), she visits her grandsons, Simon and Joseph Luckinbill, in New York City, where she maintains an apartment to make her frequent trips more comfortable. Already the boys are "I Love Lucy" fans, proving that the show will succeed in entertaining yet another generation. "That's *Nana?*" Simon asked with delight as he watched Lucy Ricardo cavorting on his television screen. "She acts *crazy!*"

No format appeared so unlikely to succeed as the crazy adventures of a carrot-top clown and a Cuban bandleader with an accent so thick you could cut it with a cleaver; yet for nine happy years the lives of millions of Americans, and countless more worldwide, ran on one tether with the Ricardos. They and the Mertzes became America's favorite foursome; they were faces that launched a million laughs, and the laughs have gone on, uninterrupted, for more than thirty years.

"It wasn't just slapstick comedy," Lucille Ball maintains. "It was a new thing called 'situation comedy,' with a beginning, a middle, and a happy ending. It wasn't *my* genius either. It was the genius of craftsmen behind the scenes, and rehearsing over and over and over again until we had it down perfect.

"We had great identification with millions of people. They could identify with my problems, my zaniness, my wanting to do everything, my scheming and plotting, the way I cajoled Ricky. People identified with the Ricardos because we had the same problems they had. Desi and I weren't your ordinary Hollywood couple on TV. We lived in a brownstone apartment somewhere in Manhattan, and paying the rent, getting a new dress, getting

TV's most famous foursome at play.

As Desi once said, " 'I Love Lucy' was never just a title."

a stale fur collar on an old cloth coat, or buying a piece of furniture were all worth a story.

"People could identify with those basic things—baby-sitters, traveling, wanting to be entertained, wanting to be loved in a certain way—the two couples on the show were constantly doing things that people all over the country were doing. We just took ordinary situations and exaggerated them," Miss Ball concludes.

Jack Gould of the New York *Times* summed up his feelings about the success of "I Love Lucy" by saying, " 'I Love Lucy' is very human—and so are we."

A French actor explained his addiction to the sitcom: "It has the reality of *l'amour* or as we say, 'sex.' While it is possible to believe that other husband and wife comedy teams share the same bedrooms, it is not possible to believe that they do so with pleasure. Lucy and Ricky Ricardo skirmish in the daytime so they can 'reconcile' at night."

Like the foreign actor, there are countless "Lucy" addicts out there. The popularity of the classic television series knows no age barrier. Children adore it as much as their adult counterparts. Ask any fan why he or she is "hooked" on "I Love Lucy," and nine chances out of ten, the response will be simply, "It's funny." What better reason is there to explain the appeal of a comedy?

In her wildest imagination, did Lucille Ball ever expect "I Love Lucy" to become a hit?

"Of course not," she admits readily. "But TV was in its infancy, and I figured it would go for a year. We had like a two-, three-year plan, but we figured if it went for a year . . . The parts all happened to come together: the people, the writers, the producers. The combination worked. Hell, we're still on the air today! I guess it did."

The First Season: 1951-52

THE FIRST SEASON: 1951–52

Executive Producer: Desi Arnaz
Producer: Jess Oppenheimer
Writers: Jess Oppenheimer, Madelyn Pugh, and Bob Carroll, Jr.
Director: Marc Daniels
Director of Photography: Karl Freund, A.S.C.
Music: Wilbur Hatch (Conducting the Desi Arnaz Orchestra)
Associate Producer: Al Simon
Art Director: Larry Cuneo
Film Editor: Dann Cahn
Assistant Director: James Paisley
Original Music: Eliot Daniel
Stage Manager: Herb Browar
Sound: Glen Glenn Sound (Cameron McCulloch in charge)
Choreography: Lee Scott
Fashions: Orbach's
Makeup: Max Factor (Hal King)

Filmed at General Service Studios

Sponsor: Philip Morris & Co.
Agency: The Biow Co., Inc.

"THE GIRLS WANT TO GO TO A NIGHTCLUB" 10/15/51

Episode #2 Filmed on Saturday, September 15, 1951 Rating/Share: 38.7/56 Music: "Guadalajara"

It's the Mertzes' eighteenth wedding anniversary, and Ethel wants to celebrate by going to the Copacabana, while Fred itches to attend the fights. An argument ensues, culminating with Ethel and Lucy informing Fred and Ricky that they'll go nightclubbing without them—with dates! Admitting to themselves that perhaps they were too hasty, the men decide to sneak into the Copa with dates of their own, just to keep an eye on their wives. Ricky calls his friend Ginny Jones, a singer at the Starlight Roof, and asks her to arrange dates for Fred and himself, and Lucy, very soon thereafter, calls her to arrange dates for her and Ethel. When Ginny spills the boys' plans to Lucy, Lucy decides that she and Ethel will impersonate their husbands' blind dates. Dressed as country bumpkins, Lucy and Ethel arrive at the Ricardo apartment. After Ricky sings a chorus of "Guadalajara," some funny hillbilly schtick unfolds, until Lucy "gives herself away" by reaching for some cigarettes hidden in a desk drawer. All is forgiven, and the two couples kiss and make up. In the tag, the men prevail and it's a night at the fights for an anniversary celebration.

"BE A PAL" 10/22/51

Episode #3 Filmed on Friday, September 21, 1951 Rating/Share: 40.3/60 Supporting cast: Hank—Richard J. Reeves, Charlie—Tony Michaels Music: "Mama Yo Quiero"

Lucy thinks Ricky is losing interest in her. Ethel suggests the book-of-the-week selection by Dr. Humphreys, *How to Keep the Honeymoon from Ending*. Chapter One suggests that the wife dress up for breakfast. But even with Lucy in her most profound feminine attire, Ricky barely looks up from his newspaper. Chapter Two—"The Be a Pal System"—prompts Lucy to join Ricky, Fred, Hank, and Charlie in a poker game. She beats them badly, which only serves to stimulate the marital discord. Chapter Three proposes that the wife surround the husband "with things that remind him of his childhood." Naturally, Lucy takes the suggestion a step too far, decorating the apartment like Cuba, with palm trees, sombreros, a flock of chickens, and even a mule. A funny sequence finds Lucy lip-syncing to a Carmen Miranda record, moments before Ricky confirms his eternal love for Lucy with a finale kiss.

NOTE: Lucille Ball asked Carmen Miranda for permission to impersonate her before filming the comedy routine.

"THE DIET"   10/29/51

Episode #4   Filmed on Friday, September 28, 1951   Rating/Share: 37.9/56   Supporting cast: Piano player—Marco Rizo   Music: "Cuban Pete/Sally Sweet"

To her dismay, Lucy discovers she's put on twenty-two pounds since marrying Ricky. Ethel: "On behalf of the tubby trio, I welcome you to our flabby foursome." A phone call from Ricky's agent reveals that Joanne, a singer featured in Ricky's Tropicana nightclub act, is getting married and will be quitting the show. Needless to say, Lucy wants the job. At auditions the next day, Lucille McGillicuddy (Lucy Ricardo) can have the part provided she loses twelve pounds in four days to fit into the ex-singer's size-twelve outfit. Lucy tries jogging ("the fourth-floor dash"), but loses only five ounces. At dinner, Lucy munches celery while Ricky and the Mertzes dine on steak and potatoes. In a funny scene, Lucy wrestles the Mertzes' dog Butch for a scrap of meat. With only five hours left in which to lose five more pounds, Lucy resorts to a "human pressure cooker" (a steam cabinet), finally weighing in at the required 120 pounds. Hours later in the nightclub act, Ricky sings "Cuban Pete" and Lucy warbles "Sally Sweet." She's a hit, but after the show, she collapses, suffering from malnutrition.

NOTE: The songs were featured in the Arnazes' 1950 vaudeville tour. . . . This was the first of many on-screen appearances for Marco Rizo, Desi's longtime pianist.

"LUCY THINKS RICKY IS TRYING TO MURDER HER"   11/5/51

Episode #1   Filmed on Saturday, September 8, 1951   Rating/Share: 36.5/56   Supporting cast: Jerry—Jerry Hausner

Engrossed in a new whodunit, *The Mockingbird Murder Mystery,* Lucy is a nail-biting wreck. Adding to her problems, Ethel's amateur try at fortune-telling reveals Lucy's imminent death. To make matters even worse, Lucy overhears a telephone conversation between Ricky and his agent, Jerry, and misinterprets the names of dogs in a new act for Ricky's girl friends. When Jerry routinely asks Ricky about Marilyn, a singer, Ricky responds: "I've decided to get rid of her . . . I'll probably miss her some, but in a couple of weeks I can get a new one." Naturally, Lucy thinks Ricky is referring to her. Panic-stricken (Lucy: "I'm not even cold yet, and already Ricky's lining up girls to take my place!"), she intends to take action. She outfits herself with a bulletproof skillet, certain that Ricky is out to kill her. Her strange behavior causes Ricky to worry, and he tries to slip her some sleeping powder, which Lucy thinks is poison. Lucy: "I got a mickey from Ricky!" She hastens to the Tropicana and confronts Ricky with a gun. There she sees the dog act made up of Ann, Mary, Helen, Cynthia, Alice, and . . . Theodore, and finally realizes that Ricky has no plans to do away with her.

NOTE: This was the first episode of the series filmed.

"THE QUIZ SHOW"   11/12/51

Episode #5   Filmed on Friday, October 5, 1951   Rating/Share: 38.0/60   Supporting cast: Freddie Fillmore—Frank Nelson, Announcer—Lee Millar, Mrs. Peterson—Hazel Pierce, Harold, the tramp—John Emery, Arnold, the first husband—Phil Ober

Lucy's careless accounting habits force Ricky to cut off her allowance and charge accounts. When Ethel arrives with tickets for a radio quiz show that awards one-thousand-dollar cash prizes, Lucy jumps at the chance to attend. After her qualifying round on "Females Are Fabulous," "based on the theory that any woman is willing to make an idiot out of herself in order to win a prize," host Freddie Fillmore tells Lucy of her money-winning stunt. She will have to introduce Ricky to her "long-lost first husband." That night Lucy is a bundle of nerves as she awaits the arrival of the bogus spouse. Meanwhile, a tramp appears at the door and Lucy assumes he is the "long-lost husband." When she discovers her mistake and throws him out, a second "first" husband arrives on the scene, whom Lucy introduces to Ricky as per the radio show requirement. Alas, she wins the thousand-dollar jackpot, but after paying all her overdue bills is left with only fifty cents.

NOTE: Phil Ober was Vivian Vance's first husband.

"THE AUDITION"   11/19/51

Episode #6   Filmed on Friday, October 12, 1951   Rating/Share: 41.9/62   Music: "Babalu," "How Dry I Am"

When Lucy learns that talent scouts from a television network are going to catch Ricky's nightclub act, she hounds her husband for a chance to be in the show: "You need a pretty girl in your act to advertise the sponsor's product. She eats it, or drinks it, or waxes the floor with it, or cuts potatoes with it, or drives off in it . . . or smokes it!" When this falls on Ricky's deaf ears, Lucy parades around the apartment with a lampshade on her head, humming "A Pretty Girl Is Like a Melody" and imitating a Ziegfeld girl. When Buffo the Clown has a bike accident at a rehearsal, Ricky sends him to the Ricardo apartment to rest up, and Lucy connives to take his place in the show. As network officials watch Ricky sing "Babalu," Lucy meanders onstage as "The Professor," wearing a broken-down tuxedo and carrying a "loaded" cello, looking for "Risky Riskadoo." She performs some funny bits with the instrument, then impersonates a seal by playing a motley group of horns. The TV bigwigs are so impressed, they offer *her* a contract. Later Lucy agrees to remain a wife and give up show business (this week).

NOTE: This episode resembles the March 1951 "Lucy" pilot. . . . Vivian Vance did not appear in this show. . . . The TV network representatives were played by producer Jess Oppenheimer and Harry Ackerman, a CBS vice-president.

"THE SÉANCE"   11/26/51

Episode #7   Filmed on Friday, October 19, 1951   Rating/Share: 44.9/64   Supporting cast: Mr. Meriweather—Jay Novello

Preoccupied with numerology and horoscopes, Lucy assures Ricky that it's a "yes day" until she realizes she had consulted yesterday's newspaper. A Gemini, Ricky was advised "to climb in a hole and pull the hole in after you." Consequently, when Mr. Meriweather, a theatrical producer, phones, Lucy immediately says no, without even listening to what the man said. This infuriates Ricky, so they go to see Meriweather at his office to make amends, only to discover that he, too, is a horoscope/Ouija board/numerology nut. Lucy tells him they're conducting a séance that evening and he might be able to contact his long-departed Tillie. Ethel portrays the medium Raya (Fred: "Well done, medium Raya."), or, as she is more commonly called, Madame Ethel Mertzola, complete with crystal ball. They contact Tillie, Meriweather's cocker spaniel, and the man's late wife, Adelaide. The producer is so pleased with the results of the séance that he hires Ricky for a new show.

NOTE: In numerology, Ricky was a 5, Ethel a 7, Lucy a 3, Mr. Meriweather a 1, prompting the latter to observe, "We're all odd, aren't we?"

"MEN ARE MESSY"   12/3/51

Episode #8   Filmed on Thursday, October 25, 1951   Rating/Share: 42.1/65   Supporting cast: Kenny, the press agent—Kenny Morgan, Jim White, the photographer—Harry Shannon, Maggie—Hazel "Sunny" Boyne   Music: "Straw Hat Song"

"Men are nothing but a bunch of mess-cats," complains Lucy Ricardo while Ricky insists, "A man's home is his castle." To make a point, Lucy divides the apartment into two equal halves. If Ricky wants to be a slob in his half, it's fine with Lucy. When Ricky's press agent, Kenny Morgan, lines up a publicity spread in *Halfbeat* magazine, Lucy decides to teach her sloppy husband a lesson. Jim White, the photographer, arrives at the Ricardos' and finds it looking like Tobacco Road. Ricky: "It's a regular pigpen!" Lucy: "It ain't a regular one, but it'll do." Lucy playfully poses for photographs amid a pile of junk, until she realizes the cameraman is from *Look* magazine, not the musicians' journal.

NOTE: Kenny Morgan, who at that time was married to Lucille Ball's cousin Cleo, was Desilu's PR representative.

"THE FUR COAT"   12/10/51

Episode #10   Filmed on Friday, November 9, 1951   Rating/Share: 44.1/67   Supporting cast: Thief—Ben Weldon

Ricky arrives home with a $3,500 mink coat that he has rented for an act at the club. Lucy immediately jumps to the conclusion that it's her anniversary gift and showers her man with grateful kisses. Thrilled, Lucy wears the coat night and day, and even does the dishes in it. Ricky implores Fred to dress as a burglar and "steal" the coat at gunpoint. But before Mertz appears, a *real* thief arrives and almost makes off with the fur. When Lucy learns from Ethel of Ricky's nefarious ploy, she plots to teach him a lesson by buying a cheap imitation fur coat and, in full view of Ricky, proceeds to "restyle" it. She cuts it in half and removes the sleeves, saying, "Congratulations, Ethel. You're the first woman ever to wear a mink T-shirt." Ricky promptly collapses, but after being told of the prank, buys Lucy a new hat and dress.

"LUCY IS JEALOUS OF GIRL SINGER" 12/17/51

Episode #11   Filmed on Friday, November 16, 1951   Rating/Share: 41.4/62   Supporting cast: Rosemary—Helen Silver   Music: "Jezebel," "El Cumbanchero"

An item in the morning gossip column prompts Lucy to assume that Ricky is seeing another woman, but he assures her that the newspaper piece is merely publicity. To apologize for her lack of wifely faith, Lucy prepares Ricky's favorite dish, *arroz con pollo,* but her mood changes abruptly when she finds a piece of black lace in Ricky's pocket. He tries to explain that it was torn off accidentally from Tropicana dancer Rosemary's gown during the rehearsal of "Jezebel." To keep an eye on Ricky, Lucy manages to wangle her way into the chorus line and upstages Rosemary during the number. Later that night at home, Ricky tells Lucy there was a "strange girl" in the chorus—ugly, and a terrible dancer. He knew all along that it was Lucy. They kiss and make up.

NOTE: *Arroz con pollo* (chicken with rice) was Desi Arnaz's favorite dish. . . . This episode appears to have been mistitled. Rosemary is clearly a "girl dancer," not a "girl singer."

"DRAFTED"   12/24/51

Episode #9   Filmed on Friday, November 2, 1951   Rating/Share: not available

When a letter from the War Department arrives, requesting Ricky to appear at "Fort Dix, Monday at 3 P.M.," Lucy concludes he's been drafted. Actually, Ricky's been invited to the New Jersey camp to entertain. Since Fred knows an appropriate Civil War routine from his vaudeville days (first mention of his show business past), Ricky invites him to go along. Not knowing of these plans, the girls begin knitting their men socks, and also arrange for a going-away party Sunday night with a guest list to include the Sedgwicks, the Orsattis, the Buzzells, and Billy Josephy. But now Ricky and Fred determine, based on their wives' knitting, that the girls are expecting babies, and plan a similar party (a shower) that same night.

NOTE: The Sedgwicks, Orsattis, Buzzells, and Willard Josephy were real-life friends of the Arnazes. . . . The original print of this episode included a special four-minute tag that was introduced by the "Lucy" announcer Johnny Jacobs as "Lucy and Ricky will be back with a little surprise!" The Christmas Eve (original air date of "Drafted") "surprise" featured the four principals dressed as Santas and singing "Jingle Bells" while skipping around the Ricardos' yule tree. As if magically, a fifth St. Nick appears, leaving the principals to quizzically wish the "Lucy" audience a Merry Christmas. The "real" Santa Claus was played by actor Vernon Dent. . . . Desi hums a few bars of the song he and Eddie Maxwell wrote in July 1951 titled "There's a Brand New Baby in Our House."

"THE ADAGIO"   12/31/51

Episode #12   Filmed on Friday, November 23, 1951   Rating/Share: 46.2/71   Supporting cast: Jean—Shepard Menken

Lucy volunteers for Ricky's Parisian apache dance number for an upcoming Tropicana show. Fred offers to teach Lucy the finer points of the terpsichorean art until Ethel manages to produce the real thing, Jean Valjean Raymand, who is the nephew of the woman who runs the French hand laundry. The Frenchman has more than dance lessons on his mind, and when Ricky finds him hiding in the hall closet, the fireworks commence. Jean challenges Ricky to a duel with pistols behind Radio City Music Hall, but they finally decide to stage a fake fight in the bedroom to teach Lucy a well-deserved lesson.

NOTE: Lucille Ball once dislocated her shoulder doing an apache dance at age twelve for a Masonic musical revue.

"THE BENEFIT"   1/7/52

Episode #13   Filmed on Friday, November 30, 1951   Rating/Share:
51.6/72   Music: "Shine On, Harvest Moon," "Auf Wiederseh'n, My
Dear," "We'll Build a Bungalow"

Ethel wants Ricky to headline a benefit show for her "Middle East Sixty-
eighth Street Women's Club," but Lucy refuses to ask him unless she can
be on the bill, too. Ethel is not thrilled, especially after hearing Lucy's off-
key rendition of "Shine On, Harvest Moon," but finally gives in. After the
posters (ballyhooing Mr. and Mrs. Ricky Ricardo) are printed, Lucy informs
Ethel that Ricky refuses to do it. Lucy: "You still have me. After all, what's
Ricky got that I haven't got, except a band, a reputation . . . ?" Ethel: ". . .
and talent!" After some wheedling, Ricky says he'll do it—an old vaudeville
routine known as "Songs and Witty Sayings." Lucy is delighted until she
gets a gander at the material—Ricky has all the punch lines. She decides to
rewrite the jokes, which are later delivered between choruses of "We'll Build
a Bungalow."

"THE AMATEUR HOUR"   1/14/52

Episode #14   Filmed on Friday, December 7, 1951   Rating/Share:
50.1/72   Supporting cast: Mrs. Hudson—Gail Bonney, Timmy
Hudson—David Stollery, Jimmy Hudson—Sammy Ogg   Music: "I'm
Breaking My Back," "Ragtime Cowboy Joe"

After buying a $59.95 dress without Ricky's permission, Lucy insists she'll
get a job to pay for it. Unfortunately, Mrs. Ricardo discovers she's unqualified
for the jobs listed in the *Times*—stenographer, bookkeeper, cook, lady
wrestler. Lucy: "This is terribly unfair. . . . Apparently you can't get a job in
this town unless you can do something!" A baby-sitting job, paying a
whopping five dollars an hour, sounds perfect, until she discovers that it isn't
an infant she'll be sitting with but two rambunctious eight-year-old identical
twin boys, Jimmy and Timmy Hudson. Practical jokers, the boys nearly burn
Lucy at the stake. When Mrs. Hudson calls from the beauty parlor asking if
Lucy will take her sons to the Blue Bird Club Amateur Contest that night in
her place—Lucy can keep the hundred-dollar prize money if they win—she
agrees. With Ricky as the coincidental emcee, Lucy and the twins perform
"Ragtime Cowboy Joe" and win the hundred dollars.

NOTE: Lee Scott was credited with the choreography. . . . The frog's name
was Elmer. . . . William Frawley did not appear in this episode.

"LUCY PLAYS CUPID" 1/21/52

Episode #15   Filmed on Thursday, December 13, 1951   Rating/Share: 51.8/73   Supporting cast: Miss Lewis—Bea Benaderet, Mr. Ritter— Edward Everett Horton

The Ricardos' neighbor, Miss Lewis, has fallen for Mr. Ritter, the local grocery man, claiming he's the "bee's knees," but the spinster's too shy to invite him to dinner herself. Lucy offers to do it for her—shades of Cyrano de Bergerac—but Ritter gets the wrong idea and thinks Lucy is the one who's crazy about him. Mr. Ritter: "I like you, too. You're just my type, Red." In order to throw him off the scent, Lucy plans to deck herself out like a hoyden at dinner that night. Ritter is aghast, especially when he encounters Lucy's twenty-five children (Lucy: "Six are missing."). Finally, Miss Lewis appears— flashing her "come hither" look, which Lucy taught her earlier—and captures the beloved grocer.

NOTE: Bea Benaderet appeared on Lucy's radio show, "My Favorite Husband," and was Lucy's first choice to play what eventually became the Ethel Mertz character. . . . The Lucy/Mr. Ritter dinner scene featured the ill-matched pair sitting on crates from a California bottler, not a New York concern. . . . Vivian Vance and William Frawley did not appear in this episode.

"LUCY FAKES ILLNESS"   1/28/52

Episode #16   Filmed on Tuesday, December 18, 1951   Rating/Share: 57.4/77   Supporting cast: Hal March—himself   Music: "When the Saints Come Marching In"

Contemplating a nervous breakdown because Ricky won't hire her for his new act, Lucy consults a book, *Abnormal Psychology,* for a solution. Three symptoms of her frustration are likely to appear, according to the text: She will assume the identity of a celebrity, develop a hopeless case of amnesia, and revert to her childhood. When Ricky arrives home, he is bombarded with not just one complex, but all three: Lucy impersonates Tallulah Bankhead, can't recognize herself in the mirror, and recklessly rides a tricycle around the living room. Ricky wants to call in psychiatrist Dr. Stevenson to help Lucy, but Fred first warns him that Lucy is faking. Therefore, Ricky decides to enlist the aid of an actor friend, Hal March, to play a phony physician. Doctor: "Just as I feared. . . . You've contracted . . . the gobloots. . . . It came into the country on the hind legs of the boo-shoo bird. . . . We may have to operate. . . . We'll have to go in and take out your zorch." Lucy believes him and prepares for her death. Ricky finally spills the beans whereupon Lucy insists on being in the nightclub act. Now Ricky is the one feigning amnesia.

NOTE: Ricky claims that he and Lucy have been living in the Mertz building for five years.

"LUCY WRITES A PLAY"   2/4/52

Episode #17   Filmed on Saturday, December 22, 1951   Rating/Share: 55.6/75   Supporting cast: Club chairwoman—Myra Marsh, Stage manager—Maury Thompson

Thwarted by her failure to break into show business as an actress, Lucy takes to the typewriter and pens "a tender, heartwarming story of a Cuban tobacco picker"—*A Tree Grows in Havana.* Naturally she wants Ricky to play the lead when the production premieres at a women's club play competition, but he absolutely refuses, so Lucy has to settle for Fred. Since Mertz's Spanish accent leaves something to be desired, Lucy transforms the setting to England and retitles her effort *The Perils of Pamela.* However, when Ricky learns that a big Hollywood producer, Darryl P. Mayer, will be the judge, he wants back in. But what he doesn't know is that the original script has been scrapped. The night of the show, he makes his entrance as per the Cuban version, while Lucy, Fred, and Ethel are doing the English rendition. The result is another maniacal mix-up.

NOTE: This was the first mention of the Wednesday Afternoon Fine Arts League. . . . Maury Thompson, who played the stage manager, was the show's script clerk.

"BREAKING THE LEASE"   2/11/52

Episode #18   Filmed on Saturday, January 5, 1952   Rating/Share: 53.4/73   Supporting cast: Bum—Bennett Green, Party guests—Hazel Pierce, Barbara Pepper   Music: "Sweet Sue," "I Want a Girl Just Like the Girl That Married Dear Old Dad," "El Cumbanchero," "La Raspa," "The Mexican Hat Dance"

After a fun evening around the piano singing "Sweet Sue" and other favorites, the Mertzes retire to bed, leaving Lucy and Ricky alone to pursue a short encore. Ethel then telephones, demanding quiet. Lucy: "Ethel, you were just up here and said it sounded great." Ethel: "Well, I'm down here now, and it sounds lousy!" One noise leads to another until Ricky threatens to move. The next morning, Ethel informs Lucy that they owe them the next five months' rent to pay off their lease. When Ricky hears this, he decides to break the contract by becoming "the most undesirable tenants" imaginable. After a day of constant racket—the Ricardos even resort to wielding a riveter's hammer against a garbage can lid—they decide to have Ricky's sixteen-piece band rehearse in the apartment. The jam session lasts until 4 A.M., when Lucy suggests the band play "El Breako the Leaso," a special version of "The Mexican Hat Dance." When the disgruntled Fred and Ethel arrive at the door, covered with plaster (Fred sports a chandelier), they reluctantly surrender the lease. On moving day, Lucy and Ethel become emotional as they tenderly recall the fun times they've had during the past nine years. Tears are shed and all is forgiven.

NOTE: This was the first Ricardo-Mertz fight, a story device that was repeated many times.

"THE BALLET"   2/18/52

Episode #19   Filmed on Friday, January 11, 1952   Rating/Share: 53.9/73   Supporting cast: Madame Lamond—Mary Wickes, Burlesque comic—Frank Scannell   Music: "Martha"

Ricky is searching for a ballet dancer and a burlesque comic for his new nightclub revue. Lucy, who once played a petunia in a school rendition of *Dance of the Flowers,* wants the ballet job. Enrolling in a dance class run by the strict Madame Lamond, she tries desperately to learn the demanding art. The results are disastrous, and Lucy finally gives up. She next hires a burlesque comic who teaches her the "Slowly I Turn/Martha" bit. When Lucy is summoned to the club to replace a sick performer, she assumes it is the comic, but it is the ballet dancer they need. Lucy arrives in her clown getup and while Ricky sings "Martha," she squirts seltzer water at everyone and pitches a custard pie in Ricky's face. To get even with her, Ricky douses her with a bucket of water when she returns home that night.

NOTE: First mention of Fred's vaudeville partner, Ted Kurtz. . . . Lucille Ball ad-libbed brilliantly when her foot accidentally got caught in the ballet practice bar.

"THE YOUNG FANS"   2/25/52

Episode #20   Filmed on Friday, January 18, 1952   Rating/Share: 56.5/76   Supporting cast: Peggy Dawson—Janet Waldo, Arthur Morton—Richard Crenna   Music: "Babalu"

When a teenage girl, Peggy Dawson, drops her steady beau, Arthur Morton, for suave Ricky Ricardo, Lucy accepts the dubious challenge of teaching the clumsy schoolboy how to dance. Unfortunately, Arthur gets carried away and proclaims his love for Lucy. To discourage the youthful duo, Mr. and Mrs. Ricardo dress up in old clothes and wire-rimmed glasses, winding up looking like their own great-great-grandparents. Ricky barely manages to sing "Babalu" for Peggy, as Lucy comments, "He's baba'ed his last lu." These disconcerting charades—including Peggy's having to "keep jiggling" Ricky's leg to keep his blood flowing—prompt the young "fans" to rush out of the Ricardo apartment *together*.

NOTE: Vivian Vance and William Frawley did not appear in this episode. . . . "Teenager" Richard Crenna was twenty-four years old when this was filmed. . . . This is the only first season show to carry the credit, "Directed by William Asher," who was on the General Service Studios lot at this time to direct the pilot film for Desilu's "Our Miss Brooks" TV sitcom starring Eve Arden, Gale Gordon, and the aforementioned Richard Crenna.

"NEW NEIGHBORS"   3/3/52

Episode #21   Filmed on Friday, January 25, 1952   Rating/Share: 58.0/78   Supporting cast: Tom O'Brien—Hayden Rorke, Mrs. O'Brien—K. T. Stevens, Sergeant Morton—Allen Jenkins

Lucy and Ethel can't wait to get a closer look at the O'Briens' (new neighbors in the building) belongings, but Ricky makes Lucy promise "not to set foot" in their apartment. Next day, she crawls in ("he didn't say I couldn't set *knees* in"), along with Ethel, to snoop. When the curious pair hear the O'Briens approaching, Lucy quickly hides in the closet. Not realizing the couple are actors rehearsing a play, Lucy jumps to the conclusion that they're going to "do away with the tenants on the upper floor and assume their identities to blow up the Capitol." Panicked, Lucy dons a slipcover, disguising herself as an armchair, and slowly makes her way out of the O'Brien household. Lucy alerts Sergeant Morton, who thinks she's crazy; then barricades their apartment door and takes up arms with Ricky and the Mertzes. The foursome winds up in jail after nearly blowing off the police sergeant's head, and Ricky is despondent over the headlines "Orchestra Leader Jailed in Shooting Spree."

NOTE: K. T. Stevens and her actor-husband, Hugh Marlowe, were among Vivian Vance's closest friends.

"FRED AND ETHEL FIGHT"   3/10/52

Episode #22   Filmed on Wednesday, January 30, 1952   Rating/Share: 59.5/61   Supporting cast: Soda jerk—Hazel Pierce

Lucy and Ricky try to patch up the Mertzes' quarrel (Fred: "She said my mother looks like a weasel!") by inviting them each to dinner without the other knowing. They manage to set the couple straight all right, but not without ending up in a squabble of their own, with Ricky moving to the Tropicana. To get him back, Ethel suggests Lucy try a subtle sympathy ploy: "Pretend you were hit by a bus." At the same time, Fred encounters Ricky at a local drugstore lunch counter, and he urges Ricky to be a hero by saving Lucy "from a burning apartment building." The sight of Lucy, covered from head to toe with bandages, casts, and a splint, trying to escape from the "burning" building, is hilarious. But now Fred and Ethel are fighting again, this time over whose fault all this was. This leads Ethel to run home to mother.

NOTE: Scene in the drugstore featured a huge advertising sign depicting Johnny, the "Call for Philip Morris" man; Desilu endeavored to accommodate its sponsor whenever possible. . . . This episode was based on a real-life incident: in 1944, the Arnazes invited three couples to their ranch home for dinner. An argument broke out between one of the couples, the wife bursting into tears and locking herself in Lucy and Desi's bedroom. The Arnazes made peace maneuvers and soon the husband and wife were back in each other's arms. Desi reminisces: "Once this good deed was accomplished we all settled down for a pleasant evening again, and Lucy and I began laughingly recalling some of our own former quarrels. Then our laughter died and we began quarreling in earnest. Do you know what the upshot of that evening was? The other couple went off happily, but Lucy and I decided to get a divorce!" . . . This show was filmed on Wednesday so that Desi and the crew could work on the "Our Miss Brooks" pilot, which was filmed by Desilu on Saturday, February 2, 1952. . . . "Lucy" stage manager, Herb Browar, played a practical joke on Lucille Ball during the dress rehearsal for this episode. For the scene featuring Lucy in her cast lying in bed, he replaced the standard reading matter with a very graphic anatomy book, opened to a page featuring a male specimen. Lucille took a long look at the page, threw a glance in the direction of Browar, and cracked up, laughing.

"THE MOUSTACHE"   3/17/52

Episode #23   Filmed on Friday, February 8, 1952   Rating/Share: 58.6/81   Supporting cast: Mr. Murdoch—John Brown   Music: "I'll See You in C-U-B-A"

When Ricky grows a moustache for a possible movie role *(Moon Over Bagdad)*, Lucy takes reciprocal action. She doesn't like kissing a man with a moustache and insists he shave it off at once. Having a little fun with her, Ricky hints he might keep it on for good, even after the movie stint. This really annoys Lucy, so she borrows a fake beard from Fred and attaches it to her face with what appears to be spirit gum. When Ricky comes home, she kisses him—to give him a taste of his own medicine. He is amused by her joke, but asks her to remove the false whiskers. She can't. They've been glued on with Bulldog Cement, not mere glue, and Lucy fears she'll have to be a bearded lady for life. But what really makes her distraught is that Ricky is bringing home the movie producer, Mr. Murdoch, for whom she naturally wants to audition. Her valiant efforts to hide the white mane behind the veil of a harem-girl outfit fail, and Ricky loses out on the role.

NOTE: Ricky shows Murdoch his scrapbook, which features clippings from *Too Many Girls* and his Copacabana dates—highlights of Desi Arnaz's early career. . . . This is the first instance of Vivian Vance and William Frawley doing a song-and-dance act in the show. . . . John Brown, who played Mr. Murdoch, was the second actor to play Harry Morton on "The George Burns-Gracie Allen Show" (January through June 1951).

"THE GOSSIP"   3/24/52

Episode #24   Filmed on Friday, February 15, 1952   Rating/Share: not available   Supporting cast: Bill Foster—Richard J. Reeves, Milkman—Robert Jellison

When Lucy is forbidden to gossip, she tapes her mouth shut and, in charades, acts out the latest bit of news for Ethel "about Betty and her husband, Jack." Ricky is disappointed that she didn't keep her word, but at the same time feeds Fred a juicy tidbit "about Joe, the trombone player, and what a wolf he is." Finally, the boys bet the girls they can keep from gossiping longer. The winners are to be served breakfast in bed for a month. Ricky has a surefire plan: He'll talk in his sleep, making up a tantalizing tale about neighbor Grace Foster and the milkman; Lucy is sure to spill it to Ethel. The following day, Lucy blurts out the news to Ethel while Ricky and Fred are listening through the furnace pipes, the snooper's friend. Fred: "Ethel, this is your conscience. . . . You've been gossiping." Lucy: "Ethel, you have the loudest conscience I have ever heard." Ricky: "Lucy Ricardo, you've been gossipin' too." Lucy: "Oh, fine. Mine has an accent." The next scene depicts Lucy serving breakfast to Ricky, with Ethel performing the same deed for Fred. Suddenly, the milkman rushes into the Ricardo bedroom, followed by Grace Foster's husband, Bill, who is wielding a pistol. The gossip was true after all, and Ricky spilled it first. Seems the tables are turned, so the boys reluctantly head for the kitchen. With Ricky and Fred out of earshot, Lucy thrusts ten dollars into the milkman's hand with instructions to split the dough with Mr. Foster for their brilliant performance.

"PIONEER WOMEN"   3/31/52

Episode #25   Filmed on Friday, February 22, 1952   Rating/Share: 66.0/86   Supporting cast: Mrs. Pettebone—Florence Bates, Mrs. Pomerantz—Ruth Perrott

Determining they have washed 219,000 dishes since being married, Lucy and Ethel demand dishwashers in an effort to rid themselves of dishpan hands—something the Society Matrons League would frown upon. The men insist the women have it too "soft" and bet them fifty dollars that they "cry uncle" first, after agreeing to live life as it was before the turn of the century, without modern conveniences. Lucy and Ethel take to churning their own butter (cost: $23.75 per pound), baking their own bread (Lucy puts in thirteen cakes of yeast, instead of three, producing a mammoth loaf), and wearing old-fashioned clothes. Ricky complies by riding a horse home from the club, bathing in an ancient bathtub, and, along with Fred, wearing period clothing. Unexpectedly, Mrs. Pettebone and Mrs. Pomerantz of the Society Matrons League drop in on Lucy and Ethel for a surprise inspection "to check on them." Lucy tries to explain but gets tongue-tied. Ricky explains that the ladies caught them in a rehearsal for a Gay Nineties bit for the Tropicana. When the highfalutin society women display some reluctance to accept Lucy and Ethel because of their show business leanings, Lucy becomes irate and informs them she has "no desire to join your phony baloney club." Ricky calls off the bet, and the foursome enjoys homemade bread and home-churned butter.

NOTE: Ruth Perrott, who played one of the society matrons, was a featured character ("Katie, the maid") on Lucy's "My Favorite Husband" radio comedy and was probably considered for the role of Ethel Mertz. . . . The name Pettebone was inspired by Jean Pettebone, a CBS photographer, and Pomerantz by Charles Pomerantz, a Philip Morris press representative headquartered in Los Angeles.

"THE MARRIAGE LICENSE"   4/7/52

Episode #26   Filmed on Thursday, February 28, 1952   Rating/Share: 70.4/90   Supporting cast: Bert Willoughby—Irving Bacon, Mrs. Willoughby (Mother)—Elizabeth Patterson   Music: "I Love You Truly"

When Lucy discovers that Ricky's name is misspelled (Bicardi) on their marriage license, she concludes their vows are invalid. She returns from City Hall, via East Orange, New Jersey, despondent: "We've been revoked." Now she wants to re-create the entire courtship and ceremony, with plans to go to the Byram River Beagle Club in Greenwich, Connecticut. They head for New England where Lucy finds the exact spot where Ricky proposed to her in 1940. Against his better judgment, Ricky gets down on his knees to propose, while Lucy feeds him the antedated dialogue. They run out of gas, whereupon they wander into the Eagle Hotel run by Bert Willoughby and his wife. The former just happens to be the town's justice of the peace and can perform the marriage ceremony for them. After "Mother" Willoughby sings the appropriate, if off-key, "I Love You Truly," vows are exchanged, and the Ricardos are married . . . for a second time.

NOTE: According to ARB, this episode was the first TV show to be seen in 10 million U.S. homes. . . . Lucille Ball and Desi Arnaz really were married in 1940 at the Byram River Beagle Club, and also reenacted their vows in 1949 in a Catholic ceremony. . . . Lucy's maiden name was Lucille Esmerelda McGillicuddy. . . . Irving Bacon later played Ethel Mertz's father (Episode

#113) and Elizabeth Patterson was hired a year after this episode was filmed to essay the recurring role of Mrs. Trumbull, the Ricardos' elderly neighbor.

"THE KLEPTOMANIAC" 4/14/52

Episode #27 Filmed on Friday, March 7, 1952 Rating/Share: 63.3/85 Supporting cast: Dr. Tom Robinson—Joseph Kearns

When Ricky discovers a large amount of cash in Lucy's purse (Lucy: "It's my mad money." Ricky: "There's two hundred dollars here." Lucy: "I get awfully mad.") and a closetful of silverware and other valuables—unaware that Lucy is collecting items for a club bazaar—he immediately jumps to the conclusion she's a kleptomaniac. At first, Fred finds it hard to believe the heartbreaking news: "She's a poor, sick creature. . . . Hey, that dirty crook just stole my clock!" Ricky's only hope is to call in a psychiatrist, Dr. Robinson, who tries to hypnotize Lucy. What the doctor, Ricky, and Fred don't know is that Lucy is wise to her hubby's plan. She puts on quite an act, "reliving" her childhood and telling of her graduation to pickpocketing: "I've picked a peck of pockets!" The climax comes in the form of a baby elephant, which Lucy says she stole from the Clyde Beatty Circus.

"CUBAN PALS"   4/21/52

Episode #28   Filmed on Friday, March 14, 1952   Rating/Share: 64.5/86 Supporting cast: Carlos Ortega—Alberto Morin, Maria Ortega—Rita Convy, Renita Perez—Lita Baron   Music: "The Lady in Red," "Similau"

Lucy is at a disadvantage when her husband's Cuban friends, Carlos and Maria Ortega, visit: Lucy's *español* is a sad sampling of pigeon Spanish. When she learns that "little" Renita Perez, with whom Ricky once danced in Cuba, is arriving in town, she insists he dance again with her, claiming it will "help the good neighbor policy." What she isn't expecting is that "little" Renita has developed into a voluptuous *señorita*. Jealous, Lucy poses with Ethel as charwomen and they invade the Tropicana during rehearsals of "The Lady in Red" number, just to keep an eye on Ricky and Renita. Determined to keep the two apart, Lucy gets Fred to dress as a cabbie and take Renita on a "shortcut through Philadelphia" instead of to the club. At the Tropicana, when Ricky introduces Renita and her usual dance partner, Ramon, who will perform the "African Wedding Dance," Lucy appears instead of the sultry Latin. It's a funny few minutes with Lucy trying to escape the clutches of the voodoo-masked Ramon.

NOTE: In the first scene, Desi Arnaz made a few mistakes while translating Lucy's English into Spanish, but he covered nicely. Watch for it.

"THE FREEZER"   4/28/52

Episode #29   Filmed on Friday, March 21, 1952   Rating/Share: 60.4/87 Supporting cast: Deliveryman #1—Frank Sully, Deliveryman #2—Bennett Green, Butcher—Fred Aldrich, Women in butcher shop— Kay Wiley, Barbara Pepper, Hazel Pierce   Music: "Cielito Lindo," "Mama Inez"

Lucy and Ethel acquire a huge, walk-in meat freezer from Ethel's butcher-uncle, Oscar, provided they pay the fifty-dollar moving charge. Next, the pair orders two sides of beef from Johnson's Meat Company, unaware of the immensity of their request. Later that day, Lucy and Ethel watch with growing horror as deliverymen unload seven hundred pounds of meat at a cost of sixty-nine cents a pound, or a total of $483. Lucy's first notion is to glue the cow back together, but the deliveryman insists he can't take it back even if she "taught it how to walk again." Next stop is a local butcher shop, where Lucy tries to unload the beef on unsuspecting customers: "Are you tired of paying high prices? Are you interested in a little high-class beef? You want a bargain? . . . I have sirloin, tenderloin, T-bone, rump; pot roast, chuck roast, ox tail, stump. . . . We do everything ourselves. We rope, we brand, we butcher, we do everything but *eat* it for ya—seventy-nine cents a pound!"

They promptly go out of business when the neighborhood butcher gets wise to their competitive tricks. In an effort to move the beef from the basement freezer into the unlit furnace before Ricky finds out about the $483 meat bill, Lucy accidentally gets locked inside, freezing into a "human popsicle." When Fred turns on the furnace to help thaw Lucy, the meat starts cooking, the aroma rising through the heating ducts. In shock and on the verge of tears, Lucy explains, "Just get a knife and a fork and a bottle of ketchup and follow me to the biggest barbecue in the world. . . ."

NOTE: This was the first episode to carry the credit: "Executive Producer: Desi Arnaz."

"LUCY DOES A TV COMMERCIAL" 5/5/52

Episode #30 Filmed on Friday, March 28, 1952 Rating/Share: 61.1/88 Supporting cast: Director—Ross Elliott, Joe—Jerry Hausner, Script clerk—Maury Thompson

Lucy connives to appear in a commercial on the "big TV show" Ricky is emceeing. To prove to Ricky how good she is doing commercials, she removes the "works" from their TV set, installs a window shade where the picture tube was, and, when Ricky arrives home, proceeds to do an impromptu Philip Morris cigarette commercial, dressed as Johnny. Hubby is not impressed with her performance and less than pleased to learn she has removed the workings of the set piece-by-piece instead of just sliding out the chassis. The following morning, Lucy gives Ricky the silent treatment, still trying to win the commercial job. She has a better idea: she'll tell the girl Ricky *did* hire that Ricky's "already hired another girl." Standing before a backdrop that reads "Join the Parade . . . Buy Vitameatavegamin Today," Lucy rehearses her speech at the TV studio: "Hello, friends. I'm your Vitameatavegamin girl. Are you tired, rundown, listless? Do you poop out at parties? Are you unpopular? The answer to all your problems is in this little bottle: Vitameatavegamin. Vitameatavegamin contains vitamins, meat, vegetables, and minerals. Yes, with Vitameatavegamin, you can *spoon* your way to health. All you do is take a tablespoon after every meal [Lucy samples product]. It's so tasty, too. Just like candy. So why don't you join the thousands of happy, peppy people and get a great big bottle of Vitameatavegamin tomorrow. That's Vita . . . Meata . . . Vegamin." After repeated rehearsals, Lucy gets bombed because the liquid tonic is 23 percent alcohol. Further attempts to polish her performance prove hilarious, with Lucy garbling her words and slurring the speech. This is Lucille Ball at her comic best.

NOTE: Maury Thompson, the script clerk, played himself. . . . A good deal of time and effort was expended by stage manager Herb Browar to find just the right liquid concoction to fill the Vitameatavegamin bottles. It had to ooze out of the bottle, not flow freely, plus it had to taste good to Lucy. After trying and dismissing a half-dozen products, including honey, Browar stopped off at a health food store on Santa Monica Boulevard in West Hollywood and found the perfect liquid: apple pectin. Lucy loved the taste, and they proceeded to fill the bottles with it on dress rehearsal day (Thursday). . . . Vivian Vance did not appear in this episode. . . . Ricky gestures offstage before his musical number and says, "Mr. Hatch, if you please." Wilbur Hatch was the conductor of Desi Arnaz's orchestra.

"THE PUBLICITY AGENT"   5/12/52

Episode #31   Filmed on Friday, April 4, 1952   Rating/Share: 64.7/89   Supporting cast: Reporter—Peter Leeds, Photographer— Bennett Green, Assassins—Richard J. Reeves, Gil Herman   Music: "I Get Ideas," "Babalu"

To increase business at the Tropicana, Lucy concocts a publicity scheme that is prompted by a newspaper item claiming that the Shah of Persia has all of Benny Goodman's records. Lucy decides to become the Maharincess of Franistan, who travels halfway around the globe to see her singing idol, Ricky Ricardo. She books a suite at the Waldorf-Astoria hotel, calls all the newspaper editors in town, and enthusiastically pursues her plan. Meanwhile, Ricky chides his press agent, Kenny Morgan, for dreaming up such a "cheap" stunt, but Kenny insists he didn't plant the story. It must be for real. Lucy, as the royal princess, is introduced at the Tropicana to Ricky and swoons every time he starts singing "I Get Ideas." But after singing twenty-five songs (every other one "Babalu"), Ricky deduces it must be Lucy (who else would "ask for more"?). To get even with her, he lines up two friends, Bill Foster and Joe, who dress up like Arab-type thugs and scare the veils off Lucy and Ethel. Warding them off, Lucy admits, "I'm not a maharincess; I'm a Henna-rinsess!"

NOTE: When Ricky enters the Waldorf suite as "Tiger," he is wearing special "platform" shoes that elevated him more than six inches. Watch for it.

"LUCY GETS RICKY ON THE RADIO" 5/19/52

Episode #32   Filmed on Friday, April 11, 1952   Rating/Share: 57.9/85   Supporting cast: Freddie Fillmore—Frank Nelson, Office boy—Bobby Ellis, Radio announcer—Roy Rowan

When a planned evening of intellectual conversation falls flat, the Ricardos and Mertzes opt for a night in front of the TV set. When the set breaks down, radio prevails and the four friends listen to the "Mr. and Mrs. Quiz" show, hosted by Freddie Fillmore. To everybody's amazement, Ricky knows all the answers (year of the Gettysburg address, the name of the youngest U.S. president, and the forty-eighth state), prompting Lucy to register him as a contestant. When Lucy tells Ricky about his upcoming radio stint, he becomes furious and reveals that the only reason he knew the answers was because he happened to be at the radio station while the program was being taped. Ricky: "All I know is that Columbus discovered Ohio in 1776." Lucy beats a hasty retreat to Freddie Fillmore's office to withdraw Ricky's name as a contestant, but Fillmore is so excited about having "a big-name entertainer" on his show, Lucy can't bring herself to break the news. But she does manage to "steal" the answers to the three questions, later committing them to memory. Unfortunately, just before showtime, the questions are switched and Lucy's memorized answers provide the hilarity. "Question one—What is the name of the animal that fastens itself to you and drains you of your blood? . . . The collector of Internal Revenue; question two—What is a senator's term of office? . . . The sap runs every two years; question three—Why did the French people put Marie Antoinette under the sharp blade of the guillotine? . . . To scrape the barnacles off her hull." Much to their collective surprise, the Ricardos answer the bonus five-hundred-dollar query correctly—"What did George Washington say while crossing the Delaware?"—because Ricky happens to blurt out, "Please let me sit down. This is making me sick."

"LUCY'S SCHEDULE"   5/26/52

Episode #33   Filmed on Friday, April 18, 1952   Rating/Share: 51.7/81   Supporting cast: Alvin Littlefield—Gale Gordon, Phoebe Littlefield—Edith Meiser

After Lucy louses up a dinner appointment with the new Tropicana boss, Alvin Littlefield, and his wife Phoebe, by being late, Ricky promptly puts his wife on a rigid time schedule (Ricky: "Ten minutes for this, fifteen minutes for that."). Ricardo informs Littlefield of this at a meeting to discuss the possibility of Ricky being made manager of the Tropicana, adding, "I've got her jumping around like a trained seal!" Seeing is believing, so Ricky invites the Littlefields to dinner to watch Lucy "perform." When Lucy gets wind of the plot, she schemes with Ethel and Mrs. Littlefield to teach their time-conscious hubbies a well-deserved lesson. The various dinner courses are rushed to the table and then whisked away in seconds, with Lucy finally donning a catcher's mitt to catch hot biscuits being thrown by Ethel from the kitchen. Littlefield has seen quite enough: "This is no way to run a house . . . but it is the only way to run a nightclub . . . Mr. Manager."

NOTE: This was the first television appearance by Gale Gordon with Lucille Ball. Eleven years later, they began an eleven-year association on "The Lucy Show" (1963–68) and "Here's Lucy" (1968–74). Gordon had appeared on Lucy's radio program, "My Favorite Husband," from 1948 to 1951 and had been considered the first choice for what eventually became the Fred Mertz role on "Lucy." . . . Edith Meiser, who played Phoebe Littlefield in this and a subsequent episode, appeared in 1941 with Vivian Vance in Cole Porter's Broadway musical, *Let's Face It.*

"RICKY THINKS HE'S GETTING BALD" 6/2/52

Episode #34   Filmed on Friday, April 25, 1952   Rating/Share: 56.0/90   Supporting cast: Mr. Thurlough—Milton Parsons

When Ricky takes to sporting a hat around the apartment, Lucy fears he's worrying needlessly about going bald. She visits a store that specializes in hair restoration products and devices. Its manager, Mr. Thurlough, demonstrates some of the cures, but Lucy feels these are too drastic in Ricky's minor case. Later, she and Ethel dream up a better stunt—they'll invite a group of bald men to the apartment to prove to Ricky how well off he really is. Lucy: "I want this place looking like a sea of honeydew melons." Thurlough arrives with a number of bare-pated men (Mssrs. Johnson, Miller, and Davis), each demanding ten dollars for his services and a meal. Lucy pays up just before Ricky phones from work to inform her he won't be home for hours. Lucy dismisses the bald-headed aggregation and opts for the drastic measures previously shunned. When Ricky arrives at home, Lucy warns him, "Yours roots won't know what hit 'em" as she proceeds to use vibrators, mustard plasters, a plunger, and heat cap ("you have to bake for twenty minutes"). Hoping he'll dislike the treatment, Lucy says he'll have to "do it every other night for six months." Strangely, Ricky likes the notion, and Lucy sighs, defeated.

NOTE: Lucille Ball was a frustrated hairdresser herself. When she was growing up, her aunt owned a beauty shop and Lucy would go often to observe. At the Chatsworth ranch, Lucy had a mini-beauty parlor and liked nothing better than giving friends permanents and trying the latest egg rinses. . . . When this episode was originally filmed, the "Caesar's salad" scene was the climax of Act One. Once the show was edited, Jess felt the ending—the bald men "party"—was weak, so he reshot a few expository scenes and reedited the thirty minutes so that the "block" comedy scene with the vibrators and the eggs came at the end of Act Two. . . . This episode may have been inspired by Jess Oppenheimer's own baldness.

"RICKY ASKS FOR A RAISE"   6/9/52

Episode #35   Filmed on Friday, May 2, 1952   Rating/Share: 54.2/83   Supporting cast: Maurice, the headwaiter—Maurice Marsac, Alvin Littlefield—Gale Gordon, Phoebe Littlefield—Edith Meiser

When Ricky's attempts to secure a raise from his boss, Mr. Littlefield, fail, Lucy decides to fight back. Noticing a newspaper ad announcing the opening of Xavier Valdez—"King of the Konga"—at the Tropicana, Ethel conjectures: "Wouldn't it be wonderful if no one shows up for Xavier's opening?" This prompts the redhead to make seventy-five bogus reservations in various names—Mrs. Worthington Proudfoot, Scarlett Culpepper, Lucille McGillicuddy—and with the help of the Mertzes' old vaudeville friend, quick-change artist Hal King, Lucy, Fred, and Ethel set off to invade the Tropicana and prove Ricky's popularity once and for all. In costume, the three parade into the club and then, upon hearing that "Ricky Ricardo isn't appearing here anymore," leave abruptly. They pull this trick a few times (including one scene featuring William Frawley in drag), until it is clear to Mr. Littlefield that he cannot afford to be without Ricky Ricardo. This speculation goes directly to Ricky's head: "I guess I didn't realize how popular I was. . . . I can write my own ticket anywhere in town."

NOTE: Hal King was the "I Love Lucy" makeup artist. . . . As the tag of this episode, Lucy and Desi appeared in the Ricardo bedroom, sitting atop a steamer trunk. They wished viewers a pleasant summer and alerted them to a new situation comedy that would replace "Lucy" for the summer months, a new show starring Gale Storm and Charles Farrell, "My Little Margie." "I think you're going to like it," Lucy hinted.

The Second Season: 1952-53

THE SECOND SEASON: 1952–53

Executive Producer: Desi Arnaz
Producer: Jess Oppenheimer
Writers: Jess Oppenheimer, Madelyn Pugh, and Bob Carroll, Jr.
Directors: Marc Daniels and William Asher
Director of Photography: Karl Freund, A.S.C.
Musical Director: Wilbur Hatch (Conducting the Desi Arnaz Orchestra)
Production Manager: Argyle Nelson
Supervising Editor: Dann Cahn
Original Music: Eliot Daniel
Assistant Director: James Paisley
Sound: Glen Glenn Sound (Cameron McCulloch in charge)
Makeup: Max Factor (Hal King)

Filmed at General Service Studios

Sponsor: Philip Morris & Co.
Agency: The Biow Co., Inc.

"JOB SWITCHING"   9/15/52

Episode #39   Filmed on Friday, May 30, 1952   Rating/Share: 64.4/60   Supporting cast: Mr. Snodgrass—Alvin Hurwitz, Foreman— Elvia Allman, Candy maker—Amanda Milligan

In need of money, Lucy writes on the back of a rubber check: "Dear Teller. Be a lamb and don't put this through until next month." Infuriated, Ricky declares: "Well, Lucy, what have you got to say?" Lucy: "Now I know why they call them tellers. They go around blabbing everything they know." Disgruntled by Lucy's spendthrift ways, Ricky insists she would feel differently about money if she had to "bring home the bacon." With Ethel's support, Lucy agrees to switch roles for a week—the girls will get jobs if the boys stay home to do the housework and cooking. The females' first stop is the Acme Employment Agency ("People We Place Stay Put") where Mr. Snodgrass interviews them. Fibbing about their experience, Lucy and Ethel land jobs as candy makers at Kramer's Kandy Kitchen. The factory foreman assigns Lucy to the candy-dipping section where disaster soon strikes, ending in a chocolate war with a co-worker. Ethel fares no better in the boxing department, and soon both girls are transferred to "wrapping," where their task is to wrap each piece of candy as it goes by on a conveyor belt. Unfortunately, they find it impossible to keep up with the swift-moving contraption and, in one of the funniest scenes ever telecast, are forced to stuff the excess candies into their mouths, hats, blouses, etc. As "housewives," Ricky and Fred are doing no better. Ricky makes a mess of the ironing and a bigger mess of the kitchen when he attempts to cook *arroz con pollo* for dinner (Fred bakes a seven-layer cake that is as flat as a pancake). The men hurriedly retreat from the shambles to buy five-pound boxes of chocolate for the wives, as a peace offering. You can imagine the looks on Lucy and Ethel's faces when they arrive home from their first day on the job—defeated and fired. The four finally agree to call off the "switch."

NOTE: This is one of Lucille Ball's favorite "I Love Lucy" episodes.

"THE SAXOPHONE"   9/22/52

Episode #40   Filmed on Friday, June 6, 1952   Rating/Share: 67.5/65   Supporting cast: Jule—Herb Vigran, Man in closet—Charles Victor   Music: "The Glow Worm"

When Lucy learns that Ricky and his band will be going out of town on a series of one-nighters, she wants to go along. Finding her old saxophone in the attic, she demonstrates her musical abilities by playing "The Glow Worm," the only song she learned to play in high school in Celeron, New York. To be like "one of the boys," Lucy attends Ricky's band auditions dressed in a wild zoot suit, complete with swinging watch chain: "Hey, man.

. . . Hiya, cats! . . . Give me some skin." Lucy auditions valiantly for her bandleader husband, but her sad rendition of "The Glow Worm" costs her the job. Determined to keep Ricky from going on the road without her, Lucy plots to make him jealous. Using Fred Mertz's derby and gloves, she leads Ricky to believe that she spent the afternoon with another man. This sends her husband into a proper jealous rage, until Fred happens to ask what his hat and gloves are doing in the Ricardo apartment. To teach Lucy a lesson, Ricky calls Jule at the musicians' union and arranges to have three or four guys, posing as Lucy's lovers, take up temporary residence in the Ricardo closet. The "lovers" arrive and the joke works perfectly, until the union man phones Ricky to tell him he couldn't get anyone to help out. Now Ricky is frantic, without realizing Lucy arranged the call.

NOTE: Lucille Ball went to high school in Celeron, New York. . . . When the writers first dreamed up this episode, they went to Lucy and asked her if she could play the saxophone. Her response: "No, but give me a week." By the time rehearsals started on June 2, 1952, she knew enough to get by.

"THE ANNIVERSARY PRESENT"   9/29/52

Episode #36 Filmed on Friday, May 9, 1952 Rating/Share: 69.1/66 Supporting cast: Grace Foster—Gloria Blondell, Jule—Herb Vigran Music: "Down Argentine Way"

The Ricardos' eleventh wedding anniversary is approaching and Lucy finds herself dropping some none-too-subtle hints in Ricky's direction. Little does she realize that her husband has already made plans for the anniversary, having arranged to buy at a discount a string of pearls for Lucy through a neighbor, Grace Foster, who happens to work at Joseff Jewelry company. But Ricky's many surreptitious trips to Grace's apartment (while Mr. Foster is out of town) to inspect the pearls have got Lucy suspecting the worst: Ricky is having an affair with Mrs. Foster. When Lucy and Ethel overhear what's going on in Grace's apartment (2-A), using the snooper's friend (furnace pipes), they decide to don some discarded painters' overalls and make their way up a scaffold to spy on the "lovers." Naturally, havoc follows when Lucy spies Ricky fondling Grace's neck. Finally, before surprising Lucy with the gift, Ricky pretends he *is* having a tryst with the Foster woman, then exclaims: "Grace and I have decided . . . these are the pearls I will give you for our wedding anniversary." Lucy is agog and all is forgiven.

NOTE: The Arnazes *were* married eleven years when this episode was filmed. . . . Joseff Jewelry is a company, headquartered in Burbank, California, that supplies jewelry for movies and TV shows.

"THE HANDCUFFS" 10/6/52

Episode #37 Filmed on Friday, May 16, 1952 Rating/Share: 67.7/64 Supporting cast: Jerry, the agent—Paul Dubov, Mr. Walters —Will Wright, Emcee—Veola Vonn Music: "In Santiago, Chile"

After Fred demonstrates his magic prowess with a set of trick handcuffs, Lucy snaps a similar pair on Ricky and herself, in an effort to persuade her husband to stay home that night instead of attending a TV show rehearsal. Much to their mutual horror, they discover the manacles date back to Civil War times (Fred got them at a police benefit in 1919) and no keys exist to open them. Ricky is furious when he realizes he will miss the important rehearsal. The pair's efforts to sleep while still cuffed together are a delight. The next morning, a locksmith, Mr. Walters, arrives with an impressive collection of keys, but none will open the contraption. He knows he has the key at home, but that's in Yonkers, over two hours away. Ricky is panicky— his television show, live from Television Center, Studio A, is only a few hours away. He tells the locksmith to meet him at the studio with the promised key. Still shackled to Lucy, Ricky appears on the "Guest Stars" TV show. With Lucy's right arm acting as his own, Ricky manages to answer questions put to him by the show's hostess/emcee. Lucy's hammy antics are priceless and continue throughout Ricky's song. Finally, Mr. Walters arrives and frees the couple just in time for Ricky's bows.

NOTE: Director Marc Daniels worked out these handcuff routines with his wife (and "I Love Lucy" camera coordinator), Emily, before instructing Lucille and Desi.

"THE OPERETTA"   10/13/52

Episode #38   Filmed on Friday, May 23, 1952   Rating/Share: 64.5/62   Supporting cast: Club president—Myra Marsh   Music: "We're the Pleasant Peasant Girls," "Lily of the Valley," "I Am the Queen of the Gypsies," "We Are the Troops of the King"

After a meeting of the Wednesday Afternoon Fine Arts League, treasurer Lucy admits to Ethel that for the past two years she has secretly balanced her household budget by borrowing from the club's treasury and vice versa, and now there isn't a dime left in either fund to pay the expenses of putting on an operetta to commemorate the club's twenty-fifth anniversary. The scheme: Save the hundred-dollar royalty fee by writing the operetta themselves ("Ethel Romberg and Lucy Friml") and rent the sets and costumes (for the eighteen-scene play) with a postdated check. Lucy plays Camille, the snaggle-toothed old queen of the gypsies; Ethel portrays Lily, a neighboring village girl; Fred takes the part of Friar Quinn, owner of the inn on the River Out; and Ricky plays the hero, "good Prince Lancelot." In the midst of the performance, men from the costume and scenery rental company arrive and proceed to repossess the items.

NOTE: This was director Marc Daniels' last "Lucy" episode and, coincidentally, his favorite. . . . According to *Newsweek* (1/19/53), this was the first episode of her parents' TV series that Little Lucie was allowed to stay up and watch.

"VACATION FROM MARRIAGE"   10/27/52

Episode #41   Filmed on Friday, August 1, 1952   Rating/Share: 66.8/90

The Ricardos and Mertzes have decided that their marriages are in a rut. Lucy: "We've all let ourselves become four big, dull clumps. . . . We are knee-deep in a pool of stagnation." A library book suggests a "week's vacation from marriage" as the solution. Once separated, the girls miss their boys and vice versa. Ricky: "You know . . . I miss Lucy." Fred: "I can top that. I miss Ethel!" Refusing to swallow their pride, the girls dress to the hilt and appear at the Ricardo apartment, hoping to make the boys jealous. Ethel: "We've been to 21 four times this week . . . that's 84." The revelation doesn't sway the husbands, so Lucy and Ethel return to the Mertz apartment defeated. When they later decide to check on their husbands, they find them missing from the Ricardo apartment. Forced to the roof because they hear their husbands approaching in the hall, they get locked outside and their efforts to elicit help from a neighbor, Mrs. Saunders, fail. Finally Ricky and Fred discover the girls shivering on the roof and douse them with water from a handy hose. Lucy says finally: "I want to be in a rut with you," and embraces Ricky.

"THE COURTROOM"   11/10/52

Episode #42   Filmed on Friday, August 8, 1952   Rating/Share: 66.5/91   Supporting cast: Judge—Moroni Olsen, Process server—Harry Bartell, Bailiff—Robert B. Williams

The Ricardos give the Mertzes a new twenty-inch television set on the occasion of their twenty-fifth wedding anniversary. Ricky's hasty tuning adjustments cause the set to blow up, and Fred retaliates by kicking in the Ricardos' TV tube. A legal battle develops, landing the foursome in court. With Ricky as defense attorney, Lucy describes, in gruesome detail, what happened. Her testimony is like the classic fish story and culminates when Lucy exposes her shapely legs for the judge. When Fred calls Ethel to the witness stand, she tries the same flirtatious ploy until Fred stops her: "What are you trying to do . . . lose the case for us?" Finally, the judge decides to reenact the drama by dragging in his own TV set from his chambers. By the time the demonstration is completed, the judge's television set is a shambles, too.

NOTE: Just a year before (Episode #2) the Mertzes celebrated their eighteenth wedding anniversary.

"REDECORATING"   11/24/52

Episode #43   Filmed on Friday, August 15, 1952   Rating/Share: not available   Supporting cast: Dan Jenkins—Hans Conried, Women on party line—Margie Liszt, Florence Halop

A visit to the "Home Show" prompts Lucy and Ethel to dream of households with new furniture. A contest, in which they each entered one hundred cards, will award the lucky winner with five rooms of new furnishings. All the wives have to do is wait for a phone call from the "Home Show" the next day; but Ricky has managed to obtain four tickets to the "new Rodgers and Hammerstein musical." Temptation notwithstanding, Lucy opts to wait for the all-important phone call. So he can attend the musical, Ricky asks Fred to make a phony phone call informing Lucy she has won. Naturally, when the call comes through Lucy is elated and immediately summons a secondhand furniture dealer. For seventy-five dollars, she sells dealer Dan Jenkins all her furniture and promptly spends the cash on new paint and wallpaper to brighten the apartment. The scene depicting Lucy and Ethel wallpapering the Ricardo bedroom is priceless. When Ricky arrives home and learns that Lucy has sold all their furniture, he chases after Jenkins to buy it back. The price—after the dealer adds on for "overhead, electricity, advertising . . ."—five hundred dollars. Ricky manages to wheedle Jenkins down to three hundred and ninety-five dollars, but only because "I like the way you sing 'Babalu.' " After viewing the new striped wallpaper in the bedroom, Ricky learns from Fred that he never made the phony "Home Show" phone call, which means that Lucy really did win the furniture.

NOTE: Dan Jenkins was a favorite writer of Lucy and Desi's, first with the *Hollywood Reporter* and then with *TV Guide*. . . . This episode was prompted by Miss Ball, who said of the existing stage furniture, "I just got tired of it."

"RICKY LOSES HIS VOICE"   12/1/52

Episode #44   Filmed on Friday, August 22, 1952   Rating/Share: 74.1/91   Supporting cast: Mr. Chambers—Arthur Q. Bryan, Flappers—Gertrude Astor, Hazel Pierce, Helen Williams, Marion B. Enfield (aka Barbara Pepper)   Music: "Sweet and Lovely," "Carolina in the Morning," "Five Foot Two, Eyes of Blue," "Charleston," "Mississippi Mud," "The Varsity Drag"

When Ricky arrives home with a bad case of laryngitis, Lucy banishes him to bed. However, the Cuban is concerned about the imminent reopening of the Tropicana, and Mr. Chambers, his new boss, is counting on him to stage a good show. Ricky's throat becomes so sore that he resorts to using a blackboard and chalk to communicate. This prompts dutiful wife Lucy to contact Chambers to tell him that Ricky is in no shape to perform his duties, but before she has a chance to break the news, Chambers informs her that he is going out of town for a few days, adding: "I have every confidence [Ricky's] going to turn out a great show!" Deciding not to tell Ricky and stage the show herself, Lucy hires "some talent that has been grossly overlooked in the past"—Fred and Ethel. Mr. Mertz unearths an old vaudeville script, "Flapper Follies of 1927," and even manages to line up all the showgirls from the original production. At the opening of the show, Ricky is aghast when a chorus line of middle-aged double-chinned flappers cavort to his singing of "Sweet and Lovely." Fred and Ethel do "Carolina in the Morning" and Lucy scores with a ukelele number, "Mississippi Mud," and the finale—featuring ex-vaudevillian Mr. Chambers—is "The Varsity Drag" with all joining in the twenties' fun.

NOTE: The furniture "won" at the "Home Show" in the preceding episode ("Redecorating") was unveiled for the first time in this episode. . . . The Tropicana set was substantially redressed for this episode: the bandstand became more colorful for future segments. . . . Among the aging showgirls featured in the musical numbers was Barbara Pepper, who in July 1933 boarded a cross-country train in New York with a few other young women to become Goldwyn Girls—one of them was Lucille Ball. . . . In the opening scene, listen for the error pianist Marco Rizo makes when Ricky tells him to "call Lucy and tell her I'll be home right away." Instead of responding, "Okay, Ricky," Rizo slips and says, "Okay, Des."

"LUCY IS ENCEINTE"   12/8/52

Episode #50   Filmed on Friday, October 3, 1952   Rating/Share: 67.7/87   Supporting cast: Maître d'—William R. Hamel, Stage hand— Richard J. Reeves   Music: "The Lady in Red," "Rock-a-bye Baby," "We're Having a Baby"

Overweight and feeling "dauncey," Lucy decides to see her doctor for a checkup. Ethel: "You don't suppose . . . you're going to have a baby." Lucy is incredulous, but—sure enough—the tests are positive. After eleven years of marriage, the Ricardos are expecting their first child. Lucy has dreamed "a million times" about this event—breaking the news to Ricky. Her first attempt is at lunch, but, alas, Señor Ricardo is in a bad mood: "Sometimes I think I go back to Cuba and work on a sugar plantation." Next, she journeys to the Tropicana, but with all the onlookers present, Lucy finds it impossible to discuss such a personal matter. In the meantime, Fred and Ethel are absolutely overwhelmed with the idea that they'll be the baby's godparents. In fact, Fred already has purchased a baseball bat, glove, cap, and ball for "little Freddie." Lucy, however, is desperate; she must tell the father-to-be as soon as possible or "wait and let the baby tell him." At the club that night, Lucy slips a note to the headwaiter during Ricky's "The Lady in Red" number. Not knowing it was penned by Lucy, Ricky reads it aloud to the audience: "My husband and I are going to have a blessed event and I just found out today. I've heard you sing 'We're Having a Baby.' Would you sing it for us?" He obliges first by singing "Rock-a-bye Baby" and in the midst of the number—in a wonderfully sentimental scene— discovers that it was Lucy who wrote the note. Thereupon he sings "We're Having a Baby" to Lucy—and the two parents-to-be are awash in tears.

"PREGNANT WOMEN ARE UNPREDICTABLE" 12/15/52

Episode #51   Filmed on Friday, October 10, 1952   Rating/Share: 68.1/92   Supporting cast: Deliveryman—Bennett Green   Music: "Cheek to Cheek"

The Ricardos are trying to agree on a name for the baby: Gregory or Joanne, Gregory or Cynthia, John or Mary? Lucy: "I want the names to be unique and euphonious." Ricky: "Okay. Unique if it's a boy and Euphonious if it's a girl." The following morning, Ricky offers to cook Lucy's favorite breakfast— waffles. After a series of kitchen mishaps, Lucy exclaims, "Do me a favor. Don't cook breakfast for me . . . I'm not strong enough." Suddenly, however, she gets the misguided idea that Ricky is interested only in "little Sharon or Pierpont," not in her. Ethel conveys these thoughts to Ricky, who immediately showers Lucy with "inappropriate" gifts—a rattle, a baby's bonnet, etc. To patch things up Ricky invites his wife to the Tropicana for dining and dancing. This manages to do the trick, except now Lucy fears Ricky doesn't love the baby. "You haven't even mentioned little Robert or Madelyn," Lucy sobs.

NOTE: Robert and Madelyn referred to Robert G. Carroll, Jr., and Madelyn Pugh—the two talented "Lucy" scribes.

"LUCY'S SHOW BIZ SWAN SONG" 12/22/52

Episode #52 Filmed on Friday, October 17, 1952 Rating/Share: 64.9/90 Supporting cast: Jerry, the agent—Jerry Hausner, Clown— Pepito Music: "Carolina in the Morning," "Strolling Through the Park," "By the Light of the Silvery Moon," "Goodnight Ladies," "Sweet Adeline"

After a little harmonizing ("Carolina in the Morning"), Fred and Ethel are given the nod by Ricky to audition for his new Gay Nineties revue. Lucy, of course, also wants in, despite Ricky's insistence that the approaching stork should have dampened her show biz aspirations. Lucy: "Would you begrudge an expectant swan her song?" At auditions the next day, Pepito, the Spanish Clown, performs his world-famous baby-crying act, and the lion tamer routine, and rides the world's tiniest bicycle. Next in line, according to agent Jerry is an act called "'McGillicuddy and Mertz." Lucy and Ethel attempt "By the Light of the Silvery Moon" and are promptly rejected. Lucy: "What a lousy excuse he gave us." Ethel: "You mean telling us we stank?" Ricky finally offers Fred and Ethel a chance to appear in the revue—as one half of a barbershop quartet, along with him and George Watson. Lucy manages to get to Watson first and, hence, becomes the fourth member of the "Sweet Adeline" foursome, with typically chaotic results.

NOTE: Pepito, the Spanish Clown, was instrumental in devising the vaudeville routines Lucy and Desi performed on their 1950 road tour. He also appeared in the "Lucy" pilot film done on March 2, 1951. His segment in this episode was an afterthought: when the original film was being edited, it was discovered that the episode came up short, leaving a three-minute gap. Desi called his friend Pepito and invited him to Hollywood to do a few routines which were filmed on November 7, 1952, the night "Lucy Becomes a Sculptress" was done.

"LUCY HIRES AN ENGLISH TUTOR" 12/29/52

Episode #53 Filmed on Friday, October 24, 1952 Rating/Share: 68.1/91 Supporting cast: Percy Livermore—Hans Conried Music: "Babalu," "Notre Dame Victory Song," "Tippy Tippy Toe" (by Eliot Daniel)

Ashamed of her sloppy English and the inevitable effects it could have on the baby, Lucy hires a tutor, after telling Ricky: "Please promise me you won't speak to our child until he's nineteen or twenty." The teacher, Mr. Livermore, arrives and proceeds to teach the Ricardos and Mertzes lesson number one: "Never use the words 'okay,' 'swell,' and 'lousy.' " The instruction period goes downhill thereafter, finally prompting Lucy to crack,

"I would say 'okay.' . . . That's a swell way to get off to a lousy start!" Ricky becomes concerned about the cost of the tutoring until it becomes evident Lucy made a deal with Livermore: In return for free diction lessons Ricky is to allow Livermore to perform his song, "Tippy Tippy Toe," at Ricardo's "nocturnal bistro." To get even with Lucy, Ricky enlists Livermore's aid, promising him an audition with all the record companies if he'll agree to speak English (?) the way Ricky does. Livermore acquiesces; and Lucy, patently disgusted, gives up the idea of English lessons.

"RICKY HAS LABOR PAINS"   1/5/53

Episode #54   Filmed on Friday, October 31, 1952   Rating/Share: 71.7/91   Supporting cast: Dr. Rabwin—Louis D. Merrill, Jerry—Jerry Hausner, Clubwoman—Hazel Pierce

Six months' pregnant, Lucy is given a "surprise" baby shower by five members of the Wednesday Afternoon Fine Arts League. It later dawns on Lucy that Ricky has become jealous of the baby because all the attention is concentrated on her and the upcoming blessed event. When Ricky starts complaining of nausea, dizzy spells, and pains in his stomach, Lucy consults Dr. Rabwin, who diagnoses the problem as "morning sickness." Assuring Lucy that her husband's ailment is merely psychosomatic, the doc suggests she make him the "center of attention" for a while. Ethel suggests a baby shower for Ricky. Lucy changes the idea to a "daddy shower," whereupon Fred turns it into a stag party. A little apprehensive about the turn of events, Lucy decides to crash the daddy shower/stag party disguised as a newspaper reporter with Ethel posing as her photographer-partner. "Pete" and "Sam"— of the New York *Herald Times Tribune*—arrive at the party that is attended by many of Ricky's friends, including Jerry, his agent. It doesn't take long for the guest of honor to realize the intrusion by the girls, and the party comes to an abrupt halt. In the final scene, pregnant Lucy enjoys a late night snack of pistachio ice cream covered with hot fudge and sardines.

"LUCY BECOMES A SCULPTRESS"   1/12/53

Episode #55   Filmed on Friday, November 7, 1952   Rating/Share: 66.6/88   Supporting cast: William Abbott—Shepard Menken, Clerk at art supply store—Leon Belasco, Mr. Harvey—Paul Harvey

No child should grow up without an artistic influence in his life, so Lucy looks into some possibilities at a local art supply shop. William Abbott, who runs the store, leads her to believe she has an incredible sculpting talent and fast-talks her into buying fifty pounds of modeling clay. Ricky and the Mertzes don't think much of Lucy's new leanings and after an ill-fated modeling stint by Fred, they insist she give up the art because it is obvious she has no talent. Better to prove his point, Ricky informs her that he is bringing home an art critic, and if he judges her work to be less than promising, she must give it up entirely. In retaliation, Lucy consults a book that describes how to make a plaster mold of one's head, and hence, a perfect replica. When this method fails, she simply encases her head in a thin layer of clay and becomes her own "bust." Mr. Harvey, the critic from the *Times,* arrives and is ecstatic over Lucy's "talent." In fact, he wishes to purchase the sculptured head for five hundred dollars. But when he proceeds to remove the bust off the table, Lucy lets out a shriek, and Harvey rushes out mumbling under his breath.

"LUCY GOES TO THE HOSPITAL"   1/19/53

Episode #56   Filmed on Friday, November 14, 1952   Rating/Share: 71.8/92   Supporting cast: Mr. Stanley—Charles Lane, Nurse in hospital lobby—Adele Longmire, Nurse with wheelchair—Peggy Rea, Orderly— Bennett Green, Tropicana maître d'—William R. Hamel, Policeman— Ralph Montgomery, Nurses—Barbara Pepper, Ruth Perrott, Hazel Pierce, Little Ricky—James John Ganzer   Music: "Voodoo"

With the baby due momentarily, Lucy is trying to remain cool and calm, despite Ricky's nervous demeanor (Lucy to Ethel: "He keeps staring at me like I'm going to explode."), so she invites the Mertzes over to act as buffers. Pretty soon, Lucy has to contend with three nervous Nellies, so she retires to the bedroom to rest. Meanwhile, Ricky suggests that the three of them "rehearse" Lucy's trip to the hospital so that when the time comes, it can be carried out with dispatch. Ethel is charged with phoning Lucy's doctor, Joe Harris; Fred promises to take care of the suitcase; and Ricky will see to it that Lucy is prepared for the taxi ride. They rehearse their roles twice and all goes smoothly, until Lucy appears in the doorway and calmly announces: "Ricky, this is it." Despite the careful and tranquil preliminaries, pandemonium results and it's a minor miracle that Lucy arrives at the hospital at all. While Lucy is taken to her room (354), Ricky retreats to the fathers' waiting area where he encounters Mr. Stanley, the father of six girls. Realizing he has little time to get to his nightclub job, Ricky asks Fred to bring his makeup kit "for the voodoo number" to the hospital. In full witch-doctor drag, Ricky departs hurriedly for the Tropicana, leaving Fred to do the parental pacing. Lucy finally delivers a boy, and Ricky races back to the hospital for his first look (and fainting spell) at Ricky Ricardo, Jr.

NOTE: Dr. Joseph Harris was Lucille Ball's physician. . . . This episode—seen by more people than any other TV show of its time—is one of Desi Arnaz's favorites. . . . At the conclusion of the episode, footage of the new baby (James John Ganzer) was accompanied by this voice-over: "Yes, there's a new baby, a wonderful baby at the Ricardos'. And we at Philip Morris rejoice in the blessed event. We know that all our millions of friends join with us in extending congratulations and good wishes to the Ricardos. May their lives together be filled with as much joy and laughter and carefree happiness as they have brought all of us week after week. To Lucy, to Ricky, and to the new baby: love and kisses from Philip Morris and from all America."

"SALES RESISTANCE"   1/26/53

Episode #45   Filmed on Friday, August 29, 1952   Rating/Share: 71.3/92   Supporting cast: Harry Martin—Sheldon Leonard, Mrs. Simpson—Verna Felton   Music: "Cielito Lindo," "There's a Brand New Baby at Our House" (by Desi Arnaz and Eddie Maxwell)

With Lucy still at the hospital, Ricky sings "There's a Brand New Baby at Our House," as Fred and Ethel look on. The three then recall with amusement Lucy's lack of sales resistance as a flashback carries us to the time Lucy spent $7.98 on a useless Handy Dandy Kitchen Helper. After Ricky insisted she return it for a refund, Lucy bought a Handy Dandy Vacuum Cleaner for $102.60. When the salesman, Harry Martin, sold it to her, he said it cost only "eight dollars and ninety-five cents . . . for the works." Unfortunately, that was all Lucy got—the works, and not the electric cord, the metal cover, or any attachments. When Ricky learned of her extravagant purchase, he demanded its immediate return. But Lucy was scared stiff that Martin would probably sell her a Handy Dandy Bulldozer! Instead, she decided to unload the contraption on some other unsuspecting soul, starting off with Mrs. Simpson, a gruff, untalkative housewife who lived on the next block. Using the Harry Martin sales pitch, Lucy failed to get rid of the machine and returned home a bedraggled, discouraged wreck. Lucy: "One more hour and they'd have reported the death of another salesman." Even "sales resistant" Ricky was unsuccessful when he tried to return the vacuum to Martin; he wound up buying a Handy Dandy Refrigerator.

NOTE: This episode, like the following four, utilized a "flashback" intro. These five episodes were originally written and filmed *before* the seven "baby shows" were written and filmed. In order to allow Lucille Ball enough time to relax before her baby was due (two months) and give her sufficient time to rest up after the boy's birth (two months), these episodes were saved for telecast *after* the baby shows aired; hence, the flashback approach. . . . A Westinghouse vacuum cleaner was used. . . . Arnaz composed the opening song (part of the flashback section) with Eddie Maxwell on the occasion of Lucie Arnaz's birth on July 17, 1951.

"THE INFERIORITY COMPLEX"   2/2/53

Episode #46   Filmed on Saturday, September 6, 1952   Rating/Share: 69.9/90   Supporting cast: Dr. Henry Molin—Gerald Mohr   Music: "Who?"

When no one laughs at Lucy's jokes or wants her for a bridge partner, she comes to the conclusion she is inferior. The next morning, she oversalts Ricky's fried egg, leaves the pits in his orange juice, and burns his toast. She cries: "I'm a big fat flop!" Depressed, she retreats to her bed, where she intends to remain for life. Ricky worries and tells Ethel he's going to consult a "physio-chiatrist." Dr. Henry Molin suggests flattery, by someone other than Ricky, as the answer. He says he'll arrange to have someone—who will call himself Chuck Stewart—arrive at the Ricardo apartment at 8 P.M. Who shows up but the handsome doctor himself, who proceeds to sweep Lucy off her feet . . . a little too far. Ricky doesn't take too kindly to the "treatment" and throws the headshrinker out, opting for a less expensive solution. With the Mertzes' help, he bends over backward in praise of Lucy's joke-telling and card-playing . . . even Lucy's singing. Alas, Lucy is cured.

NOTE: Henry Molin was a film editor for "I Love Lucy."

"THE CLUB ELECTION"   2/16/53

Episode #47   Filmed on Friday, September 12, 1952   Rating/Share: 69.0/92   Supporting cast: Jerry, the agent—Jerry Hausner, Lillian Appleby—Doris Singleton, Mrs. Knickerbocker—Ida Moore, Marion Strong—Margie Liszt, Grace Munson—Hazel Pierce, Club president—Lurene Tuttle, Clubwoman—Peggy Rea   Music: "Cuban Cabby," "Cielito Lindo"

While Ricky holds his newborn son, Ethel recalls the time she and Lucy ran for president of the Wednesday Afternoon Fine Arts League. The flashback takes us to the nominations meeting where the first order of business is approving a new member, Ruth Knickerbocker. When the current club president opens the floor for nominations, Marion Strong and Grace Munson get nods, with Ethel's name being offered up as a presidential hopeful. Jealous, Lucy huddles with Lillian Appleby and promises her a new cashmere sweater and handbag in return for a nomination. Mrs. Appleby agrees and there begins a battle for the club presidency between friends, Lucy and Ethel. The deciding vote belongs to new member Knickerbocker, so Lucy and Ethel separately entertain her, hoping to corral the needed vote. Ricky sings "Cuban Cabby" in a Tropicana nightclub scene, before Lucy and Ethel break the news that they have both won the election and will share the presidential honors.

NOTE: Doris Singleton's role as *Lillian* Appleby was changed to *Caroline* Appleby in later "Lucy" episodes. . . . Jerry Hausner provided the baby cries in the scene introducing the flashback, for which he was paid a hundred dollars.

"THE BLACK EYE"   3/9/53

Episode #48   Filmed on Friday, September 19, 1952   Rating/Share: 67.5/92   Supporting cast: Florist—Bennett Green

Lucy is reading a murder mystery to her husband when Fred and Ethel overhear a bit of dialogue: "Hit me—I dare you!" Thinking the Ricardos are having a terrible spat, they phone upstairs, hoping to break up the quarrel. Ethel: "Is there anything I can bring you? Cookies, ice cream, . . . iodine?" Moments later, Ricky playfully tosses the book at Lucy, hitting her accidentally in the eye. When the Mertzes spy the resulting shiner, they cannot accept the "farfetched" explanation Lucy offers. Taking it upon himself to patch up the Ricardos' "misunderstanding," Fred sends flowers to Lucy, but accidentally signs his own name to the card, not Ricky's. "Darling, I love you, I love you, I love you. Eternally yours, Fred," the message reads. When Lucy opens the box and sees the signature, she can't help but wonder, "Fred who?" Sarcastically, Ethel assures her it isn't Fred MacMurray, just before finding her husband hiding in Lucy's closet. Without seeking an explanation, Ethel belts Fred in the eye. He, in turn, smacks Ricky in the eye for starting the whole mess. After things have cooled down, Fred apologizes, finding the book-in-the-eye story quite plausible, indeed. In fact, he and Ethel have re-created the scene and now she, too, has a shiner. The four, black-eyed friends laugh uproariously, and everything returns to its usual state.

"LUCY CHANGES HER MIND"   3/30/53

Episode #49   Filmed on Friday, September 26, 1952   Rating/Share: 65.6/89   Supporting cast: Waiter—Frank Nelson, Harry Henderson— Phil Arnold, Tom Henderson—John L. Hart, Woman in fur salon— Sally Corner

First, Lucy can't decide which dress to wear for dinner, then has trouble choosing a restaurant. But once seated at the Jubilee restaurant, she quickly makes up her mind about what to eat—roast beef. The bespectacled waiter takes her order, then Ethel's—lamb chops. Lucy asks if she can change her order; she'd prefer lamb chops. When Ricky mentions steak ("rare, thick, and juicy"), Lucy changes her mind again. To add insult to injury, Lucy keeps changing tables at the restaurant, finding one too drafty, another viewless. Fred: "Stand by for another troop movement." The waiter becomes so flustered, he quits on the spot. Ricky is properly furious with Lucy, pointing out that she never finishes anything she starts and is guilty of constantly changing her mind. The next day, Lucy happens upon an old, unfinished love letter she once wrote to Tom Henderson, who's now a furrier. She decides to finish the letter and leave it around for Ricky to read. But Mr. Ricardo gets tipped off to the scheme by Mr. Mertz and doesn't bat a jealous eye when Lucy flaunts the letter in his face. Determined to make Ricky foam with envy, Lucy travels downtown to Henderson's fur salon where she spies a short, dumpy man. This can't be Tom, Lucy reasons, unless he "shrunk." With Ricky and Fred approaching, Lucy hops into the salon window and to make Ricky jealous starts "flirting" with a handsome male mannequin. All goes smoothly until the dummy separates in the middle, which makes for some superior Lucille Ball schtick.

"NO CHILDREN ALLOWED"   4/20/53

Episode #57   Filmed on Friday, March 20, 1953   Rating/Share: 68.3/89   Supporting cast: Little Ricky—Richard Lee and Ronald Lee Simmons, Mrs. Mathilda Trumbull—Elizabeth Patterson, Clubwomen—June Whitney, Charlotte Lawrence, Vivi Janiss, Peggy Rea, Margie Liszt, Kay Wiley, Baby crying—Jerry Hausner

Like all newborn babies, Little Ricky is cranky. The result—sleepless nights not only for Lucy and Ricky, but also for other tenants of the Mertz apartment building, most notably the elderly Mrs. Trumbull. She reads from her lease: "It is expressly understood that at no time will children be allowed to live in said building." Lucy and Ethel's attempts to humor the neighbor fail, and the conversation ends with Mrs. Trumbull warning Mrs. Mertz that she and other tenants may move out. Ethel takes an uncharacteristic firm stand: "My friendship with the Ricardos means more to me than all the money on earth." At first, Lucy and Ricky deeply appreciate the Mertzes' loyalty, until it becomes painfully clear Ethel won't let them forget her generosity. She repeats her "friendship-with-the-Ricardos" story ad nauseam to anyone who will listen until Lucy is forced to crack: "That speech has had more performances than *South Pacific!*" This leads to a giant battle during which Little Ricky is left unattended in the apartment. Realizing their stupidity, the foursome races back to the Ricardos', only to discover a not-so-crabby Mrs. Trumbull holding the infant in her arms.

NOTE: This was the first episode filmed since November 14, 1952, allowing Lucille Ball four months in which to prepare for and rest up from the birth of her baby. . . . This was Elizabeth Patterson's first appearance as Mrs. Mathilda Trumbull. . . . Note the mistake Vivian Vance makes when, after the clubwomen arrive to play bridge, she makes reference to that "old Mrs. Trimble who lives upstairs," not Mrs. Trumbull.

"LUCY HIRES A MAID" 4/27/53

Episode #58 Filmed on Friday, March 27, 1953 Rating/Share: 67.8/91 Supporting cast: Mrs. Porter—Verna Felton, Baby crying— Jerry Hausner

Lucy's sleepless nights caring for the baby prompt Ricky to hire a maid. Before the woman arrives, Lucy and Ethel discuss how to handle household help. Lucy has even prepared a list of do's and don'ts that she intends to read to her new employee. When Mrs. Porter arrives, she has her *own* list of do's and don'ts. The maid's first chore is to fix Lucy's lunch, a pitiful peanut butter sandwich. The maid had already polished off a jar of jelly, half a roast beef, and an entire head of lettuce (Mrs. Porter: "If I didn't have a salad, I'd have starved to death!"). In short, the maid takes over the entire Ricardo household, and Lucy wants to fire her but she can't muster up enough courage to do so. Instead, she transforms the apartment into a pigpen, hoping the maid will leave in disgust. Only after messing up the house does Lucy learn that Ricky already had dismissed the servant.

"THE INDIAN SHOW"   5/4/53

Episode #59   Filmed on Friday, April 3, 1953   Rating/Share: 63.8/90   Supporting cast: Jerry—Jerry Hausner, Juanita—Carol Richards, Actors posing as Indians—Richard J. Reeves, Frank Gerstle   Music: "Pass That Peace Pipe," "By the Waters of Minnetonka"

Ricky believes Lucy's show business aspirations have ended now that she has assumed the role of mother, but it's not so. The moment she hears that Ricky is staging a new Indian show at the Tropicana, she—along with the stagestruck Mertzes—wants to be a part of it. Lucy reads up on the subject in a book, *Blood-Curdling Indian Tales,* and is despondent when Ricky hires the Mertzes but not her. Nevertheless, Lucy manages to appear in the "By the Waters of Minnetonka" number by making a special "deal" with the regular performer, Juanita. But who's caring for Little Ricky? Big Ricky wants to know. Lucy has the infant strapped to her back like a papoose all through the number.

"LUCY'S LAST BIRTHDAY"   5/11/53

Episode #60   Filmed on Friday, April 10, 1953   Rating/Share: 56.7/86   Supporting cast: Jerry—Jerry Hausner, Mrs. Trumbull—Elizabeth Patterson, Maître d'—William R. Hamel, Friends of the Friendless—Ransom Sherman, Byron Foulger, Barbara Pepper   Music: "Happy Birthday to You," "Friend of the Friendless" (by Eliot Daniel and Harold Adamson), "I Love Lucy"

Lucy is feeling sorry for herself because everyone has apparently forgotten her birthday. Mrs. Trumbull's efforts to cheer her with a small cake and some confetti meet with only gloomy enthusiasm. Lucy decides to take a walk, leaving Little Ricky with the elderly neighbor. Ending up in Central Park,

Lucy is confronted by a motley group of musical itinerants known as the "Friends of the Friendless." They learn of her plight and offer a brassy chorus of "Happy Birthday." Her fury rekindled, Lucy decides to teach Ricky and the Mertzes a lesson in "the true meaning of friendship" and enlists the aid of the friendly band. Pounding a bass drum, Lucy marches into the Tropicana with her new friends. Standing bravely before the well-dressed aggregation, Lucy offers her tale of woe: "I was just a bit of flotsam in the sea . . . I was a mess." As she looks about the nightclub, she recognizes the faces of her dear friends—the Mertzes, the Orsattis, the Sedgwicks, the Morgans—who jump up and yell a happy birthday surprise. Lucy is overwhelmed as Ricky says, "I've got a wonderful present for you . . . Do you want to hear it?" Ricky sings the "I Love Lucy" theme song while Lucy, tears streaming down her face, is given presents galore. Finally, she drops them all to plant a big kiss on Ricky's glowing face.

NOTE: This was the only time the theme song lyrics were heard. The words were written by Harold Adamson. Columbia Records released it in 1953 with "There's a Brand New Baby at Our House" on the flip-side (#39937).

"THE RICARDOS CHANGE APARTMENTS" 5/18/53

Episode #61   Filmed on Thursday, April 16, 1953   Rating/Share: 60.5/98   Supporting cast: Mrs. Benson—Norma Varden

Lucy thinks the Ricardos need a larger apartment now that they have the baby, so she tries all her tricks to cajole Ricky to switch apartments with Mr. and Mrs. Benson, who have recently married off their daughter and don't need the extra bedroom. Lucy fills her apartment with junk, including a sliding pond and teeter-totter, to give it a "cramped" appearance; but Ricky is worried about the additional twenty dollars per month the larger flat will cost until Lucy promises to pay the extra cost out of her household budget. Mrs. Benson, who is still bemoaning the "loss" of her precious daughter, finally agrees to exchange apartments. Lucy, Fred, and Ethel perform the moving chores themselves (Lucy is the foreman, much to the Mertzes' consternation), and the Ricardos end up in a new apartment (3-B) with a window in the living room.

NOTE: Roy Rowan joined the company with this episode as the official "Lucy" announcer, replacing Jerry Hausner. The job paid seventy dollars a week.

"LUCY IS MATCHMAKER"   5/25/53

Episode #62   Filmed on Saturday, April 25, 1953   Rating/Share: not available   Supporting cast: Eddie Grant—Hal March, Club members—Doris Singleton, Peggy Rea, Maître d'—William R. Hamel, Man in hotel corridor—Phil Arnold

When a friend of the Mertzes, Eddie Grant, stops by for an unexpected visit and finds they are not at home, he leaves a message for them with Lucy. When she learns that the lingerie salesman is an eligible bachelor, she immediately begins brewing plans to fix him up with her girl friend, Sylvia Collins. The plan backfires (of course) and, through a clever montage of misunderstandings, Lucy and Ethel wind up in Eddie's hotel room, wearing some very skimpy negligees. The girls have some tall explaining to do when Ricky and Fred arrive on the scene. Ricky: "Lucy! You here . . . dressed like that! You must be out of your mind!" Fred: "Ethel! You here . . . dressed like that! *He* must be out of his mind!" It's all a big mistake—Eddie was merely trying to show his appreciation for the girls' hospitality by selling them some lingerie wholesale.

"LUCY WANTS NEW FURNITURE"   6/1/53

Episode #63   Filmed on Friday, May 1, 1953   Rating/Share: 59.6/90

Without Ricky's permission, Lucy buys a new sofa and coffee table for $299, using the old furniture as a down payment. Until she can find the proper moment to break the news to him, she hides the new pieces in the kitchen— leaving the living room practically barren. Denied the use of the kitchen, Lucy serves Ricky dinner in the living room. When she forgets the knives, salt, and butter (Lucy: "Butter on bread??? I'll never get used to your Cuban dishes!"), and has to make repeated mad dashes through the Mertz apartment to retrieve the items from her own kitchen, Ricky gets suspicious and finally discovers the new furniture hidden in the kitchen. Now Ricky intends to take the furniture to the club and keep it there until Lucy can pay for it out of her allowance, adding, "Cut down on some of your 'stravaganzas." But Lucy wants desperately to attend the Carrolls' party at the Tropicana on Saturday night for which she'll need a new dress and have to get her "hair dyed . . . *done!*" She tries earnestly to make her own dress and give herself a home permanent. Unveiling the finished fashion, Lucy says proudly: "I made it with my own two hands." Ethel: "It looks like you made it with your own two feet!" Her hair turns out no better, prompting Fred to exclaim, "Well, if it isn't Little Orphan Annie!" When Lucy sobs, Ricky gives in—he'll buy her a new dress, let her get her hair done, and bring home the furniture.

"THE CAMPING TRIP"   6/8/53

Episode #64   Filmed on Friday, May 8, 1953   Rating/Share: 51.5/58   Supporting cast: Jerry—Jerry Hausner, Clubwomen—Doris Singleton, June Whitney

When Lucy begins to notice the widening separation of interests between Ricky and herself, she decides to develop an interest in the sports pages of the newspaper in hopes of striking a mutual bond. With unknowing disgust, Lucy comments on an item: "They're racing little girls at Churchill Downs. First race won by a three-year-old." A summer camping trip is in the offing and Lucy itches to tag along. Fred: "If Lucy goes, Ethel will want to go, and I can be miserable at home." The men hatch the perfect scheme: Ricky will take Lucy on a weekend "trial run" and make life in the woods so rough on her, she won't want to join them for the summer sojourn. Ethel overhears the dastardly doings and informs Lucy, who puts together her own bag of tricks. On the overnighter, Lucy manages, with an assist from Ethel, to outfish, outhunt, and out-everything her husband. All goes smoothly until she challenges her outdoorsman hubby to a round of duck hunting, even though Ricky insists there are no ducks within a hundred miles of their campsite. According to plan, Ethel—perched high in a nearby tree—throws down a dead "duck" after Lucy fires her rifle. When Ricky retrieves the butcher-shop-acquired pullet, he comments: "Pretty good shooting. Not only did you kill the duck, you knocked off its feathers, and cleaned it too!" Finally, Lucy tells her handsome husband that she really doesn't want to share everything with him, just a kiss.

"RICKY AND FRED ARE TV FANS"   6/22/53

Episode #66   Filmed on Friday, May 22, 1953   Rating/Share: 43.8/64   Supporting cast: Restaurant counterman—Larry Dobkin, Cop—Allen Jenkins, Desk sergeant—Frank Nelson

When Lucy and Ethel become TV boxing match widows, they decide to go out for a bite to eat, leaving their husbands in front of the Ricardo TV set.

Much to their dismay, the atmosphere at a local café seems no better: All of the customers, a cop, and even the restaurant counterman are glued to the tube. Unable to get the latter's attention to get some change, Lucy helps herself and is caught with her hand in the cash register. She manages to escape the cop's clutches by yelling, "Look, a knockout!" and, with Ethel, takes refuge on the roof of their apartment building, where she snips the TV antenna wires and the power lines as well. Officer Jenkins catches the pair in the act and hauls them down to the police headquarters where they are questioned by Sergeant Nelson, who recognizes them as "Pickpocket Pearl" and "Sticky Fingers Sal." Lucy insists she's not a notorious criminal, suggesting that the flatfoot call Ricky (MUrray Hill 5-9975) and straighten out the misunderstanding. After a good deal of confusion, due mainly to the Ricardos' phone being off the hook, Lucy and Ethel manage to prove their innocence and they return home just as the fight broadcast is winding up. Ricky and Fred aren't even aware that the girls have been gone.

NOTE: The Wednesday-night fights on TV were a must for Desi at his San Fernando Valley home.

"NEVER DO BUSINESS WITH FRIENDS" 6/29/53

Episode #67   Filmed on Friday, May 29, 1953   Rating/Share: 41.8/83   Supporting cast: Mrs. Trumbull—Elizabeth Patterson, Joe— Herbert Vigran

After the Ricardos acquire a new washing machine, they sell their old one, despite Ricky's apprehensions, to the Mertzes for thirty-five dollars. The next day, the old machine breaks down, erupting like Vesuvius. Amid soap bubbles and spilled water, Lucy and Ricky offer their sympathy: "Gee, Fred, that's too bad." The Mertzes, however, feel differently ("Good thing we found out in time!") and take the stand that since no money changed hands yet, the deal is invalid. Possession, contends Ricky, is nine tenths of the law. Seeing red, the Mertzes call the machine a "lemon" and the Ricardos storm out. The following day, Lucy finds the old machine outside her back door. This leads to a tug-of-war with the broken-down contraption, which Mrs. Trumbull manages to break up. She suggests that her nephew Joe, who works at an appliance store, have a look at it. He does and is willing to pay fifty dollars for it. Now the Mertzes want to claim possession again, as do the Ricardos. Another mad tug-of-war ensues, climaxing with the ancient washer cascading over the porch railing and smashing on the pavement below. This is all too much to take seriously, and the Ricardos and Mertzes laugh over it and make up.

NOTE: This episode contained one of those little story errors that crept into the scripts frequently. In the segment "Sales Resistance" (Episode #45), Fred buys a new Handy Dandy Washing Machine for Ethel. That show ran about five months before this episode. Ethel must have been taking in wash for the entire city to turn that machine into a wreck in such a short time!

The Third Season: 1953-54

THE THIRD SEASON: 1953–54

Executive Producer: Desi Arnaz
Producer: Jess Oppenheimer
Writers: Jess Oppenheimer, Madelyn Pugh, and Bob Carroll, Jr.
Director: William Asher
Director of Photography: Karl Freund, A.S.C.
Music: Wilbur Hatch (Conducting the Desi Arnaz Orchestra)
Production Manager: Argyle Nelson
Editorial Supervisor: Dann Cahn
Assistant Director: Jerry Thorpe
Film Editor: Bud Molin
Rerecording Editor: Robert Reeve
Original Music: Eliot Daniel
Art Director: Ralph Berger
Set Dresser: Theodore Offenbecker
Sound Recorder: Cameron McCulloch
Makeup: Max Factor (Hal King)
Miss Ball's Wardrobe Supervised by: Elois Jenssen
Sound: Glen Glenn Sound

Filmed at Motion Picture Center

Sponsor: Philip Morris & Co.
Agency: The Biow Co., Inc.

"RICKY'S *LIFE* STORY"   10/5/53

Episode #65   Filmed on Friday, May 15, 1953   Rating/Share: 62.6/85   Supporting cast: Dance teacher—Louis A. Nicoletti   Music: "Lady of Spain," "The Loveliest Night of the Year," "Babalu"

When *Life* magazine prints a story about Ricky but features only a picture of Lucy's left elbow, she rebels in typical style: "Just think . . . when Little Ricky goes to school and some of his playmates ask who his parents are, just what is he going to say? 'My father is Ricky Ricardo, the internationally known entertainer . . . and then there's my mother, whose name escapes me . . .' " Lucy still yearns for a show business career. Fred advises Ricky to teach Lucy a lesson by showing her "how hard show business really is." They concoct a bogus performing job for Lucy—a "challenge dance" routine for which she rehearses six hours a day for three days. Saddled with all the difficult dance steps, Lucy poops out, but on her way home overhears a stage hand mention that they "still need a girl for the balcony scene." Ricky relents after Lucy promises never to ask again, but matters take a turn when Lucy discovers that Ricky has tricked her. To teach *him* a lesson, she decides to "upstage" him during his "Lady of Spain" number. The audience loves Lucy's flying antics, but Ricky thinks the applause is meant for him. He does an encore, then another number, and, finally, after spying Lucy, a rousing rendition of his signature tune, "Babalu," with Lucy as the conga drum.

NOTE: *Life* magazine of April 6, 1953, featured a cover story about the Arnazes titled "TV's First Family," printing a picture of Lucie and Desi IV. . . . When Lucille Ball read a first draft of this script, she instructed the prop man to rent from Columbia Studios the same flying belt she had worn in the movie *The Fuller Brush Girl* a few years earlier.

"THE GIRLS GO INTO BUSINESS"   10/12/53

Episode #68   Filmed on Friday, September 11, 1953   Rating/Share: 56.2/79   Supporting cast: Mrs. Hansen—Mabel Paige, Policeman— Emory Parnell, Customers in dress shop—Barbara Pepper, Kay Wiley

Certain they will become millionaires overnight, Lucy and Ethel decide to buy Hansen's Dress Shop. The asking price: three thousand dollars. Lucy talks Mrs. Hansen down to fifteen hundred dollars, just as two women customers snap up two hundred dollars in merchandise. Exclaiming, "It's a gold mine," Lucy figures that, at that rate, the store will gross nineteen thousand dollars a day! They gladly pay Mrs. Hansen the original asking price. The new partners get into an immediate argument over a name for the new business—Ethelu's, Lucyeth's, Lucy and Ethel's Dress Shop, Ethel and Lucy's Dress Shop. The first day they make five sales—to each other.

However, their future brightens when a man offers to buy the store for thirty-five hundred dollars. Then they find out he sold it for fifty thousand dollars to make way for a skyscraper.

NOTE: This episode was filmed on the night of the "red scare" incident described fully in Chapter 7.

"LUCY AND ETHEL BUY THE SAME DRESS"   10/19/53

Episode #69   Filmed on Thursday, September 17, 1953
Rating/Share: 57.3/80   Supporting cast: Marion Strong—Shirley
Mitchell, Caroline Appleby—Doris Singleton, Clubwomen—Ruth
Perrott, Hazel Pierce   Music: "When the Red, Red Robin Comes Bob,
Bob, Bobbin' Along," "Friendship," "Vaya con Dios"

The Wednesday Afternoon Fine Arts League is staging its yearly talent show (just three months after the last one), which is to be televised on Charlie Appleby's TV station at midnight Monday. Lucy promises the girls that Ricky will emcee the show, despite the fact he earlier wanted nothing more to do with the ladies' group. Offering that "next to sugar, Cuba's biggest export is ham," Lucy uses a little reverse psychology to get Ricky to appear. She tells him she has the perfect emcee—Dan Jenkins, who plays tissue paper and comb. Ricky changes his mind and even helps Lucy and Ethel rehearse their duet, "Friendship." But sparks fly when Lucy brings out the dress she intends to wear—it's identical to the one Ethel bought (Lucy got hers at Gimbels and Ethel found hers at Macy's). To avoid a fight, both decide to return their dresses. But later we learn that neither took back her dress, thinking the other would, and while they perform their song on TV, they rip each other's dresses to shreds until Ricky and Fred have to break up the on-camera scuffle.

NOTE: Dan Jenkins referred to the *TV Guide* writer of the same name. . . . This was the first regularly scheduled Thursday film date; most previous episodes were filmed on Fridays when the show was headquartered at General Service Studios.

"EQUAL RIGHTS" 10/26/53

**Episode #70 Filmed on Thursday, September 24, 1953
Rating/Share: 60.2/84 Supporting cast: Xavier, the waiter—
Lawrence Dobkin, Cops—Fred Aldrich, Louis A. Nicoletti, Cop at
police station—Richard J. Reeves**

After a heated argument about equal rights, during which the girls insist they want to be treated exactly as if they were men, the Ricardos and Mertzes go off to an Italian restaurant (on Thirty-ninth Street near Eighth Avenue) for dinner. When Xavier, the waiter, on Ricky's insistence, presents four separate checks, the girls discover they have no money. They are ordered by the management to wash dishes (so many that Lucy suggests, "I think he takes in dirty dishes from other restaurants"), and the girls decide to get back at the boys by phoning them from the bistro, informing them that they are being robbed and mugged. Ricky subsequently calls the police, then rushes down to the restaurant himself only to find Lucy and Ethel unharmed. To counter the subterfuge, Ricky and Fred disguise themselves as crooks, burst into the kitchen, and surprise the girls. Just then, the cops arrive and arrest Ricky and Fred. At the police station, Lucy and Ethel are uncertain about bailing them out. "Mean-looking, aren't they?" Lucy snarls, before relenting.

NOTE: A second's work with a prop often had Lucy practicing for hours. In this show, the script required her to seize a paper bag from a table, blow it up, and then punch it to make an explosion. "I worked three hours to get it right," Lucy said. "We changed the size, shape, and weight of the bags and the way they were stacked. Finally it came out right."

"BABY PICTURES"   11/2/53

Episode #71   Filmed on Thursday, October 1, 1953   Rating/Share: 61.4/82   Supporting cast: Caroline Appleby—Doris Singleton, Charlie Appleby—Hy Averback   Music: "In Acapulco"

The Mertzes and Ricardos take an oath not to brag about Little Ricky, now thirteen months old, even though Charlie and Caroline Appleby will no doubt drag out pictures of their son Stevie (born four days before Little Ricky) when they arrive for an evening get-together. Ricky also doesn't want to jeopardize a TV emcee stint Charlie has offered him, so when Caroline asks Lucy to "guess what little Stevie did before we left," Lucy can't resist countering, "Don't tell me he took a picture of *you* for a change." To get even, Lucy dresses Little Ricky in his finest duds and decides to pop in on Caroline the next day unannounced. The two mothers exchange barbs. Lucy: "When do you expect little Stevie to reach normal size?" Caroline: "He just seems small to you because you are so used to looking at little fatty here." After putting the two boys in a playpen, the women continue their sarcastic exchange. Caroline: "Has Little Ricky ever said, 'Morning, Mommy'?" Lucy: "In English or Spanish?" Caroline: "You mean he speaks Spanish?" Lucy: "Only when he's mad." The session ends when Lucy accuses little Stevie of "scratching himself and peeling bananas with his feet." Certain that her outspokenness will cost Ricky the TV job, Lucy tries to talk him out of it: "[Television's] only a passing fad, like goldfish-swallowing and flagpole-sitting." Naturally, Ricky is furious when Charlie cancels the show, but Lucy insists she can remedy the situation. After singing "In Acapulco," Ricky introduces on camera Stevie Appleby as "a beautiful, adorable, and intelligent child."

"LUCY TELLS THE TRUTH"   11/9/53

Episode #72   Filmed on Thursday, October 8, 1953   Rating/Share: 61.4/84   Supporting cast: Caroline Appleby—Doris Singleton, Marion Strong—Shirley Mitchell, Casting director—Charles Lane, Professor Falconi—Mario Siletti, Woman at audition—Dorothy Lloyd

Fed up with Lucy's constant fibbing, Ricky and the Mertzes bet her a hundred dollars that she can't go twenty-four hours without telling a lie. Lucy accepts the challenge before realizing she must attend a bridge game at Caroline Appleby's. Obliged to be candid, she untactfully tells Caroline what she *really* thinks of her new Chinese Modern furniture. Marion Strong gets frank opinions about her new hat and way of laughing (Lucy: "Marion, stop cackling. I've been waiting ten years for you to lay that egg!"). Lucy also finds herself in the untenable position of having to answer truthfully questions about her age (thirty-three), weight (129 pounds), and the original color of her hair ("mousy brown"). At home, she accuses Fred of being a "tight-wad," Ethel of "looking tacky," and Ricky of being a "coward" for not letting her have her fling at show business. Lucy: "You're scared to death I'll steal the show!" Ricky takes her to a TV show audition where she is asked to list her talents: "Lucille McGillicuddy—singer, dancer, comedienne, monologist, mistress of ceremonies, after-dinner speaker, saxophonist, star, bit player, or extra." When questioned on the matter of experience, Lucy hedges by saying she has just finished an eleven-year run at Ricardos ("a three-ring circus") and has appeared in "3-D" (not three-dimensional films, but her apartment number). She finally lands the job of assistant to Professor Falconi, a knife thrower. Lucy has managed to tell the truth and Ricky and the Mertzes pay up.

NOTE: The Ricardo apartment number was changed from 3-B to 3-D for this episode to fulfill the joke about "3-D".

"THE FRENCH REVUE"   11/16/53

Episode #73   Filmed on Thursday, October 15, 1953   Rating/Share: 60.0/81   Supporting cast: Robert DuBois—Alberto Morin, Stage hands—Richard J. Reeves, Fred Aldrich, Maître d'—Louis A. Nicoletti   Music: "Louise," "Valentine," "Frère Jacques," "Apache"

Unable to read the menu at a French restaurant, the Ricardos and Mertzes almost order "four orders of closed on Sunday." Because Ricky plans a French revue at the Tropicana, Lucy hires Robert DuBois, the waiter at the bistro, to teach Ethel and herself some conversational French. In return for the free lessons, Lucy promises DuBois a part in the revue. The girls become adept at saying pencil, pen, table, and cat in French. At first, Ricky is mad that Lucy has horned in (Ricky: "There's one word that's the same in Spanish, French, and English—no!"), but finally agrees to hire the waiter on the basis of his excellent "Louise" rendition. However, much to Lucy's consternation, Ricky forbids her to "come near the club." She does her best to get into the Tropicana, first by disguising herself with a lampshade and then by stowing away inside a bass fiddle case. Nothing works until opening night when she appears as a fat matron with pince-nez, then quickly changes into a chorus girl outfit to join four other gals for "Valentine."

"REDECORATING THE MERTZES' APARTMENT"   11/23/53

Episode #74   Filmed on Thursday, October 22, 1953 Rating/Share: not available   Music—"Lily of the Valley"

Lucy's new mink stole never gets worn after she offers to help the Mertzes paint their apartment and reupholster their twenty-year-old furniture. Ethel, it seems, is too ashamed to hold the next meeting of the Wednesday Afternoon Fine Arts League at her place because of the way it looks. Lucy's so-called painting party turns into a free-for-all when Fred turns on a fan to blow the paint fumes out the window at the same time Lucy is removing feathers from an overstuffed chair. After ruining the Mertzes' furniture, Lucy gives them her living room set, including the two-piece sectional sofa. When Ethel admires Lucy's new one-piece sofa, she asks: "What happened to your mink stole?" Lucy: "You're sitting on it."

NOTE: Miss Ball made one of her very infrequent mistakes in this show when she said to Ricky, "Let's paint the furniture and reupholster the old furniture," instead of "Let's paint the apartment and reupholster the old furniture." It was Desi who managed to save the exchange of dialogue by ad-libbing. Look for it.

"TOO MANY CROOKS" 11/30/53

Episode #75   Filmed on Thursday, October 29, 1953   Rating/Share:
60.1/85   Supporting cast: Mrs. Trumbull—Elizabeth Patterson,
Policeman—Allen Jenkins, Madame X—Alice Wills

Fred's birthday is approaching and the Ricardos decide to buy him a custom-made tweed suit as a surprise. Lucy sneaks into the Mertz apartment to borrow one of Fred's old suits (to serve as a model), but Mrs. Trumbull, unaware of Lucy's true intentions, sees her and tells Ethel. Because of a robbery scare in the neighborhood involving a "Madame X," Ethel immediately jumps to the conclusion that Lucy is she. But when Lucy spies Ethel, wearing Fred's hat and coat, lingering on her fire escape, she assumes that Ethel is the crook at large. After a funny scene involving fingerprints on Ricky's silver cigarette case, Lucy decides to play a trick on Ethel, hoping to expose her as Madame X. She tells her friend she's going out for the evening, but instead hides behind a chair in the living room, fully expecting Ethel to break in. However, the *real* Madame X appears (although Lucy doesn't know it) and a struggle ensues. The noise summons Ethel, and Lucy suddenly realizes she's made a mistake.

NOTE: The night this episode aired, Desi threw a surprise thirteenth wedding anniversary party for Lucy at Mocambo. In the midst of the celebration, a TV set was rolled in and the guests enjoyed the show.

"CHANGING THE BOYS' WARDROBE" 12/7/53

Episode #76   Filmed on Thursday, November 5, 1953   Rating/Share:
67.2/79   Supporting cast: Zeb Allen—Oliver Blake, Jerry—Jerry
Hausner, Alberto—Alberto Calderone, Phil, the photographer—Lee
Millar, Award presenter—Paul Power   Music: "Granada"

Off to see the new Marilyn Monroe movie, Lucy and Ethel are disgusted that the boys insist on wearing their oldest clothes in public. The following day and without the husbands' permission, the girls give the ratty clothing to a secondhand man. When shop owner Zeb Allen phones Ricky at the club, asking if he wants to buy back his old clothing, Ricky and Fred start plotting. They get some Brooks Brothers' boxes and put the old clothing in them (including Fred's Golden Gloves of 1909 sweater and Ricky's University of Havana sweatshirt), telling the wives they have bought new outfits. Meanwhile, desperate to drum up some publicity for Ricky, Jerry arranges to have his star client named "one of the ten best-dressed men," and Fred as his "fashion consultant." Elated, Ricky, now dressed in a tuxedo, instructs Lucy to "get dolled up" and join him at the club. Lucy and Ethel get their revenge by dressing in ragged attire and arriving at the Tropicana just as a photographer snaps their pictures for a newspaper layout.

"LUCY HAS HER EYES EXAMINED" 12/14/53

Episode #77   Filmed on Thursday, November 12, 1953
Rating/Share: 55.2/80   Supporting cast: Arthur Walsh—Arthur Walsh,
Bill Parker—Dayton Lummis, Eye doctor—Shepard Menken   Music:
"Stompin' at the Savoy," "The Varsity Drag," "There's No Business
Like Show Business"

When Ricky brings home Bill Parker, a motion picture talent scout who
happens to be casting *The Professor and the Co-ed,* Lucy and the Mertzes
break into a rip-roaring chorus of "There's No Business Like Show Business,"
hoping to get parts in the picture. Parker suggests that Lucy practice the
jitterbug and he'll be glad to audition her at Ricky's club the next evening.
Arthur "King Cat" Walsh teaches Lucy the finer points of jitterbugging to a
classic Benny Goodman number. When Lucy notices that Ricky has another
headache, she insists he see an eye doctor. When the doctor perceives that
Lucy's eyes are the ones in need of care, he administers drops that will blur
her vision for several hours. Knowing of her imminent jitterbug audition,
Lucy tries to knock out the drops from her eyes, but it doesn't work.
Nonetheless, Lucy performs her number, and Fred and Ethel, bedecked in
raccoon coats, sing "The Varsity Drag."

NOTE: Ethel translates *Variety* headline—"Parker Preps Prod for Pitts Preem"—
so Lucy can understand—"Parker Prepares Production for Pittsburgh Premiere."

"RICKY'S OLD GIRL FRIEND"   12/21/53

Episode #78   Filmed on Thursday, November 19, 1953
Rating/Share: 52.8/76   Supporting cast: Carlota Romero—Rosa
Turich, Young Spanish woman—Lillian Molieri, Jerry—Jerry Hausner

A magazine quiz titled "How to Rate Your Marriage, or Is Your Spouse a
Louse?" causes problems for the Ricardos. When questioned on the matter
of "old lovers," Lucy lists her ex-boyfriends (among them are Billy, Jess,
Jerry, Bob, Maury, Argyle, Bud, Wilbur, George, Phil, Karl, and Martin). To
get even, Ricky invents Carlota Romero, an old Cuban flame. Lucy flies into
a jealous rage and refuses to speak to Ricky. By coincidence, a singer by
that same name is appearing in New York at the Opal Room, according to
a newspaper item in the New York *Gazette.* The next evening, press agent
Jerry arranges for Carlota Romero (with whom Ricky did work many years
ago when she was part of the Five Romero Sisters) to see Ricky again. Much
to Lucy's delight, Carlota is now a heavy-set, middle-aged woman whom
Lucy describes as "so full of . . . well, so full."

NOTE: The names of Lucy's "boyfriends" were taken from the show's staff, namely Billy (Asher, director), Jess (Oppenheimer, producer/head writer), Jerry (Thorpe, assistant director), Bob (Carroll, Jr., writer), Maury (Thompson, camera coordinator), Argyle (Nelson, production manager), Bud (Molin, film editor), Wilbur (Hatch, musical director), Karl (Freund, director of photography), and Martin (Leeds, a Desilu vice-president).

"THE MILLION-DOLLAR IDEA"   1/11/54

Episode #79   Filmed on Saturday, November 28, 1953
Rating/Share: 62.7/83   Supporting cast: Dickie Davis—Frank Nelson

Having spent her allowance until June 12, 1978, Lucy is determined to come up with a "million-dollar idea." She decides to market "Aunt Martha's Old-fashioned Salad Dressing by advertising on a three-hour, morning TV show hosted by Dickie Davis that is carried on Charlie Appleby's TV station. For the commercial, Ethel poses as Mary Margaret McMertz, a home economist who invites "an unbiased opinion from an average housewife . . . picked at random from our audience." The "average housewife" is Lucy, of course, posing as Isabella Klump, who raves about the dressing so convincingly, she elicits twenty-three immediate orders. Lucy and Ethel set up their salad dressing plant in the Ricardo kitchen and proceed to fill the first orders (forty cents a jar, three cents of which goes to Caroline Appleby as commission) until Ricky informs them, after a little figuring, that they are losing money. He demands that they fill the existing orders "and get out of business" just as Fred drags in a huge mail sack filled with more orders. To "unsell" the product, the girls go back on TV: This time Lucy is scruffy Lucille Mc-Gillicuddy, who feigns food poisoning, exclaiming, "Looks like Aunt Martha had too many old-fashioneds!" But viewers love the "comedy" and the gals rack up a total of 1,153 orders, which they finally fill by purchasing brand-name dressing and pasting an Aunt Martha label on the jars.

NOTE: A very popular radio personality of the 1940s was Mary Margaret McBride, who had her own program on which she chatted with her audience and interviewed celebrities.

"RICKY MINDS THE BABY"   1/18/54

Episode #80   Filmed on Thursday, December 3, 1953
Rating/Share: 59.4/78   Supporting cast: Little Ricky—Joseph and Michael Mayer

Lucy complains that Ricky spends so little time with his son that the boy hardly knows him. Agreeing, Ricky changes his vacation plans so he can spend all his time with Little Ricky. In one brilliant scene that runs nearly five minutes, Ricky recites *Little Red Riding Hood* in Spanish. The child joins his father for breakfast ("a Spanish omelet with green peppers, green onions, and mushrooms"), allowing Lucy a few extra hours of sleep, which is interrupted when she overhears the menu. Bored with nothing to do, Lucy decides to go shopping with Ethel, until she sees Little Ricky wandering around in the hallway by himself. Ricky and Fred have been so involved in a TV football game, they hadn't noticed him wander off. To teach Ricky a lesson, Lucy phones her husband and nonchalantly asks about Little Ricky. Panic sets in when the father realizes his son is missing. After a well-timed series of "baby-snatchings," the segment ends with Little Ricky safely in his crib.

NOTE: Jess Oppenheimer remembers this to be the only show filmed without a studio audience. The people showed up, but had to be turned away. The company was afraid the babies would not be able to perform on cue . . . Fred and Ethel mention they are married twenty-three years in this show; in "The Courtroom" episode, aired a year *earlier*, they were married twenty-five years. And a year before *that*, they were celebrating their eighteenth wedding anniversary at the fights!

"THE CHARM SCHOOL"   1/25/54

Episode #81   Filmed on Thursday, December 10, 1953
Rating/Share: not available   Supporting cast: Bill Hall—Tyler McVey,
Lou Ann Hall—Vivi Janiss, Tom Williams—Maury Hill, Eve Whitney—
Eve Whitney Maxwell, Phoebe Emerson—Natalie Schafer

The Ricardos are playing host to the Mertzes and Bill and Lou Ann Hall, when suddenly another friend, Tom Williams, brings his knockout date, Eve Whitney. A honey, the boys swarm around her, making fools of themselves— much to Lucy and Ethel's disgust. Lucy: "What's Eve Whitney got that we haven't got? Nothing! We've got just as much as she's got, only lots more!" Ethel: "Yeah, but all the 'lots more' is in all the wrong places." They decide to take advantage of an offer for a free analysis at Phoebe Emerson's Charm School. Phoebe tests Lucy and Ethel who wind up with respective scores of 32 and 30 (out of a possible 100 points). The "uncharming" pair sign up for a full course. Soon Lucy dons a sexy, black sequined gown to surprise Ricky. Even Ethel, wearing a tight-fitting, leopard-design dress, looks great, causing Ricky to ask "Who's that?" Fred: "Who's that? *What's* that?" The girls demand a night out, and the boys hurriedly dress in outlandish garb (Ricky as a cavalier, Fred looking like Mr. Peanut) to show how "ridiculous" they look. They decide to go back to the way they were before: "four natural, lovable slobs."

"SENTIMENTAL ANNIVERSARY"   2/1/54

Episode #82   Filmed on Thursday, December 17, 1953
Rating/Share: 61.1/82   Supporting cast: Party guests—Barbara
Pepper, Hazel Pierce, Bennett Green

For their thirteenth wedding anniversary, Lucy buys Ricky a set of golf clubs and he presents her with stone marten furs, but their real wish is spending the anniversary alone at home where Lucy has a candle-lit dinner planned. The Mertzes, on the other hand, have arranged a surprise party for them, and when Ethel asks Lucy where they'll be that night, Lucy quickly concocts a dinner meeting with Rodgers and Hammerstein. As the party guests start arriving, Lucy and Ricky move their champagne dinner into the hall closet. Finally, they manage to divert the guests' attention so they can slip out the front door and make a proper grand entrance, "surprised."

NOTE: This episode was filmed just two weeks after Lucy was feted with a surprise thirteenth wedding anniversary party at Mocambo by Desi. . . . The "Lucy" company took a two-week Christmas vacation following the filming of this show.

"FAN MAGAZINE INTERVIEW"   2/8/54

Episode #83   Filmed on Thursday, January 7, 1954   Rating/Share: 62.4/83   Supporting cast: Eleanor Harris—Joan Banks, Jerry—Jerry Hausner, Minnie Finch—Kathryn Card, Minnie's neighbors—Elvia Allman, Hazel "Sunny" Boyne   Music: "Vesti La Giubba" (from *Pagliacci*)

Agent Jerry informs Ricky that magazine writer Eleanor Harris will arrive at 7 A.M. the following morning to interview the "happily married" Ricardos for an "average-day-in-the-life-of" story. The average day starts out with Lucy, in a lavish lace apron, cooking breakfast for Ricky "darling," who enters the kitchen in a smoking jacket, exclaiming, "Oh, I didn't know we had company. I woke refreshed, and with a song on my lips." On the guise of borrowing a cup of half-and-half, earring-clad Ethel arrives, followed shortly by Fred, who sports a suit, tie, and derby "to fix the faucet." The "average day" continues when Jerry informs Ricky he's sent out three thousand invitations to ladies on the Tropicana mailing list, signing Ricky's name to them and inviting each of them for dinner and dancing . . . as Ricky's "date." When Lucy discovers a sample invitation (inscribed to Minnie Finch) in Ricky's

jacket pocket, she flies into a rage and takes Ethel with her to search for this Finch woman. Minnie Finch, like her neighbors, is a slovenly dressed old lady. Lucy is properly relieved when she finds out it was just a publicity stunt, and the Ricardos return to their "happily married" state once again.

NOTE: Eleanor Harris was a real magazine writer who wrote about Lucy and Desi as far back as 1940. She also authored a paperback book titled *The Real Story of Lucille Ball* that was published in 1954, about the time this episode was aired. . . . Minnie Finch was played by Kathryn Card, who, almost thirty episodes later, would play Lucy's mother, Mrs. McGillicuddy, in a number of "Lucy" shows. . . . This was Jerry Hausner's last "Lucy" appearance. He had been in the pilot and many early episodes, but a shouting match between Desi and him during the filming of this show caused an irreparable rift.

"OIL WELLS"   2/15/54

Episode #84   Filmed on Thursday, January 14, 1954   Rating/Share: 63.9/85   Supporting cast: Sam Johnson—Harry Cheshire, Nancy Johnson—Sandra Gould, Ken, the detective—Ken Christy

When new tenants (Apartment 4-B) Sam and Nancy Johnson of Texas tell the Ricardos and Mertzes about some available oil stock—"a sure thing . . . but only a few shares left"—Ricky and Fred immediately express their disapproval. Lucy complains: "Our one big chance to live on Easy Street, and we're married to a couple of roadblocks." The next day, the Ricardos learn, with some surprise, that the Mertzes bought the remaining oil stock (ten shares for twelve hundred dollars), despite Fred's previous attitude. An argument ensues, and Lucy accuses the Mertzes of "jumping our claim." The landlords finally soften (and sell them half their shares) when Lucy hints: "We were counting on the extra money for Little Ricky's college education." According to Ricky, the girls "cross their chickens before their bridges are hatched" when they rush out and buy (on approval) a mink coat and fur stole. Of course, level-headed Ricky is no better—they catch him in the act of pricing a "custom-built periwinkle blue Cadillac with a horn that plays 'Babalu' (twelve thousand dollars)." But when a detective friend of Fred's, Ken, comes looking for the Johnsons, our shareholding foursome jumps to the conclusion they have been swindled. Using a tape recorder, Lucy confronts the Johnsons, hoping to get evidence. Despite Mr. Johnson's insistence that the "oil stocks are as safe as U.S. government bonds," Lucy demands her money back. Mrs. Johnson: "Oh, give her back her nasty old money." Sam does and Lucy goes off to tell Ricky and the Mertzes that she has saved the day; not quite—moments later, Ken tells Fred about "some dopes who sold their stock back just before a gusher came in."

"RICKY LOSES HIS TEMPER"   2/22/54

Episode #85   Filmed on Thursday, January 21, 1954   Rating/Share: 56.8/80   Supporting cast: Mrs. Mulford—Madge Blake, Morris Williams—Byron Kane, Sir Hume—Max Terhune

Ricky throws a terrible temper tantrum when Lucy purchases another new hat. She wagers he will lose his temper before she buys another hat. The bet: $49.50, cost of the hat. But when Lucy returns the headdress to the Jeri Hat Salon, clerk Mrs. Mulford interests her in a new chapeau ("a turquoise cocktail hat with little pearls"), which Lucy promptly purchases. Now she has to get Ricky to blow his Latin top before the new hat is delivered the next day. Lucy tries everything to provoke her husband, but nothing makes the Cuban lose his complacent composure. She even resorts to a "trick" drinking glass, but when Ricky ends up with tomato juice on his white tuxedo, he only comments, "It's a lovely shade of red." Next, agent

Morris Williams starts dickering with Ricky over the performing fee of his client, ventriloquist Sir Hume. The agent requests five hundred dollars; Ricky calmly offers two hundred. Suddenly, Ricardo realizes he accomplishes more by remaining calm and calls off the wager with Lucy, generously offering to buy her a new hat. Seconds later, Lucy's jeweled chapeau arrives by messenger, and Ricky realizes he actually won the bet.

NOTE: Actress Madge Blake played Aunt Anastasia in the Arnazes' film, *The Long, Long Trailer*. . . . In the opening scene, Ricky is seen perusing the January 22, 1954, issue of *TV Guide*.

"HOME MOVIES"   3/1/54

Episode #86   Filmed on Thursday, January 28, 1954   Rating/Share: 58.5/83   Supporting cast: Bennett Green—Stanley Farrar   Music: "I'm an Old Cowhand," "Vaya con Dios"

Ricky's feelings are hurt when the Mertzes walk out and Lucy falls asleep in the middle of his home movies. The next day, Lucy implores her friends to apologize to Ricky. But when Fred eloquently comments, "I'm just dying to see those lousy movies again," Ricky informs the trio that they will never have to see another film of his . . . not even the TV pilot he is making. Taking theatrical matters into their own amateurish hands, Lucy and the Mertzes make their own film—a "Western-musical-drama" shot entirely in the Ricardo living room. When TV producer Bennett Green arrives to see Ricky's pilot, "Ricky Ricardo Presents Tropical Rhythms," he is treated to a spliced-in sampling of Lucy's theatrical travesty. Ricky's on-screen singing of "Vaya con Dios" is not-so-professionally intercut with "I'm an Old Cowhand," making for a ridiculously jumbled montage. Ricky is ashamed, but Green loves the "comedy" and calls Ricardo a "genius." Lucy: "How did you ever think of it, dear?" Ricky: "I don't know . . . just came to me."

NOTE: The name Bennett Green was derived from Desi's stand-in, Bennett Green.

"BONUS BUCKS"   3/8/54

Episode #87   Filmed on Thursday, February 4, 1954   Rating/Share: 57.8/83   Supporting cast: Laundryman—Tony Michaels, Grocery boy—Don Garner, Laundry checker—Frank Jacquet, Laundry deliveryman—Bennett Green, Woman in laundry—Patsy Moran, Man at newspaper—John Frank

A newspaper is conducting a "Bonus Buck" contest, and Lucy and Ethel are checking all their dollars in hopes of unearthing a winner. After Ricky discourages them by reminding them of the incredible odds, he discovers in

his wallet a winning bill (B78455698), worth three hundred dollars. He plants the buck in Lucy's purse so she will experience the thrill of discovering it herself. However, the next day, Lucy, ignorant of Ricky's thoughtfulness, uses the prize single to pay a grocery boy, who, in turn, passes it to Mrs. Mertz as change. Both gals immediately claim ownership, and a resulting argument ends with the bill being torn in half. To save their friendship, both families intend to split the spoils, so each retains half a bill. Not trusting Lucy, Ricky takes possession of their half, placing it in the pocket of his pajamas before taking a shower. Meanwhile, the Speedy Laundry man arrives and Lucy gives him Ricky's sleepwear. The Ricardos now must retrieve their bill at the commercial laundry, where Lucy gets caught in the starch vat with obvious and amusing results. The pair locates the split single and races by taxi to the newspaper office, arriving moments before the 3 P.M. deadline. They claim the three-hundred-dollar prize, but after paying for damages to the laundry, taxi fare, and a speeding ticket are left with only a dollar, the same amount they started with.

NOTE: Such contests proliferated in the 1950s, usually under the name "Lucky Bucks." However, Desilu's contract with sponsor Philip Morris precluded them from ever using the word "lucky," the name of a competing cigarette.

"RICKY'S HAWAIIAN VACATION" 3/22/54

Episode #88 Filmed on Thursday, February 11, 1954
Rating/Share: not available Supporting cast: Freddie Fillmore—Frank
Nelson Music: "King Kamehameha," "A Hawaiian War Chant,"
"Cielito Lindo," "La Cucaracha," "I Get the Blues When It Rains,"
"Honey," "Let's Have Another Cup o' Coffee," "I'm Putting All My
Eggs in One Basket," "How Deep Is the Ocean"

Lucy is determined to accompany her husband on a concert tour of Hawaii,
even though he can't afford to take her. To wangle a free trip, she composes
a sob story letter to Freddie Fillmore, host of the TV game show "Be a Good
Neighbor," requesting the complimentary passage to the islands for the
Mertzes . . . and their old "mother"—Lucy. Fillmore, himself a devilish
prankster, contacts Ricky and arranges for him to be present at the taping.
While Ricky sings "I Get the Blues When It Rains," Lucy is doused with
gallons of water; when Ricky warbles "Honey," she is sprayed with honey.
After being bombarded with eggs, coffee, and pie in the same manner, time
runs out on her stunt and Lucy loses . . . in more ways than one.

NOTE: This was Frank Nelson's third appearance as game show host Freddie
Fillmore.

"LUCY IS ENVIOUS" 3/29/54

Episode #89 Filmed on Tuesday, February 16, 1954 Rating/Share:
59.5/83 Supporting cast: Cynthia Harcourt—Mary Jane Croft, Al
Sparks—Herbert Vigran, Henry—Dick Elliott, Martha—Kay Wiley,
Elevator operator—Louis A. Nicoletti

Cynthia Harcourt, a wealthy ex-schoolmate of Lucy's, is collecting for charity.
Informing Lucy that their mutual friend Anita "gave six," Cynthia is instructed
by Lucy to "put me down for five." But when the uppity friend arrives to
collect the pledged funds, Lucy is shocked to learn that her "five" meant
five hundred dollars. Not to be outdone by her wealthy friend, proud Lucy
intends to earn the necessary cash. Ethel sees an encouraging advertisment
in *Billboard* magazine—Al Sparks needs someone "brave" for a publicity
stunt involving a new movie, *Women from Mars;* the salary, five hundred
dollars. Taking the job despite the evident risks, Lucy and Ethel dress in
Martian drag and "invade" the top of the Empire State Building. The stunt
makes headlines and, for Lucy, the needed five hundred dollars.

NOTE: This is one of Jess Oppenheimer's least favorite "Lucy" scripts.

"LUCY WRITES A NOVEL"   4/5/54

Episode #90   Filmed on Thursday, March 4, 1954   Rating/Share: 51.5/75   Supporting cast: Mr. Dorrance—Pierre Watkin, Mel Eaton— Dayton Lummis, Messenger—Bennett Green

When Lucy learns of a housewife who made a fortune by writing a novel, she decides to do likewise. Much to their collective dismay, Ricky and the Mertzes discover that Lucy has incorporated in her book bits about them, and they begin a frantic search for the manuscript, finally finding it hidden in a window shade. Entitled *Real Gone with the Wind,* the story boasts such characters as Nicky Nicardo and Fred and Ethel Nurtz, whose characteristics are a little *too* true to life. The three "critics" take drastic action by burning the book. When Lucy returns from a shopping jaunt, she notes the fire. Ethel: "Nothing like a good book and a roaring fire." Ricky: "You mean, nothing like a good book *in* a roaring fire!" Ethel suggests a new title— *Forever Ember.* However, Lucy has taken precautions and surprises them by producing three carbon copies. When a hundred-dollar advance arrives from a publisher, Dorrance & Company, Lucy wastes no time in beginning a sequel, *Sugar Cane Mutiny.* In the midst of the second effort, she learns that the publisher has made a mistake—they don't want her novel after all. Dramatically, Lucy says: "I can't cry. . . . This is deeper than tears. Sorry, Book-of-the-Month . . . you had your chance, Bennett Cerf." When Mr. Dorrance phones Lucy a few days later, he suggests she contact Mel Eaton, who might be interested in her literary efforts. Eaton is: He wants to include her work in his new book, *How to Write a Novel* . . . in the chapter titled "Don't Let This Happen to You."

NOTE: Dorrance & Company is a genuine publisher based in Philadelphia.

"LUCY'S CLUB DANCE"   4/12/54

Episode #91   Filmed on Thursday, March 11, 1954   Rating/Share: 59.1/85   Supporting cast: Caroline Appleby—Doris Singleton, Marion Strong—Shirley Mitchell   Music: "Twelfth Street Rag"

In an effort to replenish its depleted exchequer, the Wednesday Afternoon Fine Arts League decides to form an all-girl orchestra. Saxophonist Lucy is rejected when Ethel comments to the membership: "When Lucy plays . . . it sounds like a mouse with a head cold." Lucy plots to gain entry into the female quintet by offering Ricky's professional services, without his permission, of course. After much hemming and hawing, Ricky relents, and the all-girl quintet bcomes a sextet with a seasoned bandleader. At the first rehearsal, Ricky is appalled by the girls' meager musical talents when they attempt their big number, "Twelfth Street Rag." They sound pitiful. Things take a turn for the worse, if that's possible, when an item appears in a newspaper hinting that "Ricky Ricardo has formed an all-girl orchestra." To save his reputation, Ricardo plants six members of his own band, dressed as women, in the club orchestra for its dinner-dance engagement.

"THE BLACK WIG" 4/19/54

Episode #93 Filmed on Thursday, March 25, 1954 Rating/Share: 55.8/77 Supporting cast: Roberta—Eve McVeagh, Doug—Douglas Evans, Waiter—Louis A. Nicoletti, Man on the street—Bennett Green

When Ricky forbids Lucy to get "one of those new Italian haircuts," she rebels by borrowing a wig from her hairdresser Roberta (who insists Lucy looks like a different person with it on) with the intention of testing Ricky's fidelity. The salon manager, Doug, tips off Ricky to the scheme, so when Lucy starts flirting, Ricky flirts back: "I could even teach you to rumba." Lucy returns home fuming mad; a divorce would be the easy way out, she reasons. Ethel: "Yeah, stay married to him. That'll teach him!" Posing as the "other" woman, Lucy makes a date with Ricky, telling him she'll bring along a friend. The friend, of course, is Ethel, who enlists the help of "Mother" Carroll, an old vaudeville friend who runs a local costume shop. The girls appear at Tony's Italian Restaurant at the appointed hour. Lucy is dressed in a slinky gown and black wig, while Ethel, unable to rent one *complete* costume from her friend, wears mismatched portions from three different outfits—Eskimo, oriental, and American Indian—prompting Lucy to crack: "You look like an ad for a trip around the world!" The waiter, playing along with Ricky and Fred, tells the girls that their "dates" have just left with a blond and a redhead. Lucy now figures her plan has backfired: "I wish I were dead." Ethel: "I wish you were dead, too!" As they start to leave, Ricky and Fred sneak out from the kitchen and surprise them. And, as usual, all is forgiven.

NOTE: Desi Arnaz offered to teach Lucille Ball how to rumba on their first meeting at RKO studios in 1940.

"THE DINER" 4/26/54

Episode #92 Filmed on Thursday, March 18, 1954 Rating/Share: 51.1/77 Supporting cast: Mr. Watson—James Burke, Drunk—Fred Sherman, Delivery boy—Don Garner, Patrons—Marco Rizo, Nick Escalante, Alberto Calderone, Joe Miller

When Ricky becomes fed up with the nightclub game, he considers going into business for himself. The Mertzes want in, and the four friends decide on a diner as the perfect enterprise. Lucy and Ricky have the "name"; Fred and Ethel have the "know-how" (having worked in a diner in Indianapolis). For two thousand dollars, they purchase Bill's Place from Mr. Watson, who says business is so good, he has "to close once a week to let the seats cool off." After a little bickering, the new partners decide to call their diner A Little Bit of Cuba. Business is brisk, thanks largely to Ricky's nightclub following. But suddenly the Mertzes feel they have got the short end of the deal—they're doing all the work while the Ricardos stand around, acting as hosts. How about switching duties? Fine, says Lucy before admitting she knows zero about restaurant cooking. Ethel assures her that it's easy: "You just put the meat on the griddle, and when your face gets redder than the meat, it's done!" Heated words are exchanged after which the partners decide to divide the restaurant into two separate eateries, with the Mertzes naming their half A Big Hunk of America. When the only customer of the day—a drunk—shows up, a hamburger price war erupts, then a pie fight. In the midst of it, Mr. Watson wanders in, suggesting that he "misses the old place." The Ricardos and Mertzes gladly sell back the diner to him for twelve hundred dollars. Watson, it turns out, makes his living by selling the diner to people who want to go into business for themselves, and then buying it back from them at a reduced price.

"TENNESSEE ERNIE VISITS"   5/3/54

Episode #94   Filmed on Thursday, April 1, 1954   Rating/Share: 57.3/80   Supporting cast: Ernest Ford—Tennessee Ernie Ford   Music: "Wabash Cannon Ball," "Turkey in the Straw," "She'll Be Comin' Round the Mountain"

A special-delivery letter from Lucy's mother arrives ("Dear Lucy: How are you, and how is Xavier . . . ?"), informing them that "a friend's roommate's cousin's middle boy, Ernest" is coming to New York from Bent Fork, Tennessee, and will Lucy and "Xavier" show him some hospitality? "Cousin" Ernie appears and soon disrupts the Ricardo household with his early-morning warbling of "Wabash Cannon Ball." In an attempt to get rid of the overbearing house guest, Lucy dresses like a "wicked city woman"—the type Ernest's mother warned him about—and proceeds to seduce him. Unfortunately for Lucy, Ernie likes the "vamping" and decides to extend his visit, commenting: "Ya took me to yer bosom . . . I've got a home."

"TENNESSEE ERNIE HANGS ON"   5/10/54

Episode #95   Filmed on Thursday, April 8, 1954   Rating/Share: 55.6/80   Supporting cast: Ernest Ford—Tennessee Ernie Ford, Host of TV show—Richard J. Reeves   Music: "Wabash Cannon Ball," "Y'all Come"

The second segment of a two-parter starring Tennessee Ernie Ford opens with Cousin Ernie finding in the hallway a "planted" one-way bus ticket back to Bent Fork, his hometown. This was the Ricardos' infallible scheme to get rid of the unwanted guest. But being a good samaritan, Ernie tries to locate the ticket's rightful owner, which just happens to be the first person he approaches. Lucy's next infallible plan is to pretend that she and Ricky are penniless and can't afford to buy food, something Ernie has a special fondness for. The idea *almost* works, but Ernie learns that his cousin is the host of a variety show, "Millikan's Chicken Mash Hour," that awards two-hundred-dollar talent prizes. Cousin Ernie rounds up his "cousins," the Ricardos and Mertzes, dresses them like country bumpkins, and goes on the air as "Ernie Ford and His Four Hot Chicken Pickers" singing "Y'all Come." With his share of the winnings, Ernie buys a ticket back to Bent Fork, and the Ricardo household returns to "normal."

"THE GOLF GAME"   5/17/54

Episode #96   Filmed on Thursday, April 15, 1954   Rating/Share:
54.2/81   Supporting cast: Jimmy Demaret—himself, Tournament
announcer—Louis A. Nicoletti, Caddy—George Pirrone

When Lucy and Ethel become lonely golf "widows," they decide to take up
the game, but their husbands do not share their "togetherness" enthusiasm.
Fred: "It's against the law." Ricky: "Mamie [Eisenhower] doesn't play." The
wives are not swayed, so the boys plot to make their first round incredibly
difficult by concocting a cockamamie collection of rules for the new duffers
to follow. After playing a few holes, Lucy and Ethel meet golf pro Jimmy
Demaret, who sets them straight, golf-wise. Lucy: "There's a rotten Cuban
in Denmark." They convince Demaret to help teach their husbands a lesson.
Since Ricky and Fred are teamed with Demaret in a National Golf Day
championship tournament, Lucy and Ethel decide to act as their caddies.
When Demaret himself employs some of the "unconventional" golf rules—
like asking "May I?" before attempting a shot—Ricky's eyes bug out . . .
more so than usual.

"THE SUBLEASE"   5/24/54

Episode #97   Filmed on Thursday, April 22, 1954   Rating/Share: not
available   Supporting cast: Mrs. Hammond—Virginia Brissac, Mr.
Beecher—Jay Novello

When Ricky decides to take Lucy and Little Ricky with him on a two-month
summer booking in Maine, real estate saleswoman Mrs. Hammond informs
them that she can find a suitable tenant who would be willing to sublet their
apartment for three hundred dollars per month. At first, landlord Fred doesn't
like the idea and reminds his tenants in 3-D that their lease calls for "approval
of the sublessee by the lessor." The Mertzes thereafter turn down six
prospective tenants, prompting Lucy to crack, "The Mertzes wouldn't even
approve Ike and Mamie." Patient Mrs. Hammond suggests that, to be fair,
the Ricardos should split the monthly profit of a hundred and seventy-five
dollars with the Mertzes. Suddenly Fred sees the light and approves the next
potential tenant, Mr. Beecher, a timid man who seeks peace and quiet
following a nerve-racking murder trial on which he served as a juror. After
the sublessee has been approved, Ricky learns that the Maine engagement
is canceled. The Ricardos want their apartment back, but Beecher won't
budge. There's nothing left to do but move in with Fred and Ethel—lock,
stock, and Little Ricky. Life with the Mertzes is hell, and vice versa, so Lucy
and Ethel dream up a scheme to scare Beecher into leaving. Meanwhile,
Fred has located and paid two months' rent on a temporary apartment for

the Ricardos. Just then, Ricky bursts in with the good news—the band has been booked in Del Mar, California, for the summer.

NOTE: The Arnazes actually spent the summer of 1954 in seaside Del Mar, relaxing from their strenuous "Lucy" chores.

The Fourth Season: 1954-55

THE FOURTH SEASON: 1954–55

Executive Producer: Desi Arnaz
Producer: Jess Oppenheimer
Writers: Jess Oppenheimer, Madelyn Pugh, and Bob Carroll, Jr.
Director: William Asher
Director of Photography: Karl Freund, A.S.C.
Music Director: Wilbur Hatch (Conducting the Desi Arnaz Orchestra)
Production Manager: Argyle Nelson
Editorial Supervisor: Dann Cahn, A.C.E.
Assistant Director: Jack Aldworth
Film Editor: Bud Molin, A.C.E.
Rerecording Editor: Robert Reeve
Original Music: Eliot Daniel
Art Director: Ralph Berger
Set Dresser: Theodore Offenbecker
Sound Recorder: Cameron McCulloch
Makeup: Max Factor (Hal King)
Property Master: Dick Henrikson
Miss Ball's Wardrobe: Elois Jenssen
Sound: Glen Glenn Sound

Filmed at Motion Picture Center

Sponsors: Philip Morris & Co. and Procter & Gamble
Agency: The Biow Co., Inc.

"THE BUSINESS MANAGER" 10/4/54

Episode #100   Filmed on Thursday, June 17, 1954   Rating/Share: 50.9/72   Supporting cast: Andrew Hickox—Charles Lane, Mrs. Trumbull—Elizabeth Patterson

In thirteen years of marriage, Lucy's household budget has never been in worse shape, prompting Ricky to hire a business manager. After inspecting Mrs. Ricardo's accounts, Mr. Hickox congratulates his new client . . . for having "the first set of books that have baffled me in twenty years." When Lucy is presented with only $5.00 as spending money for the month, she hatches a scheme that will net plenty of extra cash. She purchases groceries for other tenants in the building and charges them to a credit account Hickox set up, pocketing the neighbors' money. "It's my hobby," Lucy tells one of her grocery customers, Mrs. Trumbull. When Ricky spies the mountainous roll of greenbacks in Lucy's purse and Mrs. Trumbull's latest food order scrawled on a memo pad—"buy can All Pet"—he immediately concludes that Lucy is playing the stock market . . . and winning. Following the "tip," Ricky buys stock in Canadian Allied Petroleum (can All Pet) and fires Hickox, who said it was a bad investment. Ricky soon pockets an easy $1,000 from the stock maneuver, splitting it with his "genius" wife. Ricky: "I suppose you are going to put it right back in the market." Aware of her $473 grocery bill, Lucy says, "Yeah, that's what I am going to do with it, all right."

NOTE: The Arnazes' actual business manager and Desilu vice-president was named Andrew Hickox. . . . This show presented an unusual creative problem for the writers. Right up until the day of the dress rehearsal, they had not come up with the name of the stock—can All Pet. They tried hundreds of combinations and rehearsed during the week without a clue as to what it would be when suddenly someone (no one recalls who) created the perfect name.

"MERTZ AND KURTZ"   10/11/54

Episode #102   Filmed on Thursday, July 1, 1954   Rating/Share: 47.1/65   Supporting cast: Barney Kurtz—Charles Winninger, Little Barney—Stephen Wootton   Music: "They Go Wild Over Me," "By the Beautiful Sea," "On the Boardwalk of Atlantic City," "I Found a Peach on the Beach," "I Want a Girl Just Like the Girl That Married Dear Old Dad," "Oh By Jingo"

Fred Mertz wants to impress his ex-vaudeville partner Barney Kurtz (their old act had been billed "Laugh Till It Hurts with Mertz and Kurtz"), by making him believe he's a big real estate tycoon. Lucy agrees to help out by posing as the Mertzes' maid Bessie. Barney, who says he travels around the world entertaining "crowned heads," is duly impressed with Bessie and the Mertzes' obvious affluence. But when a letter from his daughter arrives, informing him that grandson Barney, Jr., will be coming to New York to see his grandfather perform, he admits he is a "fraud." He isn't a seasoned world traveler at all; he's a cook in the Bronx. Feeling sorry for the washed-up vaudevillian, Ricky allows him to perform at the Tropicana. As little Barney looks on proudly, the Ricardos, Mertzes, and Barney stage a revue around the theme of Atlantic City with nostalgic tunes.

"LUCY CRIES WOLF"   10/18/54

Episode #98   Filmed on Thursday, June 3, 1954   Rating/Share: 49.2/68   Supporting cast: Mrs. DeVries—Beppy DeVries, Crooks— Fred Aldrich, Louis A. Nicoletti

A newspaper account about a woman who was robbed and then ignored by her husband in her dire moment of need prompts Lucy to assume the same will happen to her. Would Ricky rush home from the Tropicana if Lucy phoned in a similar predicament? He assures her he would: "Right between the Baba and the lu." But when Lucy tests Ricky's valor once too often, he decides to teach her a lesson. While Lucy perches on the apartment ledge, feigning being kidnapped, he and the Mertzes have their fun. Fred: "Are you going to call the police?" Ricky: ". . . bad publicity." Knowing full well that Lucy can hear everything he's saying, Ricky offers Ethel his wife's clothes. Ethel: "I will have to have them altered. They're much too big in the hips." For Little Ricky's sake, Ricky admits he'll remarry, but "I'll wait a respectable length of time . . . about ten days." This is more than Lucy can stand, and she reappears upset. Ricky assures her that they knew all along she was just "yelling tiger" (crying wolf). When Lucy really *is* being carried off by two thugs, Ricky and the Mertzes think she's bluffing again, much to Lucy's dismay.

"THE MATCHMAKER"   10/25/54

Episode #99   Filmed on Thursday, June 10, 1954   Rating/Share: not available   Supporting cast: Dorothy Cooke—Sarah Selby, Sam Carter—Milton Frome, Messenger—Bennett Green

Lucy makes big plans to further a romance between Dorothy Cooke and Sam Carter by inviting the wedding-shy pair to dinner so they can observe firsthand an ideal marriage, the Ricardos'. Lucy's scheme—starting off with a nice chicken dinner, then a peek at Little Ricky asleep in his crib, topped off with the telling of romantic tales in front of the fireplace—falls flat on Cupid's bow and arrow. Ricky itches to retire to bed early because of a morning recording session, the baby frets, and the chicken burns beyond consumption. Lucy's matchmaker-meddling sets off a big tiff between the

Ricardos, ending with Ricky storming off in a rage. Marital bliss resumes when a telegram arrives shortly thereafter from Mr. and Mrs. Sam Carter, who insist their marriage was inspired by the Ricardos' thirteen years of wedded joy.

"MR. AND MRS. TV SHOW"   11/1/54*

Episode #101   Filmed on Thursday, June 24, 1954   Rating/Share: 48.7/67*   Supporting cast: Harvey Cromwell—John Litel, Mr. Taylor— Lee Millar   Music: "Sweet Sue"

Over lunch at 21 with Harvey Cromwell of Cromwell, Thatcher, and Waterbury (advertising agency), Lucy discusses Ricky's chances of hosting a new TV show. Ricky is reluctant when he learns that the sponsor, Phipps Department Store, prefers a husband-and-wife format. Nonetheless, Ricky agrees to do the show. But when Lucy learns that he hadn't wanted her in the show at all, she decides to get even by sabotaging the "Breakfast with Lucy and Ricky" dress rehearsal being conducted at the Ricardo apartment.

* This episode was originally intended for broadcast on November 1, 1954, but it was pulled at the last minute because the Republican Party had purchased the half-hour for a political message. It eventually aired for the first time on April 11, 1955, and received the above rating.

What Lucy doesn't know is that the so-called rehearsal is actually being broadcast to the entire city of New York in an effort to achieve that "unrehearsed," spontaneous look. As the show begins (Ricky: "Why, hello there . . . I didn't see you come in. Won't you have breakfast with us?") Lucy promptly complains of a backache from sleeping on a Phipps mattress; then comments, after savoring the Phipps-prepared breakfast, "Food always tastes different when they fix it. I don't know what they do to it!" She then disappears into the bedroom only to reappear moments later in a potato sack—an example of what Phipps's fashion department can do for a woman. She adds insult to Ricky's injury by singing her own lyrics to the sponsor's theme song—"Phipps is a great big bunch of gyps!"

NOTE: Lee Millar was the son of actress Verna Felton, who appeared on "I Love Lucy" twice in 1953.

"RICKY'S MOVIE OFFER"   11/8/54

Episode #103   Filmed on Thursday, September 16, 1954
Rating/Share: 47.4/66   Supporting cast: Ben Benjamin—Frank
Nelson, Pete—James Dobson, Mrs. Trumbull—Elizabeth Patterson
Music: "Ah, Sweet Mystery of Life," "In a Little Spanish Town,"
"Habañera" (from *Carmen*)

When Hollywood movie scout Ben Benjamin arrives at the Ricardos' to discuss a possible screen test for Ricky, he is greeted by Lucy and Ethel, who suspect him of being a burglar and smash a vase over his head. The East Side neighborhood quickly gets wind of the talent scout's presence, and soon the Ricardo living room becomes an audition hall. Mrs. Trumbull enters, offering a weak rendition of a love song; neighbor Mrs. Sawyer requests a tryout for her poodle; and Pete the grocery boy yearns to be the next Harry James. Lucy can't imagine how the movie news leaked: "I didn't tell a soul and they all promised to keep it a secret!" On the night Benjamin is to audition Ricky, everyone converges on the Ricardo apartment, hoping to nail down a role. Finding a part in the script for a "Marilyn Monroe type," Lucy outfits herself in a slinky red gown, blond wig, and oversized beauty mark. Fred and Ethel make an appearance as a matador and *señorita;* and Mrs. Trumbull saunters in clicking her castanets, followed closely by a trumpet-tooting Pete. In the midst of this three-ring circus, Ricky phones from Benjamin's hotel suite with the news that he has already auditioned and been given the nod for a screen test for *Don Juan.* Ricky: "Anything new at home?" Lucy: "Everything here is about as usual."

NOTE: Madelyn Pugh and Bob Carroll, Jr.'s literary agent was named Ben Benjamin.

"RICKY'S SCREEN TEST"   11/15/54

**Episode #104   Filmed on Thursday, September 23, 1954
Rating/Share: 45.0/63   Supporting cast: Director—Clinton
Sundberg, Assistant director—Ray Kellogg, Boom man—Louis A.
Nicoletti, Clapstick man—Alan Ray   Music: "Canta Guitarra"**

Lucy is excited about the possibility of living in California while Ricky makes
a movie: "Where do you want to live . . . Hollywood or Beverly Hills? . . .
The important thing is to find someone who can build us a swimming pool
in the shape of a conga drum." According to a story in *Variety,* Ricky is a
"sure thing" to star in *Don Juan,* a $3 million color film. Lucy begins to
have certain apprehensions when the story reveals: "Being considered for
the female lead are such names as Marilyn Monroe, Ava Gardner, Jane
Russell, Yvonne DeCarlo, Arlene Dahl, Betty Grable, and Lana Turner."
When Lucy becomes convinced that her minor "part" in Ricky's upcoming
screen test will make her a big star, Ricky deflates her hopes by informing
her she's needed only to "feed me the lines"; the back of her head is all
that will be seen. Ethel: "Lucy, what are you going to do?" Lucy: "I don't
know, but the back of my head isn't going to take this lying down." During

the screen test, she tries *every* method and means to get her face on camera, much to the director's growing annoyance.

NOTE: The following is the *Don Juan* screen test dialogue as acted by Lucy and Ricky—

LUCY: Hark! Do I hear a foot fall? Is it you, Don Juan?
RICKY: Yes, it is I, O lovely one. Would that I had the power to tell you what is in my heart tonight.
LUCY: What do you mean, my dearest?
RICKY: I have come to say farewell.
LUCY: No, say not so.
RICKY: Would that I could ask you to fly with me, but I know you are devoted to your husband, Count Lorenzo.
LUCY: Yes. Much as I love you, I must stay with him, for he is old and feeble, and he needs me.
RICKY: But for him, I would sweep you into my arms and carry you over yon garden wall.
LUCY: Oh, that I could cut these ties that bind me.
RICKY: Do not cry, my dearest. It was not meant to be. I have no right to win your heart. I had no chance to win your love. So now, I'm afraid I must say farewell.

"LUCY'S MOTHER-IN-LAW"   11/22/54

Episode #105   Filmed on Thursday, September 30, 1954
Rating/Share: 46.5/67   Supporting cast: Professor Bonanova—
Fortunio Bonanova, Assistant to professor—Virginia Barbour,
Ricky's mother—Mary Emery, Party guests—Pilar Arcos, Rodolfo
Hoyos, Messenger—Bennett Green   Music: "Bim Bam Boom"

Ricky's Spanish-speaking mother arrives for a visit while Lucy is in the middle of her apartment-cleaning chores. Moments after the unexpected arrival, a cablegram from Mother Ricardo appears. Lucy: "It's in Spanish, but I have a feeling you're arriving today." Lucy tries hard to make the relative feel welcome, but her efforts meet with disaster at every turn. She burns the *arroz con pollo* dinner, loses her in-law on the subway, and scorches one of the woman's dresses. When Ricky makes plans to invite some Cuban friends to the apartment that evening, Lucy realizes she will be unable to converse. Therefore, she employs Professor Bonanova, a mind reader who uses tiny mikes to perform his nightclub act, to translate the *español* for her. At the festive get-together Lucy manages to speak fluent Spanish, much to Ricky's astonishment. Everything goes smoothly until the professor is forced to depart suddenly, robbing Lucy of her bilingual talents.

"ETHEL'S BIRTHDAY"   11/29/54

Episode #106   Filmed on Thursday, October 7, 1954   Rating/Share: 47.3/66   Supporting cast: John's voice—Richard D. Kean, Cynthia's voice—Mary Lansing

With his wife's birthday approaching, Fred entrusts Lucy to select the proper present. Upon seeing the gaudy hostess pants, Ethel whines, "I wanted a toaster!" This sets off a heated argument between the two friends, until Lucy takes the pants, saying, "I'll wear them myself . . . after taking in the seat eight inches!" The boys appear just as Ethel complains: "She called me a hippopotamus." Lucy: "Oh, I did not, Ethel. I said you're a little hippy. . . . On second thought you *do* have the biggest potamus I've ever seen." Lucy storms out of her landlords' apartment, saying, "Happy birthday, Mrs. Mertz, and I hope you live another seventy-five years!" Since the girls now refuse to go to the theater together (Ricky bought four tickets to *Over the Teacups* as Ethel's birthday gift), the men scheme to rekindle the friendship by fooling them into believing the other has exchanged the tickets. Upon arriving in the balcony, Lucy and Ethel realize they will be sitting next to each other as they watch the sentimental production. The play moves them to tears, and the two make up.

"RICKY'S CONTRACT"   12/6/54

Episode #107   Filmed on Thursday, October 14, 1954   Rating/Share: 49.7/67   Music: "When You're Smiling"

After two weeks of waiting for a phone call from Hollywood concerning his *Don Juan* screen test, Ricky is despondent. His constant companion is the telephone, which he even takes to bed at night. He further forbids Lucy to phone any of her girl friends for fear Hollywood might be trying to get through. One day while the Ricardos are out, Ethel takes over the phone vigil (in case Ben Benjamin calls) and comments to Fred: "What a shame there can't be a message saying Hollywood called." With only good intentions in mind, Fred puts pen to paper, scrawling, "Hollywood called. You got the job!" Intending to destroy the fake message, Ethel is distracted by another phone call. When Lucy returns, Ethel hands over the stack of messages, including the "Hollywood" memo. Lucy spies it, after Ethel's departure, and immediately phones Ricky at the club, leaving a message with Marco, the pianist. Enter Ethel, who tries to locate the fraudulent note before Lucy sees it, but—alas—it's too late. Now Lucy and the Mertzes try to figure out their next move. Lucy: "We'll just tell him the truth. Of course, I'll be holding Little Ricky at the time. He wouldn't dare hit a woman with child." Just then, Ricky floats in: "Hello, baby. We're on our way to Hollywood." It turns out that Benjamin has phoned Ricky at the club with the good news.

"GETTING READY"   12/13/54

Episode #108   Filmed on Thursday, October 21, 1954
Rating/Share: 47.6/66   Music: "California, Here I Come"

After a little Lucy Ricardo indecisiveness, Ricky lays down an ultimatum: She must make up her mind about the trip to California. Is it to be via plane, train, or bus? Lucy's final decision: car. When the Hollywood-bound pair informs the Mertzes of their plan to travel cross-country by auto, Ethel gets teary-eyed. Lucy: "Even after we win the Oscar, we'll still be the dearest, closest friends." Ethel longs to go with her friends and complains to Fred that they never get to go anywhere. Not so, says Fred, who reminds his wife of her visit to Minnesota. Ethel: "I went to Mayo Brothers to have my gallstones taken out!" After a little good-natured haggling, the Mertzes are invited to go along on the trip; Ricky even agrees to pay their expenses. Now all they need is a car, but finding suitable, reasonably priced transportation is not easy. Fred recalls a friend who owns a used-car lot and returns with a Cadillac convertible. The Ricardos are delighted until they see the vehicle—a vintage roadster more than twenty-five years old. Fred defends his three-hundred-dollar purchase: "Two other people wanted to buy this car." Lucy: "Where were they from . . . the Smithsonian Institution?" All their efforts to dispose of the antique auto fail, and it appears Ricky is out some money.

"LUCY LEARNS TO DRIVE"   1/3/55

Episode #109   Filmed on Thursday, October 28, 1954
Rating/Share: 52.8/69

To replace the clunker Cadillac, Ricky buys a brand-new, 1955 Pontiac convertible (180 hp, with automatic transmission) for the upcoming trek to Hollywood. Against his better judgment, he agrees to teach his wife how to drive. When they return from the first lesson, they're not on speaking terms. Lucy tells Ethel: "Oh, he makes me so mad! . . . How was I supposed to know we didn't have enough room to make a U-turn in the Holland Tunnel?" Before Ricky departs for the Tropicana, he reminds his ex-student to notify the insurance agent about a policy for the new convertible. Now Ethel itches to learn how to drive, and "experienced" Lucy decides to teach her. Within seconds, Ethel collides with the old Cadillac, locking together the two bumpers. Fearing Ricky's temper, Lucy attempts to take the two cars to be repaired, but meets with an added disaster on a hill—another crack-up. When Ricky sees the tangled mass of steel, he shakes his head in disbelief. Luckily, he's insured . . . or is he? Lucy forgot to call the insurance man; but Ricky, having been married to Lucy for fourteen years, has made the policy arrangements himself.

NOTE: Alert "Lucy" lovers realize that, according to Episode #64 ("The Camping Trip"), Ethel already knew how to drive.

"CALIFORNIA, HERE WE COME!"   1/10/55

Episode #110   Filmed on Thursday, November 4, 1954
Rating/Share: 50.1/65   Supporting cast: Mrs. Trumbull—Elizabeth
Patterson, Mrs. McGillicuddy—Kathryn Card   Music: "California,
Here I Come"

The day before their departure for California, Lucy's mother, Mrs. Mc-Gillicuddy, arrives, suitcase in tow, ready to accompany her daughter and son-in-law "Mickey." Ricky won't hear of it and finally refuses to take her along, lamenting: "Everyone we've ever known is coming with us to California." Overhearing Ricky's comment, the "Tag-along Mertzes" decide not to go, which, in turn, prompts Mrs. McGillicuddy to cancel. Now Lucy says she isn't going either. Confusion ensues, but everything is straightened out and departure time for the sextet is scheduled for 6 A.M. It takes Fred four hours to pack the car with all the junk the ladies want to take along, and, upon viewing the mad mélange of paraphernalia strapped to the shiny Pontiac, Ethel comments: "I could have loaded it better with a pitchfork!" They decide to send the excess baggage ahead by rail. Mrs. McGillicuddy then changes her mind about the long motor trip, opting for a plane ride to California with Little Ricky. Twelve hours later, but with all problems solved, the Ricardos and Mertzes are finally on their way west. As they cross the George Washington Bridge, the four excited travelers sing "California, Here I Come."

NOTE: This was Kathryn Card's debut as Mrs. McGillicuddy, although she previously had appeared on "Lucy" in "Fan Magazine Interview."

"FIRST STOP"   1/17/55

Episode #111   Filmed on Thursday, November 11, 1954
Rating/Share: 50.6/65   Supporting cast: George Skinner—Olin
Howlin   Music: "I'm Afraid to Come Home in the Dark"

Tired and hungry after a long first day on the road, the Ricardos and Mertzes pull up to a rundown café outside Cincinnati. Owner George Skinner greets them cheerily, then serves up the "specialty of the house"—stale, cellophane-wrapped cheese sandwiches (he's all out of steak, roast beef, and chicken). Hoping to find something better elsewhere, Ricky pays the check ($4.80) and they leave, only to return several hours later, fooled by some purposely misleading road signs. Ricky: "We're not in the same place, are we?" Lucy: "We are, unless there's a chain of these across the country." Because it is late and they are hopelessly tired, the four decide to rent Skinner's only cabin for sixteen dollars. As everyone quietly prepares for bed, a freight train passes precariously close, causing the shaky cabin to quake severely. Unable to rest with the noise, the four weary travelers decide to leave without paying for the room. When they get to their car, they discover the steering wheel is missing. By coincidence, Skinner has one just like the one they had, and he'll sell it to them for . . . sixteen dollars. Reluctantly, Ricky pays, and the Hollywood-bound contingent is on its way west again.

NOTE: This was the first time the "I Love Lucy" crew ventured out of the studio to film location footage.

"TENNESSEE BOUND"   1/24/55

Episode #112   Filmed on Thursday, November 18, 1954
Rating/Share: not available   Supporting cast: Ernest Ford—
Tennessee Ernie Ford, Sheriff—Will Wright, Teensy and Weensy—
Rosalyn and Marilyn Borden (The Borden Twins), Gas station
attendant—Aaron Spelling   Music: "Old MacDonald Had a Farm,"
"Birmingham Jail," "Ricochet Romance"

The Ricardos and Mertzes are arrested for speeding, (forty miles an hour in a fifteen-mile zone) in Bent Fork, Tennessee (population: 54). Ricky decides to pay the fifty-dollar fine and leave, but Lucy feels they have been taken advantage of. When she rebels, the sheriff imposes a stiff twenty-four-hour sentence. Just then, the travelers realize they have a friend in Bent Fork— "Cousin" Ernie. Ernie arrives and helps the westward-bound jailbirds in a scheme to escape by sawing through the steel bars with files. While Ernie warbles "Birmingham Jail," the New Yorkers free themselves, but are caught by the sheriff and thrown back into the poky. To clear his friends, Ernie agrees to marry one of the sheriff's chubby daughters, Teensy, the identical twin sister of Weensy. The Ricardos and Mertzes finally manage to make their escape during a square dance/going-away party/hoedown featuring the tubby twins singing "Ricochet Romance."

"ETHEL'S HOME TOWN"   1/31/55

Episode #113   Filmed on Thursday, November 25, 1954
Rating/Share: 53.1/69   Supporting cast: Will Potter—Irving Bacon,
Billy Hackett—Chick Chandler   Music: "Short'nin' Bread," "My
Hero" (from *The Chocolate Soldier*), "Chopsticks"

After a brief stopover at the Teresa Ann Motel in Amarillo, Texas, the foursome arrives in Albuquerque, New Mexico, home of Ethel Mae Potter Mertz. Ethel's father, Will Potter, greets them with the news that the entire town "is in an uproar" over the visiting Hollywood-bound celebrity. Assuming that Potter is speaking of him, Ricky's head starts swelling until he learns the celebrity is Ethel Mae, who, apparently, has been telling some white lies in her letters home. Ethel's former boyfriend, *Chronicle* reporter Billy Hackett, shows up to photograph the "star" for a "Local Girl Makes Good" story. Feeling upstaged, the Ricardos and Fred plot to teach Ethel a lesson. On the night of Ethel's homecoming performance at the Little Theater (marquee: "Ethel Mae Potter—We Never Forgot Her"), they fiercely upstage her by incorporating some old vaudeville schtick into her serious singing of "My Hero" from *The Chocolate Soldier* and a chorus of "Short'nin' Bread." They manage to make their point, but Mrs. Mertz gets the last laugh when Hackett wants a photo of the foursome to be captioned, "Ethel Mae Potter and Company."

NOTE: Vivian Vance was raised in Albuquerque, New Mexico, and became the star player in the town's Little Theater. . . . Vance's mother's name was Mae. . . . Irving Bacon was only eight years older than Vivian, and seventeen years younger than Frawley, who was playing his son-in-law!

"L.A. AT LAST!"   2/7/55

Episode #114   Filmed on Thursday, December 2, 1954
Rating/Share: 49.9/63   Supporting cast: Bobby, the bellboy—
Robert D. Jellison, Headwaiter—Harry Bartell, Willliam Holden—
himself, Eve Arden—herself, Bill Sherman—Dayton Lummis, Mr.
Sherman's secretary—Dani Sue Nolan, Waiter—Alan Ray

Upon their arrival in Hollywood, the Ricardos and Mertzes check into the
Beverly Palms Hotel (rooms 315 and 317, respectively) and meet their
bubbly bellboy Bobby. Ricky goes off to M-G-M, leaving Lucy and the
Mertzes to hunt movie stars. Lucy: "I wonder if there's any place where they
gather in a big herd?" There is—Hollywood's famed Brown Derby restaurant.
Seated at a circular booth surrounded by caricatures of celebrities, the three
tourists spy movie star William Holden in the adjoining booth. Lucy creates
quite a ruckus as she stares at the star who, in turn, teaches her a lesson by
staring back. Embarrassed and feeling ill at ease, Lucy hastily leaves the
popular bistro, but not before causing an entire tray of desserts to splatter
on Holden. Coincidentally, Ricky encounters the star later that day at
M-G-M's Culver City studios, in the office of executive Bill Sherman. Holden
offers to drive Ricky to his hotel and, as a favor, meet his wife, Lucy, "a
fan." When Ricky arrives with Holden in tow, Lucy is in the bedroom.
Obviously, she is not thrilled when Ricky informs her that "one of the biggest
stars in the motion picture business" is waiting to meet her. Forced into
being polite, Lucy disguises herself with frumpy glasses, a kerchief, and a
long putty nose to "meet" the famous celebrity. During the encounter, Lucy's
pliable nose grows to Pinocchio proportions, prompting her to crack: "This
California sun sure makes your skin soft!" When Holden offers to light her
cigarette, he accidentally sets her fake proboscis ablaze. Lucy nonchalantly
extinguishes her flaming nose in a nearby cup of coffee, just before Holden
recognizes her. Much to Lucy's surprise and delight, Holden turns out to be
a good sport—he doesn't let on to Ricky what transpired at the Derby.

NOTE: William Holden plugged his new movie, *The County Girl,* which co-
starred Grace Kelly. . . . The putty nose routine is Lucille Ball's favorite
comedy bit. . . . The script received an Emmy nomination the following
year. . . . The dessert that was dumped on Holden was actually applesauce
"pie." . . . Dani Sue Nolan, who played Sherman's secretary, was director
Bill Asher's wife. . . . After "I Love Lucy," Holden went to Japan to make
The Bridge on the River Kwai. Japan was one of the first foreign countries
to show "Lucy." Bill was a big star, but when he walked down the street in
Tokyo, people came up to him and yelled (the equivalent of) "Love Lucy
. . . love Lucy." . . . According to Milt Josefsberg, one of Jack Benny's
longtime comedy scribes, when Benny found out that none of his writing
staff had seen the Bill Holden segment, he arranged for a special showing
for them. Jack loved that episode; so did Josefsberg, who went on to write
for Lucy years later.

"DON JUAN AND THE STARLETS"   2/14/55

Episode #115   Filmed on Thursday, December 9, 1954
Rating/Share: 51.3/67   Supporting cast: Ross Elliott—Ross Elliott,
Girl #1—Dolores Donlon, Girl #2—Beverly E. Thompson, Girl #3—
Shirlee Tigge, Girl #4—Maggie Magennis, Maid—Iva Shepard

Lucy becomes jealous when four gorgeous starlets arrive at the hotel to pose for publicity pictures with Ricky. Naturally, she connives to be included in the shots, but studio representative Ross Elliott explains: "Mrs. Ricardo, if you stand there, you'll be in the picture." Why shouldn't Lucy be in the picture? Elliott: "*Don Juan* is all about love; it has nothing to do with marriage." Lucy is further upset when Ricky goes off to his first Hollywood premiere without her . . . and on the arms of the four beautiful gals. She decides to wait up for her gallivanting husband, but instead falls asleep on the sofa, not waking until late the next morning. When she finds Ricky's bed apparently unused, she jumps to the conclusion that he spent the night out with the starlets. (What really happened is that he did return home, but had to leave early the next morning for a "call" at M-G-M, and the maid made up his bed without Lucy's knowledge.) Trying to be helpful, Fred covers for Ricky, saying he slept in their hotel room, but the fib doesn't hold water. Lucy is ready to ask for a divorce since Ricky's explanation of the mixup falls on deaf ears. Finally, the hotel chambermaid clears up the confusion when she admits to having made up Ricky's bed.

"LUCY GETS IN PICTURES"   2/21/55

Episode #116   Filmed on Thursday, December 16, 1954
Rating/Share: 51.7/68   Supporting cast: Frank Williams—Lou
Krugman, Showgirl—Onna Conners, Bobby—Robert Jellison, Stage
hand—Louis A. Nicoletti   Music: "A Pretty Girl Is Like a Melody"

Lucy is dying to appear in a Hollywood movie, her desire further sparked
when she learns the Mertzes have got parts in a picture (through their old
vaudeville friend Jimmy O'Connor) and Bobby the bellboy has landed a
speaking role in a hospital drama. She decides to take drastic action: "I went
to Schwab's today to get discovered. But they won't let you sit at the counter
unless you order something. So I sat through four chocolate malteds and
three ice cream sodas." Ethel: "And no one did any discovering?" Lucy:
"Oh, I did. About an hour ago, I discovered I was turning a light shade of
green." Finally, Lucy lands a part in an M-G-M musical in which she is to
play a Busby Berkeley-type showgirl who is shot during a nightclub sequence.
Much to director Frank Williams' chagrin, Lucy has trouble wearing an
enormous feathered headdress in the staircase number. After numerous
ruined "takes," the director replaces Mrs. Ricardo, giving her "death scene"
to another showgirl. "Wouldn't you like to see me die?" Lucy asks the
director earnestly. "Don't tempt me, Mrs. Ricardo," he responds. Determined
to get on camera, Lucy excuses herself from the set after she is offered the
part of a girl already dead on a stretcher, only to return with her name
emblazoned on the soles of her high heels.

NOTE: Lucy makes reference to Lillian Appleby instead of properly calling
her Caroline Appleby. . . . Lucille Ball sent actor Lou Krugman a wire
following filming of this episode: "Dear Lou. Appreciate your top thesping
last night so much. Stop. Just wanted you to know. Stop. Please come again
soon. Stop. Love, Lucy." . . . Desilu pianist Marco Rizo wrote a special song
for his boss and called it "Lucy's Mambo," unveiling it for the studio audience
the first time the night of the filming of this show.

"THE FASHION SHOW"   2/28/55

Episode #117   Filmed on Thursday, December 23, 1954
Rating/Share: 55.2/70   Supporting cast: Don Loper—himself, Amzie,
the sales clerk—Amzie Strickland, Mrs. Gordon MacRae—Sheila
MacRae, Mrs. William Holden—Brenda Marshall Holden, Mrs. Dean
Martin—Jeanne Biegger Martin, Mrs. Van Heflin—Frances Neal Heflin,
Mrs. Forrest Tucker—Marylin Johnson Tucker, Mrs. Alan Ladd—Sue
Carol Ladd, Mrs. Richard Carlson—Mona Carlson   Music:
"Embraceable You"

While bemoaning the lack of a suntan, Lucy yearns for a Don Loper original so she'll fit into the Beverly Hill lifestyle. Ricky relents, warning Lucy to purchase only one outfit, provided it costs under a hundred dollars. At the famed couturier's salon, the sales clerk shows Lucy and Ethel some outfits, but the price tags—nothing like those at Gimbel's basement—shock them. In the meantime, Sheila MacRae walks in and tells Mr. Loper that Joel McCrea's wife, Frances, will be unable to appear at an upcoming fashion show benefiting the charity Share, Inc. Lucy quickly picks up on their conversation and talks her way into replacing Mrs. McCrea as a celebrity fashion model—the most appealing part of the arrangement being that Lucy gets to keep the dress she models. Ashamed more than ever over her New York pallor, Lucy spends the next day basking in the warm California sun and winds up looking like a Maine lobster. This condition makes wearing a tweed suit at the charity function quite unbearable, but Lucy manages.

"THE HEDDA HOPPER STORY"   3/14/55

**Episode #118   Filmed on Thursday, February 3, 1955
Rating/Share: 50.3/69   Supporting cast: Hedda Hopper—herself,
Charlie Pomerantz—Hy Averback, Bobby—Robert Jellison, Mrs.
McGillicuddy—Kathryn Card, Lifeguard—John Hart   Music: "Cuban
Pete," "Green Eyes," "Sheik of Araby"**

Lucy's mother arrives in Hollywood with Little Ricky. Mrs. McGillicuddy: "Long time, no see, Mickey." She describes the wonderful plane trip on which she met a newspaper woman who wants to do a story on Ricky. Interrupting the family chat, Ricky's new press agent, Charlie Pomerantz, enters, exclaiming: "Dad, I'm going to make you the Cuban Liberace!" He concocts a publicity stunt that is sure to land Ricky in Hedda Hopper's gossip column—all he has to do is save a drowning woman at the Beverly Palms Hotel pool during a tea the following day. At poolside, Ricky sings "Cuban Pete," before preparing himself for the rescue act in which Lucy is to be the "victim." When they spy an object that resembles one of Miss Hopper's kooky hats passing in the background, Lucy makes a mad dash for the pool and falls in. But, alas, it was a false alarm; it wasn't one of Hedda's famous chapeaux—rather a bowl of fruit. After a few more fake drownings, the Ricardos give up and return, soaking wet, to their hotel suite where they discover Hedda Hopper, the "newspaper woman" Mrs. McGillicuddy encountered on her airplane trip. Through clenched teeth, they ask: "Mother dear, why didn't you tell us it was Hedda Hopper?" Mrs. McGillicuddy: "You didn't ask me."

NOTE: Charles Pomerantz was connected with "I Love Lucy" as the West Coast press representative for Philip Morris. . . . Commercials presented on this episode introduced the Marlboro cigarette.

"*DON JUAN* IS SHELVED" 3/21/55

Episode #119 Filmed on Thursday, February 10, 1955
Rating/Share: 51.5/69 Supporting cast: Mrs. McGillicuddy—Kathryn
Card, Bobby—Robert Jellison, Dore Schary/George Spelvin—Philip
Ober, Miss Ballantine—Jody Drew, Jim Stevens—John Hart

When an item in *Variety,* hinting at the imminent shelving [canceling] of
Ricky's picture *Don Juan,* proves correct, Lucy, the Mertzes, and Mrs.
McGillicuddy take matters into their own hands by penning five hundred fan
letters to Ricky and dressing as bobby-soxer members of the Ricky Ricardo
Fan Club. To assure Ricky's reinstatement, Lucy hatches another idea—
she's going to hire an actor to pose as a famous film producer and have him
present when M-G-M Studios chief Dore Schary arrives at the hotel to talk
to Ricky. At the Beverly Palms Hotel pool, Lucy spots the perfect sap,
offering him $7.50 for the acting stint. What she doesn't know is that the
man is actually Dore Schary, who happens to have a good sense of humor.
Schary: "I don't usually work this cheap, but things are tough what with
television and stuff." Posing as George Spelvin, Schary is quickly coached
by Lucy in the proper portrayal of a cinema producer; with Fred's help,
Lucy outfits the executive in some outlandish clothing. When Ricky arrives
for the meeting with his boss, he obviously recognizes Schary, and Lucy and
the Mertzes are horrified. Dore never reveals Lucy's sinister shenanigans,
but does inform Ricky that even though *Don Juan* has been canceled,
M-G-M wants to pick up his option in the hopes of locating a suitable motion
picture property for him. When Schary departs, Lucy reasons that the fan
mail must have done the trick, whereupon Bobby the bellboy enters with a
huge bundle of unstamped, unsent mail.

NOTE: M-G-M's Dore Schary was supposed to play himself in this episode
but backed out at the last moment. Vivian Vance's then-husband, Phil Ober,
stepped in, prompting the real Schary to comment, "He'll do a better job
playing me."

"BULL FIGHT DANCE" 3/18/55

Episode #120 Filmed on Thursday, February 17, 1955
Rating/Share: 51.2/68 Supporting cast: Ross Elliott—Ross Elliott,
Propman—Ray Kellogg Music: "Let Me Go Lover," "Dear Old
Donegal," "Humoresque," "Old Folks at Home"

Lucy's been asked by *Photoplay* magazine to write an article entitled "What
It's Like to Be Married to Ricky Ricardo." In the midst of her writing, a press
agent from M-G-M, Ross Elliott, calls to let Ricky know he will be hosting a
coast-to-coast TV benefit for the Heart Fund. Naturally, Lucy wants to appear

in the show, but Ricky turns her down. She resorts to a little "friendly" blackmail. Unless he allows her to perform, she is going to rewrite the *Photoplay* piece to imply that Ricky Ricardo "is a dirty rat." They rehearse a counterpoint arrangement of "Old Folks at Home" (aka "Swanee River") and "Humoresque," but Lucy can't seem to get it right. Next, Ricky offers her a spot in the Spanish dance number—playing the bull to Ricky's matador. Ethel: "For once, the bull will be full of Lucy!" Displeased with the turn of events, Lucy transforms the bull's image from that of a snarling beast to a mincing creature resembling Elsie, the Borden cow. The benefit show, broadcast from CBS Television City, features Fred and Ethel singing "Dear Old Donegal" and Lucy upstaging Ricky during the bullfight scene.

"HOLLYWOOD ANNIVERSARY"   4/4/55

Episode #121   Filmed on Thursday, February 24, 1955
Rating/Share: 51.1/72   Supporting cast: Mrs. McGillicuddy—Kathryn Card, Bobby—Robert Jellison, Ross Elliott—Ross Elliott   Music: "Anniversary Waltz," "La Vie en Rose"

It's anniversary time again and, alas, Ricky has forgotten the exact date. He even goes so far as to wire the hall of records in Greenwich, Connecticut, where he and Lucy were married fifteen years ago. His wife makes a big issue of his forgetfulness, and this tips off an argument. As his only defense, Ricky insists he's already arranged a big party at the Mocambo nightclub, which was supposed to be a surprise. Now, much to his astonishment, an item in a gossip column appears, bearing out his party "plans" and mentioning a long list of invited, celebrity guests. Lucy sees the newspaper piece and forgives Ricky. But when a telegram from the Greenwich county clerk arrives, containing the Ricardos' exact wedding date, Lucy flies into a rage and refuses to speak to Ricky. She'll go to the Mocambo that night, but not with Ricky. She presses Bobby the bellboy into service as her escort, but when they arrive at the nightspot, they are seated at a separate table away from the Ricardo anniversary celebration. Lucy softens when Ricky pays her a compliment and sings "Anniversary Waltz."

NOTE: This episode was inspired by a true-life incident that happened on November 30, 1953, when Desi surprised Lucille with a thirteenth anniversary party at Mocambo.

"THE STAR UPSTAIRS"   4/18/55

Episode #122   Filmed on Thursday, March 3, 1955   Rating/Share: 47.5/67   Supporting cast: Cornel Wilde—himself, Bobby—Robert Jellison   Music: "When Irish Eyes Are Smiling"

Cornel Wilde becomes the one hundredth movie star Lucy has seen in Hollywood when she learns he is occupying the penthouse directly above the Ricardo suite. Determined to gain a glimpse of the handsome actor, Lucy first disguises herself as Bobby the bellboy, then hides under the star's luncheon cart to gain entry into Wilde's suite. Things go smoothly until she's locked out on Cornel's terrace and must make her way down the side of the building using a few blankets as rope. As Ethel looks on horrified, Ricky enters, demanding to know Lucy's whereabouts. Ethel: "She's hanging around the hotel."

NOTE: Van Johnson was originally set to play "the star upstairs" but at the last minute had to drop out because of "sponsor conflict." Apparently he was a spokesman for Lucky Strike cigarettes and, as *Daily Variety* reported, "can't do anything in any media for a rival sponsor for the year's period of the ciggie deal."

"IN PALM SPRINGS"   4/25/55

Episode #123   Filmed on Thursday, March 17, 1955   Rating/Share: 44.0/62   Supporting cast: Rock Hudson—himself, Mrs. McGillicuddy— Kathryn Card

The Ricardos and Mertzes are becoming bored with each other. Each one is fed up with the others' annoying habits—Ricky's constant finger-tapping, Lucy's incessant coffee-stirring, Ethel's noisy eating, and Fred's loose change-jingling (Ethel: "For twenty-five years I felt I've been married to the Good Humor man!"). The only solution is to split up for a brief vacation. With a flip of a coin (Lucy: "Heads, we win; tails, you lose.") the girls are on their way to sunny Palm Springs. After only a short stay, Lucy laments: "I miss Ricky." Ethel: "I can top that. I miss Fred." Back in Los Angeles, the men are faring no better. The Hollywood Stars baseball game has been rained out, and they're beginning to miss their wives, bad habits and all. When Dore Schary's secretary phones to ask Ricky to meet her movie executive boss in Palm Springs, he and Fred are delighted by the "coincidence," an excuse to be reunited with their spouses. At poolside in Palm Springs, Lucy and Ethel meet handsome Rock Hudson, who introduces himself before going into a long-winded story about a script girl he knows, Adele Sliff, who had a quarrel with her husband over his annoying habits. The tale hits home, and the girls start whimpering. Just then, Rock summons Ricky and Fred (who asked the star to concoct such a story) into the scene, whereupon the two couples melt into each other's arms. Lucy gets the last laugh when she admits to being the voice of Schary's secretary.

NOTE: Adele Sliff was the "I Love Lucy" script supervisor.

"THE DANCING STAR"   5/2/55

Episode #125   Filmed on Thursday, March 31, 1955   Rating/Share: 41.5/65   Supporting cast: Van Johnson—himself, Caroline Appleby— Doris Singleton, Marco Rizo—himself   Music: "How About You?"

Caroline Appleby arrives in Hollywood en route to Hawaii and decides to visit her "dear" friends, Lucy and Ethel. Naturally, she wants to meet some of the movie stars whom Lucy has supposedly befriended. When Lucy learns of Caroline's stopover, she is left with no alternative but to trick her. While Mrs. Appleby watches from a balcony high above the hotel pool, Lucy flirts with Van Johnson. But what Lucy's friend from New York can't see is that Johnson is fast asleep. When Lucy discovers that Caroline, who suffers from nearsightedness, has lost her glasses on the plane, she compounds her chicanery by mentioning that she and Johnson are partners in a dance act being featured at the hotel nightclub. What a shame that Caroline has no glasses and can't watch a rehearsal. But the airline suddenly returns the missing spectacles and Caroline is dying to see Lucy perform with the movie idol. Desperate, Lucy races to Johnson's side and pleads with him for a chance to be his "partner" for just a few minutes. Lucy: "I'll name my next child after you . . . if I have one. If I don't, I'll change the name of the one I have." Johnson reluctantly agrees and, while Marco Rizo accompanies the duo on the piano, Lucy and Van dance to "How About You?" as Ethel and Caroline look on. Caroline is thrilled, envious of Lucy's being able to "rub elbows with the stars." Lucy confirms the "awful" truth: "Our elbows are practically raw!" That night, much to Lucy's surprise and delight, Johnson phones and asks her to be his dance partner (Hazel, his usual companion, is ill). After a little initial nervousness, the nightclub number goes well. Caroline rushes backstage to congratulate Lucy and lets her know she has decided to stay an extra day in order to attend the "open house" Lucy plans to throw for all the stars.

NOTE: Originally, Van Johnson was to appear in "The Star Upstairs," but, due to sponsor conflicts that were apparently worked out later, he had to back out. Ray Bolger, who was involved with Desilu on the Motion Picture Center lot, was to have been "The Dancing Star." . . . Peggy Carroll created the choreography.

"HARPO MARX"   5/9/55

Episode #124   Filmed on Thursday, March 24, 1955   Rating/Share: 42.9/63   Supporting cast: Harpo Marx—himself, Caroline Appleby— Doris Singleton   Music: "Take Me Out to the Ball Game"

Lucy is frantic because she has promised Caroline Appleby that there would be "real movie stars" at an "open house" she envisioned, assuming, of course, that Mrs. Appleby would already be on her way to Hawaii. Remembering that her New York chum is practically blind without her spectacles, Lucy and Ethel scheme to steal the eyeglasses and use movie star masks to fool her. Caroline arrives at the Ricardo suite ("Any stars yet?") whereupon Lucy quickly makes off with Appleby's glasses before excusing herself "to go next door and borrow a cup of sugar." Meanwhile, down by the hotel pool, "sun-worshipers" Ricky and Fred encounter funnyman Harpo Marx (there for a benefit) who kindly agrees to stop by and visit Lucy. Disguised as Gary Cooper, Clark Gable, Jimmy Durante, and others, Lucy manages to fool the nearsighted friend. But suddenly, while Lucy is away changing into another disguise, Harpo Marx appears. Ethel assumes it's Lucy until Lucy herself arrives dressed as Harpo Marx. After an unusual harp rendition of "Take Me Out to the Ball Game," Harpo and Lucy enact a classic mirror bit, re-creating the famous pantomime scene from one of the Marx Brothers' movies, *Duck Soup*. The episode concludes with Fred and Ricky, dressed as Chico and Groucho, making an appearance, hoping to help Lucy impress Caroline . . . who has already left for Hawaii to join husband Charlie.

"RICKY NEEDS AN AGENT"   5/16/55

Episode #126   Filmed on Thursday, April 7, 1955   Rating/Share: 39.2/63   Supporting cast: Walter Reilly—Parley Baer, Miss Klein— Helen Kleeb

Lucy poses as Ricky's no-nonsense, fast-talking (and nonexistent) talent agent, Lucille McGillicuddy, when she meets with M-G-M executive ("vice-president in charge of Ricky Ricardo") Walter Reilly in an effort to pressure the studio into using Ricky in another film. Employing a well-known bargaining technique, Lucy, the agent, tells Reilly that "Dick and Oscar are just wild about the boy" and want to star the Cuban "in their next Broadway musical." Reilly quickly confers with Dore Schary by phone and then informs a speechless Miss McGillicuddy: "Metro doesn't want to stand in Ricky's way . . . so we're releasing him from his contract." Shocked, Lucy insists M-G-M reconsider, perhaps by starring Ricardo in remakes of successful films—for instance, *Gone with the Cuban Wind; It Happened One Noche; Seven Brides for Seven Cubans; The Ricardos of Wimpole Street; Andy Hardy Meets a Conga Player; Meet Me in St. Ricky; Ricky, Son of Flicka.* But the executive is a busy man and his secretary, Miss Klein, shows a hesitant Lucy to the door. Heartbroken and dejected, she returns to the hotel and decides to tell Ricky what she has done. As expected, his Cuban temper flares violently and he storms out, blood in his eye. All ends happily when Lucy manages to convince the studio that "some crazy woman" is going around town impersonating Ricky's agent. Whew.

"THE TOUR"   5/30/55

Episode #127   Filmed on Thursday, April 14, 1955   Rating/Share: 31.8/53   Supporting cast: Richard Widmark—himself, Maid—Juney Ellis, Bus driver—Benny Rubin, Women on bus—Audrey Betz, Barbara Pepper

While Ricky lunches with Richard Widmark and Fred goes off to a baseball game, Lucy and Ethel embark on a Grayline Bus sightseeing tour. After taking in the local sights—the La Brea Tar Pits, Pacific Palisades, Holmby Hills—the tour winds through the tree-lined streets of Beverly Hills as the driver points out homes owned by various movie stars—Joan Crawford, Alan Ladd, Betty Grable and Harry James, Shirley Temple, Ava Gardner. Lucy becomes annoying to the driver when she starts interrupting his patter. As the bus passes Richard Widmark's mansion, Lucy jumps up and addresses the tour entourage: "My husband is having lunch with Richard Widmark right now!" The bus driver is not impressed: "I'll be sure to tell Lana about it at dinner." Spying a grapefruit tree in Widmark's backyard, Lucy yearns for a souvenir to go with the autographed Robert Taylor orange she picked up at the Farmer's Market. Warned by the driver that they will be left behind if they disembark from the bus, Lucy and Ethel decide to take their chances. Getting the souvenir fruit proves more difficult than Lucy imagined—the tree is behind a huge wall that surrounds the Widmark estate. When she reaches for a sample, Lucy loses her balance and falls over the wall, getting trapped in the process. As she sneaks through the house to rejoin Ethel on the street, Widmark and Ricky arrive. Quickly, Lucy takes refuge inside a huge bearskin rug in the movie star's trophy room. When she tries sneaking out on her hands and knees, Widmark's St. Bernard dog, Cap, stops her and Lucy is exposed. Despite everything, Widmark remains a gentleman and even autographs the infamous grapefruit for Lucy.

NOTE: Richard Widmark managed to plug his 1955 Columbia film *A Prize of Gold.* . . . The exterior shots when Lucy and Ethel get off the tour bus include Lucille Ball's home, where a similar wall surrounds her property.

The Fifth Season: 1955-56

THE FIFTH SEASON: 1955–56

Executive Producer: Desi Arnaz
Producer: Jess Oppenheimer

Writers: Jess Oppenheimer, Madelyn Pugh, Bob Carroll, Jr., Bob Schiller, and Bob Weiskopf

Director: James V. Kern

Director of Photography: Karl Freund, A.S.C.

Music: Wilbur Hatch (Conducting the Desi Arnaz Orchestra)

Production Manager: Argyle Nelson

Editorial Supervisor: Dann Cahn, A.C.E.

Assistant Director: Jack Aldworth

Film Editor: Bud Molin, A.C.E.

Rerecording Editor: Robert Reeve

Music Editor: E. C. Norton

Original Music: Eliot Daniel

Art Director: Ralph Berger

Set Dresser: Ted Offenbecker

Sound Recorder: Cameron McCulloch

Makeup: Hal King

Property Master: Dick Henrikson

Camera Coordinator: Maury Thompson

Miss Ball's Wardrobe: Edward Stevenson

Sound: Glen Glenn Sound

Filmed at Motion Picture Center

Sponsors: Procter & Gamble and General Foods
Agencies: Biow-Beirn-Tiogo, Inc., and Young & Rubicam, Inc.

"LUCY VISITS GRAUMAN'S" 10/3/55

Episode #128 Filmed on Friday, September 9, 1955 Rating/Share: 42.7/61 Supporting cast: Tourist couple—Gege Pearson, Hal Gerard, Policemen—Ben Numis, Clarence Straight

With only a week left in Hollywood, Lucy bemoans her lack of souvenirs while Ricky inspects a box full of goodies including a tin can run over by Cary Grant's left rear tire, chopsticks from Don the Beachcomber, a Robert Taylor orange and Richard Widmark grapefruit (shriveled to an unrecognizable state), menus from the Brown Derby, and a napkin boasting Lana Turner's lip-prints. Lucy's next souvenir-hunting stop—Grauman's Chinese Theatre, where *The Tall Men* with Clark Gable and Jane Russell is playing. There, she and the Mertzes view the many stars' foot and handprints, imbedded in cement slabs located in the famed theater's forecourt. When Lucy notices that John Wayne's concrete "block is loose," she decides to take home a souvenir to end all souvenirs. Later that day, Lucy returns to the theater with a crowbar and pail of fresh cement, much to Ethel's apprehension. Lucy: "If you're going to get cold feet on a routine souvenir hunt . . ." Fred arrives in the midst of their devious doings, proclaiming the scheme "real Bellevue bait." They manage to steal the slab, but not without Lucy's foot getting stuck in the pail of wet cement. When Ricky discovers the stolen slab at the hotel, he mutters some unprintable Spanish to which Lucy retorts: "I've got the feeling it isn't 'Hot diggity, just what I always wanted!' " He demands the "souvenir's" immediate return whereupon Lucy and Ethel drop it, causing it to break into a million tiny cement chips.

NOTE: This was the first script for "I Love Lucy" written by Bob Schiller and Bob Weiskopf.

"LUCY AND JOHN WAYNE" 10/10/55

Episode #129 Filmed on Thursday, September 15, 1955 Rating/Share: 41.1/61 Supporting cast: John Wayne—himself, George, the masseur—Ralph Volkie, Man with poster—Louis A. Nicoletti, Little Ricky—Mike Mayer

Ricky is reading a newspaper account that describes the recent theft from Grauman's Chinese Theatre of John Wayne's footprints by a "dishwater blond and a frowsy redhead." Ricardo calls the theater, explains the situation, and agrees to have the slab back before the premiere that night of *Blood Alley*, Wayne's latest film. While the girls are having their hair done by Irma, the hotel beautician, Ricky calls "the Duke" to explain the predicament. Being a good sport, the actor agrees to come to the Beverly Palms Hotel and plant his footprints in a fresh slab of cement. But when Lucy and Ethel see the replacement, they erase the impressions, assuming they are the work of "Freddie the Forger," who earlier had tried unsuccessfully to duplicate Wayne's prints. Duke is good enough to oblige a second time, but this effort is obliterated by Little Ricky, who decides to plant his own prints in the fresh mixture. Next, Lucy and Ethel sneak into Wayne's studio with another slab of wet cement, intending to ask Wayne to oblige yet a third time. Posing as the actor's masseur, George, Lucy gains entrance into the star's dressing room, but the deception doesn't work. Finally, Wayne arranges for "a six-month supply" of prints, and the gals are relieved to learn they will not have to face theft charges.

NOTE: The "I Love Lucy" hairdresser was named Irma Kusely. . . . Wayne's fee for appearing was scale, $280, but the true value was tied up in plugs for *Blood Alley*. . . . The scene featuring Little Ricky slopping around in the cement slab took an hour and a half of expensive overtime because three-year-old Mike Mayer stubbornly refused to do it. Even Lucy's cajoling didn't make him budge. Finally, Mrs. Mayer deciphered the mutterings of her son, discovering that he didn't want to spoil his new red shoes. Lucy promised to buy him a new pair and the film was shot.

"LUCY AND THE DUMMY"   10/17/55

Episode #130   Filmed on Thursday, September 22, 1955
Rating/Share: 46.5/66   Supporting cast: Chip Jackson—Lee Millar
Music: "I Get Ideas"

When Chip Jackson of M-G-M asks Ricky to perform at a studio party to be attended by the executives, he refuses, preferring to go deep-sea fishing instead. However, Lucy has other ideas and tells Jackson that Ricky will be glad to appear. Using a rubber replica of Ricky's head attached to a stuffed dummy (Lucy calls it "Raggedy Ricky"), Lucy steals the spotlight as she dances to "I Get Ideas." In the middle of the number, Lucy dramatically announces that "Ricky" has taken ill, and she drags the dummy into the wings. Lucy will complete the act herself—"The show must go on," she insists—but the dummy gets caught on her Spanish *señorita* outfit, refusing to come loose. The performance is hilarious, and the studio offers her a one-year contract as a comedienne. She dreams of the big career in show business she has wanted for so long, but her allegiance to Ricky and the baby comes first and she decides to turn down the studio offer.

NOTE: Although it is not included in the syndication prints, before Lucy comes out and does her Spanish *señorita* number, Chip Jackson announces a "special treat," whereupon TV audiences on October 17, 1955, got a chance to preview the Samuel Goldwyn film musical *Guys and Dolls*. The three-minute insert featured Frank Sinatra singing "Adelaide," causing quite a confusion for the crooner, who was unaware of the promotional gimmick:

friends called him the following day to say, "I saw you on 'I Love Lucy' last night."

"RICKY SELLS THE CAR"   10/24/55

Episode #131   Filmed on Thursday, September 29, 1955
Rating/Share: not available   Supporting cast: Messenger—
Bennett Green, Union Pacific ticket agent—Donald L. Brodie

When Ricky manages to sell the Pontiac convertible to Ralph Berger at M-G-M for more than he originally paid for it, he decides to return East via train, utilizing the economical "family plan." But what about the Mertzes, who traveled to California in the car with them? Ethel: "I presume that when he sold the car, the back seat went with it!" Lucy assures her friends that Ricky hasn't forgotten them, but when the envelope containing only three Union Pacific Domeliner tickets arrives, it becomes painfully evident that Ricky has. Feelings hurt, Fred and Ethel leave in a huff and prepare to journey cross-country on a fifty-dollar antique Harley-Davidson. When Ricky returns from the studio after saying his good-byes and learns of his oversight, he and Lucy rush to the hotel garage where they find their "former" friends ready to depart on the luggage-laden cycle. The Mertzes' trip, however, is short-lived—Fred accidentally backs the vintage contraption into a brick wall. Ricky agrees to buy the Mertzes train tickets, but is unable to secure compartments for them, only a pair of upper berths. Unaware of this situation, Lucy gives the expensive tickets to her friends and now has to figure out a way to switch them. Ricky: "You're vice-president in charge of sneaky switches." After much calculated confusion, including Ethel's mistaken belief that Lucy has the hots for Fred, the Easterners are ready to return home.

NOTE: Desilu's art director was named Ralph Berger.

"THE GREAT TRAIN ROBBERY"   10/31/35

Episode #132   Filmed on Thursday, October 6, 1955   Rating/Share:
42.1/62   Supporting cast: Conductor—Frank Nelson, Mrs.
McGillicuddy—Kathryn Card, Mr. Estes, the jewelry salesman—Lou
Krugman, Jewel thief—Harry Bartell, Detective—Joseph Crehan, Sam,
the porter—Sam McDaniel, Newspaper reporter—Louis A. Nicoletti,
Passengers—Hazel "Sunny" Boyne, Saul Gross, Hubie Kerns, Evelyn
Finley, Lila Finn, Gil Perkins, Hazel Pierce, Roy Rowan

Having safely boarded the New York-bound train, Lucy realizes she has left her purse containing the tickets on the Union Station platform. With just a few moments before the scheduled departure, Ricky rushes off to retrieve

the pocketbook while Lucy pleads with the conductor to hold the train. He flatly refuses, so Lucy is left with no alternative but to pull the emergency brake, causing the train to come to an abrupt halt. Conductor: "Madame, did you stop this train by pulling that handle?" Lucy: "Well, I didn't do it by dragging my foot." A mixup with Mrs. McGillicuddy's tickets results in Lucy's having a run-in with a gun-wielding jewelry salesman when she assumes he is responsible for her "missing" mother and son. Panicked, Lucy pulls the emergency brake again. When questioned by a detective concerning a jewel thief suspected of being aboard the train, Lucy warns the shamus about the gun-toting man in the next compartment. However, the real jewel thief fools Lucy into believing he's with the FBI and wants her to cooperate with him in locating the salesman with the valuable jewelry collection. When Lucy realizes that she's made a mistake, she again beats a hasty path to the emergency brake. The ensuing chaos permits the criminal to be captured, and Lucy winds up a heroine.

"HOMECOMING"   11/7/55

Episode #133   Filmed on Thursday, October 13, 1955
Rating/Share: 44.3/63   Supporting cast: Mrs. Trumbull—Elizabeth
Patterson, Nancy Graham—Elvia Allman, Neighbors—Eva June Mayer,
Roy Schallert, Charlotte Lawrence, Barbara Pepper, Bennett Green,
Hazel Pierce

Upon their return to Gotham, Lucy and the Mertzes are surprised to learn that Ricky has suddenly become a famous celebrity. His many fans clamor for a chance to get a glimpse of the star whom Mrs. Trumbull calls "another Valentino." Lucy is a bit annoyed by all the attention Ricky is getting, so when reporter Nancy Graham requests an interview with *her*, she is delighted. Graham arrives for "The Lucy Ricardo Story" and Lucy begins her prerehearsed tale: "I was born Lucille McGillicuddy in the thriving metropolis of Jamestown, New York, in nineteen . . . Let's just say I was born. I graduated Jamestown High School in . . . Let's just say I graduated four years after I started. . . ." Lucy soon realizes, much to her ego's chagrin, that Graham only wants to know about . . . him. "Him" is Ricky Ricardo. The reporter convinces Lucy that her movie star husband is "special," that he now "belongs to the world." This prompts Lucy to begin treating Ricky like a king. The overattention is more than her husband can stand, so he decides to teach his devoted spouse a lesson by becoming "the most revolting movie star" she's ever encountered. He has her shining his shoes, typing his song lyrics, cooking his favorite meals, lighting his cigarette, and answering his phone calls—all at the same time. His demands become so insistent, so beleaguering, that Lucy finally rebels: "You can shine your own shoes! . . . And if you want another roast pig, you can crawl in the oven yourself, you big ham!" Ricky is happy to have Lucy back as a wife, not a fan.

"THE RICARDOS ARE INTERVIEWED"
11/14/55

Episode #134   Filmed on Thursday, October 20, 1955
Rating/Share: 44.3/61   Supporting cast: Johnny Clark—John
Gallaudet, Edward Warren—Elliott Reid, TV director—Monty
Masters, Cameraman—Bennett Green   Music: "Rancho Grande"

Lucy and Ricky are scheduled to make a TV appearance on a "Person-to-Person"-type interview program, "Face to Face," hosted by Ed Warren. Since the show is to originate from the Ricardos' meager East Sixty-eighth Street digs, Ricky's new Associated Artists agent, Johnny Clark, suggests that the pair move to a more fitting abode on swanky Park Avenue. Lucy, of course, does not want to leave the Mertzes, and vice versa. But with only good intentions in mind, Fred and Ethel deliberately pick a fight with the

Ricardos, hoping they'll pack up and move to a better address. This ploy eventually results in an all-out fight, culminating in the severing of friendly relations between the two couples. The night of the TV show, the Ricardos and Mertzes try hard to be civil to each other, but another argument breaks out . . . on the air.

NOTE: John Gallaudet was one of William Frawley's closest friends and a pallbearer at the latter's 1966 funeral.

"LUCY GOES TO A RODEO"   11/28/55

Episode #135   Filmed on Thursday, October 27, 1955
Rating/Share: 46.9/63   Supporting cast: Johnny Clark—John
Gallaudet, Rattlesnake Jones—Dub Taylor, Madison Square Garden
announcer—Doye O'Dell   Music: "Cuban Pete," "Red River Valley,"
"Down by the Old Mill Stream," "Birmingham Jail," "The Old
Chisholm Trail," "Lily of the Valley," "Home on the Range,"Mockingbird"

Fred wants Ricky to perform at his lodge show next Friday, but the Cuban can't oblige—he's scheduled to do a radio show that day. However, Lucy and Ethel offer their talents for the lodge shindig, suggesting *The Pleasant Peasant* operetta that their ladies' club staged a while ago. Fred prefers a Western theme for the lodge show and enlists the services of his old friend Rattlesnake Jones, who's in town to see his brother perform in a Madison Square Garden rodeo. Fred and Ethel audition for Jones by singing "Birmingham Jail," and Lucy tries out by yodeling "Home on the Range." Her lousy performance prompts Jones to suggest she try her hand at bell-ringing the melody of "Down by the Old Mill Stream." Suddenly, Ricky learns from his agent that the radio show date is really a rodeo show engagement. Desperate because he has to put together a Western show in two days, Ricky even hires Lucy and the Mertzes to appear with him at the Garden show. After Ricky's rousing rendition of "Texas Pete" ("Cuban Pete" with a cowboy hat), the rodeo announcer introduces "Lucille Mc-Gillicuddy and Her Western Bell-Ringers."

NOTE: Actor Doye O'Dell hosted a local Los Angeles TV show titled "Western Theater."

"NURSERY SCHOOL"   12/5/55

Episode #136   Filmed on Thursday, November 3, 1955
Rating/Share: 42.8/59   Supporting cast: Dr. Gettleman—Olan E.
Soule, Dr. Barnett—Howard Hoffman, Nurse #1—Iva Shepard,
Nurse #2—Maxine Semon, Orderlies—Alan Ray, Robert Brubaker

Ricky wants his son to attend nursery school, but Lucy doesn't share his scholarly enthusiasm. After reading from Dr. Spock's book—"Nursery school does not take the place of home . . ."—Lucy thinks the subject is closed. Ricky reads on: ". . . it adds to it. It is particularly valuable for the only child, for the child without much chance to play with others, for the child who lives in a small apartment." Ricky believes Spock's baby-care bible. Lucy: "What does he know? He was never a mother!" However, Ricky prevails and the boy is sent off to nursery school. He enjoys the experience, and all the adults seem pleased, until young Ricky develops a cold. Lucy blames the school: "It's a hotbed of bacteria!" The child's pediatrician, Dr. Gettleman, diagnoses the problem as tonsillitis and suggests a tonsillectomy. When Lucy learns she is not permitted to spend the night with Little Ricky in his hospital room (#602), she disguises herself as a nurse and creates untold hospital havoc. Ricky comes looking for his wife and finds her curled up in Little Ricky's hospital crib, fast asleep.

"RICKY'S EUROPEAN BOOKING" 12/12/55

Episode #137 Filmed on Thursday, November 10, 1955
Rating/Share: 46.4/73 Supporting cast: Mr. Feldman—Harry
Antrim, Mr. Jamison—Barney Phillips, Dorothea Wolbert—Dorothea
Wolbert, Hazel Pierce—Hazel Pierce, Recording engineer—Louis A.
Nicoletti, Pied Pipers—Lee Cotch, Clark Yokum, Allen Davies,
Sue Allen Music: "Forever Darling"

When Lucy learns that Ricky is going on a European tour with his band,
she naturally assumes she will be included. Not so, contends Ricky—the
extra cost would be prohibitive. However, she can go along if she can raise
the money to pay her own " 'spenses." Ricky decides to take Fred along to
act as band manager and he, like Lucy, is thrilled about the prospect of
going to Europe. Says Ethel, conspicuously left out: "I don't want to see
Europe anyway . . . It's so *old!*" She, too, can go if she raises her own
expense money. Ricky estimates that the wives need a total of $3,000.
Desperate for money, they search under the cushions of the furniture, empty
pockets, clean out cookie jars, etc.—but the take is only $200.16. To raise
the other $2,800, the gals decide to raffle off a television set, claiming the
proceeds will benefit a worthy charity, the just-formed (by Lucy and Ethel)
Ladies Overseas Aid. Lucy justifies the nefarious scheme: "We're ladies. We
want to go overseas. And, boy, do we need aid!" They approach kind Mr.
Feldman, a local store owner, about purchasing a set. The shopkeeper,

impressed with the virtue of the plan, offers to donate the TV set and hold the drawing in his shop. But as Lucy is about to leave for the drawing, a representative from the D.A.'s office, Mr. Jamison, arrives and informs Mrs. Ricardo that she will be imprisoned for fraud if the raffle takes place. Lucy: "I can't go to prison! I'm going to Europe!" Rushing to the raffle in hopes of halting the drawing, Lucy appears doomed until Mr. Feldman surprises everyone by producing Dorothea Wolbert, president of the *real* Ladies Overseas Aid charity, who happily accepts the $3,000 cache. The girls' trip to Europe appears unlikely until Ricky is offered free passage by a steamship company in return for the band's playing on the transatlantic trip. Now he can afford to take along Lucy and Ethel—and the four friends are officially Europe-bound!

NOTE: A little early publicity for Lucy and Desi's film, *Forever Darling*, was generated when the Pied Pipers appeared in a scene in this episode recording the film's theme song. It is in this setting that Ricky receives the call from a steamship company with the favorable passage offer. No mention of the *Constitution* yet because the deal had not been firmed up at this point.

"THE PASSPORTS"   12/19/55

**Episode #138   Filmed on Thursday, November 17, 1955
Rating/Share: 44.2/62   Supporting cast: Helen Erickson Kaiser—
Sheila Bromley, Sidney Kaiser—Robert Forrest, Dr. Peterson—
Sam Hearn   Music: "Skip to My Lou," "Mad'moiselle from
Armentières" (aka "Hinky-Dinky Parlez-vous")**

Lucy needs her birth certificate if she intends to apply for a passport; and the Jamestown bureau of statistics has no record of her being born. However, passport officials assure Ricky that if Lucy can produce two people willing to sign affidavits swearing that they have known her since birth, they will waive the birth certificate requirement. Consequently, Lucy heads straight for her former baby-sitter Helen Erickson Kaiser, who now lives in Manhattan. Helen is about to put her signature on the paper when her lawyer-husband Sidney arrives. He takes one look at the document and refuses to allow his wife to sign it. It seems that Helen has apparently lied about her age to Sidney and couldn't possibly have been Lucy's baby-sitter. Lucy's frantic and even threatens to stow away in a steamer trunk. Trying one on for size, she promptly gets locked in. When Dr. Peterson, the McGillicuddy family physician, arrives to identify Lucy for the passport people, he is unable to see her to make a positive identification. But when Lucy recalls a song that she and the old doctor used to sing years ago, "Skip to My Lou," Peterson is certain that the girl inside the trunk is Lucille McGillicuddy. Lucy later learns she was born in *West* Jamestown when a special-delivery letter from her mother arrives with the needed certificate.

NOTE: According to the Postal Service, there is no *West* Jamestown, New York.

"STATEN ISLAND FERRY"   1/2/56

Episode #139   Filmed on Thursday, November 24, 1955
Rating/Share: 45.2/63   Supporting cast: Passport clerk—Charles Lane, Ferry attendant—Stanley Farrar

Fred suddenly remembers he suffers from seasickness. Lucy tries to allay his fears, insisting the problem only exists on small vessels: "We're going on the *Constitution,* one of the best." A visit to the huge liner fails to relieve Fred of his doubts; he gets sick even though the ship is tied to the dock. Lucy suggests some new seasickness pills and a trial run on the Staten Island Ferry as a surefire cure. Before embarking on the ferry trip, Lucy is reminded that the Passport Office closes at 5 P.M.; she must be back before then to file her application. Amid the "high" seas of New York harbor, Fred does fine, thanks to the pills. Lucy, on the other hand, begins to feel queasy, so she swallows a handful of seasickness tablets, unaware of their side effects. After five trips to Staten Island, a ferry attendant awakens the two, fast asleep on a bench. With only six minutes left to apply for their passports, Lucy and Fred burst into the government office where the officious clerk tries desperately to get sleepyhead Lucy to sign the application. It's a comedy of errors that ends happily for the four travelers.

"BON VOYAGE"   1/16/56

Episode #140   Filmed on Thursday, December 1, 1955
Rating/Share: 50.3/66   Supporting cast: Mrs. McGillicuddy—Kathryn Card, Mrs. Trumbull—Elizabeth Patterson, Officer—Tyler McVey, Dock agent—Ken Christy, Helicopter dispatcher—Jack Albertson, Helicopter pilot—Frank Gerstle, Dock worker—Bennett Green

After a brief bon voyage party in their *Constitution* stateroom, the Ricardos join the Mertzes on the ship's deck to wave their final good-byes to Little Ricky, Mrs. McGillicuddy, and Mrs. Trumbull. Lucy can't bear to leave her little boy behind and rushes off the ready-to-sail ship to give the baby one last kiss. While saying her final farewells on the dock, Lucy's skirt gets caught in the chain of a Western Union messenger's bike. She struggles valiantly to free herself, finally slipping out of her skirt completely, but, alas, she misses the boat. Advised to catch the pilot boat that would take her to the *Constitution,* she misses that too, leaping bravely aboard the boat coming in, not the one going out. It is next suggested that she hire a helicopter at Idlewild; high above New York harbor, Lucy begins to have second thoughts about going to Europe at all. The chopper pilot assures her there is nothing to worry about as he slowly lowers the tardy voyager onto the deck of the London-bound liner.

NOTE: Goateed "Lucy" writer Bob Carroll, Jr., can be seen standing beside Vivian Vance in the bon voyage scene. . . . Less than two weeks after this episode was filmed, Desilu started production on a pilot for a series about a helicopter, "The Whirlybirds."

"SECOND HONEYMOON" 1/23/56

Episode #141 Filmed on Thursday, December 8, 1955
Rating/Share: 51.1/66 Supporting cast: Social director—Tyler McVey,
Passenger with Rocky, the dog—Louis A. Nicoletti, Woman—Virginia
Barbour, Kenneth Hamilton—Harvey Grant, Man in deck chair—
Herbert Lytton, His wife—Paula Winslow, Marco Rizo—
himself Music: "Cielito Lindo"

The romantic shipboard atmosphere, coupled with the fresh sea air, has rekindled the Mertzes' twenty-five-year-long marriage. Ethel: "The love bug has bitten my Freddie." Lucy is a little jealous; she and Ricky have been unable to spend any time together because of his band commitment. Understanding his wife's loneliness, Ricky suggests she sign up for some tournaments in the hopes of meeting new friends. Lucy asks the ship's social director to find her a Ping-Pong partner, but he has trouble finding someone single "since there are mostly couples." Lucy: "With everyone paired off, I'm surprised the ship isn't called the S.S. *Noah's Ark!*" A partner finally materializes—Kenneth Hamilton—and he is, indeed, single. Unfortunately, he's also only elementary school age. The precocious youngster becomes Lucy's constant companion (they win the Ping-Pong championship) and even dances with her in the Boat 'n' Bottle Bar that night. Desperate for some time to spend with Ricky, Lucy plots to "kidnap" him the next evening. While he is dressing for the show, Lucy locks their stateroom door and tosses the key through the porthole to Ethel. But much to Lucy's surprise, Ricky has managed to get the night off, planning an entire evening of dining and dancing. In a frantic effort to locate Ethel, Lucy sticks her head through the porthole and then finds she's unable to free herself. It takes men with acetylene torches to free Lucy, but Ricky still manages a romantic serenade.

"LUCY MEETS THE QUEEN"   1/30/56

Episode #142   Filmed on Thursday, December 15, 1955
Rating/Share: 54.3/74   Supporting cast: Bellboy—Sam Edwards,
Man on the street—Robert Shafter, Maid—Nancy Kulp, Dancers—
Betty Scott, Patti Nestor

In London, Ricky tries to explain the confusing British monetary system to Lucy, who has trouble even with dollars and cents. She reacts: "No wonder the people left here to go to America." Sightseeing at Buckingham Palace, Lucy and Ethel encounter a smileless palace guard and decide to get him to break a time-honored tradition by making him laugh. Lucy: "Did you hear about the book the dog psychiatrist wrote? . . . *Is Your Cocker Off His Rocker? . . . Is Your Poodle Off His Noodle?. . . Collie Off His Trolley?*" Nothing works, the guard remains steadfastly stoic. Lucy soon finds out that Ricky is to be presented to the Queen after his London Palladium performance. Knowing that only performers are allowed a royal audience, she desperately wants to be a part of the circus-themed revue. Despite a cramp in her knee, caused by overpracticing her curtsies, Lucy does fine as a dancer, until a big leap in the finale results in a severe charley horse. Unable to effect the required bow, Lucy must pass up her one and only chance to meet the Queen. Suddenly, Ricky rushes backstage and tells her that Her Majesty wants to meet the girl who did the wonderful comedy dance routine.

NOTE: The choreography was by Jack Baker.

"THE FOX HUNT"   2/6/56

Episode #143   Filmed on Thursday, December 22, 1955
Rating/Share: 48.2/65   Supporting cast: Sir Clive Richardson—
Walter Kingsford, Angela Randall—Hilary Brooke, Groom—
Trevor Ward

Lucy is jealous after Ricky danced the night away with Angela Randall, a budding British starlet, but he claims he was only trying to be polite. Lucy plots to get Ricky out of London, and away from Miss Randall, by persuading Sir Clive Richardson, an English movie producer, to invite the Ricardos and Mertzes to his Berkshire Manor estate for the weekend. After going to great pains to wangle the invitation, Lucy is shocked to discover that Angela Randall is the stage name of Angela Richardson, Sir Clive's attractive daughter. Lucy attempts to cancel the weekend visit by saying she forgot about the cricket matches, but Sir Clive reminds her that this is not cricket season. Lucy: "Well, these are very young crickets." At the Richardsons' country estate, Lucy is introduced to her horse for the hunt, Danny Boy, whose size frightens the New Yorker. Lucy: "Do you have a large lamb?" After a number of false starts, Lucy is off on her first fox hunt. Many hours later, Lucy hobbles into the stable area, *sans* Danny Boy, covered with brambles.

Lucy: "I have a strange feeling I'm not alone." She isn't—she's sharing the tangle of brush with the fox. Lucy has won the hunt!

"LUCY GOES TO SCOTLAND"   2/20/56

Episode #144   Filmed on Friday, January 6, 1956   Rating/Share: not available   Supporting cast: Mayor Ferguson—Larry Orenstein, Townspeople—John Gustafson, John Hynd, Robert E. Hamlin, Ann Ellen Walker, Norma Zimmer, Betty Noyes, Dick Byron, Chuck Schrouder, Betty Allen   Music: "Tis Nay a Bra Bricht Nicht," "A McGillicuddy Is Here," "I'm in Love with a Dragon's Dinner," "Two Heads Are Nay Better Than One," "Dragon Waltz"

About to leave Blighty and with no available time to visit the home of her Scottish ancestors, Lucy dreams of the McGillicuddy clan's village of Kildoonan. She returns to the friendly little town, expecting to be welcomed with open arms. The townspeople welcome her joyously in song, but then inform her that she has returned just in time to be fed to a terrible two-headed dragon that appears every thirty years to appease his appetite with a McGillicuddy and Lucy is the last available member of the clan. Enter Scotty MacTavish MacDougal MacCardo (Ricky Ricardo in kilts), son of Enchilada MacCardo, who came to Scotland on the Spanish Armada. Lucy and Scotty quickly fall in love and he promises to defend her against the hungry two-headed beast. The Dragon (Fred and Ethel) appears and sings "Two Heads Are Nay Better Than One," then listens to Lucille and Scotty trying to talk him out of his high-calorie plans. When the time arrives for Scotty to save Lucille, he loses his courage. Awakened by her nightmare, Lucy pelts Ricky with her pillow, shouting, "You coward!"

NOTE: Lucille Ball is part Scottish. . . . Larry Orenstein, who played the mayor of Kildoonan, also wrote the original score. . . . One of the townspeople was portrayed by Norma Zimmer, who, years later, would become famous as Lawrence Welk's Champagne Lady.

"PARIS AT LAST"   2/27/56

Episode #145   Filmed on Thursday, January 12, 1956   Rating/Share: 49.7/67   Supporting cast: Counterfeiter—Lawrence Dobkin, Charpentier, the artist—Shepard Menken, Waiter—Maurice Marsac, Chef—Rolfe Sedan, Tour guide—Fritz Feld, Arresting officer—Trevor Ward, Policemen at station—Ramsey Hill, John Mylong, Drunk—Vincent Padula, Tourist—Hazel Pierce

On a sidewalk in gay Paree, Lucy encounters a friendly Frenchman who offers to exchange her American dollars for francs, at a rate of four hundred and fifty francs for every buck (a bonus of a hundred francs). The generous guy claims "low overhead" as the reason why he can be so benevolent, so Lucy gladly exchanges twenty dollars for nine thousand francs. Nearby, she admires the work of a Parisian painter and eagerly purchases his "masterpiece" for a thousand francs. Fred and Ethel happen along, and Lucy shares her sudden "wealth" with them, exchanging ten dollars of Fred's money. Next stop for Lucy, while the Mertzes enjoy a conducted tour of the city, is lunch at a typical sidewalk café, À La Porte Montmartre. When the waiter brings her escargots, she grimaces: "Waiter, this food has snails in it." She can hardly bring herself to eat them ("I think one of your American cousins ate my geranium."), so asks the waiter for a bottle of catsup. When the chef learns of her gauche request, he creates such a ruckus that Lucy decides to pay the check and leave. Suddenly, she is accosted by a gendarme—and accused of passing counterfeit francs! Hauled off to the Bastille, she summons Ricky from their Hotel Royale suite, lamenting: "Nobody speaks English. They're all foreigners!" Ricardo rushes to her rescue and through a cleverly devised translation method (featuring a German drunk who speaks Spanish and a French cop who speaks German) manages to clear his confused wife of counterfeiting charges.

NOTE: Bob Carroll, Jr., was featured in the sidewalk café scene. . . . In the same sequence, the Desilu prop department made an error by placing a bottle of California wine—Paul Masson—on the table.

"LUCY MEETS CHARLES BOYER"   3/5/56

Episode #146   Filmed on Thursday, January 19, 1956   Rating/Share: 50.4/68   Supporting cast: Charles Boyer—himself, Waiter—Jack Chefe

When Lucy and Ethel spy handsome Charles Boyer seated alone at an outdoor café in Paris, they prepare to carry out their usual movie star assault. While the girls powder their noses, Ricky, fearing the worst, approaches Boyer and warns him about his wife—the scourge of Hollywood. Forewarned, Boyer decides to play a little trick on Lucy. When she sits down at his table, he tells her that his name is Maurice DuBois, he's a struggling actor, and he is annoyed that so many people mistake him for Boyer. Satisfied, but disappointed, Lucy departs. Later that day, she reads an item in Art Buchwald's column that Ricky is supposed to meet with Boyer regarding a possible acting assignment on his "Four Star Playhouse" TV series. Naturally, she begs to tag along. Feigning a king's case of jealousy, Ricky forbids it. This prompts Lucy to prove her faithfulness by hiring Charles Boyer-look-alike Maurice DuBois to pose as the famous actor and have him unsuccessfully flirt with her in Ricky's presence. When Boyer/DuBois arrives at the Ricardos' hotel suite, he proceeds to make love to Lucy, who responds by nonchalantly

peeling an orange. But when Ethel tips off Lucy via phone that Ricky is playing a trick on her and that DuBois really *is* Charles Boyer, she nearly chokes on the fruit and becomes totally flustered by the presence of the French star. Her efforts to get his autograph leave him with ink on his shirt; she rips his raincoat and destroys his hat; and, finally, slams the door into his head. The scourge of Hollywood lives up to her name.

NOTE: Don Sharpe, whose name was mentioned in this story, was Lucy and Desi's TV agent and was instrumental in the creation of Four Star Productions of which Boyer was a principal. . . . Jerry Miggins, the Desilu propman, had a friend at American Express who made arrangements to fly in copies of the Paris edition of the *Herald Tribune* for Boyer to read during the opening café scene.

"LUCY GETS A PARIS GOWN"   3/19/56

Episode #147   Filmed on Thursday, February 16, 1956
Rating/Share: 48.4/63   Supporting cast: Waiter—John Bleifer

Lucy decides to go on a hunger strike until Ricky agrees to buy her a Jacques Marcel dress. The plan works perfectly (even though Ethel has been smuggling food to Lucy)—Ricky finally gives in and buys her an expensive outfit. Eager to take a picture of her in the high-fashion gown, Ricky goes looking for their camera, only to find a roast chicken in its place (Lucy: "It's a 3-D picture of a roast chicken?"). Angered by Lucy's deviousness, Ricky returns the dress. Then, he plots with Fred to get even with his wife. He employs a local tailor to put together some crazy outfits made from burlap potato sacks, along with hats fashioned from a horse's feedbag and a restaurant ice bucket, and presents them to the girls with Jacques Marcel labels sewn in. Thrilled, the wives proudly strut down the street with their Paris originals. But Ricky and Fred can't contain their secret any longer, and break down laughing. To punish the husbands, the girls demand *real* Jacques Marcel outfits, at a total cost of five hundred dollars. Much to their dismay, the next day, Lucy and Ethel spot Marcel's gorgeous models wearing the exact copies of their burlap-sack fashions. Unfortunately, the gals have burned theirs, the originals.

"LUCY IN THE SWISS ALPS"   3/26/56

**Episode #148   Filmed on Thursday, February 23, 1956
Rating/Share: 43.9/62   Supporting cast: Swiss band leader—Torben
Meyer   Music: "Schnitzelbank," "La Cucaracha," "Swiss Yodel"**

When band manager Fred fouls up by sending the orchestra to Locarno, Switzerland, instead of Lucerne, Lucy tries to appease Ricky's ruffled nerves by suggesting a healthy hike in the Alps. All goes well until an unexpected snowstorm forces the foursome into a deserted mountaintop cabin. Lucy hints that an avalanche, like the one featured in *Seven Brides for Seven Brothers,* could prove fatal. Moments later, she makes the dreadful mistake of slamming the shack's door, causing a mountain of snow to cover the tiny cabin. After being trapped for five hours, the victims become famished. Suddenly, Lucy remembers a sandwich in her knapsack; she quietly attempts to devour it without the others discovering her treasure. No such luck—the Mertzes and Ricky pounce on her for a portion of the food. After they've polished off the last crumb, Ethel reveals she would prefer dying with a clear conscience—she confesses she wasn't eighteen when she married Fred, but nineteen. Fred: "I've got news for you—you were twenty-four!" Fred clears his soul by telling the Ricardos he's charged them an extra ten dollars a month in rent; Ethel reveals she gave back the sawbuck every month. When asked if he would like to get something off his chest, Ricky responds: "I'm no fool. . . . We might be saved!" Within seconds, the distant sound of music is heard, and they are rescued by a Bavarian band playing a sad version of "La Cucaracha."

"LUCY GETS HOMESICK IN ITALY"   4/9/56

Episode #149   Filmed on Thursday, March 1, 1956   Rating/Share: 48.4/68   Supporting cast: Desk clerk—Vincent Padula, Giuseppe— Bart Bradley, Woman on phone—Ida Smeraldo, Mrs. McGillicuddy— Kathryn Card, Teresa—Kathleen Mazalo   Music: "Happy Birthday to You"

In Florence, Italy, four thousand miles away from Little Ricky on his third birthday, Lucy suddenly has the motherly urge to phone New York and speak to her son. Making the transatlantic call is a problem in itself, compounded by the fact that the hotel's only phone is located in the lobby and the Ricardos' "bridal suite" (Room 47) is on the fourth floor. While Lucy is waiting for the long distance call to go through, a street urchin shoeshine boy, Giuseppe, wanders into the lobby, offering to shine Mrs. Ricardo's shoes. While he is several years older than Little Ricky, Lucy can't help but get teary-eyed at the thought of being so far away from her own boy. Finally, the call comes through, and Ricky and the Mertzes descend the many flights of stairs to be beside Lucy during the conversation. Unfortunately, it's 5 A.M. in New York when Mrs. McGillicuddy answers the phone and Lucy sadly decides not to have her mother wake the child. Lucy tries phoning the next day, but this time Little Ricky is in nursery school. Heartbroken, Lucy decides to hold a birthday party for Little Ricky in absentia with the shoeshine boy as the guest of honor (it's his birthday too—he's eight and a half!). Soon the party grows to enormous proportions—eleven Italian bambinos, each claiming a birthday, arrive for the gala affair. In the midst of the festivities, Ricky summons Lucy to the lobby telephone—he's managed to get through to Little Ricky in New York. With tears in her eyes, Lucy wishes her son a happy birthday, and the foreign children sing the birthday song to him in Italian.

NOTE: The young actor who played the shoeshine boy, Bart Bradley, is the same person who, twenty-two years later, played Binzer on the ABC series, "Vega$," under his real name, Bart Braverman. Recalling this episode, he said: "Lucille Ball was the most delightful, kindest, sweetest, most charming woman I've ever met. Other actors are not so kind because they feel child performers are obnoxious and precocious and an unfortunate evil. They deal with them on that level."

"LUCY'S ITALIAN MOVIE"   4/16/56

Episode #150   Filmed on Thursday, March 8, 1956   Rating/Share: 47.1/63   Supporting cast: Vittorio Fellipi—Franco Corsaro, Bellboy— Saverio Lo Medico, Woman in vat—Teresa Tirelli, Vineyard boss— Ernesto Molinari, Grape picker—Rosa Barbato

En route to Rome by train, Lucy is spotted by famous Italian cinema director Vittorio Fellipi and chosen to play a part in his new movie, *Bitter Grapes*. Assuming the picture concerns the Italian wine industry, Lucy sets out to immerse herself in the role. In an effort to "soak up some local color," she journeys to Turo, a small town on the outskirts of Rome, well known for its traditional wine-making methods. Dressed in typical peasant clothes and carrying a cluster of grapes, Lucy nonchalantly wanders into a vineyard inhabited by a motley conglomeration of Italian-speaking women. When the male supervisor spots Lucy's feet (one of the local women likens them to "big pizzas"), she is quickly dispatched to the wine-making area. Lucy steps into the huge, grape-filled vat along with a local gal, Teresa, and the two proceed to stomp the grapes into chianti. Lucy finds the work fun and has a great time skipping through the mush and frolicking with her co-worker. When the diversion wears off and Lucy decides to take a short rest, her partner disapproves. This difference of opinion leads to a grape fight as Lucy and Teresa battle it out in the wine vat, scrapping like street urchins. Grape-stained and defeated, Lucy returns to her Rome hotel where film maker Fellipi awaits her. He explains, somewhat belatedly, that the film has nothing to do with the grape industry; the title is merely symbolic. Her part was to be that of a typical American tourist. In her present condition, Mrs. Ricardo will be unable to begin filming her scene the next day. Lucy: "Can't I be an American who's so homesick, she's blue?" No, says Vittorio . . . who turns around and hires Ethel for the role.

NOTE: Lucille Ball once commented that bouncing around in that grape vat was like "stepping on eyeballs." . . . The grapes were supplied by the Grape Growers' Association of California. They sent so many that the crew took them home on Thursday night, after the filming, so they wouldn't go bad over the weekend.

"LUCY'S BICYCLE TRIP"   4/23/56

Episode #151   Filmed on Thursday, March 22, 1956   Rating/Share: not available   Supporting cast: Farmer—Mario Siletti, French guard—Francis Ravel, Italian guards—Felix Romano, Henry dar Boggia

After an exhausting day bicycling from Italy toward the French Riviera, the Ricardos and Mertzes decide to look for a place to spend the night. The terrain is rural and the best accommodations are to be found in the barn of a friendly farmer. With fresh hay as mattresses and a cow as a roommate, the four tired travelers bed down for the night. Bright and early the next morning, the peasant host arrives with their breakfast—cheese and a huge loaf of Italian bread. To wash it down—milk. Unfortunately, the milk is still inside the cow and it becomes Lucy's task to coax it into a pail. Rested and satiated, the bikers continue their journey toward Nice, coming to a stop at the Italian and French border. Everyone but Lucy is permitted to cross the guard-patrolled border, for her passport is in a purse that was sent ahead to Nice with the rest of the luggage. Reluctantly, Ricky and Fred bicycle on to Nice to retrieve the required passport. Remaining behind at the border, Lucy and Ethel find it impossible to persuade the rule-spouting guards to allow her to pass without the document. When Ricky phones from the Plaza Hotel in Nice, unable to unlock the suitcase containing the pocketbook that holds the passport, Lucy realizes she has the key with her. Ethel is sent to Nice with the key, as Lucy remains behind at the boundary gate. More confusion reigns before the mixup is unraveled, but Lucy finally is on her way to Nice for the next leg of her European trip.

NOTE: The bicycles were courtesy of Schwinn. . . . Jerry Miggins, the "Lucy" propman, recalls that they used honey as "goat nip" for the scene where Lucy is awakened by a goat in the barn.

"LUCY GOES TO MONTE CARLO"   5/7/56

Episode #152   Filmed on Thursday, March 29, 1956   Rating/Share: 42.5/66   Supporting cast: Casino manager—John Mylong, Gambler—Gordon Clark, Croupier #1—Jacques Villon, Croupier #2—Louis A. Nicoletti

Upon their arrival in Monte Carlo, Ricky forbids Lucy to go near the gambling casinos, suggesting instead that she and Ethel have dinner and go to a movie. The women enjoy their dinner at Le Grill restaurant, which just *happens* to be in a casino. Strolling out, Lucy spots a chip on the floor and, being unable to find its owner, places it on the roulette table. Moments later, she is 875,000 francs richer. Frightened by Ricky's possible reaction, Lucy chooses to hide the money in Ethel's lingerie case. When Ricky accidentally opens the valise, looking for Fred's bank account books, he discovers the loot and accuses Mertz of embezzlement. A fierce argument commences, and Fred quits as band manager. To save the fifteen-year friendship, Lucy tells the husbands that the money belongs to Ethel, who inherited it from her French aunt, Yvette. Fred: "You mean my little honeybunch is loaded?" Lucy finally confesses the truth and then decides to get rid of the "ill-gotten gains." She rushes down to the casino and proceeds to gamble away the money. Meanwhile, Ricky has learned the truth about the bundle of cash and he's delighted about Lucy's good fortune. But by the time he reaches the gambling palace to tell Lucy she can keep the cash, Lucy has already lost the fortune.

NOTE: The gambler wearing the fez in the early casino scenes was Bob Carroll, Jr., "Lucy" writer. . . . The Desilu prop department went to the Earl Hays Press on Santa Monica Boulevard at Las Palmas Avenue in Hollywood to have the French francs printed for this episode.

"RETURN HOME FROM EUROPE"   5/14/56

Episode #153   Filmed on Thursday, April 5, 1956   Rating/Share: 38.4/62   Supporting cast: Evelyn Bigsby—Mary Jane Croft, Stewardess—Mildred Law, Customs officer—Frank Nelson, Airline officer—Ray Kellogg, Newsreel interviewer—Bennett Green   Music: "Rock-a-bye Baby"

The Ricardos and Mertzes are packing for their Pan American Airlines flight (No. 155) home when Ricky warns his souvenir-crazed wife that any baggage over sixty-six pounds will cost extra to ship. She finds it impossible to leave anything behind, particularly a twenty-five-pound hunk of rare Italian cheese, a gift for her mother. Assuming babies travel free, Lucy disguises the cheese as an infant and smuggles it aboard the aircraft. Seated next to her during the flight is Mrs. Evelyn Bigsby, mother of four-month-old Carolyn. To be friendly, Mrs. Bigsby asks Lucy what her baby is named. Lucy: "Cheddar, er . . . *Chester!*" When the stewardess offers to warm the babies' bottles, Lucy admits she didn't bring any, adding: "He's too fat anyway." Being a good neighbor, Mrs. Bigsby offers Lucy one of Carolyn's bottles. When the heated bottle is presented, Lucy gulps its contents: "He doesn't like to drink by himself." One hour into the flight, Lucy learns that babies do not travel free and that passage will cost thirty dollars. Ethel and she attempt to solve the problem by devouring the mammoth hunk of cheese. When Lucy returns to her seat minus little Chester and lets Mrs. Bigsby in on her gag, the woman screams. In New York, a U.S. Customs official is trying to piece together the details. Meanwhile, a newsreel cameraman is itching to get footage on Ricky and the band, who are about to open at the Roxy Theater. When the musicians attempt to play "Home Sweet Home," the music they make is silent. Leave it to Lucy—she stuffed the instruments with the cheese ("the trombone was easy, but that piccolo . . .").

NOTE: Another example of using real people's names—Evelyn Bigsby was a writer for a TV magazine who often penned articles about "I Love Lucy" and other Desilu programs. . . . Jerry Miggins, "Lucy" propman, rented the musical instruments from Ellis Mercantile Company in Hollywood and then spent all day on April 6, 1956, getting the cheese out of them before returning them to the rental company. . . . This was the last episode produced by Jess Oppenheimer, who, the following week, joined the NBC Television Network as a program executive.

The Sixth Season: 1956-57

THE SIXTH SEASON: 1956–57

Producer: Desi Arnaz

Writers: Madelyn Martin, Bob Carroll, Jr., Bob Schiller, and Bob Weiskopf

Directors: James V. Kern (Episodes #154–166), William Asher (Episodes #167–179)

Directors of Photography: Robert de Grasse (Episodes #154–157), Sid Hickox (Episodes #158–179)

Music: Wilbur Hatch

Associate Producer: Jack Aldworth

Production Manager: Argyle Nelson

Editorial Supervisor: Dann Cahn, A.C.E.

Assistant Directors: Ed Hillie (Episodes #154–157), Jay Sandrich (Episodes #158–179)

Film Editor: Bud Molin, A.C.E.

Rerecording Editor: Robert Reeve

Music Editor: E. C. Norton

Original Music: Eliot Daniel

Art Director: Ralph Berger

Set Dresser: Ted Offenbecker

Sound Recorder: Cameron McCulloch

Makeup: Hal King

Hairdresser: Irma Kusely

Camera Coordinator: Maury Thompson

Miss Ball's Wardrobe: Edward Stevenson

Casting: Kerwin Coughlin

Sound: Glen Glenn Sound

Filmed at Motion Picture Center

Sponsors: Procter & Gamble, General Foods, and Ford Motor Company

Agencies: Grey Advertising, Young & Rubicam, Inc., and J. Walter Thompson

"LUCY AND BOB HOPE"   10/1/56

Episode #154   Filmed on Tuesday, June 5, 1956   Rating/Share: 48.7/71   Supporting cast: Bob Hope—himself, Little Ricky—Keith Thibodeaux, Paul, manager at Club Babalu—Lou Krugman, Mr. Krausfeld—Peter Leeds, Male spectator—Dick Elliott, Female spectator—Maxine Semon, Little boy—David Saber, Trainer—Henry Kulky, Stadium guard—Ralph Sanford, Hot dog vendor—Bennett Green Music: "Nobody Loves the Ump" (by Eliot Daniel and Larry Orenstein), "Thanks for the Memory" (by Leo Robin and Ralph Rainger)

Lucy, the Mertzes, and Little Ricky are attending a Cleveland Indians-New York Yankees baseball game at Yankee Stadium when Bob Hope shows up. This is the perfect opportunity for Lucy to talk to Hope about appearing at Ricky's new night spot, the Club Babalu. Disguising herself as a moustachioed hot dog vendor, Lucy gains admittance to the box section where the comedian is seated. Matters take a dark turn as Lucy's distracting antics cause a ball to strike Hope on the head. Summoned to the ballpark to confer with Bob about the opening night material, Ricky finds the funnyman treating

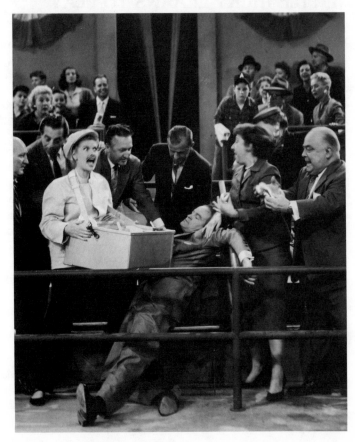

the bump on his head in the Indians' locker room. Enter Lucy, now dressed as a ballplayer, making a second stab at persuading Hope to appear at Ricky's club. When she sees her husband, Lucy attempts to escape, but Ricky pulls her back. The two performers discuss a possible bit for the show, and naturally Lucy wants in. Ricky naturally says no. But Lucy later makes a plea to Mr. Hope: "You have no idea how talented I am." He believes her and demands that she be a part of the baseball song trio. At the nightclub's grand opening, Bob Hope and the Ricardos sing "Nobody Loves the Ump," and Hope does a special-material version of his theme song, "Thanks for the Memory."

NOTE: Ten years prior to this filming, Desi Arnaz was the orchestra leader on Hope's NBC radio show. . . . Jack Baker choreographed the baseball number, which was written by Eliot Daniel and Larry Orenstein. . . . This was Keith Thibodeaux's debut as Little Ricky. . . . Due to Hope's busy performing schedule, he could not memorize his lines and had to rely on cue cards held by propman Jerry Miggins, who also had the dubious job of throwing the baseball that hits Hope on the noggin.

"LITTLE RICKY LEARNS TO PLAY THE DRUMS"   10/8/56

Episode #157   Filmed on Thursday, June 28, 1956   Rating/Share: 47.8/65   Supporting cast: Little Ricky—Keith Thibodeaux, Mrs. Trumbull—Elizabeth Patterson

Even though the Ricardos made a solemn promise not to influence their son's future, Lucy buys the boy a doctor's kit and Ricky gets him a little snare drum. The five-year-old opts for the shiny new drum from Schirmer's Music Store, and there begins a four-day nonstop concert consisting of a monotonous but rhythmic beat. The sound becomes so unbearable that Lucy and Ricky find themselves functioning to the unending beat. When Lucy squeezes oranges for Ricky's juice, she does it to the rhythm of Little Ricky's drumming. When she scrapes his toast, a similar situation prevails. Even the Mertzes, godparents of the little musician, are ready for straitjackets. The landlords decide to politely ask the Ricardos to have the child "limit" his playing. Ethel: "Just to give his little hands a rest." But the Mertzes' true feelings are exposed when the youngster pauses momentarily. Fred: "What a relief! I thought he'd never quit!" Ethel tries to soften Fred's statement: "He's just amazed at the child's stamina. He didn't think anybody could keep up that racket for four whole days!" Naturally, an argument ensues, and Fred threatens eviction, despite the Ricardos' ninety-nine-year lease. To force their departure, Fred turns off the tenants' water, gas, and electricity. As Lucy and Ricky are about to retaliate by subjecting their landlords to a rousing drum version of the "Nurtz to the Mertz Mambo," another verbal battle begins. Mrs. Trumbull halts World War III when she becomes concerned about Little Ricky, who has apparently disappeared. After a frantic search, they find him curled up on the Mertzes' sofa fast asleep—the noise was too much for him.

"LUCY MEETS ORSON WELLES" 10/15/56

Episode #155   Filmed on Thursday, June 14, 1956   Rating/Share: 43.8/62   Supporting cast: Orson Welles—himself, Miss Hanna—Ellen Corby, Paul, manager at Club Babalu—Lou Krugman, Sales clerk at Macy's—Ray Kellogg, Floorwalker at Macy's—Jack Rice, Customers— Fred Aldrich, Hazel Pierce, Bennett Green

Lucy is denied a vacation to Florida, until Ricky learns that Orson Welles has agreed to appear in a benefit at the club. To keep his meddling spouse away from the actor, Ricky changes his mind and gladly gives Lucy enough money for her Florida trip. While trying on skin-diving equipment at Macy's, she and Ethel encounter Mr. Welles, who is autographing copies of his latest record album. Dressed in a wet suit and flippers, Lucy hobbles over to Orson and immediately starts bragging to the Shakespearean expert about her wonderful performance as Juliet in a Jamestown High School production. When Welles learns Lucy's name, he offers her the part of his assistant in the act he plans to do at Ricky's Club Babalu. Lucy, of course, assumes the act is a scene from Shakespeare and proudly informs her high school drama teacher, Miss Hanna. On the night of the benefit, Miss Hanna and a group of aspiring student-actors arrive to witness Lucy's stellar Shakespearean performance. What they are treated to is a little bit of the Bard and a whole lot of prestidigitation. During Welles's brilliant levitation trick, Lucy says: "Romeo, Romeo, wherefore art thou, Romeo? . . . Get me down from here, Romeo."

"LITTLE RICKY GETS STAGE FRIGHT" 10/22/56

Episode #156   Filmed on Thursday, June 21, 1956   Rating/Share: not available   Supporting cast: Little Ricky—Keith Thibodeaux, Mr. Crawford—Howard McNear, Mrs. Van Fossen—Marjorie Bennett, Flutist—Laurie Blaine, Violinist—Diana Van Fossen, Trombonist— Jeffrey Woodruff, Accordionist—Larry Gleason, Trumpet player— Robert Norman, Bass player—Buddy Noble, Ukulele player—Earl Robie   Music: "Five Foot Two, Eyes of Blue"

Just prior to his first music school recital, Little Ricky is gripped by a full-blown case of stage fright, touched off by the nervous attentions of his parents and the Mertzes. The little drummer's teacher, Mr. Crawford, urges

Lucy and Ricky to treat the problem like the classic falling-off-a-horse syndrome. Little Ricky must get right back on the horse, or, in this case, play the drums in public. When Lucy suggests that her son play at the Club Babalu, Ricky agrees. Now the tough part—convincing Little Ricky to do it. Ethel employs reverse psychology: "Little Ricky, you don't want to play those nasty old drums, do you?" Her attempt, like Lucy's, fails. Using a tiny windup toy, Ricky manages to persuade his son to display his musical talents at the club. The night of the performance, the ukulele player, Earl Robie, comes down with the measles, which sends Little Ricky into another nervous spin; he refuses to play without his strumming cohort. It's Lucy to the rescue as she dons a striped blazer and joins "Ricky, Jr., and His Dixieland Band" as they perform an upbeat version of "Five Foot Two, Eyes of Blue."

"VISITOR FROM ITALY"   10/29/56

Episode #158   Filmed on Thursday, September 20, 1956   Rating/Share: 45.5/62   Supporting cast: Mario Orsatti—Jay Novello, Mr. Martinelli —Eduardo Ciannelli, Immigration officer—James Flavin, Pizza chef— Aldo Formica, Dominic Orsatti—Peter Brocco, Waiter—Louis A. Nicoletti

The Ricardos and Mertzes are surprised when the Venetian gondolier they met during their European travels, Mario Orsatti, arrives in New York to visit his brother Dominic. When Mario discovers a note on his brother's door explaining that he's at Sam Francesco, Lucy helps by translating the message to mean that Dominic is in San Francisco, three thousand miles away. But with only ten dollars to his name, Mario cannot afford the bus fare to California. Club Babalu owner Ricky obliges by giving the gondolier a job as a busboy. Disaster strikes, and Mario soon finds another job at Mr. Martinelli's pizza parlor. A visit by an Immigration official reveals that Mario is working illegally since he has no work permit and is in the United States on a tourist visa. Realizing that he may be deported if he returns to work at the pizza place, Lucy substitutes for her foreign friend by donning the apron of a pizza chef and setting about to fashion her first pie. Lucy makes pizza like she does everything else—hilariously—and is fired after the fiasco. Ricky ends up paying for Mario's bus fare to San Francisco and the $210.33 in damages to the pizza restaurant, just before learning from Mario's brother Dominic that he is not in San Francisco, but was visiting his sick friend, Sam Francesco.

"OFF TO FLORIDA"   11/12/56

Episode #159   Filmed on Thursday, September 13, 1956 Rating/Share: 34.7/45   Supporting cast: Little Ricky—Keith Thibodeaux, Mrs. Grundy—Elsa Lanchester, Café owner—Strother Martin

When Lucy misplaces two train tickets to Florida, she and Ethel consult the classified section, hoping to "share a ride" with someone who's driving south. They team up with a peculiar middle-aged woman, Mrs. Grundy, who's bent on getting to Florida in record time. The health-food fanatic even refuses to stop for meals, preferring to dine on watercress sandwiches while she drives. Lucy and Ethel are famished, and the prospect of one of Grundy's gastronomical delights does not overwhelm the two tag-along travelers. Lucy: "Very tasty, if you like buttered grass." While traversing the back roads of South Carolina, Mrs. Grundy's convertible develops a flat tire, and Lucy and Ethel are called upon to fix it. Grundy: "You'll find everything you need in the trunk." Ethel: "I hope we find a mechanic in there." Exhausted after their tire-changing travails, the girls fall asleep, only to be awakened by a radio broadcast: "Evelyn Holmby, the famed hatchet murderess, has escaped from a New York State prison and is believed to be heading south in a cream-colored convertible." The gals panic—they're riding in a similar car and they found a hatchet in the trunk while searching for the jack. Before they have time to escape, the lady driver, having slept a few hours in a sleeping bag, reappears and continues driving toward Miami. While the girls are dozing, Mrs. Grundy hears a radio report that leads her to believe that Lucy and Ethel are the wanted criminals. Hoping to get help, the trio finally stops at a roadside café. Instead, Grundy slips out and quickly drives off, leaving the New Yorkers stranded. The café owner then informs Lucy and Ethel that the hatchet murderess has already been captured in Kentucky. Defeated, tired, and broke, they hitch a ride on a poultry truck and arrive at the North Miami train station in order to make it appear they came by rail. When they are met by Ricky and Fred, who have been enjoying a fishing vacation, the girls try to explain how they arrived two hours before the train . . . and without tickets, which were safely tucked away in Little Ricky's wallet.

"DEEP-SEA FISHING"   11/19/56

Episode #160   Filmed on Thursday, September 27, 1956
Rating/Share: 47.1/65   Supporting cast: Little Ricky—Keith
Thibodeaux, Boat captain—James Hayward, Bellboy—Billy McLean

When Lucy and Ethel return from a shopping spree after spending one hundred forty dollars (plus tax), the husbands decide to take them on their next fishing trip to keep them out of the Eden Roc Hotel boutiques. It will be men versus women as to who will catch the bigger fish; the wager: one hundred fifty dollars. To nail down their victory, Lucy and Ethel buy a one-hundred-pound tuna at a local fish market and plan to hide it in the Ricardos' (Room 919) bathtub. Unbeknown to the scheming females, Ricky and Fred also have purchased a tuna of equal size to assure their conquest. At the end of a madcap routine, which finds each team trying to hide its "catch," the nefarious doings are exposed. With the bet still in force, the Ricardos (including Little Ricky) and Mertzes embark on a day of deep-sea fishing in the Atlantic. After a long, exhausting afternoon, the only one who's caught anything is Little Ricky. Suddenly, Lucy gets a nibble . . . followed closely by a bite on Ricky's hook. Ricky's pole goes overboard and he dives in after it, only to be reeled in by his wife. When the five fishermen discover that there is a fish lodged in Ricky's jacket, Lucy claims she won the wager because she "caught" Ricky and, hence, the fish.

"DESERT ISLAND"   11/26/56

Episode #161   Filmed on Thursday, October 4, 1956   Rating/Share: 46.7/63   Supporting cast: Little Ricky—Keith Thibodeaux, Claude Akins—himself, Jil Jarmyn—herself, Joi Lansing—herself

When Lucy and Ethel learn that their husbands have been chosen to judge a Miami Beach bathing beauty contest, they devise a scheme to keep them from officiating. Lucy instructs the dock attendant to fill the gas tank on their boat only halfway so that their precontest cruise will abort in the middle of the ocean. Then, when it's too late for the husbands to attend the contest, Lucy will "discover" a thermos of gasoline, just enough to get them back to shore. But while the gals are stocking up on suntan oil, Fred discovers the dangerous, gas-filled thermos and leaves it on the dock. Sure enough, when the time comes to turn back for the beauty contest, the motor sputters and stops. The boat eventually drifts ashore on a seemingly deserted island. Lucy and Ethel go off to explore one part of the terrain, and the husbands and Little Ricky take off in the opposite direction. The men encounter actor Claude Akins, who's dressed as a fierce, war-painted Indian, and two bathing beauties, who are filming a documentary about Florida. To teach Lucy a lesson after the gasoline incident, Ricky enlists Akins in a plot to scare the bejesus out of the girls. While Lucy and Ethel are lamenting their state, along comes ferocious Akins, pretending to be an uncivilized native warrior. When the wives have been sufficiently frightened, Ricky and Fred appear and explain the truth about Akins and the island. Lucy is deflated further when she later learns that the beauty contest has been postponed until the next day.

"THE RICARDOS VISIT CUBA"   12/3/56

Episode #162   Filmed on Thursday, October 18, 1956   Rating/Share: 45.9/64   Supporting cast: Little Ricky—Keith Thibodeaux, Uncle Alberto—George Trevino, Cigar store owner—Nacho Galindo, Ricky's mother—Mary Emery, Cigar maker—Angelo Didio, Stewardess—Barbara Logan, Nightclub emcee—Eddie LeBaron,

Ricky's relatives—Lillian Molieri, Rodolfo Hoyos, Jr., Manuel Paris, Amapola Del Vando, Abel Franco   Music: "A Lucky Guy," "Babalu"

The Ricardos and Mertzes fly to Cuba for a visit with Ricky's relatives and for the bandleader's two-day engagement at the Hotel National's Casino Parisien. Lucy is wary of meeting her in-laws, especially the formidable head of the Ricardo clan, Uncle Alberto. Ricky assures her that all will go well: "Make sure you say *muchas gracias* to Uncle Alberto all the time. He likes that." Lucy is a nervous wreck at the reunion, where nothing seems to go right for her. When Uncle Alberto asks her where she got her beautiful hair, Lucy replies: "Oh, I get it about every two weeks." She then proceeds to spill punch on his white jacket, rip his straw hat to shreds, and destroy a pocketful of expensive Cuban cigars. But when she mispronounces *muchas gracias*, calling the patriarchal uncle "a fat pig" instead, Lucy feels like a doomed woman. Lamenting the next day, she says: "After what I did last night, Cuba might cut off America's sugar supply!" To take her mind off family relations, she goes souvenir-hunting while her husband and son rehearse for their nightclub appearance. Determined to make up for the Uncle Alberto fiasco, Lucy buys him a box of his favorite cigars, Corona Grandos. Finding herself short of cash, she promises the tobacco store owner that she will return with the extra funds later. An argument develops, made worse by the entrance of Uncle Alberto himself. To avoid him, Lucy dons a big hat and apron, and proceeds to roll cigars like her co-worker. After completing a foot-long stogie Lucy retreats. The night of the big performance, Ricky sings "A Lucky Guy," then introduces Little Ricky and together they perform "Babalu." Proud Uncle Alberto leans over to Lucy and comments: "Anyone who is the mother of a boy like that is all right with me."

"LITTLE RICKY'S SCHOOL PAGEANT" 12/17/56

Episode #163   Filmed on Thursday, October 25, 1956
Rating/Share: 43.4/63   Supporting cast: Little Ricky—Keith Thibodeaux, Suzy—Candy Rogers Schoenberger

Little Ricky's kindergarten class runs short of cast members for its annual play, and the Ricardos and Mertzes are drafted. Although Ricky expected to be chosen as the play's producer and director (Clifford Terry, who runs an orange juice stand, got that job), he is given the part of a hollow tree. Lucy is to portray the wicked old witch of the forest, Fred will essay the role of Hippity-Hoppity, the friendly frog, and Ethel is lucky enough to cop the coveted Fairy Princess part (only because she fits the costume worn last year by Jimmy Wilson's hefty mother). The Ricardos become concerned when Little Ricky is chosen to play the boy lead; they don't know whether he can handle the responsibility and pressure. But certain that they and the Mertzes will be close by, Lucy and Ricky cease worrying. The pageant opens with young Suzy reading to Billy—Little Ricky—from a storybook entitled *The Enchanted Forest*. The mini-production goes well, despite Little Ricky's forgetting some of his lines, and all are glad when the finale featuring over thirty little children comes to a close.

NOTE: The settings and choreography for the play were by Pepito and Joanne Dancing Academies. Six and a half years earlier, Pepito created the vaudeville routines that Lucy and Desi performed on their 1950 road tour, an important prelude to the "I Love Lucy" show.

" 'I LOVE LUCY' CHRISTMAS SHOW" 12/24/56

**Episode # (Special)   Filmed on Thursday, November 22, 1956
Rating/Share: not available   Supporting cast: Little Ricky—
Keith Thibodeaux, Santa Claus—Cameron Grant   Music: "Jingle Bells," "Rock-a-bye Baby," "We're Having a Baby," "Sweet Adeline"**

It's Christmas Eve and Ricky warns his young son: "Santa won't bring the tree and the presents until you go to sleep." It take some effort to cajole the boy, but after Lucy convinces him that Santa will have no trouble coming down the chimney ("he brings the North Pole with him and slides down it like a fireman"), he's off to bed. The coast clear, Fred and Ethel arrive with a Christmas tree. "It's a gift from me and Ebenezer," Ethel reveals about the five-dollar fir. The four friends begin to trim the tree until Lucy discovers "a branch on the right side that spoils the shape." Fred solves the symmetry problem with a pocket saw as Ricky says to Lucy, "Our lives have sure been different ever since you told me you were going to have a baby." We flash back to the sentimental moment at the Tropicana in 1952 when Lucy breaks the baby news to Ricky (from "Lucy is Enceinte"). This reminiscence over, we discover that Fred got carried away with his saw while listening to the baby tale—the tree is now a spindly stripling. While Fred goes off in search of a replacement, Ethel and Ricky start singing "Jingle Bells," but when Lucy joins in with her off-key rendition, they recall, once again in a flashback sequence, the barbershop quartet harmonizing of "Sweet Adeline" (from "Lucy's Show Biz Swan Song"). With the last note sung, we return to the Ricardo apartment just as Fred enters with a new tree—he got this "last minute" one for only fifty cents. The foursome starts decorating the tree and discussing Little Ricky's Christmas gifts, as Ethel realizes: "It seems like only yesterday he was born." This is the perfect lead-in to a flashback of Ricky, Fred, and Ethel rehearsing Lucy's trip to the hospital (from "Lucy Goes to the Hospital"). Finally, it's Christmas morning. The four principals are up early and wearing Santa outfits. When they hear Little Ricky approaching the living room, they hasten to the kitchen so the boy won't be disillusioned by seeing four Santas. Suddenly, however, there are five St. Nicks crowding the kitchen—who's the real one? The "real" one disappears optically as the Ricardos and Mertzes stare into the camera and say, hesitantly, "Merry Christmas, everybody."

NOTE: Because this was a "special" and employed so many long flashback sequences, this "episode" was not included in the eventual syndication package. . . . The last time even a portion of it was telecast was December 1981 on Rona Barrett's short-lived NBC series, "Television: Inside and Out." . . . The final scene for this show dates back to December 24, 1951, when Desilu featured a special Christmas tag to "Drafted." It featured the Ricardos and Mertzes around a Christmas tree and *five* Santas.

"LUCY AND THE LOVING CUP"   1/7/57

**Episode #164   Filmed on Thursday, November 1, 1956
Rating/Share: 50.9/68   Supporting cast: Little Ricky—Keith
Thibodeaux, Policeman—Robert Foulk, Johnny Longden—himself,
Hazel Longden—herself, Woman from Brooklyn—Jesslyn Fax, Men on
train—Byron Kane, Lester Dorr, Man on platform—Phil Tead,
Woman on platform—Sandra Gould, Young woman on platform—
Florence Ann Shawn, Bum—William L. Erwin**

After Ricky pokes fun at Lucy's new hat, she jokingly puts on a loving cup he had planned to present to jockey Johnny Longden at a National Turf Association dinner. The problem is that Lucy can't get the trophy off her head. Ethel suggests a silversmith, but the man refuses to make a house call. Wearing a veil over the loving cup in an effort to disguise it, Lucy and Ethel board a Lexington Avenue IRT subway train and, of course, elicit more than their share of stares from the rush-hour crowds. When the pair prepares to transfer at the Bleecker Street station, Lucy gets caught in the pushing melee and is shoved back into the car. Assuming that she, like Ethel, has gotten off the train, Lucy asks a stranger: "Pardon me, sir, can you tell me where the stairs are?" New Yorker: "You have to get off the train first." Lucy: "I *am* off." New Yorker: "You're telling me!" Lucy's veil accidentally comes loose and she tries to act nonchalant with the loving cup still stuck on her head. The scenes depicting Lucy "reading" a newspaper, hoping to look inconspicuous, are hilarious. She finally manages to exit at Flatbush Avenue (the end of the line) whereupon a crowd gathers. Lucy explains her plight to a cop who, dismissing his urge to take her straight to Bellevue, is nice enough to accompany her to the Johnny Longden banquet where Ricky has been waiting patiently for the arrival of the loving cup. Finally, Ricky presents the award to the champion jockey . . . with Lucy still attached to it.

NOTE: During the summer of 1955, Desi Arnaz optioned Johnny Longden's life story for a possible motion picture, which was never made.

"LUCY AND SUPERMAN"   1/14/57

Episode #166   Filmed on Thursday, November 15, 1956
Rating/Share: 48.1/65   Supporting cast: Little Ricky—Keith
Thibodeaux, Superman—George Reeves, Caroline Appleby—Doris
Singleton, Charlie Appleby—George O'Hanlon, Martha—Madge
O. Blake, Her husband—Ralph Dumke, Stevie Appleby—Steven Kay

Lucy is planning Little Ricky's fifth birthday party for Saturday, the same day that Caroline Appleby has arranged a birthday shindig for her son Stevie. Each affair has the same guest list and neither mother wants to change the day of her affair. Caroline has hired a clown and magician, and even plans to stage a puppet show—hard acts for Lucy to top. Suddenly, however, Mrs. Ricardo remembers that Superman (George Reeves) is in town, and she asks Ricky to invite him to Little Ricky's party. Without waiting for a confirmation, Lucy phones Mrs. Appleby and announces that Superman *is* coming to her gathering. Firmly defeated, Caroline cancels her party plans. When Ricky is unable to corral the "Man of Steel," Lucy laments: "If I don't produce Superman, my name will be Supermud." She is left with no choice but to impersonate the comic strip hero. Donning a football helmet, ill-fitting tights, and a flowing cape, she climbs out on the ledge while Little Ricky's party is in full swing. When she is about to make her grand entrance through the living room window, who should show up but the "real" Superman, who makes a dashing leap into the room through the louvered windows of the kitchen. The party guests are thrilled, and so is Lucy. But much to her chagrin, she finds she has been locked out on the ledge just when a rainstorm commences. Who comes to her rescue? Superman, of course, who comments to Ricky: "You mean to say that you've been married to her for fifteen years? . . . And they call *me* Superman!"

NOTE: Among fanatic "Superman" fans and collectors, this show remains a favorite. Prints, stills, and scripts from this episode command high prices. . . . George Reeves was accompanied to Desilu by Si Simonson, the "Superman" special effects man: "George wouldn't go without me, so Lucy's director and I worked out the particulars together. But what I don't understand to this day is why George didn't get billed." The credits carried the National Comics copyright for "Superman character, feats, and narration." . . . Special casters, available at the time only in Chicago, were used on the Ricardo piano to make it seem effortless for Superman to move the instrument. . . . Technically, Little Ricky was only four, since he was born on January 19, 1953.

"LITTLE RICKY GETS A DOG" 1/21/57

Episode #165 Filmed on Thursday, November 8, 1956
Rating/Share: 45.1/61 Supporting cast: Little Ricky—Keith
Thibodeaux, Mr. Stewart—John Emery, Voice of dog—June Foray

Animal lover Little Ricky has turned the Ricardo apartment into a miniature zoo with frogs, turtles, goldfish, a parakeet, lizard, and now a puppy, thanks

to the generosity of little Billy Palmer. Lucy says the puppy must go, but her feelings quickly change when the doggie showers her with friendly kisses. When Daddy arrives home from the club and learns of the recent addition to his family, he heads straight for Little Ricky's room intending to evict the dog. Moments later, Ricky returns from the boy's room. Lucy: "Where are you going, dear?" Ricky: "To the basement to get a box." Landlord Mertz appears and demands: "That pooch has got to go!" But when he learns that Little Ricky has named the new pet Fred, he heads for the basement to prepare a proper throne for his namesake. After a sleepless night caused by Fred's yelping, a grouchy new tenant, Mr. Stewart, confronts Lucy, demanding to see for himself whether or not there is a dog being harbored on the no-pets-allowed premises. She denies the presence of any canine, so when Stewart spies some dog biscuits, Lucy claims they belong to her and proceeds to munch one. The disagreeable tenant makes life miserable for everyone, until Fred Mertz puts his foot down: "I'd rather live with a little dog than a big grouch!" Stewart storms out with plans to move. When Ethel reminds her loyal husband that he has just kissed away two hundred fifty dollars, Fred promptly faints.

NOTE: The no-pets-allowed clause in the Mertz apartment house lease apparently didn't affect Mrs. Trumbull, whose cat was mentioned on at least one occasion.

"LUCY WANTS TO MOVE TO THE COUNTRY" 1/28/57

Episode #167   Filmed on Thursday, December 6, 1956
Rating/Share: 42.1/56   Supporting cast: Joe Spaulding—
Frank Wilcox, Eleanor Spaulding—Eleanor Audley

Fed up with the dirty city, Lucy wants the fresh air and sunshine of suburban life for her family. To exaggerate her case, she moves all the living room furniture together to give the apartment a cramped appearance and sprinkles talcum powder on the mantel to simulate dust. She even powders her face to accentuate her city pallor. Ricky takes the Mertzes into his confidence and breaks the news that he has already put down a deposit of five hundred dollars on a house in Connecticut, as a sixteenth wedding anniversary surprise for his wife. When Lucy sees Ethel's eyes filling with tears, the news is spilled. Now Lucy never wants to move away from the Mertzes. Amid the tears and turmoil, Ricky attempts to get back his deposit, but the money will be returned only if the owners find the buyers unsuitable. Lucy and the Mertzes hatch a scheme, guaranteed to yield the five hundred dollars. They arrive at the Westport, Connecticut, home of Joe and Eleanor Spaulding dressed as gangsters. Lucy plays a brash gum-chewing, purse-slinging gun-moll type; Fred looks like a fugitive from the senior citizens' chapter of the Hell's Angels; and Ethel resembles the madam at a discount bordello. Just then, Ricky enters, unaware of the goings-on. He tries to explain to the Spauldings that his wife and friends have only good intentions in mind. Reluctantly, the homeowners return Ricky's deposit. But as Lucy takes a closer look at the warm, homey surroundings, she changes her mind about staying in the city, and the Ricardos become the proud owners of a home in the suburbs.

"LUCY HATES TO LEAVE"   2/4/57

Episode #168   Filmed on Thursday, December 13, 1956
Rating/Share: 42.5/57   Supporting cast: Little Ricky—Keith
Thibodeaux, Mr. Taylor—Gene Reynolds, Mrs. Taylor—Mary Ellen
Kaye

Ricky is losing sleep over the prospect of being a homeowner. He laments: "Do you realize how many times I'm going to have to sing 'Babalu' to pay for that house?" Lucy tries to reassure her husband by calling his paranoia "a bad case of homeowner's heebie-jeebies." A twenty-year mortgage and the thought of buying a houseful of new furniture enters his mind: "Maybe I can get a hit record or something." Fred tears up the Ricardos' ninety-nine-year lease, then asks permission to show their 3-D apartment to some prospective tenants, a young married couple, the Taylors. The couple agrees to rent the flat with the stipulation that they be permitted to move in immediately. The Ricardos kindly agree to vacate four days early and move in with the Mertzes. Since Lucy and Ricky have decided to sell their old furniture to the young couple, there won't be much stuff cluttering Fred and Ethel's apartment before the move to Connecticut. However, when Lucy finds out that the Taylors have plans to cut off the legs on the coffee table, she gets sentimental about her belongings and refuses to part with them. Suddenly, the Mertz abode looks like a warehouse and living under such cramped conditions becomes unbearable for the five friends. To make matters worse, the Spauldings phone with the news that their move has been delayed two weeks. The Ricardos will be unable to take possession of their new home in Connecticut until then.

NOTE: Mr. Taylor was portrayed by a friend of Bob Schiller, a young, not-very-successful actor who, until this part came along, had been financially stranded in New York. Desilu paid him five hundred dollars for four days' work, and Gene Reynolds decided to stay in California. Today, he is one of TV's most respected producers, responsible for such shows as "Room 222," "Lou Grant," "M*A*S*H," and others.

"LUCY MISSES THE MERTZES"   2/11/57

Episode #169   Filmed on Thursday, December 20, 1956
Rating/Share: 38.8/50   Supporting cast: Little Ricky—Keith
Thibodeaux, Harry Munson—Tristram Coffin, Station clerk—Jesse
Kirkpatrick, Moving man—Robert Bice, Deliveryman—Gary Gray

After fifteen years of being together, the Ricardos and Mertzes must finally part. They exchange house keys and tearful good-byes. After Ricky carries his wife over the threshold of the Connecticut house, a big basket of fruit—a housewarming gift from the Mertzes—arrives. Lucy contends that they must have been really upset and sad. Ricky: "For Fred to spend ten dollars on a basket of fruit, he must have been hysterical!" That night, with Little Ricky spending the night with his new friend, Billy Munson, the Ricardos become lonely. Suddenly, they get the idea to take the train into Manhattan and surprise the Mertzes. At the same time, the Mertzes decide to take the train to Westport to surprise the Ricardos. But when Ricky arrives at the railroad station and tries to contact Fred and Ethel by phone, he naturally doesn't find them at home. Disappointed, the new suburbanites return home and go to bed. The Mertzes make it to Connecticut, but Fred refuses to spend any more money (he's already forked out $8.16) on taxis and he insists they walk to the Ricardos'. When they find the house dark, they open the front door with the key Lucy gave them and make themselves at home. The Ricardos are awakened by the noise downstairs and suspect a burglar. After some confusion, the four friends are reunited and enjoy the basket of fruit . . . especially Fred.

"LUCY GETS CHUMMY WITH THE NEIGHBORS"   2/18/57

Episode #170   Filmed on Thursday, January 10, 1957
Rating/Share: 38.0/49   Supporting cast: Little Ricky—Keith
Thibodeaux, Ralph Ramsey—Frank Nelson, Betty Ramsey—Mary
Jane Croft, Mr. Perry—Parley Baer, Bruce Ramsey—Ray Ferrell

When Lucy determines that her old furniture doesn't quite fit into its new setting, she asks Ricky if she can replace it. He says she can, but allows her to spend only $500. New neighbor Betty Ramsey informs Lucy that she can get a 40 percent discount at Mr. Perry's furniture store. There, Lucy buys new sofas, new chairs, new lamps, new tables, new everything . . . to the shocking tune of $3,272.75. Lucy is so afraid of Ricky's Cuban temper that she phones the Mertzes in New York and pleads with them to take the first train to Westport to protect her from the furniture flak. Sure enough, when Ricky returns from New York and sees the overabundance of new furniture, he hits the ceiling, then demands that she return all but $500 worth. When Lucy tries to make an excuse for not wanting the new items (she says she'd prefer Chinese Modern), Betty Ramsey, who selected them, becomes insulted. Ricky decides to solve the problem himself by having a man-to-man talk with Betty's husband, Ralph. At first, Ralph flatters Ricky by offering him a TV gig. This, of course, makes Ricky's task a little more difficult. When he winds up giving Ramsey the impression that Mrs. Ramsey's taste in furniture leaves something to be desired, the new neighbor is ruffled. Ramsey: "Forget about the TV show. We'll get Cugat!" Enter the Mertzes, who break up the unneighborly feud by explaining to the Ramseys that the Ricardos simply cannot afford the new furnishings. The Ramseys understand, and Ralph offers Ricky that TV job again, which will pay $3,500 . . . just enough to pay for Lucy's extravagance.

NOTE: This was the first appearance of Frank Nelson and Mary Jane Croft as the Ralph Ramseys. Both performers had appeared previously on "Lucy." . . . Jerry Miggins, the "Lucy" propman who joined Desilu in 1955 after a long career at M-G-M, recalls that the new furniture that appeared in this and subsequent Connecticut-based shows (both the half-hour and hour versions) was a gift to Desilu from the manufacturer. "Everyone tried to get their stuff used on the show because it was so popular," recalls Miggins. "It was Desi's idea to use two sofas back-to-back. Desi and I spent hours arranging and rearranging all the living room furniture with Lucy directing us from the sidelines. Because of the fireplace, we couldn't seem to hit on something that worked properly until Desi's brainstorm."

"LUCY RAISES CHICKENS"   3/4/57

Episode #171   Filmed on Thursday, January 17, 1957
Rating/Share: 51.2/68   Supporting cast: Little Ricky—Keith
Thibodeaux, Betty Ramsey—Mary Jane Croft, Woman from magazine—
Mary Alan Hokenson, Man from magazine—Tyler McVey

Betty Ramsey has good news—*House and Garden* magazine wants to do a picture layout on the Ricardos' home; Ricky has bad news—the bills are piling up and he's slowly going broke. Lucy suggests they raise chickens to bring in a little extra money. Very little investment is required. Lucy reasons: "What can a little grain cost . . . fifty cents? That's chicken feed." Ricky advertises for an experienced couple who can care for the chickens in return for a percentage of the profits, and who should answer the ad—the Mertzes. Fred's poultry experience: "For the past twenty-five years, I've been hen-pecked!" Counting their chickens before they're hatched (literally), Lucy and Ethel buy five hundred baby chicks before Fred has a chance to finish the required coop. In the meantime, it is imperative that the chicks be kept warm, so they place the creatures in the den and turn up the heat to ninety degrees. Then they find that Little Ricky has accidentally left open the den door, and the baby chicks are crawling all over the house. While everyone is frantically corralling the birds, the *House and Garden* editors arrive. Unimpressed, they depart. The Ricardos don't mind—maybe next month they'll make the *Chicken Breeders' Gazette*.

"LUCY DOES THE TANGO"   3/11/57

Episode #172   Filmed on Thursday, February 7, 1957
Rating/Share: 35.4/47   Supporting cast: Little Ricky—Keith
Thibodeaux, Bruce Ramsey—Ray Ferrell   Music: "Tango"

Discouraged by the baby chicks' rate of growth, the Ricardos and Mertzes exchange their five hundred little birds for two hundred laying hens, guaranteed to produce salable eggs. After the first two weeks, the hens have laid exactly six eggs and, by calculation, that's eighteen dollars per egg. Ricky is disgusted with the whole enterprise and gives the hens one more day to shape up. Ricky: "I should have raised something I knew about, like sugarcane." Deciding to improve on Mother Nature, Lucy and Ethel buy five dozen eggs, and the gals quickly stuff them in their blouses, pockets, and shirts. When they've crammed the last one out of sight, Ricky comes home, wanting to rehearse with Lucy the tango routine for the upcoming PTA show. All goes smoothly until the final spin lands Lucy in Ricky's arms, eggs first. When he learns of the deception, he intends to get out of the egg business immediately. However, Little Ricky and his friend Bruce Ramsey have grown so fond of the hens, they decide to hide them so Mr. Ricardo can't get rid of them. The next day when Ricky is about to round up his lazy brood, the chickens are nowhere in sight. Finding a few in the Mertzes' closet, Ricky accuses Fred of being a chicken thief. A battle results and continues until Betty Ramsey phones, informing the feuding foursome that she has found chickens all over her house. Little Ricky confesses just as Bruce arrives with a basket brimming with freshly laid eggs. The Ricardos and Mertzes are back in the egg business.

NOTE: The tango/eggs routine resulted in the longest laugh ever recorded on "I Love Lucy"—sixty-five seconds. . . . The routine was not rehearsed with *real* eggs because Lucille Ball wanted the experience to be fresh when the cameras rolled; hard-boiled eggs were used for the run-throughs.

. . . The Ford Division of the Ford Motor Company sponsored this and the following "Lucy" episode, using the commercial time to introduce their new hardtop convertible. The experience must have proven worthwhile because the auto manufacturer signed on to sponsor the first five hour-long "Lucy" shows that premiered in the fall of 1957.

"RAGTIME BAND" 3/18/57

Episode #173 Filmed on Thursday, February 14, 1957
Rating/Share: 40.2/52 Supporting cast: Little Ricky—Keith
Thibodeaux Music: "Sweet Sue," "She'll Be Comin' Round the
Mountain," "Man Smart, Woman Smarter"

After Lucy volunteers Ricky's musical services for a Westport Historical Society benefit without consulting him first, he refuses to participate. But Lucy's promised an appearance by Ricky Ricardo and she intends to carry through. Ricky Ricardo, Jr., will be the stellar attraction. She decides to organize her own little orchestra with her son on the drums, Ethel at the piano, Lucy tooting her saxophone, and Fred playing his fiddle. Ethel: "The last time he played was three chins ago." Their first rehearsal is a disaster— Ethel knows only one song, "She'll Be Comin' Round the Mountain," and Lucy knows only one, "Sweet Sue." When Ricky agrees to listen to the ensemble and give his honest opinion of their talents, he decides to save his reputation as an orchestra leader by lending the combo some of his own musicians. At the benefit, Ricky sings "Man Smart, Woman Smarter" while the others support him with calypso-flavored sounds.

NOTE: Lucy claimed to know only one song, "Sweet Sue." What about "The Glow Worm"?

"LUCY'S NIGHT IN TOWN" 3/25/57

Episode #174 Filmed on Thursday, February 21, 1957
Rating/Share: 38.4/51 Supporting cast: Theater manager—Joseph
Kearns, Woman with purse—Gladys Hurlbut, Woman in box—Doris
Packer, Man in box—John Eldredge, Waiter—Louis A. Nicoletti,

Usherette—Jody Warner, Theatergoers—Roy Lazarus, Susan Johnson,
John Henson, Alan J. Gilbert, Shorty Long, Art Lund, Paul Power
Music: From *The Most Happy Fella* by Frank Loesser—"Standing
on the Corner," "Don't Cry," "Big 'D' "

In Manhattan for the evening, the Ricardos and Mertzes are enjoying dinner
before their theater date to see Frank Loesser's musical, *The Most Happy
Fella*. When Lucy checks her purse for the tickets (sixth row center, orchestra,
row F, seats 104, 105, 106, and 107), she makes the horrifying discovery
that they were for the matinee. Lucy tells a distraught Ethel: "Well, at least
I didn't forget them. You have to admit that." The gals try their darndest to
eat slowly in hopes of being so late to the Imperial Theater that they will
miss the show. Lucy insists on chewing each mouthful of food twenty-five
times and even intends to peel every lima bean. When Lucy's mistake is
exposed, Ricky tries to buy four new tickets, but is able to obtain only two
box seats. To be fair, the women will get to see the first act, and the men
will see the second act. At intermission, Lucy and Ethel inform their husbands
that the two seats behind them were unoccupied during the first act; therefore,
all four of them can enjoy the remaining half. As luck would have it, the two
ticket-holders arrive, and the girls must relinquish the seats to them, before
squeezing in next to their husbands. This causes so much confusion that
Ethel's purse containing five hundred dollars in cash (apartment house rent
receipts) flies off the balcony and lands in the orchestra section. By the time
the donnybrook is unraveled, the musical has ended.

NOTE: Desilu was one of the financial backers of Loesser's musical, which
had opened May 3, 1956, on Broadway.

"HOUSEWARMING"   4/1/57

Episode #175   Filmed on Thursday, February 28, 1957
Rating/Share: 45.1/62   Supporting cast: Little Ricky—Keith
Thibodeaux, Betty Ramsey—Mary Jane Croft, Bruce Ramsey—
Ray Ferrell

The Mertzes feel left out when the Ricardos invite only the Munsons, the
Baileys, and the Ramseys to a dinner party. Ethel, in particular, has become
envious of Lucy's friendship with Betty Ramsey. Sensing her friend's hurt
feelings, Lucy sets up a nice luncheon for the three gals. Still jealous, Ethel
barely opens her mouth during the tête-à-tête. But when Betty casually
mentions that she was born in Albuquerque, New Mexico—Ethel's hometown—the two women become inseparable. Now Lucy is jealous of the
Betty-Ethel alliance: "Ever since they had lunch here, they've been as thick
as thieves. What's so hot all of a sudden about being born in Albuquerque?
I could have been born there myself if my parents didn't live in Jamestown!"
When Lucy happens to overhear the tag end of a conversation between
Betty and Ethel through the newly installed intercom system (connecting the

main house with the Mertzes' guest cottage), she jumps to the conclusion that the pair is planning a surprise housewarming party for the Ricardos and that's why they've been so preoccupied lately. That night, Lucy convinces Ricky to dress to the nines and to expect a barrage of friends to burst through the door any moment. After hours of idle waiting, no one shows up. Lucy must have been mistaken, and she whimpers to Ricky that they have no friends. Through the same intercom, Ethel hears Lucy crying and, realizing the problem, hastily organizes a surprise housewarming party.

"BUILDING A BAR-B-Q"   4/8/57

Episode #176   Filmed on Thursday, March 14, 1957   Rating/Share: 42.1/56   Supporting cast: Little Ricky—Keith Thibodeaux

Ricky's on vacation and he's driving Lucy crazy just hanging around the house. She suggests: "Honey, why don't you call up little Freddie Mertz and ask him to come over and play?" Discussing his idleness with Ethel, Lucy realizes that her husband needs a project to keep him busy. How about that brick barbecue he's been promising to build on the patio? Ethel: "Why don't you do what I do with Fred when I want to do something? I start it, and when he sees I'm doing it all wrong, he takes over." Ethel's suggestion works like a charm—when Ricky and Fred see the gals slinging bricks and cement everywhere, they agree to do the job. In the midst of the project, Ricky discovers Lucy's wedding ring precariously near the bucket of cement. To teach her a lesson, he decides not to tell her he found it. It doesn't take Mrs. Ricardo long to realize the ring is missing from her finger and when she traces her steps back to the fireplace project, she immediately assumes the ring is in the cement mixture holding together the barbecue bricks. Late that night, she and Ethel converge on the patio and proceed to tear the new structure apart brick by brick. Ethel: "It's times like these when I wish I kept a diary so I could write, 'Dear diary, Tonight I went out to the backyard and felt through wet cement.'" When Ricky sees the travesty the next morning, he hits the ceiling: "What happened to our beautiful barbecue?" Lucy: "An earthquake?" Ricky: "They don't have earthquakes in Connecticut." Lucy: "A tornado?" Ricky: "They don't have tornadoes in Connecticut." Lucy: "Boy, this is a dull state!" Ricky: "I think it was a couple of hurricanes. . . . Hurricane Lucy and Hurricane Ethel." When Lucy explains the truth, Ricky accepts the blame, telling Lucy that her wedding ring can be found in the pocket of his old work shirt. But Lucy gave the old shirt to Ethel for a rag, who in turn gave it to Fred, who gave it to Little Ricky to use as a tail for his kite . . . which just flew away. Heartbroken, Lucy can't enjoy the first hamburger cooked on the new grill: "How can I eat when my wedding ring is somewhere over the Long Island Sound?" As she takes a reluctant bite of her burger, she discovers the ring inside. It had fallen from Ricky's pocket the day before when he bent over to pick up the platter of meat.

"COUNTRY CLUB DANCE"   4/22/57

Episode #177   Filmed on Thursday, March 21, 1957   Rating/Share:
not available   Supporting cast: Little Ricky—Keith Thibodeaux, Ralph
Ramsey—Frank Nelson, Betty Ramsey—Mary Jane Croft, Diana
Jordan—Barbara Eden, Harry Munson—Tristram Coffin, Grace
Munson—Ruth Brady

At a club dance, Ricky, Fred, and Ralph Ramsey are smitten with Harry and
Grace Munson's cousin Diana Jordan, a sultry blonde, much to their wives'
collective disgust. The next day Lucy, Ethel, and Betty Ramsey are discussing
the "spectacle." It seems that Ricky danced with Diana nine times, Ralph
eight, and Fred thirteen. They all have been invited to a party the Munsons
are giving in Diana's honor, but this time the gals are going to doll themselves
up so that their husbands will not even notice the Jordan girl. Lucy will wear
her tightest dress, Betty will sport her most exotic perfume, and Ethel will
do her hair up like Grace Kelly. Noticing something strange, the husbands
decide to play along with the wives that evening. At the gathering, the guys
bend over backward trying to be nice to their wives. Ricky's "strange"
behavior prompts Lucy to crack: "When you're this sweet, there's something
rotten in Cuba." She gathers up her female cohorts and departs. Later that
night, the husbands confess that Pat Boone–crazy Diana is too young for
them, and they return to their understanding wives.

NOTE: It is mentioned that Little Ricky is off visting Stevie Appleby in Manhattan, enjoying the zoo and a Dodger baseball game. . . . Barbara Eden was twenty-two when this episode was filmed.

"LUCY RAISES TULIPS" 4/29/57

Episode #178 Filmed on Thursday, March 28, 1957 Rating/Share: 41.2/65 Supporting cast: Little Ricky—Keith Thibodeaux, Betty Ramsey—Mary Jane Croft, Flower show judges—Peter Brocco, Eleanor Audley

Lucy is itching to cop first prize for the "Best-looking Garden" in Westport, Connecticut, and spends every waking moment tending to her beautiful patch of tulips. She is determined to dethrone Betty Ramsey, who has won the coveted Garden Club award three years in a row. Much to her dismay, Ricky has mowed only half the lawn before taking off for a Yankee ball game. This means she must complete the job if her garden is to look just right. Seating herself on the bulky machine, Lucy takes off . . . and is unable to stop. After upsetting downtown Westport, she manages somehow to mow down Betty Ramsey's tulip beds. Lucy: "I feel just rotten about it." Ethel: "Well, you could give her your tulips." Lucy: "Ethel, I feel rotten, but not *that* rotten!" Lucy replaces the mowed-down flowers with wax tulips she bought at the Village Gift Shop. When the Garden Club judges disqualify Betty's fake flowers, they proceed next door to evaluate Lucy's collection. It seems that Lucy's tulips are wax too—the result of Ricky's mowing the lawn in the dark—and they're slowly melting in the warm New England sun.

"THE RICARDOS DEDICATE A STATUE" 5/6/57

Episode #179 Filmed on Thursday, April 4, 1957 Rating/Share: 35.6/56 Supporting cast: Little Ricky—Keith Thibodeaux

It's Yankee Doodle Day in Westport, Connecticut, and the patriotic towns-people are about to unveil a monument to their Revolutionary War ancestors. For the accompanying pageant, Fred has been tapped as the town crier and Ricky has been chosen to give the dedication speech at the unveiling ceremony. Lucy is showing Ethel the beautiful stone sculpture of a patriot kneeling with a musket, when suddenly Little Ricky announces that his dog Fred has run away again. Lucy jumps in the family station wagon (Ford) and, forgetting about the attached trailer holding the statue, takes off. A few moments later we hear a terrible crash; the one-of-a-kind statue is in pieces. Desperate, Lucy contacts Mr. Silvestri, the sculptor, who wonders why Lucy wants a second statue. Lucy: "Why? . . . Well, Westport is growing and may become twin cities like Minnepaul and St. Apolis." A replacement will take two weeks to prepare. Lucy has a better idea. At the ceremony, after Ricky

gives his speech, the statue is unveiled. Dressed as a Minuteman, impersonating the sculpture, is Lucy. She goes undetected until Fred the dog decides
to lick the patriot's face. Stone figures don't laugh.

NOTE: The Desilu prop department commissioned the real-life Silvestri Studios
in Los Angeles to fashion the Minuteman statue. . . . The crowd scene
featured the real-life Arnaz children—Lucie, five and a half, and Desi, Jr.,
four (to whom Ethel says, "Are you having a good time, honey?")—the only
time they appeared on "I Love Lucy."

The Seventh, Eighth, and Ninth Seasons: 1957-60

THE SEVENTH SEASON: 1957–58

Executive Producer: Desi Arnaz
Producer: Bert Granet
Writers: Madelyn Martin, Bob Carroll, Jr., Bob Weiskopf, and Bob Schiller
Director: Jerry Thorpe
Director of Photography: Sid Hickox, A.S.C.
Music Composed and Conducted: Wilbur Hatch
Associate Producer: Jack Aldworth
Production Manager: W. Argyle Nelson
Editorial Supervisor: Dann Cahn, A.C.E.
Art Director: Ralph Berger
Assistant Director: Jay Sandrich
Film Editor: Bud Molin, A.C.E.
Rerecording Editor: Robert Reeve
Music Editor: E. C. Norton
Theme Music: Eliot Daniel
Set Dresser: Theodore Offenbecker
Sound Recorder: Cameron McCulloch
Makeup: Hal King
Hair Stylist: Irma Kusely
Camera Coordinator: Maury Thompson
Property Master: Jerry Miggins
Miss Ball's Wardrobe: Edward Stevenson
Costumer: Della Fox
Casting: Kerwin Coughlin
Photographic Effects: Howard Anderson Company
Sound: Glen Glenn Sound

Filmed at Motion Picture Center

Sponsor: Ford Division of the Ford Motor Company
Agency: J. Walter Thompson Company

"LUCY TAKES A CRUISE TO HAVANA"
11/6/57

Episode #1 Supporting cast: Susie MacNamara—Ann Sothern,
Carlos Garcia—Cesar Romero, Rudy Vallee—himself, Hedda
Hopper—herself, Little Ricky—Keith Thibodeaux, Cruise director—
Frank Nelson, Judge—George Trevino, Jailer—Nestor Paiva, Trustee—
Joaquin del Rio, Nightclub owner—Vincent Padula, Waiter—Louis A.
Nicoletti **Music:** "Our Ship Is Coming In," "That Means I Love You"

Newspaper gossip columnist Hedda Hopper arrives at the Ricardos' Connecticut home to interview Lucy and Ricky on how their romance began. A
flashback transports us back twenty years to the deck of a cruise ship headed
for Havana, Cuba. Two young New York stenographers—Lucille Mc-
Gillicuddy and Susie MacNamara—are anxious to enjoy their vacation in the
popular Latin resort city—and hope to meet a man. The ship is sorely
lacking, however, in male companions. Susie: "I have searched this boat
stem to stern, top to bottom, fore to aft, and I haven't found one available
man. I hate to tell you, Lucy. We're traveling on a floating Y.W.C.A." Lucy:
"Brother, they weren't kidding when they said this ship was on its *maiden*
voyage!" The girls do encounter a pair of honeymooners, Fred Mertz (with
hair) and Ethel, "his charming child bride of 1934," and singing idol Rudy
Vallee, who is hoping for a little peace and quiet. When the boat docks,
Lucy and Susie meet a couple of natives who run a combination taxi-

sightseeing service—Ricky Ricardo and Carlos Garcia. At a Cuban nightclub, El Tambor, Lucy and Ricky get romantic and pledge their affection for each other in a specialty drum number, "That Means I Love You." Lucy soon discovers that Ricky's real wish is for a musical career in America, and she pesters Vallee into giving the boys jobs with his orchestra. He agrees, but a misunderstanding leads to a public brawl, and Lucy and Susie land in jail. They inadvertently drink from a barrel of water that has been laced with rum. They get drunk and nearly miss their boat home.

NOTE: Dancer Barrie Chase—once Fred Astaire's TV dance partner—appeared briefly as one of a group of dancers in a production number early in the show.

"THE CELEBRITY NEXT DOOR"   12/3/57

Episode #2   Supporting cast: Little Ricky—Keith Thibodeaux, Tallulah Bankhead—herself, Ida Thompson—Elvia Allman, Butler—Richard Deacon, Maid—Phyllis Kennedy

When a moving van pulls up to the house next door to the Ricardos, Lucy and Ethel promptly take to the binoculars to find out who their new neighbor is. Lucy: "She must be either very rich or very poor." Ethel: "How can you tell?" Lucy: "From the furniture. It's either cheap, beat-up junk, or priceless antiques." In the midst of their peeping, the new resident drops by to use the telephone, and it turns out be none other than actress Tallulah Bankhead. Hoping to make friends with the star, Lucy invites her to dinner with an ulterior motive in mind—she wants to persuade the woman to appear in a PTA benefit production. (Tallulah: "P. T. what???") To impress the Broadway headliner, Lucy cons the Mertzes into posing as the Ricardos' maid and butler, but the meal turns out to be a fiasco. Once apologies have been made all around, Tallulah agrees to co-star with Lucy and Ricky in the school show, with the "Alabama foghorn" taking over the lead. The girls have a subsequent falling out when Lucy accidentally spray-paints Tallulah, head to toe, with yellow paint, then sits on one of Tallulah's freshly painted kitchen chairs while wearing her own brand-new black suit. Lucy decides to "get even" with the visiting celebrity by upstaging her in the PTA show, and, as usual, turns the whole thing into a shambles.

NOTE: Prop master Jerry Miggins recalls: "During a rehearsal for the telephone scene, Tallulah picked up the receiver and did her scene, then this look came over her face and she said, 'I've been in show business forty years and this is the first time a stage phone worked!' This meant that the phone was 'live,' she could actually hear someone on the other end. She thought that was just terrific. Later, for the Southern dinner scene, I had to supply the food. I had no intention of cooking up fried chicken myself, so I bought packages of the first frozen fried chicken dinners ever manufactured. I didn't tell anyone. Well, Tallulah raved about that chicken all night—'This is the best fried chicken I've ever eaten!' "

"LUCY HUNTS URANIUM"   1/3/58

Episode #3   Supporting cast: Little Ricky—Keith Thibodeaux, Fred MacMurray—himself, June Haver—herself, Claims clerk—Charles Lane, Maid—Maxine Semon, Bellhop—Robert Jellison, Gas station attendant—Norman Leavitt, Prospector #1—William Fawcett, Maître d'—Paul Powers, Busboy—Richard King, Desk clerk—Rick Warrick, Prospector #2—Louis A. Nicoletti

Ricky has a band engagement in Las Vegas, and Lucy, Little Ricky, and the Mertzes are traveling there with him. Lucy has special plans for her Vegas holiday—she intends to prospect for uranium in the nearby hills, even though Ricky strictly forbids it. Aboard the train, she encounters movie star Fred MacMurray, who soon falls prey to Lucy's get-rich-quick scheme. It seems that MacMurray is afraid to tell his wife, June Haver, about some Vegas gambling losses he incurred, and the prospect of recouping his losses sounds promising. Hoping to persuade Ricky, Lucy has a phony newspaper headline ("BIG URANIUM STRIKE OUTSIDE VEGAS") printed at a local novelty shop. Ricky doesn't believe the news—but the hotel chambermaid does, and soon the whole town—Ricky included—is out prospecting for riches. Lucy, Ricky, the two Freds, and Ethel find what they believe to be uranium, but, in typical Ricardo/Mertz fashion, jealousy takes over, and, in a madcap chase, each tries to beat the other back to the land office. Once again in town, the gang woefully discovers their claim is worthless.

NOTE: Lucille Ball changed her hairstyle beginning with this episode to a style similar to what she would wear the rest of her TV career. In fact, in one scene, when Lucy Ricardo reaches for a hatbox (in which she's hidden her Geiger counter) Ethel mistakenly guesses: "Oh, you've bought a new hat to go with your new hairdo?"

"LUCY WINS A RACEHORSE"   2/3/58

Episode #4   Supporting cast: Little Ricky—Keith Thibodeaux, Betty Grable—herself, Harry James—himself, George—Norman Leavitt, Man—James Burke   Music: "The Bayamo"

Little Ricky wants a horse and Lucy thinks it's a good idea even though Ricky forbids it. She enters a "Name the Horse" contest being sponsored by Corny Crinkles breakfast cereal, forwarding entries under her friends' names as well as her own. Lo and behold, the entry bearing Fred Mertz's name wins—but Fred claims the thousand-dollar steed belongs to him. Ethel: "Either you give that horse to Little Ricky, or I'm going to leave you." Fred: "Ethel, if you're trying to scare me, you've gotta do better than that!" Fred ultimately acquiesces, and Lucy finds herself saddled with the care and feeding of a love-starved horse named Whirling Jet. Lucy is determined to keep the animal despite Ricky's objections, and with the financial help of Betty Grable (who with husband Harry James is appearing in Ricky's nightclub show) she enters Whirling Jet in a harness race. Lucy: "Betty, you're just what I've been looking for—an Ethel Mertz with money!" Whirling Jet will not respond to the driver's commands, however, so Lucy disguises herself as a man and races him herself.

NOTE: James and Grable's guest appearance is highlighted by a musical number, "The Bayamo," danced by Ricky and Betty to the trumpet accompaniment of Harry James. Jack Baker created the "Bayamo" choreography with composer Arthur Hamilton, who also wrote the song.

"LUCY GOES TO SUN VALLEY"   4/14/58

Episode #5   Supporting cast: Little Ricky—Keith Thibodeaux, Fernando Lamas—himself   Music: "Melancholy Baby"

After making plans to go to Sun Valley, Idaho, on a second honeymoon, Ricky learns that he is to appear with Fred and Little Ricky on a TV show. He cancels the vacation, but not for long—Lucy and Ethel decide to go to the popular ski resort by themselves. There they meet Argentina-born Fernando Lamas, who happens to be staying at the same lodge. She hatches a scheme to make Ricky jealous, by having Ethel take a picture of them skiing together and hinting to Ricky that they have been seeing a lot of each other. While Ethel focuses the camera, Lucy leans forward a little too far, and she and Fernando head down the ski slope, she riding piggyback on his shoulders. Fernando lands in a tree with two broken ribs—and Ricky fails to fall for Lucy's jealousy plot. Fred and Ricky are lonely without their wives, however, and rush up to Sun Valley anyway. Lucy is furious that Ricky didn't believe her stories about Fernando, and rejects her husband's affection. Ricky, Ethel, and Fred—individually—interrupt Lamas's shower to ask him to "come on" to Lucy at an afternoon skating party, just so Ricky can feign jealousy and convince Lucy that he loves her. Unfortunately, Latin-lover Lamas goes a bit too far, Ricky loses his temper, and both men gain a black eye.

NOTE: A double was used for the scene depicting Lucy skiing. Good thing for Lucille Ball—the double wound up with a broken leg!

THE EIGHTH SEASON: 1958–59

Executive Producer: Desi Arnaz
Producer: Bert Granet
Writers: Bob Schiller and Bob Weiskopf
Script Supervisors: Madelyn Martin and Bob Carroll, Jr.
Director: Jerry Thorpe
Directors of Photography: Sid Hickox (Episodes #6–9) and Nick Musuraca
Music Composed and Conducted: Wilbur Hatch
Associate Producer: Jack Aldworth
Production Supervisor: W. Argyle Nelson
Production Manager: James Paisley
Supervising Film Editor: Dann Cahn (Episodes #6, 8, and 9) and Bill
   Heath
Assistant Director: Jay Sandrich
Film Editor: Bud Molin, A.C.E.
Rerecording Editors: Robert Reeve (Episodes #6–8) and Gerald S. Rosen-
   thal
Music Editor: E. C. Norton
Theme Music: Eliot Daniel
Art Director: Ralph Berger
Set Decorator: Sandy Grace
Sound Recorder: Cameron McCulloch
Makeup: Hal King
Hair Stylist: Irma Kusely
Camera Coordinator: Maury Thompson
Property Master: Charles West
Miss Ball's Wardrobe: Edward Stevenson
Costumer: Della Fox
Casting: Kerwin Coughlin
Photographic Effects: Howard Anderson Company
Sound: Glen Glenn Sound
Filmed at Motion Picture Center

Sponsor: Westinghouse Electric Company
Agency: McCann-Erickson, Inc.

"LUCY GOES TO MEXICO" 10/6/58

Episode #6 Supporting cast: Little Ricky—Keith Thibodeaux,
Maurice Chevalier—himself, Mexican boy—Alan Costello, Customs
officer—Charles Lane, Consul—Addison Richards, Bullfighter—Chalo
Chacon Music: "Something's Gotta Give," "Louise," "La
Cucaracha," "Valentine," "Mimi," "Yankee Doodle Dandy"

The Ricardos and the Mertzes are in San Diego while Ricky rehearses with
Maurice Chevalier for a show to be presented aboard a U.S. Navy aircraft
carrier, the *Yorktown*. Lucy and Ethel are eager to go across the Mexican
border into Tijuana for some souvenir- and bargain-hunting, so Ricky
deputizes Fred to go along and keep the girls in line. Lucy, however, quickly
becomes embroiled with the U.S. Customs officer when a little Mexican lad
tries to stow away in her automobile trunk, in order to see—firsthand—"a
real-life aircraft carrier." Lucy and the Mertzes seem destined for a real-life
jail term, until Ricky and Maurice arrive to bail them out. But further
complications arise when Maurice, a French citizen, cannot get back into the
United States without proper authorization. Lucy sets out to find the American
consul—who is attending an afternoon bullfight. The border police are in
pursuit, so Lucy disguises herself as a matador, and winds up in the ring
with the ferocious bull.

NOTE: Writer Everett Freeman shared writing credit with Schiller and Weiskopf
by helping brainstorm the story premise. . . . Ralph Berger was assisted by
Claudio Guzman, another art director; and Jerry Miggins worked with Sandy
Grace on set decoration.

"LUCY MAKES ROOM FOR DANNY"   12/1/58

Episode #7   Supporting cast: Little Ricky—Keith Thibodeaux, Danny Williams—Danny Thomas, Kathy Williams—Marjorie Lord, Rusty Williams—Rusty Hamer, Linda Williams—Angela Cartwright, Judge—Gale Gordon

Hoping to give his children, Rusty and Linda, two months of healthy country air, Danny Williams and his wife Kathy rent the Ricardos' Connecticut home while Lucy and Ricky are to be in Hollywood making a motion picture. On their arrival in New England, the Williamses discover that the Ricardos' film commitment has been canceled and they want their house back. Danny holds firm, however, and the Ricardos wind up "bunking in" with the Mertzes. Lucy cannot stand the thought of "strangers" living in her house, using her best dishes for every day, not watering her plants, etc., and makes a nuisance of herself by dropping in every two or three minutes to check up on things. Tempers soon flare, and the housing problem culminates in a six-way snowball fight and a day in court, where a bewildered judge tries to smooth out the badly wrinkled domestic situation.

NOTE: Danny Thomas's "Make Room for Daddy" series inherited the "I Love Lucy" time slot—Monday nights at nine—when the half-hour sitcom went off the air in 1957. . . . When Thomas originally agreed to do his series for the fall of 1953 (for ABC), he went to Desilu for production assistance and utilized their exclusive three-camera technique. . . . Desi Arnaz had been trying to get Danny Thomas on the "Lucy" show since 1955, but, at that time, there existed a sponsor conflict—"Daddy" was bankrolled by a competing cigarette company.

"LUCY GOES TO ALASKA"   2/9/59

Episode #8   Supporting cast: Red Skelton—himself, Bellboy—Sid Melton, Desk clerk—William Newell, Clerk—Hugh Sanders, Eskimo #1—Iron Eyes Cody, Eskimo #2—Charlie Stevens, Show director—Jess Kirkpatrick   Music: "Poor Everybody Else"

Lucy and the Mertzes accompany Ricky to Nome, Alaska, where his band is scheduled to appear on a Red Skelton TV show celebrating Alaska's admission to the Union—and where Fred and Ricky have bought some land, sight-unseen. The boys soon discover that they own a plot of frozen wasteland, and that, because hotel accommodations are scarce, they and their wives will have to share a single room with but one bed. The hotel clerk helps out by supplying an army cot, a hammock, and a sleeping bag, for which straws are drawn—and Lucy winds up in a hammock that seems to have a mind of its own! The following day, Red Skelton learns that the actress who was to appear with him in a Freddie the Freeloader sketch ("Dining at the

Waldorf") is unable to fly to Alaska, and Lucy naturally offers to substitute. Knowing that movie stars like to invest in real estate, Lucy interests Red in the Alaska property—unaware that Ricky and Fred have no reason to believe it's ripe with oil. Lucy and Red go out in a jeep to inspect the land and are caught in a blizzard. Their jeep is wrecked in a snowbank, and, in exchange for the land, an Eskimo volunteers to fly the duo back to Nome. Suddenly, however, Lucy and Red find themselves flying the aircraft themselves—with Ricky, Fred, and Ethel at the Nome airport trying to guide them safely to land.

NOTE: Location scenes for this episode were filmed in Lake Arrowhead, one hundred miles northeast of Los Angeles.

"LUCY WANTS A CAREER"   4/13/59

Episode #9 Supporting cast: Little Ricky—Keith Thibodeaux, Paul Douglas—himself, Mr. Robinson—Pierre Watkin, Secretary—Doris Packer, Miss Low Neck—Joi Lansing, Miss Leg Girl—Sue Casey, Miss Leg Girl #2—Lorraine Crawford, Miss Hairdo—Larri Thomas, Kibitzer—Sam Hearn, Cameraman—Louis A. Nicoletti

Lucy still believes that her life as a housewife is humdrum and boring. Lucy: "Cook the meals, wash the dishes, make the beds, dust the house. . . . For

two cents I'd go out and get myself a job." Despite Ricky's objections, she hires Ethel to baby-sit for Little Ricky and sets out to find a job. She answers an ad for a "Girl Friday" position on Paul Douglas's new "Early Bird" TV show, but her wild shenanigans to ward off other applicants infuriate the star. Her "everyday housewife" credentials impress the sponsor, however, and she lands the job. Moreover, her fresh approach endears her to the program's audience, and the breakfast-food sponsor signs her to a long-term deal—which seems to be everything she's ever wanted. Or is it? Lucy soon discovers that her early-morning work schedule is in constant conflict with her husband's late-night nightclub work, and the twosome only gets to see each other at Grand Central Station as one is coming home and the other going off to work. When Paul Douglas learns of Lucy's problem, he promises her a release from her contract, and the Ricardos go out on the town to celebrate. That night Lucy takes a sleeping pill—to make sure she doesn't wake up at the usual 4 A.M. time—and is blissfully asleep when Douglas arrives at the house, panic-stricken because he hasn't been able to arrange for Lucy's release. If she's not at the studio in two hours, the sponsors plan to sue. Ricky and Douglas frantically get her to the set on time, but when she falls asleep in a bowl of "Wakey Flakies," the sponsors fire her fast. She's happy being a housewife once again.

NOTE: In the late 1940s, before "I Love Lucy," Lucille Ball and Desi Arnaz had the same problem as depicted in this hour show—Lucy had to rise early for her movie commitments and Desi was working late at nightclubs. They used to meet in the early-morning hours on Sepulveda Boulevard—on the side of the road—to catch up on their lives!

"LUCY'S SUMMER VACATION"   6/8/59

Episode #10   Supporting cast: Ida Lupino—herself, Howard Duff— himself, Little Ricky—Keith Thibodeaux, Man—William Fawcett Music: "Row, Row, Row Your Boat," "Cielito Lindo"

Lucy and Ricky enthusiastically accept friend Harry Bailey's invitation to spend a week at his vacant Vermont mountain lodge. Shortly after they arrive, Ida Lupino and Howard Duff turn up—it seems that absentminded Harry extended similar invitations to both couples for the same week. The men decide to go fishing and leave the wives to amuse themselves with such chores as cleaning their daily catch. Bored, Lucy and Ida doll themselves up in their best evening dresses and try to woo their husbands into a romantic evening. When that fails, Lucy decides to drill holes in the bottom of the boys' rowboat. That way, they'll have to stay on shore and keep them company. Ricky and Howard, by this time, are feeling guilty about all their fishing expeditions—and decide to take their wives out onto the lake for an evening of moonlight and romance. Not even Lucy's strategically placed bubble gum can keep the punctured rowboat afloat.

THE NINTH SEASON: 1959–60

Executive Producer: Desi Arnaz
Producer: Bert Granet
Writers: Bob Schiller and Bob Weiskopf
Script Consultants: Madelyn Martin and Bob Carroll, Jr.
Director: Desi Arnaz
Director of Photography: Sid Hickox, A.S.C.
Music Composed and Conducted: Wilbur Hatch
Associate Producer: Jack Aldworth
Production Supervisor: W. Argyle Nelson
Production Manager: James Paisley
Supervising Film Editors: Dann Cahn (Episode #11) and Bill Heath
Assistant Directors: Jay Sandrich (Episode #11) and Jack Aldworth
Film Editors: Bud Molin, A.C.E. (Episode #11), Robert C. Oberbeck
   (Episode #12), and Edward Biery (Episode #13)
Sound Editor: Jerry Rosenthal
Music Editor: E. C. Norton
Theme Music: Eliot Daniel
Art Director: Ralph Berger
Set Decorators: Ross J. Dowd and Sandy Grace (Episode #11)
Sound Recorder: Cameron McCulloch
Makeup: Hal King
Hair Stylist: Irma Kusely
Camera Coordinator: Maury Thompson
Property Master: Charles West
Miss Ball's Wardrobe: Edward Stevenson
Costumers: Bob Christenson (Episode #12) and Della Fox
Casting: Kerwin Coughlin
Photographic Effects: Howard Anderson Company
Sound: Glen Glenn Sound

Filmed at Desilu-Cahuenga

Sponsor: Westinghouse Electric Corporation
Agency: McCann-Erickson, Inc.

"MILTON BERLE HIDES OUT AT THE RICARDOS' " 9/25/59

Episode #11 Supporting cast: Little Ricky—Keith Thibodeaux, Milton Berle—himself, Mr. Watson—Larry Keating, Secretary—Elvia Allman, Shorty—Sid Melton, Tumblers—Frank Mitchell, Walter Pietila, Harry—Herman Snyder Music: "Them There Days"

When Lucy tries to snag Milton Berle to emcee a benefit show for the PTA, she discovers him swamped with other business demands and unable to find the peace and solitude necessary to finish writing a book before the publisher's deadline. Unbeknown to Ricky—who doesn't think his wife ought to be bothering a big star like Berle in the first place—Lucy offers Milton the daytime use of their Connecticut home, so that the man can work on his manuscript without interruption. Uncle Miltie accepts, with the understanding that he will appear at the school function if he finishes his writing on schedule. The arrangement works out fine, until nearsighted Fred tells Ricky that a mysterious stranger has been spending entire days at the Ricardo house when he's gone. Ricky storms home; Milton tries to escape in drag (as "Mildred"), and everyone ends up enemies. But Lucy still has a glimmer of hope for patching things up, so she tries to get in to see Berle at his New York high-rise office—via the window and a construction worker's crane. Ricky arrives in the nick of time to save his wife—and Berle—from plunging to their deaths. Apologies abound and everybody stars in the PTA show, a Western spoof featuring the number "Them There Days" by composer Arthur Hamilton.

"THE RICARDOS GO TO JAPAN" 11/27/59

Episode #12 Supporting cast: Little Ricky—Keith Thibodeaux, Bob Cummings—himself, Mrs. McGillicuddy—Kathryn Card, Various roles—Teru Shimada, Linda Wong, Sondi Sodasi, May Lee Music: "Cuban Pete"

Lucy and the Mertzes accompany Ricky on a band junket to Tokyo, Japan, where they encounter Bob Cummings in the adjoining hotel suite. After Ricky refuses to spring for a string of real pearls for Lucy (she's tired of her tacky artificial ones), she's overjoyed when Cummings offers to get them from a friend at a substantial discount. Lucy must solve one problem first— she must come up with the money to pay for them. She and Ethel hit on a scheme to "borrow" the cash from Fred's never-opened money belt—then panic when Fred decides that the belt has grown too tight and announces he plans to buy a new one. Lucy reluctantly asks Cummings to return the necklace, but unwittingly gives him her original cheap strand instead of the real pearls. Hoping to catch up to him before he makes the transaction, Lucy and Ethel follow him to a men-only Geisha house. Not stopped by convention, the girls disguise themselves in full Geisha attire, slip into the club, and discover Ricky and Fred—who were supposed to be at a ball game—there, too. All is forgiven when the boys decide to buy their wives each a strand of real pearls.

"LUCY MEETS THE MUSTACHE" 4/1/60

Episode #13 Supporting cast: Little Ricky—Keith Thibodeaux, Ernie Kovacs—himself, Edie Adams—herself, Crandall—Paul Dubov, Chauffeur—Norman Leavitt, Hotel clerk—Louis A. Nicoletti, Bellboy—Dick Kallman Music: "That's All"

When Ricky gets to feeling low because he hasn't had any TV or movie offers lately, Lucy and the Mertzes remember that Ernie Kovacs and his wife, Edie Adams, who live nearby, have their own television show. Lucy plans an evening with the Kovacs, but Ernie winds up offering Little Ricky a job on his program instead of big Ricky. Lucy tries to persuade Kovacs to reconsider, but only makes a nuisance of herself. Desperate to save her despondent husband, Lucy disguises herself as the comedian's chauffeur, and plans to talk him into giving Ricky a job. She picks up Ernie at the railroad station and is pleasantly surprised to see Ricky with him. The fellows have already gotten together on a deal. Edie, calling on the car phone, tips Lucy's cover—and the guys decide to teach the meddling redhead a lesson.

NOTE: Dick Kallman was a member of Lucille Ball's acting workshop on the RKO/Desilu lot. He later starred in the NBC sitcom "Hank."

Handy-Dandy Episode Finder

This "Handy-Dandy Episode Finder" will help you locate the complete synopsis of any one of the classic 179 "I Love Lucy" segments. Even if you only know a word or a key phrase from an episode, this index will quickly point you in the right direction. The numbers listed here refer to the episode number as it appears in the log.

Index

ABOUT THE AUTHOR

BART ANDREWS is a former TV comedy writer turned literary agent whose twenty published books include *The Worst TV Shows Ever, The TV Addicts Handbook,* and *The Official TV Trivia Quiz Book.* Andrews has written material for Bob Newhart and Phyllis Diller, among others, but his true passion has long been watching reruns of "I Love Lucy." This addiction led to three previous books on Lucille Ball: *Lucy & Ricky & Fred & Ethel, Loving Lucy,* and *The "I Love Lucy" Quiz Book.* He lives in West Hollywood, California, drives a 1953 Pontiac with a licence plate that reads "I LV LCY," and collects back issues of *TV Guide.*

ABOUT THE AUTHOR